Configurations of Power

CONFIGURATIONS OF POWER

Holistic Anthropology
in Theory and Practice

EDITED BY

John S. Henderson
AND Patricia J. Netherly

Published in Cooperation with the Society for
Latin American Anthropology and the
American Anthropological Association

Cornell University Press

ITHACA AND LONDON

Copyright © 1993 by Cornell University

All rights reserved. Except for brief quotations in a review, this book, or parts thereof, must not be reproduced in any form without permission in writing from the publisher. For information, address Cornell University Press, Sage House, 512 East State Street, Ithaca, New York 14850.

First published 1993 by Cornell University Press.

International Standard Book Number 0-8014-2487-9
Library of Congress Catalog Card Number 92-52759
Printed in the United States of America
Librarians: Library of Congress cataloging information appears on the last page of the book.

⊗ The paper in this book meets the minimum requirements of the American National Standard for Information Sciences—Permanence of Paper for Printed Library Materials, ANSI Z39.48-1984.

Contents

Acknowledgments   vii

Introduction: Murra, Materialism, Anthropology, and the Andes   1
John S. Henderson and Patricia J. Netherly

PART I. ARCHAIC STATES

1. The Nature of the Andean State   11
   Patricia J. Netherly

2. The Wealth of a Native American State: Value, Investment, and Mobilization in the Inka Economy   36
   Craig Morris

3. Divine Kingship in the Formation of the Japanese State, 1868–1945   51
   Robert J. Smith

4. The State-Church Reconsidered   74
   Bruce G. Trigger

5. Political Power and the Origin of Social Complexity   112
   Elman R. Service

PART II. POWER, POLITICS, AND HIERARCHY

6. Hierarchy and Power in the Tropical Forest 137
   Irving Goldman

7. State and Household Crops among the Jola (Diola) of Senegal 160
   Olga F. Linares

8. Women, Status, and High Office in African Polities 181
   Ronald Cohen

9. Women's Writing in Heian Japan: Expressions of Power 209
   Denise O'Brien

10. Keeping Up with the Stuyvesants: House Size and Status in Seventeenth-Century New Amsterdam 228
    Nan A. Rothschild

11. Technologies of Power: The Andean Case 244
    Heather Lechtman

12. Pancho Villa and the United States 281
    Friedrich Katz

13. Old Postulates and New China 303
    Morton H. Fried

    Epilogue: Clio Rediviva 327
    Sidney W. Mintz

    Contributors 335

    Index 337

Acknowledgments

For a variety of reasons, this volume has remained in the editorial process far longer than anyone could have imagined at the outset. The authors have been remarkably creative in finding ways to keep their work abreast of continuing developments in the field without having to resort to extensive rewriting. If it has not been possible to take into account the most recent literature in every case, the fault does not lie with the authors. In any event, the essays remain fresh and incisive. In one case, death intervened, and the final revision of Morton Fried's essay involved only the most minor editorial changes.

The authors have also been astonishingly patient; each of them has our profound gratitude and admiration. We appreciate the efforts of Bev. Phillips of Cornell's archaeology program; of Jeanne J. Henderson; of copyeditor John Thomas; and of Joanne Hindman and Kay Scheuer at Cornell University Press in transforming the manuscript under difficult circumstances.

J.S.H.
P.J.N.

Ithaca, New York

Configurations of Power

INTRODUCTION

Murra, Materialism, Anthropology, and the Andes

*John S. Henderson and
Patricia J. Netherly*

This volume is intended to be an explicit statement of the importance of a particular approach to anthropology, a stance that is at once unabashedly empirical, thoroughly holistic, and broadly comparative. In one sense, of course, the book is a Festschrift in honor of John Murra, but it is not so much a memorial to him as an appreciation of his contributions to anthropology as key examples of this critical approach to the discipline.

Individually and collectively, the essays in this collection represent a distinctive stance with respect to the theory, method, data, and practice of anthropology. In their emphasis on data, their readiness to combine the methods and perspectives of ethnography, ethnohistory, archaeology, and allied fields, and in their focus on economic and political issues, the authors exemplify what the editors believe to be essential in anthropological scholarship. John Murra has been an unwavering proponent of this kind of anthropology throughout the last three decades. And though his work has been concentrated in the Andes, it is of immense general importance.

In one sense, Murra's Andean focus is simply a fortuitous result of his life history. In 1941, at the beginning of his career, he had the opportunity to do fieldwork in Ecuador as Don Collier's assistant. This experience introduced him to an area at once rich in information and relatively unstudied by anthropologists—a suitable arena in which to pursue his developing anthropological interests. At the same time, the personal impact of Andean people on Murra determined him to be not just a student of these peoples and their cultural tradition but their advocate. Ultimately, Murra's Andean involvement would become so intense as to represent an identity for him. But, in the years that intervened between his first work in Ecuador and his return to the Andes, Murra developed a deep familiarity with the literature on North American Indian societies and on the traditional states of Africa, and he did fieldwork in the Caribbean. From these experiences and interests he drew important aspects of the fundamental approach to anthropology that he would later elaborate in an Andean context: an appreciation of the importance of primary data, of British social anthropology's tradition of exquisite ethnographic description, and of the insights to be gleaned from comparative analysis about shared patterns and common institutions. The focus within British social anthropology on the economic and social organization of African states—with their emphasis on such phenomena as asymmetric reciprocity, systems of redistribution, and the articulation of kin ties with the state—also had an important impact on Murra. To some degree, he approached the ethnohistory of the Inka as though he were writing the social anthropology of a traditional African society, though the addition of a historical dimension, the ability to accommodate the study of process, transcends the British tradition.

Murra has always remained aware of his intellectual roots in American and British social anthropology. In fact, another feature of his basic approach to anthropology is his constant consciousness of the history and structure of the discipline itself, and particularly of national and ethnic differences within it. He keenly felt the obligation to foster the development of professional anthropology in the Andean republics and, more than any other North American or European anthropologist, fostered the development of institutions and individual scholars in the Andean republics, both by offering formal and informal instruction in local settings and by helping Andean students and professionals find educational opportunities in the United States and Europe. Beyond the advocacy for the modern representatives of the cultural tradition that is his subject of study, Murra's focus on the history and organization of anthropology in the Andes has kept him constantly aware of the changing political and social contexts in which anthropology is practiced there.

For many of us, the most important feature of Murra's approach to anthropology is that it maintains an essential empirical dimension without becoming atheoretical. It is a truism that theoretical stance, whether explicit or implicit, is vital in organizing the acquisition of data during fieldwork, ordering the description of data, and structuring their analysis. This is no less true for John Murra's anthropology than for that of any other anthropologist. Though he has never dwelt on the theoretical dimensions of his work—especially not in abstract latinate jargon—they are nonetheless important.

Murra has always chosen to emphasize, instead, the empirical dimensions of his work, most particularly his respect for the inherent importance of data. In fact, for Murra, as for the editors and most of the contributors to this book, the sine qua non of a contribution to anthropology is the collection of primary data and description of them in a format that makes them available to local anthropologists, not just in the foreign anthropologist's home country. Scholarly rigor is at least as essential here as in subsequent analyses, and Murra's historiographic technique and descriptive handling of primary data are models of elegance.

This kind of focus on data collection necessitates intensive and extensive fieldwork, that is, a long-term engagement in a particular region. It is this continuing involvement in an area that allows the investigator to achieve sufficient familiarity with the natural environment and cultural context to be able to pose research questions that are not only interesting and important but also potentially answerable. Only extended residence can familiarize an outsider with seasonal and other cyclical phenomena and provide an appreciation for minor "microhistorical" perturbations. Long-term fieldwork is essential to permit the archaeological research agenda to move beyond the elaboration of time-space systematics. Description is fundamental here, too, along with a basic "paleoethnographic" level of reconstruction that is enormously time consuming. Elaborating basic contextual frameworks for ethnohistory is also a long-term process, as is developing a detailed knowledge of archival holdings. At the same time, continuing involvement provides the opportunity for an understanding of the local social context of the research, for coordination with local anthropologists and representatives of local institutions, for appreciation of their priorities for research and training, even—as in John Murra's case--for a firm identification with, and advocacy of, the local cultural and anthropological tradition.

Earlier generations of anthropologists would have found Murra's insistence on the value of data unexceptionable. It is only in very recent years that some anthropologists have failed to recognize that the proper collection and description of primary data are at least as important as rigorous subsequent analysis of them.

A second major dimension of John Murra's approach to anthropology, and one his anthropological forebears would have found equally obvious, is his holistic basic stance. This breadth of vision with respect to both the theoretical perspectives of the discipline and the practice of the profession in the field has its roots in the early history of American anthropology, and it is a major aspect of the field's attractiveness. For John Murra, as for so many other anthropologists, anthropology was initially aesthetically, not just intellectually, appealing. It was a source of delight, a liberating (if disciplined) way of understanding the world.

This perspective has led Murra to cast his intellectual net broadly in the attempt to understand the Andean cultural tradition. Historical, linguistic, and even biological (at least in the ecological sense) information and perspectives are all grist for his mill. Within anthropology itself, ethnography, ethnohistory, and archaeology simply represent different tactics of investigation. They focus on different kinds of data, which call for different techniques of acquisition, description, and analysis, but they need not represent incompatible (or even different) overall research goals. In fact, the truly important questions about human societies, of the sort that Murra poses, not only lend themselves to such a multipronged approach but actually demand that all these perspectives be brought to bear. Murra's own concentration on ethnohistory—which he considers a set of techniques for using historical data to study non-Western peoples within an anthropological analytical and conceptual framework—stems in part from personal preference and in part from his life history. His ethnohistorical study of the Inka was partly a response to the U.S. Department of State's refusal to permit him to return to Ecuador to do an ethnographic study of the weavers of Otavalo. Within his broad overall perspective, Murra's research interests have always focused on politics and especially on economics. To some degree, his attraction to Marxist political and intellectual thought may account for this emphasis, though he soon moved beyond any concern with a Marxist political agenda. Murra's economic emphasis is more a matter of tactical utility than of abstract principle. The overwhelming material and economic bias of the available archaeological data is unavoidable; conquest period European documentary sources typically adopt a sharply economic and political perspective on Andean societies; even material and economic aspects of modern societies are the easiest for the outsider to begin to comprehend. But Murra's more specific research emphases have also been pragmatic: cultural reality in the Andes dictated a focus on social groups rather than on land tenure or territory.

Murra's preoccupation with economic issues reflects a tactical choice to begin with the concrete. He finds it useful to begin with an analysis of material organization and economic institutions and then to move on to work out their implications for other cultural realms. This focus is not a denial of the importance of ritual activity or symbolic dimensions of culture but a recognition that it is easier, more productive, and personally more gratifying to develop a material framework for understanding belief systems than to try to approach ideological and structural issues—which are typically far more opaque and less tractable than economic or political phenomena—directly. When ritual and ideological issues are obviously embedded in the economic and social spheres, as with cloth and maize in Andean ritual, Murra has never hesitated to consider them. In his study of the Huanuco *visita* he focused on ecological complementarity and the archipelago model, but he also sketched out the basic dual and quadripartite organizational framework that is essential for understanding economic organization. In each case, he is most sensitive to the economic implications of ritual activity, to the articulation of ceremonial concerns with material realms.

His preoccupation with economic and political issues notwithstanding, Murra insists on bringing data and approaches drawn from all subfields of anthropology as well as history and other allied disciples to bear in defining and resolving important issues. Few other anthropologists in recent years have celebrated the importance of this sort of intellectual breadth or even the value of primary data. Whether or not these approaches have come to seem old-fashioned, however, they are certainly not outmoded, as the essays in this volume demonstrate.

One dimension of the temporary decline in popularity of Murra's approach to anthropology is that it eschews high-level abstraction, except in the very rare situations where the requisite foundations have been laid. An approach that insists that detailed description and extensive analyses are necessary before any attempt to deal with large explanatory or theoretical questions has inevitably lacked appeal to schools of thought that do not value the concrete or substantive dimensions of anthropology. Murra has never disdained explanation or theory as ultimate goals of anthropological scholarship. He chooses, however, to begin with data collection, exquisite detailed description, and basic functional analysis. The next higher analytical level involves a more abstract kind of analysis that might be termed ethnological: institutional and organizational reconstruction. At the same time, though, he celebrates variability rather than mask it by premature typologizing. The development of diachronic perspectives on such patterns and reconstruction of specific historical processes represents a comparable level of historical abstraction. This level of analysis—"historical ethnology" embedded in particular historical settings—ultimately produces culture history of the sort that is richly represented in Murra's contributions to Andean anthropology. Murra has focused his energies on ethnographic description and ethnological analysis—the critical middle ground that makes cultural sense of data, providing the essential foundations for explanatory or processual analysis intended to reveal the fundamental structure and organizing principles of culture. His work includes organizational or institutional comparison, a kind of initial stage of comparative history, but he has always proceeded slowly and methodically at this level of analysis to avoid the all too common tendency to reify the abstract and mistake it for theoretical insight.

The essays in this volume echo many aspects of Murra's approach to anthropology. In general, they highlight the importance of data and description rather than theoretical abstraction. The essays in Part I, with their focus on specific aspects of economic and political organization in state-level societies, reflect the kind of institutional analysis Murra favors as well as his fundamental interest in political economy.

Patricia J. Netherly's essay appropriately opens the section with a consideration of the nature of the state, and particularly of the form it took in the Andean cultural tradition. She points out Andean states' distinctive reliance on kinship rather than territory as a key organizational principle and goes on to illustrate, from her own research, how the resulting multi-level dual and quadripartite organization actually functioned on the north coast of Peru.

Craig Morris, building on Murra's institutional analyses of Andean economies, explores aspects of Inka economic organization and resource management, including such seemingly noneconomic considerations as symbolic values of goods and the function of ceremonial cities as infrastructure for the state.

Moving beyond the Andes, Robert J. Smith provides a historical perspective on divine kingship in Japan, which survived for more than a millennium in a variety of organizational configurations. His focus is on the nineteenth-century Meiji Restoration and the conscious manipulation of myth and historical tradition in the redesign of the institution of kingship.

Bruce Trigger undertakes a wide-ranging consideration of the complementarity of state and church as institutions in early complex societies. Rejecting the notion that religious institutions serve simply to sanction and reinforce elite dominance and the power of the state, he argues that religion serves as a regulatory mechanism with respect to the state, limiting potential excesses of rulers in terms of both internal exploitation and external expansionism.

Elman R. Service broadens the focus still further with a general consideration of the nature and evolution of social complexity. Characterizing a series of societies in order of increasing complexity, he points out that inequality exists on an individual basis in all societies. The key evolutionary process, he argues, is the institutionalization of inequality with the emergence of hierarchial sets of permanent offices and the development of unequal segments of society.

The essays in Part II also illuminate features of political and economic institutions in complex societies, but their immediate focus is on more diffuse configurations of power, in simpler societies as well as in state contexts.

Irving Goldman's rich description of the importance of hierarchical concepts among tribal societies in Colombia echoes the themes raised by Service, though with a twist. Complex systems of ranking affect virtually every facet of social organization but have essentially no material correlates, a situation that provides considerable food for thought with respect to the evolution of hierarchical institutions.

Olga F. Linares also provides an ethnographic case with evolutionary implications. Her analysis of the introduction of peanuts into rice-growing areas of West Africa clearly illustrates how broadly the impact of such a change can range. She suggests that the appropriation of revenue crops by emergent bureaucracies may be a general aspect of state formation.

Ronald Cohen examines the strong tendency toward male dominance in political spheres in traditional African societies in relation to women's offices in these societies. His analysis shows that gender serves not only as a symbol of integration but as a principle underlying mechanisms and institutions that actually promote integration.

Denise O'Brien explores women's roles in relation to political and economic power in a very different way in Japan. Women's writing in the Heian period was Japan's first vernacular literature and had an immense impact on later traditions of Japanese writing. Noting that these authors were elite women, O'Brien relates their achievement to the elevated economic status that freed them to write, as well as to their access to education.

Nan A. Rothschild's analysis of housing and economic status in early New Amsterdam demonstrates a clear relationship between house size and wealth, despite the multitude of other constraints that may obscure the correlation. Rothschild argues forcefully for the need to avoid ethnocentric assumptions in explaining the relationships among social and economic factors on the one hand and space use on the other, especially when it is necessary to rely solely on archaeological data.

Heather Lechtman's consideration of Andean technology also emphasizes the importance of native points of view. Her analysis demonstrates that conceptualizing technology as the social organization of knowledge not only provides insights into symbolic or ideological aspects of technology but may also reveal otherwise imperceptible structural homologies between seemingly very different technologies.

Friedrich Katz's essay is focused on an individual historical figure—Pancho Villa, the Mexican revolutionary by whom North Americans have been alternately attracted and repelled. Cutting through the accumulated layers of official propaganda and popular myth, Katz provides glimpses of the real Villa and his changing relation with the United States. Initially, close alliances with U.S. business interests, with at least the tacit approval of government officials, provided Villa with important political and military advantages. Ultimately, his northern allies proved unreliable and actually contributed to his downfall.

Morton H. Fried's essay on today's China returns us to a broad, holistic perspective on a very complex society. Using the concept of "cultural postulates," which has something in common with the kind of institutional analysis Murra has always advocated, Fried argues that the distinctive features of the "new" China (after the Cultural Revolution) can be attributed to an attempt to institutionalize a peasant subculture.

Finally, the volume concludes with Mintz's biographical epilogue. In addition to illuminating personal reminiscence, Mintz provides useful analytical comments on some of the formative factors involved in the development of Murra's approach to anthropology.

Collectively, the contributors to this volume demonstrate the many facets of Murra's contributions to anthropology: they deal with many aspects of many societies, but their primary concern is with political and economic organization in complex societies; they recognize—even celebrate—the importance of data, description, and basic analysis; they do not deny the importance of religion and symbolic considerations, but they recognize that a proper understanding of these cultural realms requires rich data and elaborate analysis; in the same way, they do not disdain theory, but they insist that it be grounded in appropriate data and analyses, not pure abstraction. Put simply, they adopt a historical perspective on every issue and freely blend ethnographic, historical, and archaeological data. That they do so with such diversity bears witness to the scope of Murra's impact on the field. His work and theirs deserve the widest possible audience.

Part I

ARCHAIC STATES

CHAPTER ONE

The Nature of the Andean State

Patricia J. Netherly

It is curious that the study of preindustrial, or "early," states in the Americas seems to have fallen by default to the anthropologists. It has been suggested that the study of the evolution of state organization and of the causes underlying such a system raises the issue of the nature of social evolution and fundamental questions of moral and political philosophy (Cohen 1978b). As the most powerful organizational system ever developed, states force us to consider questions of the cost to and the benefits bestowed on the human populations living under their rule. Since we include under the rubric of state different orders of political organization, whose respective definitions are based on the emphasis of their different characteristics, both definition of the state and the history of its evolution have generated considerable debate.

Defining the state presents difficulties, and scholars have encountered still more in trying to determine when a polity has passed to a condition of sufficient complexity to qualify as a state. Stability through changes in rule and the pressures of succession struggles is one criterion (Goldschmidt 1962). It has also been argued that, where the polity can withstand the centrifugal pressures of fission and hold together over time, it is a state (Cohen 1978a, 1978b).

The significance of the state as a mode of organization for human history lies in its ability to mobilize human energy for a common purpose (Cohen 1978b; Netherly 1977, 1984, n.d.a., n.d.b.). To this end, a ruling group assumes directly or through others a series of managerial functions such as collecting revenue, adjudicting disputes, raising armies, and ensuring continuity by supervising and controlling succession. In this sense the state becomes a powerful adaptive mechanism for the furtherance of human society.

Explanation of the development of states, however, has had an uncertain trajectory. Some theoreticians, most notably Marx and Engels and those influenced by them, focus on the growth of inequality and the appropriation of and control over the means of production and scarce resources (Engels 1972; Fried 1967; Carneiro 1970, 1981). Others emphasize the centralization and hierarchization of relations of power with the loss of autonomy by local groups (Service 1975; Fortes and Evans-Pritchard 1940). More recently, there has been emphasis on the state as a centralized structure for the utilization of human energy (Adams 1975) or the processing of information. Such a definition has permitted archaeologists, for example, to define a state in the absence of documentation as a hierarchy of at least three organizational levels (Wright and Johnson 1975).

A more useful approach is to view state formation as a systemic process, the result of the input and mutual influence of factors such as population pressure, cirumscription of productive resources, military organization for conquest or defense, the protection of the elite, and efforts to expand their privileges. Cohen (1978a, 1978b) has shown that none of these alone is a necessary and sufficient cause for state formation and that, in fact, varied causes produce similar effects. The reason for this, he argues, is the emergence of the political order itself as a determining factor of change: "After the tendency to centralized control has been triggered, the hierarchical structure itself becomes a selective determinant that feeds back to all the sociocultural features to make them fit more closely into its overall pattern. Early states as far removed as Incan Peru, ancient China, Egypt, early Europe and precolonial West Africa exhibit striking similarities" (1978b:8).

It is not surprising, given the heterogeneity of the theoreticians, that there has been a great deal of emphasis put on the transition from lower levels of political organization to one that can be unequivocally considered a state. This has been the case in the Andean area as well as in others. Archaeologists working in the Andes have addressed this question; Isbell and Schrieber (1978) raise the question with regard to the expansionist Wari polity of a thousand years ago. More recently, Schaedel (1985) has reopened the issue with regard to the large, stratified Moche polities of the north coast of Peru.

For the purposes of the following discussion, we may consider the barebones minimum for a state system to center around legitimacy, articulation, and self-maintenance or perpetuation (Goldschmidt 1962). Legitimacy involves the right of rulers to rule, on the one hand, and a commitment on the part of the ruled to accept the rulers and their mode of operation, on the other. Articulation or organization has been understood in the West to be spatial or territorial organization—townships, counties, provinces— useful for societies whose primary focus is on the land. There are, however, other ways of integrating populations into an organizational network. The articulation can also be through the organization of the population into segments that are then arranged in a hierarchy, terminating in the paramount ruler, or, in the Andean case, rulers. If articulation is based on people rather than on territory, the apparent contradictions in Andean political economy—the peaceful sharing of access to particular resources among many polities, or the positioning of segments of a polity at a considerable distance from its core to exploit scarce resources—are resolved (Murra 1975:59-116), and the internal logic of such a system in an exacting environment becomes manifest.

The perpetuation of an orderly political system is the final requisite for state systems. Protection from conquest by outsiders, the reduction of the risks present in a hostile environment, the maintenance of order, the orderly and effective transfer of power, and the support of public institutions and public works are all aspects of self-maintenance or self-perpetuation which should be considered (Goldschmidt 1962).

Two additional aspects of early state organization have not received adequate discussion but are important in a consideration of the Andean state. One is the issue of the sacralization of the ruler. In the Andes as elsewhere this sacralization may be seen as part of the legitimation of the rulers and their rule. The second is the creation of an ethnic identity based on the state for its citizens (Cohen 1978b).

This process occurred in Europe in the course of the formation of the modern nation-state. It is doubtful whether, in archaic states, allegiance to the highest level of political organization culminating in an *ethnic* identification with the state ever became the only ethnic identification of individuals or communities at the lower levels of organization. Certainly in the Andes the nesting of loyalties and ethnic identifications was an inherent characteristic of these states.

Andean Political Organization

The achievement of Andean societies can hardly be overestimated. The Andes are a tropical mountain chain and as such are made up of a mosaic of extremely varied environments (Dollfus 1986; Troll 1958, 1968), ranging from the desert coast to high plateaus and valleys, both humid and dry, at 10,000 feet altitude and more and then down the warm and humid eastern slopes toward Amazonia. Much of John Murra's work has shown how Andean peoples developed economic strategies and institutions that permitted them to exploit this mosaic and, despite the apparent constraints, produce a surplus that afforded comfort and even wealth (Murra 1975, 1980; Troll 1958).

The social and political organization that permitted the management of these institutions and contributed to their success through a superior organization of human energy in a demanding environment has received less attention. It is fundamental, on a pragmatic level, to an understanding of the management mechanisms by which the Andean achievement was attained.

Consideration of the nature of the organization of Andean polities has been hampered by notions of what the state is. For the most part, students of the Andes have thought of the state in terms of a political tradition that counts among the primary characteristics of state organization the existence of an increasingly centralized core focused on a single ruler and dedicated to the exploitation of the labor and resources of the governed. Such a model does not work well for the Andes, where there were no single rulers and where the functions of the central core were largely delegated.

Andean political organization achieved state-level organization not once but many times. The Inka state, truncated by the European invasion, was merely the last of these states. It is the best documented because many of its institutions were glimpsed, however imperfectly, and noted by the first Spanish observers. In the past three decades the written accounts have been powerfully complemented by new information derived from archaeological research.

The Andean states present new forms of organization to the general study of archaic states in two areas. One of these is the use of principles of dual organization and opposition of polities or bounded social groups to achieve articulation. The other area, properly part of self-perpetuation, is the system of succession both within the dual divisions and as a mechanism for maintaining the dual opposition on which the political structure was based.

Kinship, as a metaphor for ranked relations of different kinds, appears in Andean polities and states as a system of articulation. The use of kinship relations to articulate different groups within an archaic state is not unique to the Andes. For this reason, and because it appears to be somewhat restricted in its use, kinship as a mode of articulation per se will not be discussed here, although it is unquestionably important to an understanding of the functioning of Andean polities at the local level and for aspects of the organization of the Inka state (Zuidema 1964, 1978, 1990).

Dual Structure

The population of an Andean community was, and in many cases still is, divided into two groups or moieties. These, in turn, may each be divided into moieties again, making a total of four sections at the next lowest level of organization. In many American Indian societies these "halves" are equal but in the Andes they are organized hierarchically; that is, one always outranks the other. Although no necessary relation between the presence of moieties and state-level organization, exists, moiety divisions are the building blocks of Andean political structure up to the state level.

Rather than a single dual structure, the Andean political organization consists of a number of structures embodying principles of duality. These principles embrace dual, quadripartite, eight-part, and more subdivisions arranged as a series of ranked moieties (Netherly 1977, 1984, 1988c). Decimal divisions are also usually ranged in a dual mode from five to ten to twenty to forty parts in conjunction with quadripartite and dual divisions at the upper levels (Netherly 1977, 1990; Zuidema 1990). Finally, there appear to be dually organized, tripartite systems with up to twelve sections organized in four divisions of three and two of six parts each (Albó et al. 1972; Harris 1986). Zuidema draw attention to these three systems thirty years ago with regard to the organizational ideology of Cuzco, the Inka capital (1964). Since that time, the study of contemporary Andean communities and those larger Andean polities which still functioned in the middle sixteenth century have provided new insights into the functioning of these systems at the local and regional levels.

Whatever the numerical system employed, dual organization into moieties formed the basis for the political structure wherein each moiety was governed by a headman or lord. This organization resulted in ranked dual rulers at the apex of each polity and for a collegium of four or more rulers when lower levels of organization were included. In the Andean states this fundamental political organization became an instrument of state policy as new territories were incorporated into an expanding imperium.

Andean political organization offers a unique view of a dual political structure at all levels because of the absence of a parallel among the preindustrial states of the Old World, but particularly because it was so effective in organizing human energy and resources. Andean political structures were built on underlying principles of social organization that have survived at the community levels until the present, which has been abundantly documented in ethnographic reports (Arguedas 1964; Houdart-Morizot 1976; Palomino Flores 1971; Platt 1986; Wachtel 1974).

Only in Bolivia, however, have traces of organization above the community level survived (Harris 1986; Platt 1986). Some Bolivian groups, such as Machaca and Laymi, even integrated an underlying asymetric tripartite division into dual organization (Albó et al. 1972; Harris 1986). It would be interesting to know just when and how this integration occurred. The integration of decimal systems into Andean dual and quadripartite political structure appears to be confined to particular levels of organization (Netherly 1977, 1990; Platt 1986; Zuidema 1964, 1990).

Dual social and political divisions are very ancient in the Andes and take many forms. Several years ago, an attempt was made to identify different kinds of dual organization and opposition as models for interpreting the patterning of prehistoric sites at the regional level as well as the architecture of particular sites (Netherly and Dillehay 1986). The direct historical approach was employed beginning with twentieth-century ethnographies and sixteenth-century documentary evidence and proceeding through the prehistoric evidence from late to early. Paired platform mounds, a form of public architecture, were found to date from four thousand years ago and earlier, well within the preceramic period, to the period of Inka domination, indicating a fundamental dual organization. The patterning and ranking of twentieth-century Andean communities across the landscape, which employs different principles of duality, was present in recognizable form in prehistoric Andean valleys.

The ethnographic studies in the central and southern Andean highlands of the past thirty years and the early ethnohistorical studies of the Inka state (Zuidema 1964 and Duviols 1979a) particularly offer abundant evidence for dual and quadripartite nature of Andean social and political organization and its antecedents in the Inka state. In recent decades much new information has appeared on the larger ethnic polities of the highlands, in large part thanks to John Murra (1967, 1968, 1975), and on the Inka state through the persistence of Nathan Wachtel and R. T. Zuidema (Wachtel 1982; Zuidema 1978, 1982, 1990). When I came to study the dismembered polities of the expansionist state of Chimor, the largest regional polity conquered by the Inka, the pervasiveness of dual organization in other areas of the Andes allowed me to recognize its presence in the societies of the north coast.

Quadripartition in Chimor

The few European accounts of the area contained no explicit descriptions of the political structure of Chimor or the subordinate north coast polities.

Inka policy had been to suppress the political structure of conquered Chimor, and north coast political organization did not excite Spanish interest until long after the potential eyewitness informants were dead (Netherly 1977, 1988b, 1990, n.d.a.). The Spanish referred to the discrete groups into which the general population was organized as *parcialidades*. They did not distinguish between levels in the use of this term, and it is consequently necessary to establish the context in each case. Nevertheless, the political structure was latent in the extensive Spanish administrative records. As the different lords appeared before Spanish officials to present petitions or to give testimony, it became apparent that their order of appearance reflected the hierarchies of the north coast political organization (Netherly 1977, 1984, 1988a, 1988c, 1990). Because of the abundance of such documentation, more details of the integration of subordinate groups into higher ones are known for the north coast polities than for many highland groups, including the Inka.

The detailed information on the particular type of dual and quadripartite organization found in the sixteenth-century north coast polities at different levels will be considered first. The implications of north coast political structure for a more complete understanding of Inka policies as expressed in the political organization of *Tawantinsuyu* will follow.

The evidence from the north coast polity of Chicama, located in the valley of the same name, is so clear that it provides an excellent example. It is by no means unique, however, and is confirmed by evidence from polities in Lambayeque and the Moche Valley (Netherly 1984, 1990). Repeated appearances by lords of different levels, who represented the groups for which they were directly responsible, made repeated appearances, which enables an understanding of the political structure as well as a method in which to ascertain the names of six of eight ranked rulers. In Figure 1.1 the names of each of these lords are shown in the appropriate place in the hierarchy. The young *cacique principal*, Don Juan de Mora, was the head of the higher-ranking moiety; he is shown alone at the highest level. In colonial documents from the mid-sixteenth century the highest-ranking lord sometimes appears alone on behalf of the entire polity. In the earliest colonial documents, these lords appear with at least one other, the lord of the lower-ranking moiety. It is not clear whether the highest-ranking lords could represent the whole polity in pre-European times, but I make the assumption that they sometimes did.

The nesting of rule at different levels, characteristic of Andean political structure, is evident in the figure where higher-ranking lords appear as rulers of smaller groups at the lower levels. Figure 1.1 is a schematic representation of a political structure based on ranked moieties. The heavy

18   Patricia J. Netherly

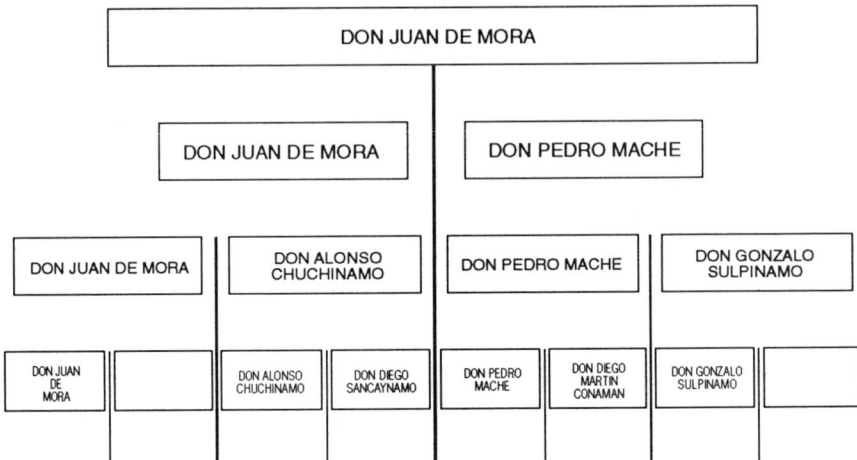

Figure 1.1. Formal political structure of the polity of Chicama.

line divides the primary moieties, with the higher-ranking submoieties at the left at the next level.

It is interesting to note that the moieties and submoieties of the Chicama polity were territorially organized with the limits set by the canal system in this desert valley oasis. If the top of the figure is seen as upstream and the heavy median line as the Chicama River, then the lands of the sections of the higher-ranking lords of each moiety are found upstream of the two lords of the secondary moieties, whose lands are closer to the sea. The lands of all the submoieties are longitudinally ranged wedges, parallel to the river so that at the level of eight sections each group has some frontage on or near the sea (Netherly 1984:232, fig. 2, 1990:464, fig. 1; Netherly and Dillehay 1986). This organization of the landscape is found in twentieth-century highland communities and in other prehistoric contexts on the coast.

Another characteristic of Andean political organization as it is found on the north coast is that rulers, even the highest-ranking, did not govern alone. Though one ruler may have been paramount at any given level, his rule was limited by the fact that he directly controlled only part of the lower levels of the polity. The necessary presence of the lords of the other principal sections of the polity served as a check on unilateral action by the lord of the higher-ranking moiety (Netherly 1977, 1988c, 1990).

This form of political organization was also present in the Inka state, despite all the Western misperception of single kings or emperors. It is one of the unique features of Andean political organization. The efficiency of this organizational structure for the mobilization of human energy is the reason for the success of the Andean states. The structure of this organization also explains why it was possible for states to expand so quickly and why lower-level political structures did not disappear once incorporated into an Andean state. The persistence of the polities at lower levels of organization also explains the lines of cleavage found when the larger aggregation broke up.

The regularities of duality and quadripartition in many of the principal north coast polities are impressive. All the same, there are instances from the mid-sixteenth century of three phratries instead of two moieties divided again into four sections; San Pedro de Lloc, ancient Lloco, is one example (Netherly 1977, n.d.a.). These examples are rare, however, and in most cases, within fifty years or so an adjustment back to a four-part structure occurred.

Decimal division on the north coast appears to have come under a superior scheme of quadripartition. The numbering system used on the north coast was base ten and the theme of forty lords (political divisions at the same level) is important in the Naymlap origin myth from Lambayeque (Netherly 1977, 1990; Zuidema 1990). The royal geneologies found in the myths of political origin may be regarded as charters of an ideal political structure (Netherly 1990). There are a number of ways to arrive at a total of forty: two sections of twenty parts, four of ten, five of eight, for example. The exact form of articulation for the north coast is not known, probably because it did not survive the Inka conquest.

The north coast polities that survived the Inka policy of disaggregation appear to have been organized on the basis of two-, four-, and eightfold divisions. The dual and quadripartite structure of pre-Inka Chimor has been traced in some detail and appears to be confirmed by the archaeological record. The "lost" decimal structure would have intervened between the imperial structure and that of the regional polities. It may also have been confined to the Lambayeque region, source of the Naymlap myth.

The integration of composite dual structures—that is, quadripartite and decimal systems articulated together into a single political organization—is also characteristic of the Inka state. The early Spanish observers, with their focus on monarchy, concentrated their attention on the Inka royals rather than on the immediate levels of articulation subordinate to them. The Spanish administrative and judicial records document the articulation between the Inka state and the regional polities, which is frequently an interface between different systems of duality. Again, as with Chimor, there are "lost" levels of imperial integration, but in the Inka case, it may be possible to recover some of the missing levels, working down from the top and up from the regional level.

Charka Political Organization

The setting for what is really an experimental reading of research carried out by other investigators lies in the highlands of the southern Andes, in northern Potosí in present-day Bolivia. There, in 1582, the lords of four polities, who had served the Inka exclusively as soldiers, petitioned to be excused from *mit'a* service stating that they were the "four nations, the Charcas and Caracaras and Chuis and Chicas" (Espinoza Soriano 1969). The phrasing in the petition and the fact that these four polities had a special status under the Inka suggests that the four groups made up a larger entity. This may have been an administrative creation of the Inka rather than a natural political aggregation, built up over time or by a pre-Inka conquest, although there seems to be a tradition of a "Charka confederacy." In Figure 1.2, I indicate the larger entity as *Charka?*, giving the polity of the four nations the name of the highest-ranking section. I use the order of presentation of the four polities in the *Memorial de Charcas* to rank them within the larger polity, following the same principles of order operative on the north coast.

As it happens, subdivisions of two of these four sections were studied in the 1970s by two young British anthropologists, Olivia Harris and Tristan Platt. Harris (1986) worked with the Aymara-speaking Laymi, once part of Chayanta, a moiety of the Charka. I infer from information given by Harris that the Charka were divided into moiety groups, the Chayanta and Sakaka, and that Sakaka was the higher-ranking of the two, since the *reducción* town of Sacaca was the principal town (*cabecera*) of the colonial *parcialidad* or polity of Chayanta. There was also a *reducción* settlement called Chayanta, which replaced Sacaca as the regional center of colonial administration in 1572 (Harris 1986:261).

The Macha, studied by Platt (1986), were a moiety subdivision of the Karakara, whose principal town was the *reducción* of Macha, suggesting that the Macha were the higher-ranking moiety within the Karakara. I have interpreted the Charka as being the higher-ranking group in the larger Charka polity made up of the Charka, the higher-ranking moiety or *anansaya*, and the Karakara, the lower-ranking moiety or *urinsaya*. Again, following the order of the polities in the *Memorial de Charcas*, the Chui

The Nature of the Andean State 21

```
                    CHARKA ?

         ANANSAYA         URINSAYA

         CHARKA     |     KARAKARA
        _____|_____
                    |
          CHUI      |     CHICHA
                    |
```

Figure 1.2. Quadripartite organization of the ethnic polities of Charka as presented in the *Memorial de Charcas* of 1582 (Espinoza Soriano 1969). The hierarchical relationships have been inferred from the *Memorial*.

made up the second section (i.e., lower-ranking moiety) of *anansaya* and the Chicha were the second section of *urinsaya*.

These relations are shown in Figure 1.2 and again in Figure 1.3. In the latter, I use a linear display conforming to one of the transformations of Andean principles of duality and quadripartition (Bouysse-Cassagne 1986; Netherly 1990). The largest Charka polity is indicated at the top, divided by a heavy median line into *anansaya*, presumably called Charka, and *urinsaya*, presumably called Karakara. At the next level, the quadripartite level, both *anansaya* and *urinsaya* are again subdivided into moieties with Charka and Karakara retaining the higher-ranking positions and the lower-ranking ones occupied by the other two ethnic groups: the Chui and the Chicha. Thus, Figure 1.2 and the first three levels of Figure 1.3 display the same hierarchical relations. The median line (*chaupi* or *taypi* in Quechua and Aymara respectively) that divides the two moieties at all levels is shown at the center in Figure 1.3. Following the Andean principle (Bouysse-Cassagne 1986; Netherly 1990), the higher-ranking moieties at each level are shown next to this line. For the Charka this level is the Sakaka, and for the Karakara, it is the Macha.

Platt (1986:229) tells us that in the sixteenth century the Karakara polity, of which Macha was the upper moiety, had ten thousand householders. The Macha polity itself had ten *ayllu*s, a referential term for social and political units at different levels of organization. He also notes that the Sakaka, the upper moiety group of the Charka, had ten thousand householders. This information is incomplete, however, and is a reflection of an Inka state manipulation of the organization of the Karakara. If the Sakaka polity had ten thousand heads of household, they were organized into ten administrative units, presumably *waranqa*, by the Inka. If the Macha, the upper moiety of the Karakara and an equivalent group on the same organizational level as the Sakaka, had ten ayllus, then they likely had ten

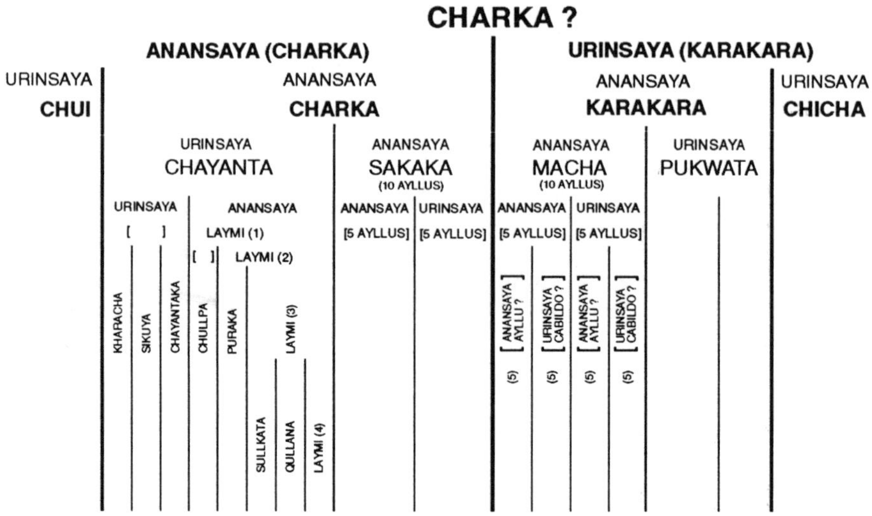

Figure 1.3. A composite diagram displaying a hypothetical rendering of the sixteenth-century relationship of the four polities of Charka as moieties. The upper levels are based on sixteenth-century documentation in Espinoza Soriano (1969) and Wachtel (1982). The lower levels of the Macha moiety as an ethnic polity are based on Platt's ethnographic evidence (1986). The lower levels of the Chayanta are based on Harris's fieldwork (1986). There is no equivalence of level between these groups that can be demonstrated today nor can the number of levels be considered the same as it was four hundred years ago. Both ethnographic cases are presented as instances of different modes of organization, each embodying elements of duality, and integrated by means of dual opposition within the same overarching Inka political framework.

thousand heads of household or ten *waranqa*. Harris (1986:261) indicates that the Chayanta was a *parcialidad* of the Charka; I would suggest it was the lower moiety of the Charka in the early sixteenth century. If the Sakaka had ten thousand heads of household, then Chayanta probably had an equivalent number. As Harris's research makes abundantly clear, however, the Chayanta were not organized into a decimal system of ten ayllus (262–263). The Pukwata, who are present on the modern landscape (see Figure 1.4), were undoubtedly the lower moiety of the Karakara in the early sixteenth century. The nature of their internal organization is not known, but if the Macha had ten thousand heads of household, then the Pukwata probably had an equivalent number.

The reorganizing hand of the Inka is very evident. The "four nations" of the Charka had been set aside as providers of manpower for the Inka armies without the obligation to render other service to the Inka state (Espinoza 1969). One would expect at the level of the largest Charka polity—consisting of the Charka, Karakara, Chui, and Chicha—a grouping of forty thousand or four groups of ten thousand heads of household. The total may have been as high as eighty thousand, though, assuming that the Chui and Chica between them made up forty thousand heads of household as well.

Inka-imposed changes also occur in the internal organization of the Macha and Sakaka polities that functioned as the higher-ranking moieties at their organizational level. The organization is suspiciously regular: ten thousand heads of household divided into ten ayllus. The retention of the term *ayllu* for the administrative *waranqa* may be an indication of its foreignness in this region. Harris shows very clearly how different the autochthonous political organization was for Laymi, part of Chayanta, and perhaps for Pukwata as well. A similar form of organization was reported for Machaca by Albó et al. (1972).

Figure 1.3 shows the modern political organization of Laymi as it existed at the time of Harris's fieldwork in the early 1970s. The political structure displays a system of what Harris calls asymmetrical dualism, which is based on the uniting of three elements in a structure of dual opposition with two polities in one moiety and one in the other. The two polities, however, are themselves in a moiety relation at the next lower level of organization. (The information in Figure 1.3 is from Harris [1986: Figs. 14.1 and 14.2]. I made one modification by renumbering the levels of the Laymi ayllu from one to four.) I have assumed that the Laymi as the highest-ranking member of each level; thus, at the highest moiety division within Chayanta, the *anansaya* moiety would also have been known as Laymi, in this case Laymi (1), giving four levels or organization instead of the three noted by Harris. In a dual system, the joining of three polities in two moieties gives a structure that begins with a dual moiety division at the highest level, then an asymmetrical quadripartition—the Laymi (2) moiety opposes an unnamed single polity, perhaps a higher level of the Chullpa ayllu—in *anansaya* and a similar asymmetrical moiety arrangement in *urinsaya* (probably a larger Chayantaka moiety encompassing Chayantaka and Sikuya opposed to a higher-level Kharacha). The next level of organization is tripartite, giving a total of six ayllus in *anansaya* and *urinsaya* together, three in each moiety. Harris shows what I have called Laymi (3) further subdivided into three ayllus, one of which notes the presence of a Qullana, or preeminent, ayllu. Its presence may indicate Inka manipulation at this level, perhaps the insertion of an ayllu of *mitmaq* into the local system, as occurred in Cuenca to the north (Houdart-Morizot 1976).

The extraordinary depth of Andean organization surviving in northern Potosí had made possible a more coherent discussion of Inka and lower-level dualities than is possible using material from other Andean regions. I have discussed only in a broad outline the organization of Macha and Laymi in the twentieth century. I have made no mention of the dual organization within the ayllus at all levels, which pits the higher puna lands and economy, based on herding and potato cultivation, against the lower valley economy, based on the cultivation of maize. The use of dual opposition and complementarity to provide access to the products of both zones is common to both the Macha and Laymi, but is found in other areas of the Andes as well (Duviols 1973; Netherly and Dillehay 1986).

A final piece of evidence for major Inka manipulation of dual political structures of the Charka and Karakara within the larger Charka polity is the disposition of the Charka lands as shown in the map published by Platt (1986, Fig. 13.3). The lands of the Macha, Pukwata, and Sakaka ayllus are laid out in long strips and include puna and valley lands with a *chaupi,* or intermediate, zone between them. This arrangement of lands across ecozones in long strips occurs elsewhere on the *altiplano* (Wachtel 1974). Harris infers that the Chayanta lands, which are now discontinuous and separated by mestizo and white landholdings, originally had the same form (1986). Figure 1.4 presents the layout of the lands of the modern and colonial polities in schematic form. The heavy line indicates the division between the former Charka and Karakara lands. The small numbers to the left indicate the relative hierarchical position of the polities presented in Figure 1.3. In the longitudinal quadripartite schema found in the Andes (Bouysse-Cassagne 1986; Netherly 1990), the chaupi line divides the two moieties, in this instance Charka and Karakara, and the highest-ranking of the moieties at the next organization level are found immediately next to the chaupi division. The lower-ranking moieties are found in the outside positions. The actual position of the ethnic lands, however, shows that Chayanta and Pukwata occupy the center positions, and the Sakaka and Macha lands lie in the outside, subordinate position. This positioning is the reverse of the structural position of these polities as given in the colonial documents.

We know the Inka dealt with the larger Charka polity in a special way, reserving this large group for military service. We also know that the internal political structure of Macha and probably Sakaka, which originally may well have shared the asymmetrical duality found in Chayanta, was altered to conform to the decimal organization of the Inka state. Some lower-level polities may have been removed from the Macha and Sakaka as *mitmaq* or *yana* and replaced with groups of different ethnic origin to assure the loyalty of these former Inka opponents.

The Nature of the Andean State 25

(1)	SAKAKA
(2)	[CHAYANTA]
(2)	PUKWATA
(1)	MACHA

Figure 1.4. Quadripartite organization of the lands of the former Charka and Karakara moieties. Note the reversed hierarchical relationships within each moiety.

I hypothesize that the position of the lands of Sakaka and Chayanta of the Charka polity and those of Pukwata and Macha of the Karakara reflect the original ranking of the moieties in pre-Inka times. The Inka modified the political structure of Macha and Sakaka, originally the *urinsaya* moieties in Charka and Sakaka, and then *redefined* their rank to *anansaya* but left the traditional lands as they were. This arrangement would have insured Inka control of their Charka fighting force, which was surely of prime importance (Murra 1986).

Even though the evidence suggests that no single Andean dual political structure existed, Andean political structures are nevertheless based on fundamental, ranked dual oppositions expressed in terms of opposed polities at all levels of organization. Tripartite, quadripartite, and decimal systems are subsumed under the dual organization. Andean governance was based on a system of ranked rulers who together represented the whole polity. The system of checks and balances among such ruling groups must have been delicate indeed, and the political reality highly complex. Nevertheless, because of its nested and ranked structure, the survival of Andean political organization was not dependent on the survival of the Andean states. The tenacity with which Andean peoples have retained a ranked dual organization is testimony to its effectiveness in organizing human endeavor and harnessing human energy.

Succession in Andean Polities as a Mechanism for Perpetuation

Let us now turn to the way the principles of Andean kinship were used to provide an orderly succession in normal cases and a reasonable—by Andean lights—succession in abnormal ones. It appears that succession normally took place within the patriline of a deceased lord. The choice seems to have been made by the collegium of lords, that is, the lords of the other sections of the polity, who belonged to different lineages. It is clear, however, that reigning lords, and presumably other senior members of their respective lineages as well, may have favored particular candidates to the point of designating them as their preferred successors before the old lord's death (Netherly 1977, n.d.a.).

The preferred succession appears to have been by younger brothers and then sons of the deceased lord; in terms of the Andean kinship calculus, these kinsmen were structurally equivalent (Zuidema 1978). Some of the most complete data on succession come from a small polity of the central coast of Peru, the *parcialidad* and *waranqa* of Guancayo in the Chillon Valley (Martinez Rengifo [1571] 1963:58-69; Netherly 1977, n.d.a.). Less complete information from the north coast, particularly Lambayeque, conforms to the same general pattern (Netherly 1977, 1988b, 1990, n.d.a; Rostworowski 1961, 1972). These provincial succession models are pertinent to the understanding of Inka succession, although the group of possible heirs was more severely restricted in the Inka case, again by use of the kinship calculus (Zuidema 1978).

One of the most important characteristics of Andean succession to high office seems to have been the preference of the younger brothers of the deceased lord in order of birth. This ranking is one of the organizational features of Andean kinship (Zuidema 1978). There seems to have been little or no distinction between the sons of a principal wife and those of secondary wives; the patrilineal link appears to be more important. Clearly this is at some variance with the data presented for the Inka by Zuidema (1964, 1978), in which a sharp distinction is made between the sons of the Inka by his principal wife, who was his full sister, and those by secondary wives, who were generally unrelated to the Inka. The number of male siblings was high in the provincial succession lists; it fluctuated between three and six as a consequence of the lords' polygyny. The Inka state, perhaps in order to minimize the possibility of rebellion and at the same time to capitalize on the leadership potential of this group, called for and got the younger sons of local and regional lords as part of the labor service contributed by these groups to the state. In the case of the *waranqa* of Guancayo in the Chillon Valley, Martinez Rengifo ([1571] 1963:63; Netherly 1977) reports that one of the labor service requirements of that polity was to send three sons of lords to serve the Inka.

A close examination of the information on succession in Guancayo shows how this functioned. Guancayo was divided into nine *pachaqa* of one hundred adult married men each. This is an anomaly, since presumably a *waranqa* would normally have ten *pachaqa* to make up the requisite one thousand households. The lord of the *waranqa* of Guancayo, the *waranqa-kuraka,* with whom the succession account begins, was Mongoy. In addition to being *waranqakuraka*, Mongoy was also lord of two *pachaqa*, one called Guancayo and the other called Guarauin. When Mongoy died, his eldest son, also called Mongoy, became lord of the *waranqa* of Guancayo and lord of the *pachaqa* of Guancayo. The *pachaqa* of Guarauin went to another son of the deceased Mongoy, named Paicongo. On the death of his brother, Mongoy, Paicongo succeeded him as *waranqakuraka*, retaining the *pachaqa* of Guarauin. The *pachaqa* of Guancayo passed to a third brother, Chuquinpayco. Thereafter, the lordship of the *pachaqa* of Guancayo passed to three younger male siblings of Chuquinpayco in turn and only then did it pass to the son of the seventh brother. Figure 1.5 shows the succession of Guancayo. Much the same pattern appears in the succession to the *pachaqa* of Guarauin. After the death of Paicongo, seven of his nine sons were lords of the *pachaqa* in turn. Only then did the succession shift to the descending generation, first to the son of Paicongo's second son and then to the son of his fifth son. Figure 1.6 shows this succession.

Succession to a polity of much larger scale, once a regional state—the Lambayeque polity of the north coast—shows similar principles at work. Lambayeque was organized by dual and quadripartite division (the information that follows pertains to the succession of the highest-ranking lords). The oral tradition recording the last lords of Lambayeque, under first

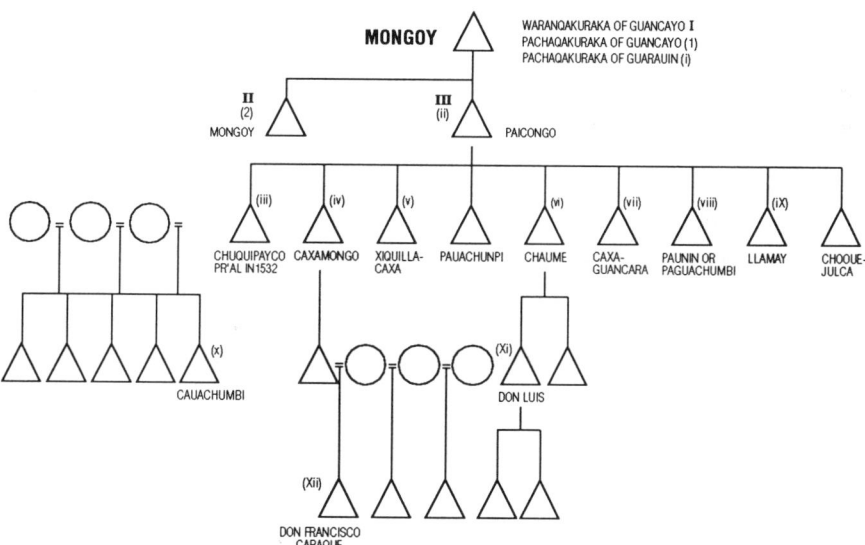

Figure 1.5. Succession in the *waranqa* of Guancayo and the *pachaqa* of Guarauin (Martínez Rengifo [1571] 1963).

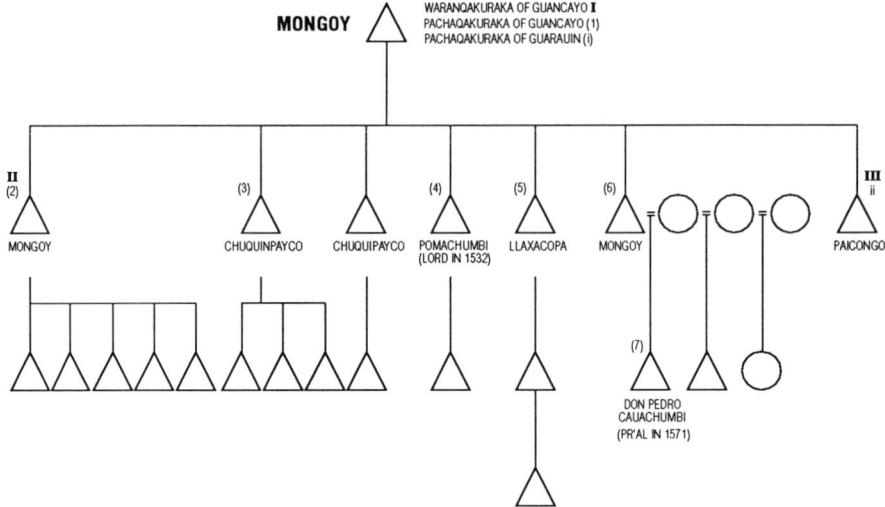

Figure 1.6. Succession in the *waranqa* of Guancayo and the *pachaqa* of Guancayo (Martínez Rengifo [1571] 1963).

Chimu and then Inka domination, was recorded by Cabello Balboa ([1586] 1951:329-30, 417, 468) in the late sixteenth century and again in the eighteenth century in a genealogical account that was presented to support the claim of one of the contestants in a case involving the colonial *cacicazgo* of Lambayeque (Vargas Ugarte 1942:480). There are many distortions in the genealogical claim, but these appear to be either errors or else an attempt to exclude the issue of the fifth brother, Cuzcochumbi, from the succession. Cabello's account written fifty years after the events is more worthy of trust.

Cabello's information is used in Figure 1.7 with the exception of the names of the murdered brothers of Xecfuinpisan. Cabello traces the succession in the more distant generations as from father to son—which may well be a convention of Andean geneologies (Netherly 1990; Zuidema 1990). In the two generations immediately before that of Don Martin Farrochumbi, lord in 1566, there is lateral succession by brothers. Indeed, one of the more interesting aspects of the account of the death of Xecfuinpisan, the lord of Lambayeque who was put to death by the lords who accompanied him as he traveled to Jayanca to meet the Spanish invaders, is the fact that Cabello relates that he put to death three of his brothers, presumably to eliminate them as potential rivals ([1586] 1951:468). Succession by siblings creates a situation in which factions can develop around

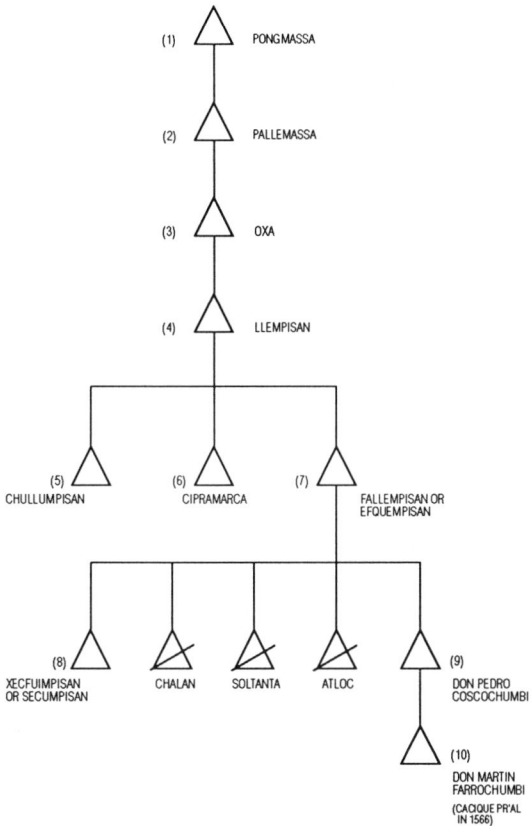

Figure 1.7. Succession in the polity of Lambayeque (Cabello Balboa [1586] 1951:329–30, 417, 468; Vargas Ugarte 1942:478, 481).

the adult younger brother of a lord, and this was surely a major problem with which the lords had to contend. The lords traveling with Xecfuinpisan were heads of the lower-ranking sections of the Lambayeque polity. The account is clear that it is they who undertook the responsibility of a discrete execution by murder of a lord who was a triple fratricide and prepared to deal with the Spanish as well.

Another kind of succession occurred when, instead of inheritance of a lordship by a group of brothers in turn, the moieties of a polity were divided and the leadership of each given to two brothers. In Huaura on the central coast in 1583, one of the *ayllu* (as the subdivisions were called in this Quechua-speaking valley) was split between two brothers and each ruled as headman. The division was so recent that there was as yet no differentiation by name of the two parts (Netherly 1977, n.d.a). It appears that this division was along moiety lines and that it occurred in order to bring the number of *ayllu* up to eight in a system of quadripartion.

A somewhat different instance illustrates the means by which the lords of a polity could serve as a pool of replacement rulers if the need arose. This instance is late, from the seventeenth century, but it is confirmed by much earlier but less complete examples. This function, which could be called the contingency function, seems to have devolved on the lord of the second moiety when there was no successor to the paramount lord. The prehispanic polities of Collique and Cinto in the Lambayeque Valley were removed to Chiclayo in the sixteenth century. This site is described as lying on the boundary between the lands of the two polities (Arroyo 1956). Indeed, the town itself was divided until the nineteenth century, with the Indians of Cinto located to the north of the plaza and those of Collique to the south. In the third decade of the seventeenth century, the *senor principal* of Collique died without leaving an heir. He was succeeded in 1623 by the *segunda persona* (lord of the second-ranking moiety), who thus accumulated the lordship of both moieties and that of the paramount lord in his person. According to witnesses in the litigation, one of the functions of the lord of the second moiety was to be available to act as a stand-in for the paramount by acting as a high-ranking substitute. What happened next, however, expresses the Andean conception of both dual division and succession. On the death of this lord, the lordship of the second moiety passed to his eldest son, who became in Spanish terms *segunda persona*. The younger son became lord of the first moiety while his father was still alive and founded a separate lineage (Netherly 1977, n.d.a.).

There is a final point to make with regard to this case. Although rule was divided at any given level, including the highest, between a collegium of two, four, or eight lords according to context, each lord was head of his own lineage. When in the literature a *segunda persona* is referred to as a "brother" of the paramount, this cannot be taken literally, as the Spanish chroniclers apparently did, because the lords of the collegium had to be heads of independent lineages. When, as in the instance cited above, a polity was divided between two brothers or brothers occupied the headships of both moieties, each founded a distinct lineage with their common father as a common ancestor. What the statement that the lord of the second moiety is "brother" to the paramount/lord of the first moiety really indicates is the hierarchical difference between them, just as an older sibling outranks a younger within their common status as siblings (Netherly n.d.a.; Zuidema 1978).

This situation is entirely different from the common practice of designating an heir who may have been a younger brother or a son or a brother's son. Although a lord could express a preference and could even join such a favorite to him as almost a coruler, he could not preempt the final decision of the collegium of lords. Furthermore, such association of an heir as a coruler was possible only because it was taking place within the *same lineage,* not across lineages (Netherly n.d.a.). Kinship is a calculus. It permits the structuring of society in such a way that everyone knows where they fit in. It became in the Andes a powerful tool of analogy and was used in many spheres to describe relationships that strictly speaking had nothing to do with it.

It may be asked what the advantages were for Andean societies of such a political organization, particularly in the light of their characteristic cohesiveness and adaptive success. From an organizational point of view, it appears that one advantage is that of articulation. In every context, one knows where one fits into the system.

A second advantage seems to be stability, at least on the regional level. The Andean states were aggregations of hierarchically organized regional states and smaller polities, characterized in the first instance by indirect rule. Whereas these larger expansionist states rose by a process of aggregation and fell by a process of disaggregation again and again in Andean history, the regional states remained remarkably stable. One might note in contrast the factional, ritual battles that took place in some African states by means of which the whole polity had to be redefined at the succession of each new ruler.

A final advantage from the point of view of political economy, where the regional states in particular were especially effective, was the reduction of risk in a disaster-prone environment (Netherly 1977, n.d.a.). The rulers of these states provided for storage and redistribution of food and seed, as well as for the effective mobilization of human energy in the face of calamity, both natural and man-made. For the Andean peoples, whose minimal political unit was the small-scale group, not the household or the individual, the benefits of state organization clearly outweighed the costs.

References

Adams, Richard N.
    1975   *Energy and Structure: A Theory of Social Power.* Austin: University of Texas Press.
Albó, Javier, and CIPCA personnel

1972   Dinámica en la estructura inter-communitaria de Jesus de Machaca. *América Indígena* 32:773–816.

Arguedas, José Maria
1964   Puquio: Una cultura en proceso de cambio. In Luis Valcarcel, ed., *Estudios sobre la cultura actual del Perú*, pp. 221–72. Lima: Universidad Nacional Mayor de San Marcos.

Arroyo, Luis
1956   *Los Franciscanos y la fundación de Chiclayo*. Lima.

Bouysse-Cassagne, Thérèse
1986   *Urco* and *uma*: Aymara concepts of space. In John V. Murra, Nathan Wachtel, and Jacques Revel, eds., *Anthropological History of Andean Polities*, pp. 201–27. London: Cambridge University Press.

Cabello Balboa, Miguel
[1586] *Miscelánea antártica*. Lima: Universidad Nacional Mayor de San
1951   Marcos.

Carneiro, Robert L.
1970   A theory of the origin of the state. *Science* 169:733–38.
1981   The chiefdom as precursor of the state. In Grant Jones and Robert Kautz, eds., *The Transition to Statehood in the New World*, pp. 37–70. New York: Cambridge University Press.

Cohen, Ronald
1978a   State origins: A reappraisal. In H. J. M. Claessen and P. Skalnik, eds., *The Early States*, pp. 31–75. The Hague : Mouton.
1978b   Introduction. In R. Cohen and E. Service, eds., *Origin of the State*, pp. 1–20. Philadelphia: Institute for the Study of Human Issues.

Dollfus, Olivier
1986   The tropical Andes: A changing mosaic. In John V. Murra, Nathan Wachtel, and Jacques Revel, eds., *Anthropological History of Andean Polities*, pp. 11–22. London: Cambridge University Press.

Duviols, Pierre
1973   Huari y llacuaz, agricultores y pastores: Un dualismo prehispánico de oposición y complementaridad. *Revista del Museo Nacional* (Lima) 39.
1979   La dinastía de los incas: ¿Monarquía o diarguía? Argumentos heurísticos a favor de una tesis estructuralista. *Journal de la Société des Américanistes* 66:67–83.

Engels, Friedrich
1972   *The Origin of the Family, Private Property, and the State*. Reprint
[1891] ed., ed. Eleanor Leacock. New York: International Publishers.

Espinoza Soriano, Waldemar
1969   El "Memorial" de Charcas: "Crónica inédita". In *Cantuta, Revista de la Universidad de Educación*. Chosica, Peru: Universidad de Educación La Cantuta.

Fortes, Meyer, and E. E. Evans-Pritchard
1940   Introduction. *African Political Systems*. London: Oxford University Press.

Fried, Morton
- 1967   *The Evolution of Political Society.* New York: Random House.

Goldschmidt, Walter
- 1962   Foreword. In Edgar V. Wynans, *Shambala: The Constitution of a Traditional State.* Berkeley: University of California Press.

Harris, Olivia
- 1986   From asymmetry to triangle: Symbolic transformations in northern Potosí. In John V. Murra, Nathan Wachtel, and Jacques Revel, eds., *Anthropological History of Andean Polities,* pp. 260–80. London: Cambridge University Press.

Houdart-Morizot, Marie-France
- 1976   *Tradition et pouvoir à Cuenca, communauté andine.* Travaux de l'Institut Français d'Etudes Andines, vol. 15. Lima.

Isbell, William H., and K. Schrieber
- 1978   Was Wari a state? *American Antiquity* 43:373–89.

Martínez Rengifo, Juan
- [1571]   La visita de Guancayo, Maca, y Guaravni 1571. In Waldemar Espinoza Soriano, La Guaranga y la reduccion de Huancayo. *Revista del Museo Nacional* (Lima), 32.
- 1963

Murra, John V.
- 1967   La visita de los chupachu como fuente etnológica. In Iñigo Ortiz de Zúñiga, *Visita de la provincia de León de Huánuco en 1562,* vol. 1, pp. 381–406. Huánuco: Universidad Nacional Hermilio Valdizán.
- 1968   An Aymara kingdom in 1567. *Ethnohistory* 15:115–51.
- 1975   *Formaciones económicas y políticas del mundo andino.* Lima: Instituto de Estudios Peruanos.
- 1980   *The Economic Organization of the Inka State.* Greenwich, Conn.: JAI Press Inc.
- 1986   The expansion of the Inka state: Armies, war, and rebellions. In John V. Murra, Nathan Wachtel, and Jacques Revel, eds., *Anthropological History of Andean Polities,* pp. 49–58. London: Cambridge University Press.

Netherly, Patricia J.
- 1977   Local level lords on the north coast of Peru. Ph.D. diss., Department of Anthropology, Cornell University.
- 1984   The management of late Andean irrigation systems on the north coast of Peru. *American Antiquity* 49(2):227–54.
- 1988a   From event to process: The recovery of late Andean organizational structure by means of Spanish colonial written records. In Richard Keatinge, ed., *An Overview of Peruvian Prehistory,* pp. 257–78. Cambridge: Cambridge University Press.
- 1988b   El reino de Chimor y el Tawantinsuyu. In Tom D. Dillehay and Patricia J. Netherly, eds., *La frontera del estado inca,* pp. 105–29.
- 1988c   Los señores tardíos en las costa y sierra norte. *Alternativa: Revista de Análisis del Norte.* (Chiclayo, Peru) 9:59–75.
- 1990   Out of many, one: The organization of rule in the north coast polities.

In Michael E. Moseley and Alana Cordy-Collins, eds., *The Northern Dynasties: Kingship and Statecraft in Chimor*, pp. 461–87. Washington, D.C.: Dumbarton Oaks Research Library and Collection.
n.d.a. Lords and ancestors: Political organization on the north coast of Peru. Ms. in possession of the author.
n.d.b. Andean realms. Ms. in possession of the author.

Netherly, Patricia J., and Tom D. Dillehay
1986 Duality in public architecture in the upper Zaña valley. In Daniel H. Sandweiss and D. Peter Kvietok, eds., *Perspectives in Andean Prehistory and Protohistory*, pp. 85–114. Ithaca, N.Y.: Cornell University, Latin American Studies Program.

Palomino Flores, Salvador
1971 La dualidad en la organización sociocultural de algunos pueblos andinos. *Revista del Museo Nacional* (Lima) 37:231–60.

Platt, Tristan
1986 Mirrors and maize: The concept of "yanantin" among the Macha of Bolivia. In John V. Murra, Nathan Wachtel, and Jacques Revel, eds., *Anthropological History of Andean Polities*, pp. 228–59. London: Cambridge University Press.

Rostworowski de Diez Canseco, María
1961 *Curacas y sucesiones*. Lima.
1972 Breve ensayo sobre el señorío de Ichma o Ychima. *Arqueología PUC* (Lima) 13.

Schaedel, Richard P.
1985 The transition from chiefdom to state in northern Peru. In H. J. M. Claesen et al., eds., *Development and Decline: The Evolution of Sociopolitical Organization*, pp. 156–69. South Hadley, Mass.: Bergin and Garvey.

Service, Elman
1975 *Origin of the State and Civilization*. New York: W. W. Norton.

Troll, Carl
1958 *Las culturas superiores andinas y el medio geográfico*. Lima: Universidad Nacional Mayor de San Marcos.
1968 *Geoecology of the Mountainous Regions of the Tropical Americas*. Colloquium Geographicum Band 9. Bonn: Ferd. Dümmlers Verlag.

Vargas Ugarte, Rubén
1942 Los Mochicas y el cacicazgo de Lambayeque. International Congress of Americanists, 27th, *Actas y Trabajos*. Lima.

Wachtel, Nathan
1974 Le dualisme chipaya: Compte-rendu du mission. Institut Français d'Etudes Andines (Paris, Lima), *Bulletin* 3(3):55–65.
1982 The *mitimas* of the Cochabamba valley: The colonization policy of Huayna Capac. In George A. Collier, Renato I. Rosaldo, and John D. Wirth, eds., *The Inca and Aztec States 1400–1800: Anthropology and History*, pp. 201–35. New York: Academic Press.

Wright, Henry T., and Gregory Johnson
1975 Population, exchange, and early state formation in southwestern Iran. *American Anthropologist* 77:267–89.

Zuidema, R. Tom
1964 *The Ceque System of Cuzco: The Social Organization of the Capital of the Inca.* Leiden: Brill.
1978 The Inca kinship system: A new theoretical view. In Ralph Bolton and Enrique Meyer, eds., *Andean Kinship and Marriage*, pp. 240–81. Washington, D.C.: American Anthropological Association.
1982 Bureaucracy and systematic knowledge in Andean civilization. In George Collier et al., eds., *The Inca and Aztec States 1400–1800: Anthropology and History.* New York: Academic Press.
1990 Dynastic structures in Andean culture. In Michael E. Moseley and Alana Cordy-Collins, eds., *The Northern Dynasties: Kinship and Statecraft in Chimor*, pp. 489–505. Washington, D.C.: Dumbarton Oaks Research Library and Collection.

CHAPTER TWO

The Wealth of a Native American State: Value, Investment, and Mobilization in the Inka Economy

Craig Morris

"The compulsory issue of culturally valued commodities in a society without money and relatively small markets can be viewed as the initial pump-priming step in a dependent relationship, since the 'generosity' of the conqueror obligates one to reciprocate, to deliver on a regular, periodic basis, the results of one's workmanship" (Murra 1962:721). There are both economic and political dimensions to the "pump-priming" mechanisms mentioned by Murra in his studies of the role of cloth in the Inka state. Such gifts and exchanges seem to have been the common denominator of both political and economic growth. In spite of the early observation of the importance of the gift in economy and society (Mauss 1954), Murra's study (see also Murra 1980) is one of the few attempts to look at the concrete data of a large-scale society in which such mechanisms were critical. Most studies and classifications of precapitalist economies and exchange systems have assumed that if such systems are dynamic they are evolving toward some form of market economy (especially the case in archaeological studies). There has been much more interest in that transition than in the growth and embellishment of nonmarket systems per se.

My purpose here is to look at some of the possibilities for expansion in reciprocity-based systems of production and exchange. How is wealth created in an archaic society in which market mechanisms play at most a marginal role? Two closely related socioeconomic processes seem to me to be central to the problem: the conversion of an increasing proportion of the time and energy of the members of the society into work or labor, and the concentration or centralization of part of that labor and its products so that improvements in the management of labor and the technologies of production can be made.

These related processes appear to be intimately associated with the emergence of a new class of goods that serve the primary function of communicating information about social positions and relationships. The value of such goods rests in the social symbols and signs they convey and only incidentally, if at all, in their usefulness as tools, containers, shelters, or garments. The control and manipulation of such goods is thus part of the process by which sociopolitical change takes place, and the creation of wealth is inseparable from the creation of power.

From a comparative point of view, what is so intriguing and important about the Inka case is the remarkable scale it achieved while retaining economic and political institutions we tend to associate with small societies in which face-to-face contact among members is still feasible. Tawantinsuyu, the Inka state, was by far the largest political unit assembled in the New World: it amassed millions of bushels of foodstuffs in its storehouses (D'Altroy 1981; Morris 1967); it built terracing and irrigation systems that permanently altered the shape and productivity of areas with appropriate climatic conditions.

There is no doubt that the Inka realm was rapidly changing at the time of the Spanish invasion, and some claim that market and commodity exchange mechanisms were significant components of the state economy (Hartmann 1968). Most interpretations of the growing archaeological and written evidence, however, see an economy and polity vast in scale but still largely based on traditional pre-Inka Andean principles. State revenues depended mainly on the labor obligations of its subjects (Murra 1980; Rowe 1946). These labor obligations were manipulated by the state to provide food both to support the labor effort itself and to produce special prestige items that were important to the state as gifts for its subjects. Administrative cities were built to support a vision of rule based on gift giving and generosity by the ruler.

These points have been elaborated previously (Morris 1987; Morris and Thompson 1985; Murra 1980). Here I use the Inka material to explore the importance of special prestige goods and associated ceremonies in turning increasingly large segments of human time into labor and the related investments of available labor made possible by increasing sociopolitical scale and centralization of authority.

Prestige Goods, State Revenues, and the Growth of Labor Time

Archaeologists have long noted the important role of goods that signal differences in sociopolitical status and the significance of craft specialization that so often accompanies such goods (Childe 1951). The idea that these goods are a kind of automatic result of surplus agricultural production has long been surpassed, although both the assurance of an abundant and reliable food supply and a substantial degree of sedentism were probably essential for the emergence of production of nonsubsistence goods on a large scale. The more difficult questions involve the motivations, both sociocultural and individual, to produce and acquire such goods. What social, political, and economic functions did they serve? Why did people want such goods? How was the society able to organize the labor supply to produce them? These basic questions of value and demand are difficult enough to study in modern economies with the tools of marketing research at our disposal. In situations that are essentially pre- or protohistoric, as is the case with the Inka and other early complex societies, the lack of reliable information makes analysis extraordinarily difficult.

Long ago John Murra (1980) showed how the principles of Inka state revenues were based on community practices that gave leaders the rights to labor. Leaders arranged for the fields of the old, the infirm, the widowed, and the orphaned, as well as for those of religious deities and shrines, to be tilled. Leaders' own fields were, at least in part, tilled by community labor. Although practices were certainly not uniform, at least in the Andean highlands such limited rights to labor almost certainly extended back for centuries. Inka practices of state revenues seem to have drastically expanded the quantities of labor available to support the enterprises of the state and its elite.

In spite of recent strides in our understanding of Andean labor categories, quantitative data still are lacking. But the process involved shifts in the proportions of time devoted to work in local fields and on local tasks in relation to work for the state. The state had access to labor in rotation through the *mit'a*. This was probably both its most traditional source of revenue and its most significant in terms of quantity. The evidence is beginning to suggest that three other labor categories were becoming increasingly important, since they offered more flexible, reliable, and nearly full-time work for especially critical jobs: (1) the *yana,* a category of men whose energies were at the disposition of the Inka (and occasionally also of local leaders) on a full-time basis; the *yana* were important for herding (Murra 1966); (2) the *aklla,* a category of women who, in addition to their apparent religious duties, were brewers and makers of cloth (Morris 1974;

Murra 1980; Rowe 1946); and (3) the *mitmaq*, a category based on groups of households rather than individuals, had its origins in the Andean principles of exploitation of multiple ecological zones described by Murra (1972). Members of the *mitmaq* were especially important because they could be moved, often as permanent colonies, great distances to perform important tasks. According to Wachtel (1982), early *mitmaq* "colonies" were placed for strategic reasons, but by the time of the Inka Huayna Capac, near the time of the European invasion, those responsible for tilling the fields of Cochabamba served functions that were primarily economic.

The shift in primary functions of some *mitmaq* from strategic to economic is only part of the apparent change. The maize fields of Cochabamba were cultivated by both temporary and permanent laborers. Apparently, *mit'a* as well as *mitmaq* institutions were employed (Wachtel 1982:213). What is particularly interesting about the Cochabamba case, beyond the enormous scale of state agricultural operations it documents, are the data on the support of the people who worked the fields. In part, at least, they had access to the produce of Inka state fields through the Inka's "generosity" and the state granaries. In addition, they were given lands for their own cultivation under their own leaders. The lower-level leaders were thus responsible for the "generosity" and redistribution (Wachtel 1982:215–17). This assignment of the management of the sustenance for state labor in part to lower levels in the hierarchy of political units seems to indicate some compromise of the principle of maintenance and generosity by the state as represented in the person of the Inka. By Huayna Capac's time, the scale to which the state was tapping its labor resources may have begun to blur some of the distinctions between categories such as *mit'a* and *mitmaq*. The drive was toward a more effective use of potential labor resources, which may not always have coincided with traditional rules of generosity or land distribution in relation to the various labor categories.

It is not possible to provide an exhaustive review of Inka labor revenues in this context. Like everything else, principles were changing and could not be rigid in rapid expansion over vast and varied geography. The effects of incorporating coastal peoples and peoples near the northern frontier in particular require careful evaluation. But, in spite of these complexities, there is no doubt of careful planning (coordination) in the use of the state's major resource, human energy. Increasingly large numbers of people were devoting increasingly larger parts of their time to state activities. How seriously this was impinging on local economic prerogatives is not clear, but there is little suggestion of large scale-dependence on the state for subsistence goods. The responsibility for local subsistence was still overwhelmingly in local hands.

As important as the increasing supply of labor in the state pool were the shifts in the sociopolitical context of production and in the kinds of work done. Although we have no quantatative information, the bulk of the state labor was probably still devoted to agriculture—for the Inka, and for fulfilling his obligations to others. But increasingly it went into the making of cloth, into warfare, and into construction and other activities of special political value. Much of this manipulation of labor was diversion from local uses to state purposes. But if we could measure it, I suspect we would see that the state had achieved a per capita increase in overall output, an increase in productivity, as well as a shift in the objectives of production.

The measure and documentation of per capita labor time is not possible with presently available evidence. Like population, it can only be measured archaeologically with extraordinary data. But, nevertheless, the summation of roads, towns, terraces, storehouses, and the rich clothing seen in the court and army at Cajamarca implies a significant increase in overall wealth in the central Andean highlands from the immediately pre-Inka period. The amassing of new wealth seems more than can be explained by extractions from the coast and elsewhere or increases that might result from technological improvements. As questions of productivity are addressed in future research, one topic that deserves special attention is scheduling. In particular, we need to look more closely at both the cultural and ecological dimensions of the annual cycle. The temporal aspect of the use of multiple ecologies needs to be studied in more detail, as do the ways that nonsubsistence, prestige goods were factored into the cycle. The calendar and its associated ceremonies (Zuidema 1964, 1982) was primary in manipulating the cycle so that human energy was effectively deployed through the seasonal cycle and the diverse geographic zones. The precision with which ecological time and space were coordinated is emerging as one of the major Andean achievements.

Although the calendar was a critical coordinating and administrative mechanism, it does not in itself explain why people gave up time from personal and local pursuits for the sake the Inka. If we reject the notion of outright slavery, we must try to see the economic and social factors that helped transform the use of human time and energy—both the transfer of labor time from local to state projects, and the conversion of what may be called, for want of a better term, leisure time to economically productive labor time.

Symbolic Value and the Mobilization of Labor

Part of what is needed to come to terms with the so-called prestige goods and the economic and political growth that accompanied their production is the expansion and modernization of theories of value. Although the element of labor (Marx 1977) is basic to analytical understandings, it is not sufficient for dealing with social and economic behavior in relation to such objects. There are certain goods which, in the absence of overt coercion, people will expend more labor to acquire than the total amount of labor necessary to produce and deliver them. Part of the difference between the labor cost of an object or service and the labor it can command is a result of various symbolic meanings associated with the goods. They are imbued with a set of culturally defined values that in effect turn them into signs of prestige, acceptance, security, and a whole repertory of benefits society can bestow. They come to have meaning in terms of a cultural code, not unlike language. A major function of the objects is, in fact, to communicate information about roles, statuses, and group identities.

It is easy to see the importance of these symbolic values in a superficial way in modern commodities: certain trademarks are worth more than others; the allure of sex and romance may account for most of the enormous difference between the production cost of perfume and its price; a gift with the imprimatur of an emperor is worth more than one without it. But analysis of symbolic aspects of goods is another matter, one that involves issues ranging through semiotics and the psychology of motivation as well as complex institutional questions. It also involves appropriating matters from the cognitive and emotional domains and defining them in economic terms. As unsatisfactorily as such redefinition must be, some attempt is necessary if we are to understand how the transformations in the quantitites and loci of expenditure of labor times were achieved. Some approximation can perhaps be made by looking at the difference, indicated above, between the labor one will expend to acquire an object, privilege, or service and the labor required to produce it. The greater part of that difference lies in the social relations, positions, and qualities the goods symbolize. Part of the difference can also be attributed to strictly circumstantial elements such as variations in who is present and where things happen in the production or exchange situations.

The evident difficulty is in measuring the portion of value that pertains to symbols, signals, sentiments, and the contexts of circulation. Even with ethnographic data such matters defy quantification except as the residue after more traditional values have been taken into account. Archaeological and early written information is even more intractable. One of the ways these notions can perhaps best serve us is in clarifying our understanding of what is sometimes referred to as mobilization exchange (Smelser 1959), that centripetal economic form in which large quantities of goods flow toward the political and economic center of the society to be consumed there in support of political ends. The term has been used mainly in relation to modern wartime economies in which personal consumption is reduced in favor of economic support of state purposes. Labor is ordinarily also increased, with the result of growth in production. The increased labor and reduced personal consumption on the part of most of the people is the result of the state's ability to persuade them of the advantage of its actions and the disadvantages and dangers of alternative courses. Normally this persuasion involves communication and ceremonies that implore a spirit of patriotic solidarity and the threat of coercion to those who do not collaborate. Since the success of mobilization is likely to depend on a kind of ratio between enthusiastic supporters and reluctant participants, the importance of the state's effort to communicate, promote, and dramatize its directives is critical. Different versions of these same factors of mobilization were probably involved as early complex societies drew wealth and power into their centers as the basis for hierarchical and geographic expansion. But, like most other concepts invented to encapsulate modern phenomena, mobilization (as in to fight a foreign war) tends to obscure the archaic institutions early complex societies used to feed, clothe, and justify their power structures.

The real advantage of looking more closely at the symbolic value of goods is the possibility they offer of illustrating the dynamics of the growth of wealth and power in this particular archaic kind of mobilization. Goods whose value largely depends on the human relationships they symbolize are at the interface of the material and cognitive realms. They are the focal point where the cultural principles guiding the structuring of a society and the more concrete relationships of production meet. In archaic societies they were, on the one hand, part of the system whereby a cultural code that legitimated a larger sociopolitical scale was established. On the other hand, they were involved with the expanded technologies and economic relationships that were evolving to provide for their production. Tension and disjunctions at such interfaces between the cultural subsystem and social and ecological relations are especially conducive to change (Geertz 1973). In early complex societies, the interplay between the meanings, productions, and exchange of sumptuary goods was a pivot of change. Each increase in sociopolitical scale involved new principles of coordination and new social relationships. It also involved new levels of wealth to support not just the elite itself but the elaborate ceremonial and symbolizing apparatus that communicated the principles and propagated the relationships that enabled larger sociopolitical scales to function.

The prominence and virtuosity of cloth among Andean goods is no coincidence: it was the major carrier of the signs and symbols that guided social relations (Murra 1962). The great elaboration of metallurgical technologies lay in a series of techniques to achieve surface color. Tools, and particularly weapons, were of secondary importance (Lechtman 1980). The emphasis, again, was on symbols of status and ceremonial paraphernalia. Even among subsistence goods, maize occupied a special, prestige role (Murra 1960). The *chicha* beer brewed from it was the essence of hospitality, the common denominator of ritual and ceremonial relationships (Morris 1979). It was the drink generous leaders were required to provide as part of their obligations of authority. The terraces and irrigation that brought new warm lands into cultivation in the "sacred" Urubamba valley and elsewhere in Tawantinsuyu were not for ordinary food but for the prestige food and drink that formed part of the substance of sociopolitical relationships. The value of maize was such that it was transported great distances. Certainly, efforts to organize the cultivation of the maize fields near Cochabamba on the eastern slopes of the Bolivian Andes and the human and animal energy to carry the maize to Cuzco (Wachtel 1982) cannot be justified in subsistence terms alone. If mere subsistence was the objective, an equal amount of labor time invested in potatoes would probably have fed more people. But mere subsistence is not what complex societies are about.

Investment of State Revenues

Traditionally we tend to not speak of investments in precapitalist economies. Whether consciously calculated or not, however, both the likely overall increase in production and the shifts of labor resources to the state were heavily based on the accumulation of goods, the improvement of land, and the construction of facilities. Economic and political expansion would not have been possible without key investments in facilities and infrastructure which made possible the production of symbolically important goods as well as the situations in which they acquired and communicated their meanings. Three forms of state investment are most evident in the archaeological and written records for the Inka: warehousing; the acquisition and improvement of land; and the building of ceremonial cities connected by roads.

Investments in Storage

The massive Inka warehousing system so admired by the Spanish has been amply confirmed archaeologically (D'Altroy 1981; Morris 1967). My studies of it in the 1960s suggested that the stored goods, mainly food, primarily served state operations. These included maintenance of the military, the bureaucracy, and the elite; construction projects; and to some extent nonagricultural production for the state. These goods also supplied ceremonial and ritual activities in state centers. Whatever their specific uses, the state stores obviously represent a major investment and a triumph of planning and organization, with the warehouses integrated into parts of the broader infrastructual system.

The Inka warehouses may be seen primarily as a key to expanding labor revenues. Andean tradition held the recipient of labor services responsible for the sustenance of the crew. Furthermore, many of the state projects and campaigns were in places where abundant and reliable food supplies were not available. If the state was to mobilize large amounts of labor, it had first to invest in the means to provide for its workers. Part of this provisioning was accomplished by increases in both the quality and reliability of food production. But it was the storehouses, prominently in view on the hills above Inka installations, that assured that the workers would be fed wherever they were needed.

The Alienation and Technological Transformation of Lands

Land as well as labor was required to produce the goods that filled the storehouses. Because of the scant data, regional variation, and many layers of social and political organization, land tenure within Tawantinsuyu is yet another ill-understood topic. The official Inka version that there were three kinds of lands—those of the community, the religion, and the Inka—is often repeated. Although this is an oversimplification, these distinctions are sufficient for my discussion here. The question becomes one of how state lands were acquired. We have no quantitative figures on the proportions of state lands as compared to the other categories, but the figures must have been large and growing. There is also the question of how state and religious lands differed in terms of the disposition of their produce. After all the sun, to which much of this land was supposedly dedicated, was the state religion.

Much of the land must have been transferred to the state from local community rights, although there are too few clearly documented cases to allow us to understand the mechanisms involved. In some cases, direct alienation was probably carried out, particularly in regions where Inka domination was accomplished through force. It was probably also common in the local division of lands to assign part of those lands that had previously gone to support local leaders and shrines to the Inka and the sun.

The use of *mitmaq* colonies to occupy and utilize lands in regions far from Cuzco was perhaps a special form of alienation, again based on much earlier Andean traditions. The Inka were taking advantage of customs of ecological complementarity that allowed polities direct access to varied ecological zones and permitted them to establish their colonies in those areas in order to bring labor to the land. The movements of people and the accompanying reassignment of land rights were sometimes on a very large scale, and by late Inka times they were used in some cases to give the state access to maize fields (Morris 1985; Murra 1960; Wachtel 1982).

Inka land policies are most clearly evident archaeologically in the great terracing systems that altered the shapes of the deep highland valleys. The terraces, frequently incorporating irrigation, increased land area, productivity, and reliability in areas where climatic conditions were correct for growing maize (Murra 1980).

Definitive studies of Inka land renovation have not been made, but there is no better topic to indicate the extent and detail of Inka coordination and planning. Terrace design was concerned with drainage, availability of water, flatness of the surface, and possibly even minor temperature differences at various levels within the terracing systems (Earls and Silverblatt 1981). The effective utilization of renovated lands was further increased by the use of Inka labor institutions to match human skills to the kind of cultivation best suited to a given system. It is this combination of sensitive ecological understandings, technological capabilities, and organizational scope that is so impressive. It had become important to increase production of food, particularly maize, and the Inka knew how to bring the land, the engineering, and the human energy together to accomplish it.

Infrastructure, Production Facilities, and Other Investments

We might examine many other aspects of Tawantinsuyu in terms of contributions to investment and growth. The herds of llamas and alpaca that were the principal component of wealth in the altiplano (Murra 1972) were managed toward state objectives. The system of roads and way stations that formed the infrastructure without which such a large territory could not have functioned also served as investment, although that certainly, is not the only way it can be viewed (Hyslop 1985; Morris 1982). The production of crafts was still organized in many different ways within the Inka realm; but archaeological research at Huanuco Pamapa uncovered a substantial production complex devoted to cloth making and brewing, probably by a group of *aklla* women (Morris 1974). The archaeological context is such as to leave no doubt of state construction and control of the facility. In 1984 and 1985 a smaller cloth production complex was excavated in the heart of the Inka compound at La Centinela, the capital of the Chincha kingdom that had been incorporated into Tawantinsuyu. The preliminary evidence suggests that the labor unit here was probably not *aklla*, but direct state control of production is indicated.

In sum, the data leave no doubt that Inka managed much of their income and resources in such a way as to achieve growth. We do not yet have a good view of the attendant decision-making processes of Inka governance, in spite of our increasing understanding of the labor institutions through which it operated. The data are already clear on one point, however. The directions in which investments were placed were still basically attuned to the traditional economy of reciprocity and redistribution and the factors that made it grow. It was toward maize, cloth, and the infrastructure for ceremonial activities that most investment was aimed.

Ceremony and Symbolic Value: The Economic Context of the Ceremonial City

We have acquired during the 1970s and 80s at least two major new documents on the Inka at the state level. One of these is the description of state lands and workers in Cochabamba referred to above (Wachtel 1982). The other is the accumulated archaeological evidence on the great systems of settlements and roads built by the state (Hyslop 1985; Morris 1982; Morris and Thompson 1985). Huanuco Pampa is the most completely preserved of the large Inka settlements. It was abandoned rapidly after the European invasion, providing unusually good associations of archaeological materials with architecture. Nearly four thousand structures surround an open central plaza about a half-kilometer long. Several years of research there have suggested that Huanuco Pampa was a city built and essentially furnished by the state. Its 497 storehouses along with the cloth-making and brewing facilities already mentioned constitute the most obvious evidence for its economic life.

The limitations of archaeology have to be taken into account, and our sample of over two hundred tested buildings is small, given the size of the site. But we found no positive evidence of a marketplace, little to indicate systematic exchange with areas outside the center itself, and except for brewing and cloth making no evidence of craft production except on an incidental, household scale. Many of the residents were probably temporary. If our present interpretations are accurate, by far the greater part of the center's buildings and open plaza areas were devoted to public ritual and feasting. Some of the participants were lodged in small houses, but more, possibly the majority, stayed in larger communal-type structures. Cooking and eating were more often than not done in larger groups. Some of the housing appears to have been separated by gender.

In short, the population structure of Huanuco Pampa was not based on families in permanent residence. Some analysis remains to be done, but the population of the city seems to reflect groupings related to the Inka labor categories mentioned earlier. The overall plan of the city—in twelve zones composed of four quarters, each subdivided into three parts—mimics the Inka pattern replicated in the calendar and best known from the *ceque* organization of shrines in the Cuzco region (Zuidema 1964). The complex planning suggests highly structured public ritual space and a concern for both hierarchy and the social interplay of the various parts (Morris 1984). The city plan provided an architectural backdrop for public functions that were the main feature of large-scale reciprocal administration.

A second aspect is economic in a more direct sense: it refers to the relations between the cities and their ceremonies and the values of the prestige goods that were displayed, used, exchanged, and in some cases manufactured there. The value of these goods depended on their role in establishing and communicating social and cultural messages. That value is inseparable from—or acquired, if you will, as a result of—the ceremonial contexts of such centers as Huanuco Pampa. Like cities in quite different cultural contexts, this was a center of social and cultural creation and innovation. Its role was primarily that of creating or reaffirming a sociopolitical situation in which people could participate and be assigned roles in the growing political structure. One of its results was that the values of certain goods increased and the importance and power of the state and its leaders also increased. A feed-back loop was established which became a spiral in which wealth could be turned into ever greater prestige, and prestige into ever greater wealth.

One of the principal issues in the growth of an economy is the way it harnesses it own energies. Human labor is obviously not a simple constant that can be measured by the size, age, and health of the population. People work to gratify needs, some of which are biologically based, others learned as part of the cognitive apparatus of culture, and still others idiosyncratic. Under circumstances that we do not yet understand clearly, the kinds of gratification, or at least the ways gratification is symbolized, can expand markedly.

The motivations to work and the motivations to consume are thus closely related, even though analytical paradigms of economics find it useful to separate them. If we ever reach a point from which we can see the actual operation of Inka revenues in more detail, I expect that we will find that much of the work took place as part of the ceremonies and feasts. Consumption and work were directly linked; the rewards of labor were direct and close at hand.

I suspect, but cannot yet conclusively demonstrate, that most of the people at Huanuco Pampa were *mit'a,* the temporary laborers who were the major source of state revenues. Yet there is little evidence of the work they did, except for the ongoing construction of the center itself. The evidence of feasting and ceremony far outweighs the evidence of production. If *mit'a* "laborers" were there, they appear more as consumers than as workers. The difference between what was done in the fields and in the urban context of Huanuco Pampa was great, but the conception of the *mit'a* category, with both its obligations *and* its rewards, was probably more of a piece.

The ceremonial cities, at least to the extent that Huanuco Pampa is representative, were devoted to expanding the reciprocal polity and economy to a large scale by mobilizing both the political and the economic support of incorporated peoples. This use of ceremonial added what was in a sense an urban dimension to reciprocal relationships. The upper-scale relationships seem rather fictional (at least in comparison to smaller societies), but they at least attempted to set up the feeling and atmosphere of a direct relationship. They did this through an elaborate symbolic portrayal of the structure of the state and of its Inka rulers, acted out against the backdrop of the ceremonial city and with all the elaborate prestige goods as props to underline the messages.

Besides establishing and learning the sociopolitical relationships that formed the upper levels of sociopolitical scale, the participants became accustomed to the rewards in esteem and in goods that accompanied these new higher levels. Some of the goods were craft products, like clothing, which fixed new identities in relation to the overall structure in a more permanent way: symbols of the relationships that could be carried away from the ceremonial context in which they were received.

What I have outlined here is at least the fragment of a complex system of social and economic relations ordered by a group of traditional labor categories and made functional through an infrastructural system of ceremonial cities. Most of the details of this impressive native Andean state still elude us, and our understanding is at best tentative. Its enormous wealth, however, is amply demonstrated. And, as is the case with any wealthy society, the production of wealth beyond subsistence depends not just on critical natural resources and appropriate technologies but also on sectors of the society being able to plan the investment of resources and mobilize the energies of the society's members to work and to consume.

References

Childe, V. Gordon
    1951   *Man Makes Himself.* New York: Mentor.

D'Altroy, Terrance Norman
    1981   Empire growth and consolidation: The Xauxa region of Peru under the Incas. Ph.D. diss., Department of Anthropology, University of California, Los Angeles.

Earls, John, and Irene Silverblatt
    1981   Sobre la instrumentación de la cosmología inca en el sitio arqueológico de Moray. In Heather Lechtman and AnaMaria Soldi, eds., *La tecnologia en el mundo andino.* Vol. 1, pp. 443–73. Mexico: Universidad Nacional Autónoma de México.

Geertz, Clifford
    1973   Ritual and social change. In *The Interpretation of Cultures,* pp. 170–92. New York: Basic Books.

Hartmann, Rosewith
    1968   *Maerkte im alten Peru.* Bonn.

Hyslop, John
    1985   *The Inka Road System.* New York: Academic Press.

Lechtman, Heather
    1980   The central Andes: Metallurgy without iron. In Theodore A. Wertime and James D. Muhly, eds., *The Coming of the Age of Iron,* pp. 267–334. New Haven: Yale University Press.

Marx, Karl
    1977   *Capital: A Critique of Political Economy,* vol. l. Trans. Ben Fowkes. New York: Random House.

Mauss, Marcel
    1954   *The Gift: Forms and Functions of Exchange in Archaic Societies.* New York: William Morrow.

Morris, Craig
    1967   Storage in Tawantinsuyu. Ph.D. diss., Department of Anthropology, University of Chicago.
    1974   Reconstructing patterns of non-agricultural production in the Inka economy: Archaeology and documents in institutional analysis. In Charlotte Moore, ed., *The Reconstruction of Complex Societies: An Archaeological Symposium,* pp. 49–60. Cambridge: American Schools of Oriental Research.
    1979   Maize beer in the economies, polities, and religion in the Inca Empire. In C. Gastineau, W. Darby, and T. Turner, eds., *Fermented Food Beverages in Nutrition.* New York: Academic Press.
    1982   The infrastructure of Inka control in the Peruvian central highlands. In George A. Collier, Renato I. Rosaldo, and John D. Wirth, eds., *Inca and Aztec States, 1400–1800,* pp. 153–71. New York: Academic Press.

1985   From principles of ecological complementarity to the organization and administration of Tawantinsuyu. In Shozo Masuda, Izumi Shimada, and Craig Morris, eds., *Andean Ecology and Civilization: An Interdisciplinary Perspective on Andean Ecological Complementarity.* Tokyo: University of Tokyo Press.

1987   Architectura y Estructura del Espacio en Huánuco Pampa. *Cuadernos del Instituto Nacional de Antropologia* (Argentina) 12:27–45.

Morris, Craig, and Donald E. Thompson

1985   *Huanuco Pampa.* London: Thames and Hudson.

Murra, John V.

1960   Rite and crop in the Inca state. In Stanley Diamond, ed., *Culture in History,* pp. 393–407. New York: Columbia University Press.

1962   Cloth and its functions in the Inca state. *American Anthropologist* 64(4):710–28.

1966   New data on retainer and servile populations in Tawantinsuyu. *Actas y Memorias del XXXVI Congreso Internacional de Americanistas* (Sevilla) 2:25–45.

1972   El 'control vertical' de un maximo de Pisos ecológicos en la economía de las sociedades andinas. In *Visita de la provincia de León de Huánuco,* vol. 2, pp. 429–76. Huánuco: Universidad Nacional Hermilio Valdizán.

1980 [1956]   *The Economic Organization of the Inca State.* Greenwich, Conn.: JAI Press.

Rowe, John H.

1946   Inca culture at the time of the Spanish conquest. *Handbook of South American Indians,* vol. 2: *The Andean Civilizations,* pp. 183–330. Smithsonian Institution, Bureau of American Ethnology, Bulletin 143.

Smelser, Neal J.

1959   A comparative view of exchange systems. *Economic Development and Cultural Change* 7 (2):173–82.

Wachtel, Nathan

1982   The mitimas of the Cochabamba Valley: The colonization policy of Huayna Capac. In George A. Collier, Renato I. Rosaldo, and John D. Wirth, eds., *The Inca and Aztec States, 1400–1800,* pp. 199–235. New York: Academic Press.

Zuidema, R. T.

1964   *The Ceque System of Cuzco,* International Archives of Ethnology, Supplement to vol. 50. Leiden.

1982   The sidereal lunar calendar of the Incas. In A. F. Aveni, ed., *Archaeoastronomy in the New World,* pp. 59–109. Cambridge: Cambridge University Press.

CHAPTER THREE

Divine Kingship in the Formation of the Japanese State, 1868–1945

Robert J. Smith

"The ties between us and our people have always stood upon mutual trust and affection. They do not depend upon mere legends and myths. They are not predicated on the false conception that the Emperor is divine" (Lu 1974:2.190–91). With these words the father of the present monarch of Japan brought to an end the ancient claim of the royal house to divine descent. The rescript in which they are contained was issued on New Year's Day, 1946, only a few months after Japan's surrender to the Allied powers. It is unclear whether his subjects, still sunk deep in the miseries brought on them by the catastrophic course of the war, were much concerned. However that may be, for any consideration of the recurrent theme of divine kingship in the history of the Japanese polity the event was a momentous one. To appreciate its historical import fully it is necessary to turn to the two earliest official documents extant, both written in the eighth century of the Christian era.

Temmu (r. 673–686) had ordered the compilation of the documents, and they represent the best efforts of their authors to legitimate his line's claim to the throne. Reflecting the heavy sinification of the court and elite that had been under way for some time, the *Kojiki* (Record of Ancient Matters) and *Nihon shoki,* or *Nihongi* (Chronicles of Japan), also make lavish use of indigenous myths. These were invoked "to support the claim, unprecedented in China, that the Japanese imperial family had the divine mission to reign as well as to rule the nation in perpetuity by virtue of their solar ancestry" (Kitagawa 1981:217). The notion of royal descent from the sun goddess Amaterasu-o-mikami can be traced at least to the end of the fourth century; from the seventh century on it was made official dogma.

In his classic study of on divine kingship, Evans-Pritchard (1962:84) reminds us that the king must be in society yet stand outside it. This is possible only when the office is made sacred and raised to a mystical plane; "it is the kingship and not the king who is divine." In Japan it was surely both.

Let us be clear about the nature of the claim to legitimacy thus defined. The kings of Japan did not rule by divine right or because they enjoyed the Mandate of Heaven or yet solely in their capacity as intermediaries between the worlds of the sacred and the profane. Their claim to the kingship was purely genealogical in character; it follows that usurpation of the throne was theoretically impossible. Japan's history is not that of dynastic successions, therefore, and the present monarch is counted as the 125th in an unbroken line of descent from the sun goddess.[1]

In this essay I am concerned to show how it came about that the institution of divine kingship survived for more than a thousand years to emerge as the fundamental symbol of the Japanese state at the end of the nineteenth century. To do this I begin not at the beginning, for at that end of the historical chronicle all is speculation and surmise, but rather with the period of transition marked by the Meiji Restoration of 1868. The critical years are from about 1850 to about 1890; it was during that space of a generation that the men who toppled the Tokugawa shogunate (1616–1868) devised the new Japanese state. This is a period of great interest to the anthropologist, although it is the historian and political scientist who have dealt with it almost exclusively. Its anthropological interest lies chiefly in the uses made of the past for present purposes. Those who supported the restoration of the "emperor," the divine king, reached back into Japanese mythohistory and outward into the Western world of constitutional monarchies in an effort to forge an institution on the basis of which they could claim legitimacy on behalf of the state they were creating. They also looked to China for its definitions of polity and the imperial institution. From these disparate elements they devised the modern Japanese monarchy and declared it to be a revival of the pure form of the institution as it had existed at the dawn of Japanese history.

By their adroit use of that institution, the men who created the Meiji (1868–1912) state achieved two signal aims. They met the challenge familiar to all who would form a state—the problem of how to "maintain or even establish the obedience, loyalty and cooperation of its subjects or

---

[1]The ancient accession and modern enthronement ceremonies are of particular interest to the anthropologist, but I lack the space to go into their rich symbolic content here. See Ellwood 1973 and Holtom 1972 for detailed accounts of both.

members, or its own legitimacy in their eyes" (Hobsbawm 1983:265). Their second achievement is a tribute to the degree of their success in the first: "Modern states are more apt to disintegrate than the number and strength of unifying factors would suggest. A shared heritage of law, of education, of language and cult, of interests and animosities, may provide large nations with strong ligaments; but these cannot make up for the lack [of what the Japanese developed], that feeling of unconditional connectedness" (Singer 1973:75).[2] Thus, not only did the Meiji oligarchs manage to legitimate their revolutionary program of social, political, and economic reform by claiming to have restored the rule of the divine king, but they also succeeded in using that institution as the basis for the development of a sentiment of national unity among his subjects.

In his discussion of state formation, Hobsbawm writes:

> The problems of state and rulers were evidently much more acute where their subjects had become citizens, that is, people whose political activities were institutionally recognized as something that had to be taken note of—if only in the form of elections. They become even more acute when the political movements of citizens as masses deliberately challenged the legitimacy of the systems of political or social rule, and/or threatened to prove incompatible with the state's order by setting the obligations to some other human collectivity—most usually class, church or nationality—above it. The problem appeared to be most manageable where social structure had changed least ... and where the ancient ways of hierarchical superiority and stratified, multiform and relatively autonomous subordination remained in force. (1983:265)

He then refers in passing to the Japanese case of state formation: "A 'modernization' which maintained the old ordering of social subordination (possibly with some well-judged invention of tradition) was not theoretically inconceivable, but apart from Japan it is difficult to think of an example of practical success" (266). Hobsbawm does not remark that in this perhaps uniquely successful enterprise the Meiji oligarchs were spared the necessity of dealing with the possibly fatal divisiveness of any sense of obligation on the part of the people to some other collectivity in the form

---

[2] Kurt Singer was a German Jew who taught economics in Japan from 1931 to 1939. He arrived there at the age of forty-five and left the country to take up a teaching position at the University of Sydney in Australia. The manuscript of his book was written some time after the end of World War II and before 1957, when he returned to Europe. Singer died in Athens in 1962 at the age of seventy-six. His book is a valuable account of Japan in the heyday of militarism, xenophobia, and the cult of emperor worship. Written after the debacle that destroyed the values that were being so assiduously inculcated in the people during his sojourn in Japan, *Mirror, Sword and Jewel* has about it an air of foreboding lacking in other contemporary accounts.

of either church or ethnicity. I return to the matter of church and state below.

Let me first review the mytho-history of the Japanese monarchy. Excluding the legendary and semilegendary kings of the archaic period, it is far and away the world's longest royal dynasty. Until the end of the Pacific War in 1945 it was held that the first of these divine kings, Jimmu, ascended the throne on February 11 in 660 B.C., establishing what was to be an uninterrupted succession. Despite the best efforts of the chroniclers and genealogists to conceal them, however, it is certain that there have been two breaks in the succession. The first was in the second century of the Christian era, the second in the early sixth. In A.D. 507, Keitai, the twenty-sixth monarch, seized the throne and took as his queen a princess of the royal line he had overthrown. From his reign to the present all occupants of the throne have been without question patrilineal descendants of the usurper; that is, they all come from what is usually called the "imperial family" (*tenno-ke*), a group of linked households patrilineally descended from a common ancestor.

Goody (1966:1–4) has argued that all monarchies must make some claim to uniqueness. Two characteristics of the Japanese royal house set it apart from all other households of its subjects. Alone among Japanese families, the *tenno-ke* has no surname and to it alone is denied the very common practice of adoption designed to secure succession into the next generation. There can be no clearer assertion of genealogical purity in the reckoning of descent. It may come as something of a surprise, however, to learn that in its claim to divine origins the royal house is not unique: most of the great military and political houses of Japan characteristically have identified as their ancestor one or another of the myriad deities who figure in the myths of the Age of the Gods. It was not until the seventh century that the kings made an attempt to raise themselves a level above others who were divinely descended by assuming the designation *akitsu-mikami*, which means something like "living god." There is no reason to believe that the claim was taken all that seriously then; it was not until the late nineteenth century that the notion was revived successfully and made part of official dogma.

I do not review the complicated history of the kings and the court from the early sixth through the late sixteenth centuries. Suffice it to say that the line of divine kings was divested of political power and secular authority in A.D. 1185 with the establishment of the Kamakura shogunate. This military regime was the first of three that for almost seven hundred years ruled Japan until the Meiji Restoration of 1868. The divine kings remained in their capital, the city now called Kyoto, and succession to the throne continued uninterrupted. We must ask why the institution survived at all. Theoretically, as we have seen, usurpation was an impossibility, but there is more to it than that. The institution might well have been abolished or allowed to wither away. A usurper might have at least attempted to lay claim to the throne through genealogical manipulation, but none did so. The divine kingship survived, I suggest, because of the complete uncoupling of the institution from the exercise of secular, political power, leaving to it a purely sacerdotal role that could be played by none other. As the embodiment of ultimate morality, the divine king served two essential functions. He was the only authentic direct intermediary between the cosmic forces represented by the deities from whom he was descended, and he alone could accord unassailable legitimacy to those who sought to rule in his name.

Those familiar with the writing of Japanese history will note that to this point I have avoided use of the word "emperor." It is of some interest that in official documents of the early years of the Meiji period the Japanese referred to the head of state as *tenno,* transliterating the characters. Later, as the government began to assert its claims to parity with other nations, they shifted to "emperor," although they might well have adopted the quite common European practice that gave us the German *kaiser* and the Russian *tsar.* They might even have called him king of Japan. Whatever their motives, the decision to translate the *tenno* into an emperor has long obscured the true nature of the institution. To most non-Japanese the term, as was surely intended, conjures up images of the public display of pomp and power designed to instill awe. Nothing could be farther removed from the role and functions of the *tenno* throughout most of Japanese history. The decision to call him emperor initiates a period of imperial aggrandizement alien to the Japanese tradition which proved to have a very short life.

To show how the Meiji oligarchs transformed the institution, let us consider the functions of the divine kings in the period just before the Restoration. The Tokugawa shoguns, third and last of the military houses to rule the country, at first maintained that they were the legitimate rulers, basing the claim on the Confucian concept of the Way of the King, by which they meant to designate themselves. The divine kings in the royal capital remained somehow superior to them but were not permitted to govern. Somewhat later, the Tokugawa shifted their ground and claimed legitimacy as deputies of the divine kings, who were said to reign but not to rule. The appropriation of neo-Confucian doctrine, Chu Hsi's Way of the King, reflects the general conviction of the Tokugawa house that in Confucianism they had found an ethical system under which it would be possible to unify the country and guarantee their control of it. The king, it was said, ruled by virtue of the Mandate of Heaven; he was thus a secular ruler, subject to the threats of usurpation, overthrow, and even loss of life should the mandate pass to his nemesis. The formula fit the facts of shogunal history very well indeed.

The problem was that Chu Hsi was necessarily silent on the subject of the divine kings. There simply was no place for them in his doctrine, and the contradiction between the Japanese state as described in the ancient chronicles (or as the nativist scholars of the eighteenth and nineteenth centuries imagined it to be described) and the reality of the Tokugawa polity began to attract the attention of a variety of ideologues and scholars. Many of these men came ultimately to a compromise. The position of the shogun, the secular ruler, was justified in neo-Confucian terms. That of the divine king, the sacerdotal monarch, was explicated in terms of the ancient tradition, usually called Shinto (the Way of the Gods) in the West. Clearly the contradiction was not resolved at all. By the middle of the nineteenth century there had emerged a school that made much of the incompatibility of these two unconnected legitimating doctrines. These men, the nativist scholars of the Mito domain in particular, formulated a theory of government and the state that in the end brought down the shogunate in the name of imperial restoration.

Among the many slogans of the time was *osei fukko* ("restore antiquity"), a call for the restoration of the rule of the divine kings. They had not ruled for centuries, as we have seen, but had remained the symbols of national independence, historic continuity, national unity, and harmony between the rulers and the ruled (Webb 1965:187). As a symbol, then, the divine king was of immense importance to the men whose aim it was to unite the country in order to make a stand against the expansionist powers of the West and to fashion a new state that could reasonably assert equality with those European powers most likely to threaten its independence. They were well aware of events in China, as the Ching empire tottered toward its collapse, and knew that throughout Asia the ancient monarchies had almost without exception fallen under the domination of foreigners or been destroyed. It seemed to them that the divine king alone could afford the new government the necessary legitimacy, just as his predecessors had done for the shogunal governments of the previous seven centuries. These men were to pursue a course of action for which there were no true precedents, asserting continuity in the name of the sovereign (Beasley 1972:302).

Thus the rhetoric of the Meiji oligarchs was at once revolutionary in its intent and profoundly conservative in its idiom. Seeking nationalist reconstruction of society and polity, they called it "imperial restoration." Their adoption of this strategy at once raises a question. Is it conceivable

Divine Kingship in the Formation of the Japanese State 57

that the shapers of the Meiji state could have created their appeals out of whole cloth and yet have led the people where they wanted to take them? The answer must be no. Had they merely falsified the past rather than combining and reordering many of its salient themes, they surely would have failed to persuade the Japanese people of the legitimacy of their position and their goals. The alternative would have been to jettison the past in its entirety, but such a course of action would have been risky in the extreme, for they would have exposed themselves to the charge of having usurped sovereign power. They chose the only course realistically open to them and set about creating a new version of the divine kingship that would best suit their purpose, which was to govern in its name. Despite their best efforts, however, they were in fact challenged by loyalists in the late 1870s who in turn rebelled in the name of true restoration, charging that the new government, like the shogunate before it, had usurped the power of the sovereign despite their claims to the contrary. The rebellion was crushed handily and the building of the Meiji state proceeded.

Many interpreters of the character of the Meiji Restoration have charged that the institution of divine kingship was forced on a hapless people by manipulative wielders of power. They assert that the people held the institution in neither awe nor affection and allege that even the existence of the divine kings was a matter of no concern to most of the populace. There can be no question that throughout the Meiji era the government did establish some unprecedented associations and sentiments specifically designed to bind the people to the throne, but there were fundamental continuities as well. We are fortunate to have an eyewitness account of a crucial event in the history of the Restoration that speaks to those continuities.

In November 1868, the king set out from his capital at Kyoto to visit his newly designated one, the shogunal capital of Edo, renamed Tokyo. A few months later he was to take up residence there in the former palace of the shoguns, a gesture obviously designed to symbolize the fusion of secular and sacred power. On this first visit he entered his capital in a palanquin of a sort probably not seen outside the confines of the royal palace for nearly a thousand years. A foreign eyewitness described the event:

> After about half of these [the domain lords and the nobles] has passed, with their attendants, led horses, guards and baggage, with occasional bodies of troops, came the Prince of Bizen, in charge of two square boxes borne high upon men's shoulders, and covered with a red and yellow damask silk. These were believed to contain the insignia or regalia, and small shrines for their safe conduct had been erected at all the halting-places along the road. After

these rode Uwajima, the Minister for Foreign Affairs, and then we saw approaching the Ho-o-ren or phoenix car.

This is a black lacquered palanquin, about six feet square, and with a dome-shaped roof; the front is closed only by curtains, and in the centre of each side is a latticed window, through which it was possible to see that it held no one. The Mikado is supposed to travel in it, but has really a more comfortable palanquin. On the summit is a splendid image, apparently of gold, of the Ho-o, or phoenix, a fabulous bird, with the head and body of a peacock and the spreading plume-like tail of the magnificent copper pheasant of Japan turned up over its head. From the four corners depend silk ropes two inches thick, held each by three men. These and the bearers of the car, which is carried high upon their shoulders and on a frame which raises its base some six feet from the ground, were on Thursday all dressed in bright yellow silk, and wore a curious circular ornament of feathers at each ear eight inches in diameter, like two outspread fan frames placed together. There were fully sixty of them immediately surrounding the Ho-o-ren, and the effect of the group, with the brilliant sun lighting up the sheen of the silk and the glitter of the lacquer, was very gorgeous and indescribably strange, comparable to nothing ever seen in any other part of the world. And now a great silence fell upon the people. Far as the eye could see on either side, the roadsides were densely packed with the crouching populace, in their ordinary position when any official of rank passes by. . . . As the phoenix car . . . with its halo of glittering attendants came on . . . the people without order or signal turned their faces to the earth, . . . no man moved or spoke for a space, and all seemed to hold their breath for very awe, as the mysterious presence, on whom few are privileged to look and live, was passing by. (Dickins and Lane-Poole 1894:2.97–98)

A second foreign observer wrote of the same occasion:

The silence that prevailed among the assembled multitudes, during his passage, was really something that might be felt. . . . it was impressive in the extreme. All the people bowed down as he approached, but this was the last time I ever saw them do so for any great man. The next time I witnessed a procession in which the Mikado figured, all was changed; His Majesty dressed in European costume rode in a carriage, free to be gazed on by all beholder. (Black 1883:2:236)

Taken together, these accounts provide us with two valuable insights into the nature of the divine kingship at the beginning of the Meiji state. It will have struck the reader as astonishing that the palanquin that was carried into Tokyo on that sunny day in 1868 was quite empty. Equally striking is the reverential awe with which its passage was greeted. In some respects this procession shares much with the great trains of the domain lords of the Tokugawa period that moved along Japan's postroads in accordance with the requirements of alternate residence in their domain capital and that of the shogun in Edo (Tsukahira 1966). It might be argued that the people of Tokyo, obliged to make obeisance to these powerful figures for more than two hundred years, only complied with long-established usage. But this procession contained something utterly without precedent—the symbolic presence of the divine king—and we may be quite sure that no multitude would have turned out on that day simply to watch another lord and his retinue pass by. That both king and royal regalia were concealed from view is beside the point; the passage of the symbols of sovereignty signaled that the world would never be the same.

The second insight is to be found in the comment of the second observer, written only fifteen years after the event, that the awesome procession of 1868 had marked the end of the isolation of the king from his subjects. For when next he emerged from his palace in his new capital, he had been transformed into something that seemed very like his counterparts in Europe. I say "seemed" because there remained important ways in which Japan's ruling monarch was treated very differently from the crowned heads of contemporaneous states.

In the course of his 45-year reign, the Meiji emperor was photographed on no more than five occasions. The earliest sitting before the camera, in 1872, resulted in two photographs in both of which he is wearing court dress. On the second occasion, in 1873, he appears in Western-style military uniform in at least two poses, only one of which was given wide circulation. This second sitting appears to have been arranged at the urgent prompting of an early diplomatic mission whose members had discovered that it was the custom in the West for such delegations to present photographs of their head of state to their host governments. A third photograph survives; taken at a distance late in his reign, it shows the elderly, full-bearded Meiji emperor in profile. What, then, of by far the best known portrait of 1888, universally assumed to be a photograph as well? It is, in fact, a photograph of a drawing of the mature Meiji emperor done by a foreign artist. It is this portrait that was enshrined in every school building in the country until 1945, the object of veneration by teachers and pupils alike on ceremonial occasions. All the realistic representations made of him during his lifetime derived from either the early 1872 or 1873 photographs or this later drawing disguised as a photograph.

It was not until 1877 that the Meiji emperor was shown full figure in any graphic medium. In the many colored woodblock prints, for example, the artist either depicted only the closed conveyance in which he rode or so composed the picture that a part of his body, but never his face, was visible.³

Surely the representation of the person of no other reigning monarch of the late nineteenth and early twentieth centuries was so tightly controlled. The emperor did make public appearances, reviewed military parades, opened government installations, and traveled about in open carriages. Thus he could be seen, but for reasons yet to be understood photographic representations of his person are extremely rare, although during his reign Japan became intoxicated with the possibilities of the new medium. There is otherwise an immense photographic documentation of the forty-five years of Meiji. It might be argued that the man simply disliked having his picture taken, but I agree with Hirai (1987) that there is much more to the matter.

All the evidence shows that "Japanese commoners in the late Meiji period were instructed by government officials and advised by the nonofficial elite to view the emperor as they would a Shinto deity" (Hirai 1987:92). Menstruating women were admonished to refrain from looking at him, just as they were warned not to enter the precincts of Shinto shrines when in that state of "pollution." It is reported that during one of his tours white paper was pasted over the lattice grills of the second-story windows of the houses along his route, much as the doors of domestic Shinto altars were sealed against pollution at the death of a household member. Instructions on proper deferential behavior due the imperial portrait parallel those for the reading of Shinto prayers before the *sacra:* "In the Man-God continuum of Shinto belief, the emperor was closer than any Japanese, alive or dead, to the divine end of the spectrum. That made him incomparably divine for the Japanese—divine enough, indeed, to worship" (Hirai 1987: 92). With respect to the paucity of photographs, it should be pointed out that Shinto deities are almost never represented graphically or in any other manner as having palpable form. And in the end, Japan's first modern divine king was enshrined in the great Meiji Shrine in Tokyo in emulation of the Shinto deities worshiped throughout the country in countless other sacred places.

How all this came about is understandable in view of the history of the royal house during the Tokugawa period. Between 1586 and 1866 there had been fifteen occupants of the throne, two of them women. I return to

---

³I am grateful to Henry D. Smith II, Professor of History at the University of California, Santa Barbara, for sharing the preliminary results of his current research into the matter of representations of the Meiji emperor. Detailed information on these and related matters can be found in Taki 1986.

these little-known queens, for their histories are of considerable importance for the light they shed on the ideal of patrilineal succession in the royal house. These fifteen divine monarchs played the classic role of intermediary between the mundane and sacred worlds, conducting the rites and ceremonies essential to the maintenance of order in the cosmos. (The present Japanese monarch is said to perform about thirty such rites annually within the confines of the palace.) Their persons so sacrosanct that they were not permitted to touch the earth, they remained hidden from public view. Their subjects did not worship the persons of the divine kings but instead made pilgrimages to the great shrine at Ise where they worshiped the ancestress of the royal line, Amaterasu-o-mikami. So complete was their seclusion that between 1626 and 1863 no monarch left the precincts of the palace save when fires or other emergencies required their removal to temporary quarters (Webb 1965:172–73). When the young Meiji visited the city of Osaka in April 1868, he became the first Japanese monarch in almost three hundred years to see the ocean, although the capital lies less than 50 miles from the coast.

What of the two queens? They were Meisho (r. 1629–43) and Go-Sakuramachi (r. 1762–70), the 109th and 117th in the line of royal succession. Before Meisho, no female had held the throne since the eighth century. Neither of the women was permitted to marry during or after her reign; both abdicated in favor of a male. Meisho was born in 1623, was enthroned in 1629, reigned until 1643, abdicated just before turning twenty, and died in 1696 (Webb 1968:74). She was the eldest daughter of her predecessor, who had no surviving sons at the time of his abdication in 1629, and it is clear that her stay on the throne was intended to be brief. Had she married, there would have been problems of protocol not only in the treatment of her spouse but also in the ultimate disposition of their offspring. According to Herschel Webb, "By ordinary Japanese family law a man's wife and children belong to his family unless he is adopted by the wife's family. The imperial family employed ancient usages forbidding inheritence through female lines, and . . . Meisho's children would not have belonged to her family but to her husband's, yet as children of an ex-sovereign they would presumably have merited some sort of special treatment that would have been difficult for theorists of imperial etiquette to work out" (1968:74). Go-Sakuramachi was also the daughter of her predecessor and was placed on the throne as an expedient measure. The eldest son of the preceding king, Go-Sakuramachi's brother, was only four years old when their father died. She was chosen to occupy the throne until her brother was deemed old enough to replace her. Accordingly, she abdicated when he reached the age of twelve.

It is highly likely that much more than imperial etiquette was involved in the decision to prevent these queens from marrying. Remember that the *tenno-ke* is a group of linked royal households, each headed by the patrilineal descendant of his predecessor. To allow into that closed domain the person of a queen's consort, much less their offspring, would have been to raise the specter of even more serious succession disputes than occurred in the normal course of events. From the circumstances surrounding the elevation of these women to the position of monarch we may infer that powerful interests within the court were committed to maintaining the patrilineal succession required by the equivalent of today's Imperial House Law.

Throughout the Tokugawa period the shogunal government took care to represent itself as the protector of the court and its provider. Increasingly intervening in matters once the sole prerogative of that court, the shogunate nonetheless was at pains to ensure the financial ability of the court and kings to perform their ceremonial functions with dignity and to live in some degree of ease. For its part, the court may be thought of as purveyor of an essential service to the true rulers of the country: it authenticated and legitimated the shogunal government through the issue of patents of appointment of its officers. The court's role was purely passive, to be sure, but the members of the court were important not for what they did but for what those outside the palace walls thought of them (Webb 1968:130–31).

What their contemporaries thought of them remained more or less unchanged from the time the shogunate undertook to refurbish and protect the court until the 1840s. At that point in Japanese history, however, the recognition of a foreign threat to the nation propelled both court and divine king into the political arena for the first time in a thousand years. Japan had been closed to foreign intercourse since the mid-seventeenth century, but in the 1840s it became increasingly apparent that the Europeans and Americans proposed to force the country to open to the outside world. The shogunal bureaucracy failed to demonstrate any marked ability to deal with the crisis, with the result that the king and court became the rallying points for those who saw the need for swift, decisive, and above all united action. The Meiji Restoration was, of course, an undertaking initiated by loyalists.

The institution of the divine kingship had served the shogunates well. Acknowledged as the ultimate source of legitimacy, it represented a symbol of enormous utility to anyone who would govern successfully. No wonder, then, that the leaders of the new state relied so heavily on the king as the legitimater of their rule, and less wonder still that they asserted that their policies derived from ancient indigenous practice and doctrine. Throughout the debate over the form the new government would take, Western example and theory were advanced by the proponents of all positions; all these spokesmen nonetheless cloaked their views in the rhetoric of tradition. Whether the inspiration was Rousseau, English common law, or the Prussian constitution, the source of the idea was attributed to Mencius, Confucius, or even the sun goddess herself. A prime example of this tendency is to be found in the announcement of the abolition of all court offices and the formation of a modern cabinet system in which it was claimed that the establishment of the cabinet was nothing less than a reversion to the ancient Japanese political theory that held that the king ruled personally, advised by his ministers (Beckmann 1957:75). Everyone concerned with the struggle over the creation of the new state was perfectly well aware that the new cabinet system had been modeled directly on the Prussian. It is a measure of the degree to which the oligarchs believed it essential to appeal to past precedent that they clothed radical reform in the garb of antiquity.

The two key documents of the Meiji period are the Constitution of the Empire of Japan (1889) and the Imperial Rescript on Education (1890). In the creation of each, this same process and the use of analogous rationales could be seen. Because both are absolutely essential to an understanding of the nature of the Meiji state, I deal with them at some length.

A major contributor to the draft of the constitution was the German jurist Hermann Roesler, without question one of the most influential foreign advisers to the new government. Roesler had come to Japan in 1878 at the request of the Foreign Office and soon extended his activities into the several other ministries struggling to create legal and administrative machinery for the new state. Deeply suspicious of the growing movement for popular rights, Roesler found his natural allies among the more conservative of his colleagues. He believed that they were guided by their feelings of loyalty to the throne and the person of the divine king. It was therefore easy enough for him to agree with their contention that the monarchy was the foundation of Japanese national life; he admired their absolute conviction and endorsed their aspirations. In their view and his, the monarchy was the only institution on which the new political order could be built successfully.

Ito Hirobumi, a towering figure in this period, offered the following explanation for the course of action taken:

> Up to this day in oriental countries, there has been no example of constitutional government. European constitutionalism is rooted in a long history and its beginnings go back to the ancient past. In our country, however, constitutional

government is a completely new phenomenon. Therefore, in establishing this new constitution we must first discover what is the "pivot" which sustains our country. If there is no cornerstone, politics will fall into the hands of the uncontrollable masses; and then the government will become powerless; and the country will be ruined. Constitutionalism in Europe has more than a thousand years of life. Moreover, religion has been the foundation of this form of government and the people thus have a fundamental consensus. In Japan, however, religion does not play such an important role and cannot become the foundation of constitutional government. Though Buddhism once flourished and was the bond of union between all classes, today its influence has declined. Though Shintoism is based on the traditions of our ancestors, as a religion it is not powerful enough to become the center of union of the country. Thus in our country the one institution which can become the cornerstone of our constitution is the Imperial House. (quoted in Pittau 1969:177, abridged by author)

Roesler set to work with these men on the constitution, which in draft form was a rather liberal version of German monarchical constitutional law. At its center stood the king; the intent was to synthesize his authority and the rights of the people. But Roesler and his closest associates came to a parting of the ways over the latters' insistence on the theory of the identity of the state and the power of the king. He simply could not bring himself to subscribe to the theory of divine descent of the royal line. His colleagues thereupon turned to other German advisers, men who had supported the Bismarck constitution, for what proved to be a highly satisfactory formula—a theory of the state as living historical entity. Roesler had posited a king who both reigned and ruled; they created instead a figure "completely outside the real political order as numen, as a pure symbol of the divine order" (Siemes 1968:27). Indeed, the *tenno* of Japan's modern century exercised far less power than either the tsar or kaiser and probably wielded even less political influence than Europe's other constitutional monarchs (Lehmann 1982:275).

It is a tribute to their sense of consistency that the oligarchs arranged to have the king grant the constitution to his subjects, permitting them later to make the claim that Japan differed from all other constitutional monarchies in that the people had not had to wrest a constitution from the sovereign through threat of force. The date of its promulgation was February 11, the mythical date of the founding of the Japanese state by Jimmu, the first of the royal line. Thus, the people had no part at all in the framing of the constitution, which was issued without public debate. The proponents of popular rights were outraged, but for all the bitterness that characterizes the political maneuvering of the period there was at one level a national consensus. T. C. Smith has suggested that the transition from Tokugawa to Meiji went as smoothly as it did because there emerged no aristocratic defense of the old regime. Unlike the European nations dealt with by Hobsbawm (1983), in Japan there was no ideological cleavage of a truly radical kind: "All were more or less reformist, more or less traditional, and more or less modern. [The past] was a barrier in some respects, in others a positive aid. Modernization appeared to most Japanese who thought about it at all, not as a process in which a life-or-death confrontation of traditional and modern took place, but as a dynamic blending of the two" (Smith 1961:382). To make matters easier, during his long centuries of seclusion in Kyoto the king had been neither a scourge nor a burden to his people (Hall 1968:41). In the view of the men who shaped the new government, then, the divine king exemplified one of the most fundamental of all Japanese conceptions of the nature of the world—that there is no recognized separation of the moral order from the natural (Hall 1968:29).

Such a conception has its obvious strengths, but it also poses a fundamental problem for those who would explain the relationship between history and the natural order. For an example of the resolution of this Confucian paradox, we may turn to the works of the Mito scholar Aizawa Seishisai, whose thought is characteristic of the first half of the nineteenth century. The problem as he defined it was that, because people must act in historical time lacking any other dimension, they must necessarily operate through expedient action, the only available technique. The paradox lies in the notion that the ultimate purpose of action is permanence and universality. Aizawa's resolution of the paradox might well have served as the motto of those who ultimately created the Meiji state: "The ultimate end of expedient and adaptive measures must always be the reconstitution of the universal order" (Koschmann 1980:99). It was the Mito scholars who provided the formulation that brought down the shogunate and paved the way for restoration. And it was Aizawa himself who borrowed political priorities from the Confucian Analects, clothed them in the trappings of Japanese mytho-history, and made them the foundation of *kokutai,* the national essence that lies at the heart of both the Meiji constitution and the Imperial Rescript on Education.[4]

---

[4]For a succinct review of the history of the concept of *kokutai,* see Earl 1964:236–39. From the book *Kokutai no Hongi,* he quotes the following passage: "The unbroken line of Emperors, receiving the Oracle of the Founder of the Nation [i.e., *Shinchoku* (vow) of Amaterasu], reign eternally over the Japanese Empire. This is our eternal and immutable national entity [i.e., *kokutai*]. Thus, founded on this great principle, all the people, united as one great family-nation in heart and obeying the Imperial Will, enhance indeed the beautiful virtues of loyalty and filial piety. This is the glory of our national entity. This national entity is the eternal and unchanging basis of our nation and shines resplendent throughout our history" (Gauntlett 1949:6).

Probably unknowingly, the Meiji oligarchs had embraced an inherently dangerous doctrine. The Confucian equation of natural law and social order leaves open the way to two equally tenable but mutually contradictory interpretations of the implications of action. "Either by rigid adherence to pure doctrine it becomes a revolutionary principle directed against the concrete order, or by its complete identification with the actual social relations it becomes an ideology guaranteeing the permanence of the existing order" (Maruyama 1974:199). Proponents of the two interpretations were locked in a struggle for power throughout the early years of Meiji. Those who championed popular rights maintained that, inasmuch as the state is a human invention, it is subordinate to those who construct it and therefore can be changed arbitrarily by human will. Those who opposed popular rights argued on the contrary that the state develops in accordance with the natural character of humankind and thus is not their creation. Therefore, states are not subject to human control; humans are subject to the control of the state. At the core of the Confucian value system, then, "was a belief in the substantial unity of the central values and norms of the existing social order with the structure of the cosmic order. This belief could generate tensions within the existing sociopolitical condition, but its more important effect was to freeze the normative order of state and society and render it absolute" (Chang 1980:267). Modern Japanese history offers abundant evidence of the accuracy of this observation, for until the end of the Pacific War in 1945 the rulers of the Japanese state attempted to exercise control in the name of the restored cosmic order, unchanging and eternal, fused with the person of the divine king.

That they even made the attempt is so astonishing that it comes as no surprise to learn that they encountered increasing difficulty in maintaining that control. What they had done, no doubt unwittingly, was to create a powerful revolutionary potential by denying the existence of the moral order as the Confucianists defined it and setting imperial will in its place. They had created, perhaps without realizing it, a society in which any person or any group of any political persuasion could move to seize power, claiming legitimacy by virtue of a correct interpretation of imperial will. Even now there have been calls for social revolution under the guidance of the royal family. Even if the oligarchs did see the danger, they may not have been unduly concerned, for at the outset they were supremely confident of their monopoly of the interpretation of that will. Nevertheless, it is important to see what they had done. With the promulgation of the constitution, the imperial will had been given a wholly arbitrary character; there was no longer a natural political order (Silberman 1974:443, 451).

The Preamble to the Constitution of the Empire of Japan reads in part:

Having, by virtue of the glories of Our Ancestors, ascended to the Throne of a lineal succession unbroken for ages eternal; desiring to promote the welfare of, and to give development to the moral and intellectual faculties of Our beloved subjects, the very same that have been favored with the benevolent care and affectionate vigilance of Our Ancestors; and hoping to maintain the prosperity of the State, in concert with Our people and with their support, We hereby promulgate . . .

The right of sovereignty of the State, We have inherited from Our Ancestors, and We shall bequeath it to Our descendants. (Beckmann 1957:150–56)

Chapter 1 (The Emperor) consists of seventeen articles, which assert that, among the emperor's powers and characteristics, he is of a line of descent unbroken "for ages eternal," is "sacred and inviolable," and as head of the empire has within himself "the rights of sovereignty."

The second major document of the Meiji state, the Imperial Rescript on Education, was promulgated a year later in 1890:

Know ye, Our subjects:
Our Imperial Ancestors have founded Our Empire on a basis broad and everlasting and have deeply and firmly implanted virtue; Our subjects ever united in loyalty and filial piety have from generation to generation illustrated the beauty thereof. This is the glory of the fundamental character [*kokutai*] of Our Empire, and herein also lies the source of Our Education. Ye, Our subjects, be filial to your parents, affectionate to your brothers and sisters; as husbands and wives be harmonious, as friends true; bear yourselves in modesty and moderation; extend your benevolence to all; pursue learning and cultivate arts, and thereby develop intellectual faculties and perfect moral powers; furthermore advance public good and promote common interest; always respect the Constitution and observe the laws; should emergency arise, offer yourselves courageously to the State; and thus guard and maintain the prosperity of Our Imperial Throne coeval with heaven and earth. So shall ye not only be Our good and faithful subjects, but render illustrious the best traditions of your forefathers.

The Way here set forth is indeed the teaching bequeathed by Our Imperial Ancestors, to be observed alike by Their Descendants and the subjects, infallible for all ages and true in all places. It is Our wish to lay it to heart in all reverence, in common with you, Our subjects, that we may thus attain to the same virtue. (Lu 1974:2.70–71)

The victory of the conservatives was complete. For the next fifty-five years this talismanic document was read aloud in full by the school principal at periodic ceremonies, made the subject of innumerable exegeses, and worked into the textbooks of ethics and morals used in the primary and middle schools. Here continuity is asserted with a vengeance, for the rescript marshals both indigenous Shinto and Neo-Confucian traditions into what is at once an assertion of unassailable legitimacy, a definition of the virtues of the subject, and a claim for the unique character of the Japanese state. The authority for the assertion of legitimacy is "the teaching bequeathed us by Our Imperial Ancestors," a reference to the vow made by the sun goddess when she dispatched her grandson to earth. She promised him that the line of his descendants would flourish, and it was his great-grandson Jimmu who became the first of the human royal line (Earl 1964:47n). The Way of the Subject, as it came to be known, is defined exclusively in terms of the Confucian virtues of loyalty and filial piety, couched in language designed to suggest that they are equally an aspect of the ancient Japanese tradition. For Buddhism, the religion of the people, there was no place at all.

Once the conservative elements had gained the upper hand, they still confronted the problem of communicating their social and political orientation to the people and converting them to the Way of the Subject. How they accomplished this task is of considerable interest. In 1891, the year following promulgation of the rescript, the Ministry of Education issued a directive to all primary schools declaring the Imperial Rescript on Education to be the foundation of moral education. That they took this route is clear evidence of a basic difference between the nations of the Western world and Japan, for in Japan there existed nothing even remotely resembling the distinction between church and state; that is, the oligarchs had no institutional context analogous to the church which could be used to instill in the people the new national morality. The quotation from Ito Hirobumi given above makes their position quite clear.

Yet they had tried to construct something like a church in the form of a state cult of Shinto. In the early Meiji period they established National Shinto as a state religion with its own system of shrines and a priesthood, supervised by the central government. Between 1869 and 1875 the promoters of the cult, whose high priest was the divine king, of course, sent out priests trained in propagation of the new faith. Both Shinto and Buddhist clergy were pressed into this service, for the government intended that large numbers of Teachers of Religion and Morals, as they were called, should go out to spread the new morality of loyalty to king and state. For a variety of reasons the effort was abandoned, and the constitution of 1889 guaranteed qualified religious freedom to the people. Shinto had not become the kind of national religion its proponents had envisaged.

They therefore required an alternative solution to the problem of instilling the virtues of imperial loyalty and filial piety in the populace, and they found it in the national system of compulsory education they themselves had created in 1872. There being no authentic church and the effort to construct one having failed, the Meiji government simply moved the entire responsibility for training in morality and ethics into the classroom, where they had a free hand. The rescript became the basic sacred text of the new religion of unquestioning patriotism, and in subsequent regulations the Ministry of Education defined the development of moral character as the central mission of primary schooling (Dore 1964:191).

The Confucian impulse is evident. There is this passage in the Analects: "Their persons being cultivated, their families were regulated. Their families being regulated, their states were rightly governed. Their states being rightly governed, the whole kingdom was made tranquil and happy." A stable family meant a stable society. The oligarchs had taken the necessary bold step of converting filial piety from a private duty into a civic virtue. They had found a way to bind the royal house to the people through the universally observed practice of ancestor worship, the dominant mode of Japanese domestic religious life for the preceding several centuries. Taking a very old idea from the *Kojiki* and *Nihon-shoki* of the eighth century, they reworked it and asserted that since all Japanese are descended from the royal house all are related. The teachers' manuals issued after 1910 made this point: "The connection between the Imperial House and its subjects is thus: one forms the main house and the others form the branch houses, so that from ancient times we have worshipped the founder of the Imperial House and the heavenly gods. Our relationship to this house is sincerely founded on repaying our debt of gratitude to our ancestors" (Caiger 1968:68). The subjects of the divine king thus partook of his divinity to the extent that they were said to be his children. The word was *sekishi*, literally "infants," and in that profound respect there were no distinctions to be drawn among them. In their relationship to the throne, therefore, all people were one, bound to it by genealogical ties and all equally members of the family-state (*kokka*), which was the land of the gods (*shinkoku*). Household and state, parent and king, ancestor and deity, all had been merged effectively into an indivisible sacred entity of ceremony and sentiment.

In their treatment of the institution of divine kingship in archaic civilizations, Berger and Luckmann unwittingly offer an almost perfect summation of what the Meiji oligarchs had wrought:

> The symbolic universe provides a comprehensive integration of *all* discrete institutional processes. The entire society now makes sense. Particular institutions and roles are legitimated by locating them in a comprehensively meaningful world. For example, the political order is legitimated by reference to a

cosmic order of power and justice, and political roles are legitimated as representations of these cosmic principles. (1966:75)

Earlier I quoted Kurt Singer on "that feeling of unconditional connectedness" the Japanese enjoyed in the 1930s, when he knew them. That connectedness does not mean that the history of modern Japan has been that of a tranquil society whose members thought and acted as one under the benign authority of a sacred monarch. To be sure, the Confucianists had produced yet another concept to undergird their definition of morality, that of *taigi meibun,* a notion that "subjects spontaneously performed the ethical duties appropriate to their subordinate positions" (Kinmonth 1981:84). Yet inspection of the historical record reveals a domestic political world far from harmonious, rendered pluralistic, contentious, and often perilous by the very terms of the constitution. Attempted coups d'etat and conspiracies from the loyalist right mark the period. Ultimately, forces within the military and elsewhere began to call for yet another restoration, claiming that the successive constitutional governments had in fact impeded the direct flow of imperial will to the people. Political parties and party cabinets would have to go, they argued, in the interests of promoting national unity under the sovereignty of the restored divine kingship. In 1940 Japan became a one-party state. Disaster was not far off.

As Japan encountered mounting hostility in the international community and the sense of awful isolation grew, government appeals for patriotic dedication and sacrifice grew ever more strident. Schools, the media, and even the organs of local government down to the village level were pressed into service to convey to the people the message of the beauty of imperial loyalty and filial piety, the need for every greater effort, and a sense that the Japanese, a unique people, were alone in the world. Their faith was deep enough to propel the people, with little dissent of any consequence, into one of history's great human catastrophes in which some three million of them died. In retrospect, it seemed that the Meiji oligarchs had succeeded all too well.

When it was over, suddenly, on August 15, 1945, it was the divine king himself who delivered the bitter message of defeat, although he did not use the word. It is appropriate to conclude this survey of the creation of the Meiji state with the announcement of its demise. The message was broadcast on radio, the first time the people had heard what was called the *gyoku-on,* the "jewel sound," the voice of the divine king:

> It is according to the dictates of time and fate that we have resolved to pave the way for a grand peace for all the generations to come by enduring the unendurable and suffering what is insufferable. Let the entire nation continue

as one family from generation to generation, ever firm in its faith in the imperishability of this divine land, mindful of its heavy burden of responsibilities, and the long road before it. United your total strength to be devoted to construction for the future. Cultivate the ways of rectitude and nobility of spirit, and work with resolution so that you may enhance the innate glory of the Imperial State and keep pace with the progress of the world. (Lu 1974:2.176–77)

A few months later he issued what the Allied occupation powers interpreted to be the rescript renouncing his divinity, contained in the quotation with which I opened this essay. Today the divine king remains as symbol of the state, as it is phrased in the new constitution, who neither reigns nor rules. He has thus been restored to a role not unlike that which the institution has occupied for most of Japan's recorded history (Hall 1968:64), the symbol of the national moral consciousness. The persistence of the divine kingship into the postwar period provides clear support of the contention that there remains at least the residue of the potential power of the powerless center around which the Meiji state was erected.

References

Beasley, W. G.
    1972   *The Meiji Restoration.* Stanford: Stanford University Press.
Beckmann, George M.
    1957   *The Making of the Meiji Constitution: The Oligarchs and the Constitutional Development of Japan, 1868–1891.* Lawrence: University of Kansas Press.
Berger, Peter L., and Thomas Luckmann
    1966   *The Social Construction of Reality.* Garden City: Doubleday.
Black, John R.
    1883   *Young Japan: Yokohama and Edo.* 2 vols. New York: Baker, Pratt.
Caiger, John
    1968   The aims and content of school courses in Japanese history, 1872–1945. In Edmund Skrzypczak, ed., *Japan's Modern Century,* pp. 51–81. Tokyo: Sophia University Press.
Chang, Hao
    1980   Neo-Confucian moral thought and its modern legacy. *Journal of Asian Studies* 39(2):259–72.
Dickins, Frederick V., and Stanley Lane-Poole
    1894   *The Life of Sir Harry Parkes.* 2 vols. London: Macmillan.
Dore, Donald P.
    1964   Education: Japan. In Robert E. Ward and Dankwart A. Rustow, eds., *Political Modernization in Japan and Turkey,* pp. 176–204. Princeton: Princeton University Press.

Earl, David Magarey
   1964   *Emperor and Nation in Japan: Political Thinkers of the Tokugawa Period.* Seattle: University of Washington Press.

Ellwood, Robert S.
   1973   *The Feast of Kingship: Accession Ceremonies in Ancient Japan.* Tokyo: Sophia University Press.

Evans-Pritchard, E.E.
   1962   The divine kingship of the Shilluk of the Nilotic Sudan. In *Essays in*
   [1948] *Social Anthropology,* pp. 66–86. London: Faber and Faber.

Gauntlett, John O., trans.
   1949   *Kokutai no Hongi: Cardinal Principles of the National Entity of Japan.* ed. Robert King Hall. Cambridge: Harvard University Press.

Goody, Jack
   1966   Introduction. In *Succession to High Office,* pp. 1–56. Cambridge Papers in Social Anthropology, no. 4.

Hall, John W.
   1968   A monarch for modern Japan. In Robert E. Ward, ed., *Political Development in Modern Japan,* pp. 11–64. Princeton: Princeton University Press.

Hirai, Atsuko
   1987   The state and ideology in Meiji Japan—a review article. *Journal of Asian Studies* 46(1):89–103.

Hobsbawm, Eric
   1983   Mass-producing traditions: Europe, 1870–1914. In Eric Hobsbawm and Terrence Ranger, eds., *The Invention of Tradition,* pp. 263–307. New York: Cambridge University Press.

Holtom, D.C.
   1972   *The Japanese Enthronement Ceremonies with an Account of the*
   [1928] *Imperial Regalia.* 2d ed. Tokyo: Sophia University Press.

Kinmonth, Earl H.
   1981   *The Self-Made Man in Meiji Thought: From Samurai to Salary Man.* Berkeley: University of California Press.

Kitagawa, Joseph M.
   1981   Monarchy and government—traditions and ideologies in pre-modern Japan. In A. L. Basham, ed., *Kingship in Asia and Early America,* pp. 217–32. Mexico: El Colegio de Mexico.

Koschmann, J. Victor
   1980   Discourse in action: Representational politics in Mito in the Late Tokugawa period. Ph.D. diss. University of Chicago.

Lehmann, Jean-Pierre
   1982   *The Roots of Modern Japan.* New York: St. Martin's Press.

Lu, David John, ed.
   1974   *Sources of Japanese History.* 2 vol. New York: McGraw-Hill.

Maruyama, Masao
   1974   *Studies in the Intellectual History of Tokugawa Japan.* Trans. Mikiso Hane. Princeton: Princeton University Press.

Pittau, Joseph
    1969   *Political Thought in Early Meiji Japan, 1868–1899*. Cambridge: Harvard University Press.

Siemes, Johannes
    1968   *Hermann Roesler and the Making of the Meiji Constitution*. Tokyo: Sophia University Press.

Silberman, Bernard S.
    1974   Conclusion: Taisho Japan and the crisis of secularism. In Bernard S. Silberman and Harry D. Harootunian, eds., *Japan in Crisis: Essays in Taisho Democracy*, pp. 437–53. Princeton: Princeton University Press.

Singer, Kurt
    1973   *Mirror, Sword and Jewel: A Study of Japanese Characteristics*. New York: Braziller.

Smith, Thomas C.
    1961   Japan's aristocratic revolution. *Yale Review* 50:370–83.

Taki, Koji
    1986   *Tenno no shozo: Zusho no seijigaku e no kokoromi—Meiji-ki zenpan ni okeru* (The imperial portrait: Toward a political science of the image in the first half of the Meiji period). *Shiso* 740:2–27.

Tsukahira, Toshio G.
    1966   *Feudal Control in Tokugawa Japan: The Sankin Kotai System*. Cambridge: Harvard University Press.

Webb, Herschel
    1965   The development of an orthodox attitude toward the imperial institution in the nineteenth century. In Marius B. Jansen, ed., *Changing Japanese Attitudes toward Modernization*, pp. 167- 91. Princeton: Princeton University Press.
    1968   *The Japanese Imperial Institution in the Tokugawa Period*. New York: Columbia University Press.

CHAPTER FOUR

The State-Church Reconsidered

Bruce G. Trigger

John Murra's career is an eloquent demonstration of how much may be learned about ancient civilizations when their study is grounded in painstaking respect for the surviving documentation and when these data are subjected to prolonged contextual analysis. His research is also informed by a keen awareness that the interpretation of these societies is significantly influenced by the perspectives from which anthropologists view them. Transcending a simplistic positivism to achieve greater knowledge of how the modern social milieu influences our understanding of the past offers, at the very least, the possibility of an improved awareness of the limitations of what we know about ancient civilizations. At best, it may result in a more objective understanding of our data. This is the kind of approach I wish to apply in this essay to a consideration of the role religion played in the maintenance of the social systems of early civilizations, with specific reference to ancient Egypt and the Near East.

Religion in the Ancient Civilizations

Archaeological evidence has revealed that civilizations developed in widely separated parts of the world during the past six millennia. Whatever influences some of these civilizations may have exerted on each other in

---

This essay was written while the author was a recipient of sabbatical leave from McGill University and a Leave Fellowship of the Social Sciences and Humanities Research Council of Canada.

their early stages, it is also evident that many structurally analogous features evolved repeatedly in instances of total isolation. Hence, they represent examples of similar causes independently producing similar effects, or of parallel cultural evolution, as Julian Steward (1955) discussed this process. These common features serve to define the early civilizations as a particular type of society. Explaining the repeated development of such a set of features is an important challenge to evolutionary anthropologists.

All early civilizations were profoundly inegalitarian. They were hierarchical societies in which the possession of wealth was directly correlated with power and status. Each was administered by a complex structure made up of rulers, officials, accountants, and soldiers who collected taxes, maintained order, and regulated many of its most important activities. Palaces, fortresses, and administrative centers loom large in the archaeological record. Equally or even more prominent are massive temples and other evidence of the important role played by institutionalized religion. Large amounts of wealth were expended on cult activities. Available evidence supports Gordon Childe's (1944:107–8) observation that a greater proportion of the productivity of these societies was devoted to support such practices than in the case of any more recent ones.

The governments of the ancient civilizations were quasi-religious. Invariably, rulers claimed to be gods, descendants of gods, or at the very least to enjoy their support (Frankfort 1948; Hooke 1958). They performed major rituals that were believed necessary to mediate between humankind and the gods and thereby to ensure the survival of society. In Egypt, only the pharaohs were believed capable of performing any act of temple worship, although in practice such rituals were delegated to groups of priests (David 1973:4). The tomb complexes of royalty, which are the third class of major monuments occurring in the archaeological record of early civilizations, reflect this ideology of kingship. The royal pyramids were by far the largest structures erected in Egypt during the Old Kingdom, and the royal burials of Early Dynastic Mesopotamia have yielded the richest surviving treasures of that ancient civilization. These tomb complexes were at the same time symbols of political power and temples for the cults of divine or divinely sponsored rulers.

The governments of the early civilizations also sought supernatural support by lavishly patronizing religious activities. The scale of their endowments provides a further indication that religion was central in the governing of ancient civilizations. Yet, however closely religious and governmental activities were linked ideologically and however tempting it is to proclaim the embedded nature of religious and sociopolitical structures, the fundamental basis on which the power of a ruler depended appears to have been his control of the administrative hierarchy and the army rather than any claim of priestly authority (Kus 1981:209). No ancient civilization was a theocracy in the sense that the authority of its rulers rested solely on a claim of divine support. Recent advances in understanding Maya hieroglyphic inscriptions have shown the traditional view of classic Maya society as a theocracy ruled by priests to be erroneous. It is now evident that, instead of being anomalous in this respect, Maya states were ruled by dynasts preoccupied with warfare and secular politics (Coe 1980:147–48). It is also clear that the secular administrative hierarchy and the property and personnel of major cults were institutionally distinguishable from one another in the early civilizations, even though the precise relationship between them varied from one civilization to another. There was also no civilization in which institutions of both types were not present (Adams 1966:120–69).

The State-Church

The aforementioned observation led Leslie White (1959:303–28) to propose the universality in early civilizations of two linked institutions that formed a special mechanism of social control: the state-church. He argued that

> the special coordinative, integrative mechanism of political control in civil societies [i.e., civilizations] is everywhere marked by a civil, political, and military aspect, on the one hand, and an ecclesiastical, clerical, and theological aspect, on the other . . . ; state and church, as we are using these terms, do not necessarily label discrete entities, but rather *aspects* of the mechanism by which civil societies are integrated, regulated, and controlled . . . ; the function of the state-church, in a word, is the preservation of the integrity of the sociocultural system of which it is a part (303, 305, 313).

White conceptualized the state, much as political anthropologists have done more recently, as "a centralized and hierarchically organized political system in which the central authority has control over the greatest amount of coercive force in the society" (Cohen 1978:36) and officials have the authority to execute people, inflict corporal punishment, seize property, and alter "the standing and reputation of a member of the society" (Krader 1968:21). In all these definitions, the state is conceived of as a political device for the control of complex societies rather than identified as a type of society. This distinction is important because the state as a political institution is associated with societies of many different types. These range from entities such as the Zulu kingdom, in which tribal elements remained dominant, through early civilizations, later preindustrial republics, kingdoms, and empires, and various types of industrial society (Krader 1968). The modes of production, systems of property-holding, ideologies, and forms of intellectual life associated with these different types of society vary radically. Indeed, the state as an institution ranges beyond the limits of what are generally recognized as class societies, which precludes grouping them under the single label of "state societies." Still, distinguishing a separate form of government for each type of state society would inhibit our understanding of those aspects of government they share and hinder a discussion of the origin and development of the state as a mechanism of social control. Conceptualizing the state as a political institution that occurs within but is not coextensive with individual societies provides social scientists a conceptual tool of major importance for cross-cultural analysis.

The principal goals White ascribed to the state are to repel invasions by foreign enemies; to protect property rights, especially by maintaining order among exploited groups; and to control disputes arising among the rich and powerful. He defined the state as a political instrument characterized by ultimate authority and decision-making powers being invested, at least in theory, in the hands of a single ruler; by an administrative hierarchy staffed by professional, specially trained personnel; by the use of force to ensure the implementation of decisions and to inflict punishment on those who do not obey authorities; and by the collection of taxes to support its personnel. The state often, but not always, suppresses blood revenge as part of its assertion of control over society. In addition to intervening in the economy through the collection of taxes, the state for various reasons may control or influence significant aspects of economic production, build roads, and supervise markets, weights, and measures (White 1959:314–23). White assumed that a professional army and police forces were an integral part of the state apparatus of the early civilizations. He also noted, however, that in many later and more complex preindustrial civilizations the army tended to become more clearly defined as an institution in its own right. Its officers were able to threaten or even control the state administrative hierarchy while maintaining a separate basis for their power.

White (1959:323–27) paid less attention to defining the structure and specific functions of what he called the church. Yet it is fairly clear what he had in mind. Religious institutions were seen as existing to perform the rituals believed necessary to regulate relations between humankind and the supernatural on behalf of society as a whole, significant groups, or prominent individuals. These institutions, like the state, have administrative hierarchies controlled by members of the upper classes. Priests are experts in esoteric lore, which they formally transmit from generation to generation and possession of which characterizes them as specialists. The temples also own property, which provides revenue to support their personnel, cult activities, and construction programs. White observed that, in some early civilizations, all the religious institutions were grouped to form a hierarchical structure paralleling that of the state. At the head of this structure stood one or more high priests, whose authority in relation to cult activities was analogous to that of the ruler in relation to the state. Secular and religious officials were sometimes closely related, though the high priest invariably was of lower status than the king and subordinate to his authority. Yet, though White assumed that the Spanish described such an all-embracing religious hierarchy for the Aztecs, Calnek, who has re-examined this evidence, affirms that "while the great temples occupied the highest rank within the inventory of religious structures . . . they did not stand at the apex of a hierarchically organized system of temple communities" (1976:295). There is likewise no proof of a rigidly organized chain of command within the Mesopotamian city-state, with the head priest of the principal deity of the city serving as the high priest. White also noted that church and state were institutionally less differentiated in some civilizations than in others. In Old Kingdom Egypt, where government centralization was more extensive than in most early states, priests tended to be civil servants who performed cult duties on a part-time basis.

There is also no evidence that as Mesopotamia became politically united a coextensive religious hierarchy developed paralleling that of the state. Instead, kings and central governments appear to have dealt on a bilateral basis with the priesthoods of different cities or major temples (Westonholz 1979:109). The same is true of Egypt: even during the New Kingdom, when major temples had full-time head priests, each cult appears to have been articulated with the government individually rather than arranged in a separate, all-embracing religious organization (O'Connor 1983:201–2). There is also no evidence of a hierarchy of religious control reaching beyond the city-state in the Aztec tributary system, even though the tribute coming from this empire was used to support temples and cult activities within the cities of the Triple Alliance (Spath 1973). The supposed all-embracing Inka religious hierarchy is an apparent case of such a structure (Rowe 1946:298–99), and there is evidence that the victorious Inka established their own religious cults in major centers (Lumbreras 1974:223). Yet, it is also possible that the Spanish misunderstood honorific titles and interpreted Inka religious organization too much along the lines of the Roman Catholic church (Murra 1980:34, 160–61). These examples raise an issue White did not pursue: the degree to which in early civilizations religious hierarchies did or did not parallel political ones, especially in large territorial states. I try to explain below why such parallels were not necessary and might have been counterproductive from the point of view of social regulation.

White also failed to note that in the early civilizations there was no corpus of exclusive dogma such as characterized the later international religions, acceptance of which was obligatory for membership in the church. Far from having a voluntaristic basis, participation in most cults was automatically determined by membership in particular families, professions, or communities. Hence, in the early civilizations, a religious institution was more an administrative structure than a church in the modern theological sense. Yet, even when account is taken of both of these qualifications, White's concept of the church is as useful for purposes of cross-cultural comparison and the analysis of early civilizations as is the more generally accepted concept of the state. The main weakness of his formulation is his failure to explain convincingly what "churches" did and why the state-church is found in all early civilizations.

White viewed the state-church as a dual institution that functioned to integrate, regulate, and control society. He also maintained that the roles played by the church were essentially parallel to those played by the state (1959:327). According to White, the church helped to preserve the integrity of the sociocultural system by (a) being involved in offensive and defensive relations with neighboring states, (b) helping to keep the subordinate classes obedient and docile, (c) carrying on intrasocietal processes such as agriculture, irrigation, handicrafts, business transactions, and public works (for this, see also Adams 1975:236), and (d) influencing the behavior of individuals by means of education and rituals (White 1959:323). He concluded that "the church performs essentially the same functions as the state" (328).

White also stressed important formal resemblances between state and church. Both owned extensive tracts of land, possessed slaves, and employed highly specialized craftspeople. The leaders of both were recruited from leading families, though there was a tendency for younger sons or junior lineages to be assigned religious offices. The church as an institution had no less vested an interest in protecting wealth and privilege than did the state. Both depended for their survival on the perpetuation of a social order based on inequality. White concluded that keeping the subordinate classes in their place was a critically important function of religions in the early civilizations (235–36).

White perceived state and church as differing mainly in the manner in which they sought to accomplish their goals. The state depended on political manipulation, coercion, and repression. Yet force and the threat of force by themselves were insufficient to counteract the threat of anarchy and insurrection in the early civilizations. The church sought to keep the masses in check by manipulating the supernatural: "Priesthoods employed theology and ritual to instill obedience and docility into the minds of the masses and make them loyal to the established order" (324). The priests taught the people that "they must be docile, patient, and humble, that they must endure privations and bitter labor, that they must not rise up against their masters but must submit to them peacefully and even with good will. . . . it is not merely their terrestrial masters whom they must serve and obey, but the eternal and almighty gods. . . . the masses are made to believe that if they fail to obey they will suffer divine wrath and punishment" (219). The priests also stressed the sanctity of the elite; rulers were either gods or human beings chosen and favored by the gods. The hierarchical structure of each civilization was believed to be based on an ideal and immutable pattern established by the gods at the time of creation. Disobedience to the state was therefore an act of sinfulness that would incur divine wrath.

The Theocratic Tradition

Despite White's avowedly materialistic orientation, his theory of the state-church can be seen in historical perspective as part of a theocratic tradition that has been prominent in American anthropology. Ironically, this tradition is deeply committed, although often implicitly rather than explicitly so, to an idealist view of human behavior. White followed Turner (1941:2.1283) in arguing that, with the development of early civilizations, the acquiescence to spirits that had previously existed in Neolithic farming villages was elaborated into subservience to an earthly elite (White 1959:314). He maintained that hunter-gatherers and tribal agriculturalists believe they must have help from the spirit world to survive; they offer their first fruits to these spirits in return for their continuing support. With the development of civilization, this gratitude and recompense was extended to priests as human representatives of the gods (325). The upper classes also claimed special links to the supernatural, as a result of either their descent from the gods or their possession of esoteric lore that won divine favor and thus promoted the fertility of the earth and the well-being of the people. When accepted, these claims permitted usurpation by kings and other officials of religious prerogatives that formerly were possessed by the heads of families as a result of their connections with the spirits of dead ancestors and with local fertility deities. The resulting religious power became an important source of political authority (see also Childe 1946:48–50; Friedman and Rowlands 1978:211).

The broader theocratic view White's formulation reflects grew out of the refusal of most American anthropologists to accept that the social control found in complex, inegalitarian societies ultimately could be based on force exercised by a small number of rich and powerful people to control a subservient majority. This conviction is primarily a projection into the past of the largely unquestioned belief that the government of the United States is derived from and sustained by the consent of the governed. More remotely, it is based on the social contract theories that dominated speculation about the origin of complex societies among western European philosophers in the eighteenth century and played an important role in the American revolution and the shaping of the new republic. According to these theories, even if the state used force to maintain order, the sanction for it doing so was a decision to which any human being, guided solely by reason and long-term self-interest, could be expected willingly to give his or her assent (Heilbroner 1961:28–57). The relative openness both of the American frontier and of American class structure appeared to support this view during the nineteenth and early twentieth centuries. Yet, in the modern equivalents of the social contract theory to which American anthropologists have subscribed in recent years, the ideas of rationality and freely given consent have been replaced by ones that evoke religious fear as the main reason an exploited majority was initially prepared to support a social system based on political and economic inequality. It was to this latter version that White subscribed.

Why did this change come about? Rationalist thought, beginning in the eighteenth century, had characterized religion as a potent means for duping primitive and uneducated people. Have anthropologists simply continued to believe that all populations not influenced by Enlightenment philosophy belong in these categories? Have they been influenced by the idea of scholars such as Lévy-Bruhl (1910) that primitive and non-Western peoples were incapable of sustained logical thought, a position reaffirmed by Hallpike (1979)? Or is the reason more deeply rooted in changes in American society which make it impossible for anthropologists any longer to understand their own society as an expression of human reason? Where reason cannot account for the development of complex, hierarchical societies, idealists find religion and superstition to be acceptable substitutes (Street 1975:7, 138).

Steward and His Successors

One of the clearest and most influential formulations of the theocratic concept in anthropology was Julian Steward's "Cultural Causality and

Law" (1949). Steward hypothesized that the earliest states developed as a result of the economic need for irrigation to support a growing population in arid environments. He believed that the control required to construct and maintain irrigation systems was provided by religious leaders, who were obeyed because they were thought to possess supernatural power and sanctions. These developments initially produced clusters of relatively small states, each with a hierarchical social structure characterized by vast privileges for the powerful. Yet he saw little evidence of militarism or the use of force in these societies. Instead, inequality was maintained as a result of the general acceptance of supernatural sanctions. In this halcyon age, highly sophisticated arts and crafts were continuously refined to provide the secular and priestly elite with luxury goods. The early civilizations tended to be open societies, since their developing economies offered plenty of opportunity for vertical mobility.

Only when it was no longer possible for irrigation systems to expand to accommodate growing populations did warfare become a significant part of an intensifying struggle to control economic resources. This change allowed soldiers to replace the older theocratic leaders, and political control came to be based increasingly on force rather than on supernatural sanctions. Decreasing opportunities for economic expansion caused membership in social classes to become fixed and led to a general decline in cultural creativity. The political and economic crises generated by growing populations periodically resulted in the collapse of these states, which brought suffering and death to rich and poor alike. In due course, a similar despotic society was reconstituted, initiating a cyclical process. This sort of irrigation society represented an evolutionary dead end from which, on its own initiative, no further economic or social progress could be expected. Steward (1949) called these two successive stages in the development of early civilizations the periods of Regional Florescence and Cyclical Conquest.

Steward's views have been extremely influential. Gordon Willey and Philip Phillips's (1958) Classic and Post-Classic stages for the development of New World civilizations were essentially archaeological versions of Steward's periods. Despite certain misunderstandings, they have also been significant in leading the British geographer Paul Wheatley (1971:320) to postulate that all the earliest cities evolved from ceremonial centers, a view that he believed was supported by the prominence of religious architecture in all the early civilizations. Though the American neo-evolutionists Morton Fried (1967) and Marshall Sahlins (1968) have paid relatively little attention to the part played by religion in the early civilizations, Elman Service (1971, 1975) has devoted much attention to this topic. His arguments concerning early civilizations are based on the concept of a chiefdom as a developmental stage between tribal society on the one hand and states or civilization on the other. The term "chiefdom" had been coined to describe certain circum-Caribbean societies by K. Oberg (1955), who had worked with Steward on the *Handbook of South American Indians*. Service (1975:15–16) and other anthropologists who use a neo-evolutionary typology have conceptualized chiefdoms as societies characterized by economic inequality and a hierarchical social and political organization but which do not rely on force as a sanction to protect the rights and privileges of the elite, which in many cases include the power of life and death over their subjects. At first it was suggested that the material basis of chiefly power is the role these leaders play in assuring the redistribution of essential goods throughout societies that had become larger and more complex. This view was derived from Polanyi's (1957:43–55) exaggerated claim that the economy was wholly embedded in the social and political organization of all premodern societies. Although it is widely acknowledged that there are major structural differences between the economies of societies at different levels of complexity, Polanyi's followers are now censured for assuming that these differences rule out the possibility of individuals seeking to strike a bargain favorable to themselves in either type of society (Ekholm and Friedman 1979).

As a consequence of a reexamination of the evidence prompted by Timothy Earle's (1977) studies of traditional Hawaiian society, it is now recognized that interpersonal barter and market exchange were inportant in the redistribution of everyday necessities in societies of the chiefdom type. In many cases, what has been called redistribution turns out to be taxes, tribute, and chiefly control exercised over the circulation of high status goods. It is now generally accepted that chiefly management of the circulation of staple products is not a universal feature of chiefdoms (Peebles and Kus 1977).

Fewer anthropologists are yet ready to recognize that absence of force is also not a characteristic of chiefdoms. It is clear, however, that when Hawaiian rulers toured their realm to collect taxes they were accompanied by a band of retainers who helped to ensure that the expected payments were made (Cordy 1981:20–21; Earle 1978:18–19). The rulers of most chiefdoms turn out to have had at least some coercive force at their disposal, and therefore these societies, in terms of their political organization, qualify as simple states (Krader 1968). So-called simple chiefdoms that lack state structures, such as the Iroquois or the Nootka, are better classified as egalitarian tribal societies with hereditary chiefships. In these societies, chiefs and their families are compelled to produce and distribute more than anyone else to validate their hereditary status (Trigger 1969:68–72). On closer inspection, the concept of chiefdom appears to have conflated many radically different types of society, thereby obscuring rather than assisting our understanding of the development of important political and economic institutions (Lewis 1981). Despite these far-reaching criticisms, many anthropologists continue to accept the chiefdom as a stage of cultural evolution in which social and economic inequality was maintained without physical force, thanks to generalized fear of supernatural sanctions and acceptance of inequality as an essential part of the natural order. The popularity of these views, despite the limited archaeological and comparative ethnographic evidence to support them, reinforces the suggestion made above that they are a projection into the past of the current American ideology.

In his *Origin of the State and Civilization*, Service (1975) adopted a more extreme position than neo-evolutionists had previously taken when he extended this interpretation to the early civilizations, which he sought to portray as being fundamentally similar to large chiefdoms. They were larger than true chiefdoms, had more complex divisions of labor, and possessed a more hierarchical social organization that was divided into true classes. Yet the authority of their government was based on supernatural sanctions rather than force. This position is similar to that adopted with respect to early civilizations by Maurice Godelier (1977).

Service supported his position with a selective range of evidence. It is true that professional armies were smaller and less differentiated from the rest of society in the early civilizations than they were in such later preindustrial ones as New Kingdom Egypt, Mesopotamia from the Old Babylonian period onward, the Persian empire, the Hellenistic states, and the Roman empire. Foreign wars were fought mainly with peasant conscripts. Yet Service ignores the Egyptian palace guards; the uniformed and professionally equiped Sumerian armies that appear even in the Early Dynastic period; and the Aztecs who, as a reward for valor in battle, were released from other labor and attached as professional warriors to the royal court. In wartime, these latter soldiers formed the core of the Aztec army (Durán 1964:122, 141–42). Service also does not adequately note evidence from Egypt, dating as early as the Old Kingdom, of the use of a police force, at least partly composed of foreign mercenaries, to enforce the decisions of state officials (Duell et al. 1938:17). Coercive force was clearly significant in political control in the early civilizations, just as it was in still earlier simple states.

The Failure of Theocratic Explanations

While stressing the common regulatory goals of the state and religious institutions, neither White nor the neo-evolutionists have explained why two apparently redundant mechanisms of control developed in all the early civilizations. White believed that the state cannot exert sufficient coercive force to control society, but he never specified to what degree, or how, control was effected by physical coercion or by supernatural sanctions. Service (1975:91), at his most extreme, implied that the latter alone could support the entire system of inequality found in early civilizations. Moreover, even if one grants that supernatural sanctions were important in securing the obedience of the peasantry to a numerically smaller and highly privileged elite, this does not explain how such a relationship could evolve in the first place. Do religious beliefs at a tribal level constitute an effective substratum for the evolution of political power? Ralph Turner (1941:2: 1283) and apparently Morton Fried (1967:137–41)—following a tradition pioneered by Numa Fustel de Coulanges (1900) and Emile Durkheim (1915)—have argued that they do. Or are such beliefs the result of an attempt to rationalize and symbolically reinforce political control that is based primarily on physical coercion? The Zulu ruler Shaka's suppression of rainmakers and usurpation of their powers is a historically documented example of the latter process occurring at a primary level of state formation (Gluckman 1940:31). Yet neither of these approaches addresses the problem of why dual political and religious systems of control are present in all early civilizations.

It is clear that the character of religious institutions in early civilizations needs to be defined with greater precision. Neo-evolutionary anthropologists have failed to pay sufficient attention to these institutions. To explain why the equivalent of White's state-church evolved in all these societies, we must ascertain functions for religious institutions and the state that are both necessary and complementary. In this way alone can we determin how and why the social and political controls associated with these societies worked and evolved.

Historical Materialism and Religion

The basis for an alternative and more productive approach to understanding religion in the early civilizations is provided by historical materialism. In their various writings, Karl Marx and Friedrich Engels analyzed the social functions of religion, especially in terms of alienation and class interests. Far from dismissing religion or belittling it, they sought to understand, from a materialist point of view, what made religion indispensible to human beings at specific stages of social development (Kiernan 1983). Although religious beliefs are more remote and appeared to be more detached from material life than any other aspect of human behavior, they were interpreted as necessary to veil the inadequacies or irrationalities of any system of production that was not based on an evolved technology and equal respect for all human beings. As Engels put it, religion is "the fantastic reflection in men's minds of those external forces which control their daily life, a reflection in which the terrestrial forces assume the form of supernatural forces" (Marx and Engels 1957:131). Religion as the fantasy of impotent or alienated human beings is the supreme embodiment of false consciousness (37).

Engels also stressed that religion had to be understood in terms of a developmental perspective. He described the transition from primitive egalitarian to class society in the following terms:

> In the beginnings of history it was the forces of nature which were first so reflected and which in the course of further evolution underwent the most manifold and varied personifications among the various people. . . . But it was not long before, side by side with the forces of nature, social forces begin to be active—forces which confront man as equally alien and at first equally inexplicable, dominating him with the same apparent natural necessity as the forces of nature themselves. The fantastic figures, which at first only reflected the mysterious forces of nature, at this point acquire social attributes, become representatives of the forces of history. (131)

Marx and Engels also noted that, although religion always contains and derives power from material borrowed from a distant past and to this degree constitutes "a great conservative force," religions adapt themselves to "every new phase of . . . world conditions" (83, 237).

Marx and Engels (233) argued that, as states developed vis-à-vis society, they produced their own ideologies. Yet, while they maintained that the ideas of the dominant class are inevitably the ruling ideas of such a society and that the primary goals of religion in a class society are to represent acquisitiveness and oppression as altruism, they argued that such religions address themselves in varying degrees to the interests of both the dominant and subordinate classes. Religion seeks to justify the privileges of rulers and to eliminate or divert feelings that could be potentially subversive. Yet, where true liberation from exploitation is impossible, religion expresses not merely the abasement of the subordinate classes but also their aspirations. It therefore preserves the lower classes from experiencing the worst ravages of despair and self-contempt. As John Plamenatz has put it, "while as yet men cannot recognize that they are alienated, it is better that some of their needs as species-beings should find illusory satisfaction than no satisfaction at all" (1975:246–47). This is what Marx meant when he wrote in "Contribution to the Critique of Hegel's Philosophy of Right" that "religious distress is at the same time the expression of real distress and the protest against real distress. Religion is the sigh of the oppressed creature, the heart of a heartless world, just as it is the spirit of a spiritless situation. It is the opium of the people" (Marx and Engels 1957:38). By opium, Marx meant painkiller.

Marx and Engels did not attempt to elaborate a comprehensive theory of religion. They related general changes in religious beliefs and practices to changes in technology and social organization, but paid no attention to the relation between religion and the personal problems of loss, suffering, and bereavement which are inherent in the human condition and ameliorated only to a limited degree by technological and social change. Their studies of the specific content of religion as it relates to social change were limited mainly to Christianity and to a lesser degree the religions of classical antiquity. Although they would probably have been prepared to agree with M.D. Coe (1981) that the rise of specific states cannot be understood *in detail* without knowledge of the religious beliefs of the people involved (Marx and Engels 1957:244–47), they have nevertheless provided a framework for a general understanding of the relation between religion and society at both preclass and class stages of development.

Whereas Marxism has considerably influenced the study of religion by sociologists and anthropologists in Western Europe and North America (Banton 1966; Glock 1973; Robertson 1970; Scharf 1970; Silvert 1967), it has had little effect on studies of early civilization among Western scholars, perhaps because of the strongly humanistic orientation of their research. The archaeologist Gordon Childe adopted a historical materialist perspective on religion in evolutionary studies of early civilization in *Man Makes Himself* (1936) and *What Happened in History* (1942). He was more concerned in these books with understanding those factors that could slow or halt social change than with ones that promote it. He distinguished between progressive societies, in which the relations of production favor the expansion of technology and there is a harmonious relationship among the means of production, social institutions, and the dominant system of beliefs, and conservative ones in which entrenched political hierarchies and inflexible systems of religious beliefs can block change. He believed that the ruling classes in early civilizations often sought to forestall technological changes that threatened their control of society. They did this by exercising bureaucratic control over craftspeople, inhibiting the pursuit of technological knowledge, and patronizing magic and superstition on a lavish scale, as well as by exercising force. They succeeded, however, only at the cost of making it more difficult for their own societies to compete with more progressive neighbors (Childe 1947). In agreement with Marx and Engels, Childe thus ascribed an important role in shaping history to both the base and the superstructure of societies. Yet he was careful to point out that, where the superstructure was dominant, its influence could only be negative. He did not ignore the concept of class conflict in his study of early civilizations. Instead, he argued that social evolution occurred very slowly in these societies because such struggles were blunted by highly effective political and religious techniques of social control. Yet, although his analysis contributed to our understanding of religion in what Marx had identified as Oriental society—the only type of class society not characterized by rapid change (Bailey and Llobera 1981; Dunn 1982)—he failed to utilize all the analytical resources of historical materialism to explain how religion accomplished what he identified as its important, although negative, historical role.

Religion, the State, and the Individual

The Economic Base

In the early civilizations of the Near East, the state exploited the peasantry by extracting significant surpluses from them for the use of the upper classes, as well as to cover the cost of the bureaucracy and to support numerous craftspeople. It is also clear that the rulers of the early civilizations did not extract these surpluses by force alone. This operation depended in part on the state being seen to provide protection and internal order that were of benefit to everyone. Such order, among other things, made possible the development of high population densities and intensive systems of agricultural production. As a result, people of all classes came to depend on the maintenance of peace and public order to assure the survival of high-density populations. The state also may have integrated vital economic tasks, such as building and maintaining irrigation systems and ensuring the circulation of materials needed by everyone, even though the precise nature of these activities and the point at which they became vital to the consolidation of the state are more variable than was thought formerly (Adams 1981; Butzer 1976; Flannery 1972). Finally, the state functioned as the supreme source of honor and status. Especially when a society was expanding economically or politically and there were chances for vertical mobility, this was of as much importance to commoners as it was to the nobility (Renfrew 1978:213).

Yet, contrary to Service's claims all early civilizations put force at the disposal of authorities to ensure that the orders of the state were carried out. This force was used to suppress overt disobedience to the state by individuals and groups and to discourage the possibility of such disobedience. Scribes who collected the grain tax in ancient Egypt were accompanied by policemen who could arrest, beat, and imprison peasants and their families if they refused to deliver what was required (Lichtheim 1976:170–71). Force was, however, relied on to cope with specific and relatively limited challenges to the authority of the state, rather than to make the entire social system work. Certain general rules governed the relationship between the capacity to use force and the overall social system. The less authorities relied on force, the less expensive was the overall cost of government. Yet, under these conditions, rulers had to depend to a greater degree on political persuasion and manipulation to control the social system, and the upper classes were limited in the amount of goods and labor they could extract for their own use. Conversely, more use of force allowed larger surpluses to be extracted from the peasants, but that required greater expenditure to maintain larger professional armies. This in turn meant that a smaller proportion of the total surplus was available for the use of the highest classes than had been available previously. Although the pyramids of Old Kingdom Egypt demonstrate what could be achieved with what appears to have been a relatively small standing army, the number of people benefiting substantially from the surpluses collected at this time seems to have been much smaller (Kemp 1983) than was the case in the New Kingdom (O'Connor 1983) or the Late Period (Lloyd 1983).

In general, the later states of antiquity in the Near East and around the Mediterranean appear to have behaved more brutally and exploitatively than did earlier ones. Beginning in Egypt by the New Kingdom and in Mesopotamia still earlier, armies became larger and were composed increasingly of professional soldiers, many of whom were foreigners recruited as mercenaries. Many of these soldiers were allotted land as a source of income. In such societies, general taxation grew heavier and a larger proportion of the population was reduced to slavery. At the same time, legal systems appear to have become more repressive and punishments more brutal (Pritchard 1955:160–96). These societies, in which the more intensive exploitation of the peasantry and laboring classes supported a larger number of privileged persons, appear to have been the natural outcome of an increasing reliance on force as an instrument of social control and of increasing competition among elites for hegemony over larger populations. They were sufficiently different from the earliest civilizations to justify the modern Marxist contention that Ancient Oriental and Slave societies represent successive stages in the early development of class societies (Friedman and Rowlands 1978:216–41).

It may be assumed that, where population densities are high and people have come to rely on a central government to maintain order and provide a political framework within which necessary economic activities can be carried on, ordinary people are willing to produce and surrender a reasonable surplus in return for these benefits. Tension is generated, however, when the standard of peasant life declines below a reasonable level of expectation, or when the upper classes increase their demands for goods and services markedly beyond traditional limits. The latter could occur either because of increasing rapacity among the upper classes or because the members of those classes increase in numbers disproportionately to the entire population (Kanawati 1977). As a general rule, it appears that, in the absence of investment in increased means for physical coercion, the upper classes as a group must keep their demands within traditionally acceptable limits if a political regime is to remain stable.

Religion and the Individual

Because of the greater availability of written documentation, the functioning of religious institutions can better be understood for the later phases of civilization in Egypt and the Near East than for the early historic period (Baines 1983; Oppenheim 1964). Little is certain about these societies before 2500 B.C. Yet what is known about religion in the later phases of the early civilizations and afterward provides a useful basis for helping to clarify the role played by religion in earlier times. It is clear, as White recognized, that religious institutions were prominent in the regulation of these societies, that such institutions were controlled by the upper classes, and that they sought to defend and perpetuate a social order based on inequality and exploitation. The question is, how did they do it?

One generally acknowledged function of religion is to provide culturally acceptable answers to the unresolvable problems posed by the conditions of human existence within a social context (Leach 1969:10). Yet, for this very reason, it is simplistic to argue, as White and Service have done, that religion can function as an instrument of social control simply by terrifying the masses with the threat of supernatural punishments and by teaching them that they are unfit to be other than servile. Instead, as Marx and Engels clearly recognized, religion in class societies has an ongoing mission to provide individuals with acceptable explanations for their inferiority and misfortunes and to convince them that, in spite of these difficulties, they live in a universe and social order that remain fundamentally just and benevolent. In societies where it is commonly acknowledged, as was the case in Egypt (Lichtheim 1973:169–84) or Mesopotamia (Jacobsen

1976:134), that individuals experience many misfortunes and acts of injustice at the hands of their superiors, there is little hope that this reassurance can be achieved simply by persuading the victims of the validity of some simple cosmological scheme. Religion must also offer individuals what appears to be an acceptable means to curb the abuses from which they suffer and to win redress for them. To achieve these multiple goals, the religious systems of ancient Egypt and the Near East had these four tasks:

1. *Uphold norms of moral conduct.* Such rules of behavior were an integral part of the early civilizations of this region, and most of them were viewed as morally incumbent on all social classes. Hence, they provided a standard by which the conduct of every person could be judged by peers and subordinates alike. While such codes reinforced certain ideals that were specific to individual societies or groups within society—such as bravery or stoicism—all of them also stressed the need for generosity and kindliness, at least when dealing with members of one's own society. In New Kingdom Egypt, the dead were believed to be required to deliver a long recitation of sins they had not committed. These included denials of murder, causing pain, robbing the poor, falsifying weights, stealing land or irrigation water, or maligning a person to his or her superior (Lichtheim 1976:125). As early as the Old Kingdom, officials boasted of having fed the hungry, rescued the weak, and clothed the naked, even when these were not relatives (Lichtheim 1973:17). In Mesopotamia, honesty and generosity were similarly exalted as norms of social behavior (Lamberg-Karlovsky 1985; Pritchard 1955:426).

2. *Explain suffering and apparent injustice, whether of natural or social origin.* Such misfortunes were frequently seen as retribution for acts committed by the victim, either consciously or unconsciously, in the present or some previous life. The offences included breaches of norms of right conduct, failure to observe necessary rituals, or behavior that had inadvertently proved offensive to a supernatural power. The conceptualizations of retribution were highly varied and framed in terms of diverse cosmologies. Where there was a belief in reincarnation, low-caste status was interpreted as a punishment for sins in a former life, including refusal to accept the social role assigned to individuals (Thapar 1966:46). During the New Kingdom, the Egyptians viewed at least some illnesses as divine punishment for sins, including blindness as a consequence of bearing false witness (Giveon 1982; Lichtheim 1976:104, 110). Likewise, in the Near East many illnesses and other misfortunes were construed as divine retribution for offending the gods by sinful conduct. Philosophical speculations about this problem reached their most profound expression in this region in the Book of Job, probably dating from the eighth century B.C. Fear of supernatural

punishment served as a curb on the behavior of rich and poor alike. It also encouraged victims of misfortune to look first to themselves as the possible cause of their trouble, before blaming their superiors or the social system.

3. *Offer hope for supernatural redress of grievances.* In New Kingdom Egypt, even the great state gods were thought to aid the unfortunate and distressed. Amon was said to rescue the poor from bondage and to support the friendless in court (Lichtheim 1976:106, 111). It was also believed that the gods punished those who oppressed such people. Even in the Old Kingdom, the gods punished plots against other human beings just as they exacted retribution for the despoiling of temples (Lichtheim 1973:64, 105). The "Instruction Addressed to Kagemni" warned that "one knows not what may happen, what god does when he punishes" (Lichtheim 1973:60). It was, therefore, regarded as appropriate to pray to the gods for wrongs to be avenged rather than to seek revenge through personal recourse to violence (Lichtheim 1976:141–42). Even if divine retribution was not obviously forthcoming in this life, ancient Egyptians could hope that the souls of their tormentors would be condemned to be destroyed after death. In the Near East, where life after death was viewed less optimistically, divine retribution could likewise be expected to be visited on wrongdoers in their lifetimes or on their descendants (Exodus 34:7). Views such as these, together with the less-documented practice of witchcraft, which provided sufferers other supernatural methods of bringing their oppressors to a bad end, encouraged them not to disrupt the social system by taking justice into their own hands. It also offered a safer way of seeking revenge to lower-class individuals, for whom the use of force against superiors almost certainly would have proved both futile and self-destructive. It therefore encouraged all but the most desperate victims of injustice not to resort to physical violence that would have disrupted the social system.

4. *Offer hope for personal success and welfare.* The ancient Mesopotamians attributed good fortune to the support of an individual's patron deity (Jacobsen 1976:155–60). The Egyptians saw their gods as bestowing wealth as a gift on those they favored (Lichtheim 1973:60, 71). Those who patiently endured injustice might hope that these same gods would offer them material compensation for their sufferings. In Mesopotamia, such compensation had to be obvious prior to death. Failure for it to be forthcoming might betoken unexpiated sins or shortcomings of a ritual nature. In societies that held more positive concepts of life after death, a reward for suffering might be expected in paradise or in the form of reincarnation in a more exalted state. The chief Egyptian hope was for a good life after death. This required not only ritual provisions but success before a

supernatural judgment in which evidence of sinful behavior on earth could lead to destruction (Lichtheim 1973:163–69).

The effect of such a complex of beliefs was, on the one hand, to curb the maltreatment of individuals resulting from the abuse of power and, on the other, to diminish aggression resulting from injustice or at least to channel it into patterns of behavior that did not disrupt the social system.

Yet, by themselves, doctrines promising supernatural rewards to those who did not disrupt the system did not necessarily do much to maintain law and order. It is even less likely that they were important enough to explain the prominence of religious institutions in the ancient civilizations of the Near East, let alone in all early ones. Such explanations did not convince everyone, especially victims of injustice, even if public opinion or state repression prevented these explanations from being questioned publicly. Indeed, if they had been highly successful, they would have permitted increasing injustice to the point that it might have seriously disrupted societies as practical systems of production and distribution. The propagation of such beliefs, although not unimportant, is incommensurate with the importance of religion. Furthermore, it does not explain its effectiveness.

It can be argued that ideals of just conduct acquire additional significance insofar as they can be seen to curb the disruptive behavior of the rich and powerful no less than that of the poor. Standards of justice provide members of the upper classes with a basis for criticizing their peers' treatment of subordinates when such treatment is disruptive to the social system. Ordinary people are likewise provided with a publicly accepted standard by which the behavior of their superiors may be judged. Thus public opinion reinforces fears of supernatural punishment in controlling the behavior of individual officials. The two together form a potent combination that operates on the symbolic as well as the social level.

One elaboration of such a mechanism of control is the belief that the misdeeds of officials can result in divine punishment of a whole society. The Bible states that in the reign of King David the Israelite kingdom was afflicted with famine for three years because the previous king had slaughtered a neighboring people in violation of a treaty sworn between them (2 Samuel 21:1–9). David's kingdom was also smitten by a plague as divine retribution for his carrying out a census, by which means he sought to increase royal power contrary to God's command (2 Samuel 24). Ideas of this sort achieved their ultimate refinement in the Chinese concept of the Mandate of Heaven (*t'ien ming*), which postulated that the sins and misconduct of kings and their officials would result in the withdrawal of the favor of heaven from their dynasty. This withdrawal was believed to manifest itself in crop failures and other natural disasters that expressed the anger of heaven, as well as in uprisings that eventually brought to power a new regime that enjoyed the favor of the gods. Beliefs of this sort transfer to the realm of the supernatural the causal mechanisms by which the growing administrative inefficiency and corruption of the officials of a weak political regime contribute to its collapse.

If religious beliefs supported rulers by doctrines of their divinity or rule by divine right, they also limited their powers and those of their officials. The role religious institutions filled in curbing violence and maintaining order in early civilizations was therefore twofold. Their effectiveness in propagating belief systems that restrained violence among ordinary people depended to a large degree on their also restraining injustice by officials and keeping inequality within traditionally accepted limits.

Religion and Group Interests

The situation during the earliest stages of the development of civilization is less clear than it is for later and better documented periods. It is generally assumed that at that time religion did not take much cognizance of individual needs; hence there was little personal piety or sense of a divine awareness of and concern for the fate of individuals. Instead of being oriented toward morality, religion was concerned with maintaining the fertility of nature, placating local spirits, and assuring the support of the dead for their living descendants. In particular, the cults of dead rulers were of national importance. The individual was defined and protected by membership in a kin group or local community, and men and women did not acquire religious status except as members of such groups. The emergence of an individual relationship to the divine resulted from a diminution in the importance of such groups (Friedman and Rowlands 1978).

In *The Dawn of Conscience,* J. H. Breasted argued that in ancient Egypt social conscience had its roots in the family and only gradually expanded to embrace the individual in relation to the whole society. As a result, gods were increasingly seen as shifting their attention from the realm of nature to human affairs. Only in the late New Kingdom did there develop a devotional spirit that postulated a personal relationship between individual human beings and gods. This new attitude involved a sense of sinfulness, accompanied by a belief in the willingness and ability of a god to forgive sins (Breasted 1933:312). In his more recent study of changes in Mesopotamian religious thought, Thorkild Jacobsen (1976) outlined a shift in emphasis from gods seen as instransitive forces of nature, to gods seen as rulers upholding a legal and moral order and shaping the fortunes of states, to a final view of gods as parents with whom the individual could establish a personal relationship.

But to what extent are such differences real rather than apparent? It is true that, in Egypt, Old Kingdom and Middle Kingdom texts lack the explicit personal piety of late New Kingdom ones, in particular the latter's sense of guilt and of the need for atonement. Also, we do not find literary compositions in which ordinary people beseech the great gods for welfare and protection. Yet, as early as the Old Kingdom, we encounter firm beliefs in the soul having to face judgment as a prerequisite for life after death and in the right of the person who has been wronged to demand justice on that occasion (Lichtheim 1973:16, 24, 107). There is also evidence of individuals calling on gods for assistance and expecting divine punishment in the present life (55). A careful examination of Old Kingdom texts shows that a strong moral element was already explicit in the concept of *maat*, or cosmic order, which was held to be the essential ingredient for a smoothly functioning kingdom (4). As early as the third millennium B.C., appeals were made to the Sumerian sun-god Utu by individuals who were unable to secure justice from fellow human beings, and a cry for help to this god was believed to have supernatural power in its own right. The goddess Inanna, as the evening star, was also held to judge cases of injustice. Later, personal deities were looked to for protection against disease, misfortune, and oppression (Jacobsen 1976:134, 138, 160–64). The evidence from Egypt and Mesopotamia thus suggests the early presence of a belief in supernatural curbs on wrongdoing which would have provided the basis for the later conceptualization of the gods as personal avengers of the oppressed. It is also possible that the latter concept was already present at an early period, although it did not receive explicit literary expression in the limited range of genres in use at the time.

It is possible, however, that in the first stages of their development some early civilizations did not conceptualize ethical relations between individuals as having cosmic or religious significance. Yet, even if this were so, religion would have played a vital role in mediating between the interests of numerous smaller groups and those of the administrative hierarchy. In all early civilizations, gods served as patron deities for regions, cities, professions, clans, lineages, households, and other social groups. Each group had a cult center and appropriate rituals the elaborateness of which reflected the social ranking of the group. The relationships among the gods thus constituted a cosmological representation of hierarchical societies, though the conceptualization varied considerably as to how the gods were related to one another and, in particular, with respect to the genealogical explicitness that was or was not used to relate major deities. Especially in southern Mesopotamia, the major deities were genealogically related to a much greater degree than were Egyptian ones (Frankfort 1961:3–29).

Political changes were sometimes reflected in alterations in the ranking of major deities. As a result of the prominence of rulers of Theban origin in the Middle and New Kingdoms, the local god Amun was identified with Re, the principal royal deity of the late Old Kingdom, as well as becoming a major national deity in his own name (David 1982:98). In Mesopotamia, the kingship of the gods passed in turn from Enlil to Marduk to Ashur as Babylon and later Assyria acquired hegemony in the region (Jacobsen 1976:167). Successful shifts of this sort were, however, extremely difficult and required considerable time to consolidated.

Though subject to such political manipulations, the gods represented the political interests of their worshipers. By identifying these interests with specific divinities, weaker groups acquired supernatural significance that exceeded their political strength, thereby enhancing their integrity and ability to cope with state domination and even to survive military defeat. In Mesopotamia, when towns or nations were conquered their chief temples were sometimes sacked and burned and the images of their gods carried off as symbols of victory (Olmstead 1948:237). It was often construed that defeat had come about as the result of a patron deity becoming angry with his or her city (Pritchard 1955:455–63). Yet attempts by victorious kings to transfer old local cults to their own capitals, such as were made by the Akkadian ruler Naram-Sin, led to unrest and sometimes to widespread rebellion (Westenholz 1979:112). Temples normally were repaired and their cults maintained so that conquerors and local worshipers alike might avoid the anger of the resident deity. By permitting or even encouraging such renovation, the conquerors had to acknowledge the continuing corporate validity of groups whom they had defeated.

The protection of the rights of subordinate groups by religious institutions is evident in ancient Egypt, where for long periods political integration was far-reaching and denied the political validity of provinces, whatever their origins, except as administrative units of the central government. The king, as we have already noted, claimed to be the sole priest of all the gods and hence the only significant intermediary between human beings and the supernatural. Yet local cults were honored by the central government from earliest times into the Roman period, with shrines, estates, and numerous special donations for their maintenance. All the gods, whether they were worshiped in the royal capital, provincial centers, or other important towns, were specifically associated with these places. Every temple marked a specific location where its major presiding deity had created the world (David 1982:127–29). They therefore served as symbols of local interests, and the attention they received from the central government acknowledged that it was aware of these interests. In later Ptolemaic times, as the power of these foreign rulers waned, pharaonic formulas of kingship proliferated and huge temples were erected to honor the gods of Egypt and court favor with the native Egyptians (Bevan 1968:214–68).

Three notable exceptions to this rule, if we may credit historical traditions as well as archaeological evidence, were the pharaohs Khufu and Khafre, the builders of the two largest pyramids in the Old Kingdom, and Akhenaton in the New Kingdom (Aldred 1968:260). These rulers were accused of closing temples and suppressing local cults in order to promote religious programs designed to enhance the power of the central government. In the Old Kingdom, this was done by building vast royal pyramids; in the New Kingdom, by promoting the cult of a single, solar deity who was proclaimed to be king of heaven and earth. The failure of both programs, as evident from the reduced size of later pyramids and the suppression of the Aton cult, represents the failure of the central government to obliterate local interests as embodied in their traditional religious cults (Trigger 1981:181–82). In a state such as Egypt, which exhibited an extremely high degree of centralization for the ancient world and tolerated little regional political dissent, religion allowed local groups to express their interests and to make claims on the central government in a fashion that was not disruptive. The honoring of local cults by the central government was a visible token of its concern for the welfare of these localities and, by implication, for their economic and political problems. Hence, in Egypt local cults served as the medium for a dialogue between rulers and ruled.

In Mesopotamia during the Early Dynastic period there is evidence of struggles for political and economic control within some city states between temple estates belonging to major deities and military leaders who were establishing themselves as hereditary kings (Kramer 1959:47). During this period, there appears to have been a substantial shift in political and economic power from temple communities to palace institutions. As tributary networks and then politically more integrated empires developed, the gods of city states became, as in Egypt, foci for expressing local interests in contradistinction to those of the central government. In Early Dynastic times in southern Mesopotamia, the paramount king was the ruler of a city-state who compelled neighboring ones, by force or threat of arms, to pay him tribute. He also adjudicated interstate disputes concerning water rights and other matters and assumed leadership in keeping foreign enemies at bay. In addition, he had many religious duties. In legal theory, he received his office, not as a result of conquest, but as a gift from Enlil, the chief diety of Nippur, the politically neutral cult center of southern Mesopotamia. He also had to visit the capitals of each subject city-state to make offerings to the gods of that state at appropriate festivals. These activities have led at least one Assyriologist to describe these paramount kings as "a sort of president over a council consisting of the heads of the individual city-states" (Westenholz 1979:109). Later Assyrian and Persian kings took great care to honor the gods of major cities such as Babylon as part of their policy of encouraging these cities to accept their rule (Brinkman 1979:229). In all these situations, as in Egypt, the relationship between local gods and kings provided a metaphor for discussing political problems arising between states and the sectional interests with which they had to contend.

It is clear that at the group level, just as with the individual, religion played a dual role in sanctioning the power of the central government and supporting opposition to it. If the concept of supernatural interest in the welfare of individuals evolved out of a belief in such concern for the group, this dual role must have antedated the concern with individual relationships discussed earlier. Sooner or later, however, with respect to the relations of both individuals and groups, religion became important in balancing the interests of the strong and the weak, the rich and the poor, the ruler and the ruled. This was a socially complex and pervasive role, one very different from the simple support of state power that White's characterization assigned to it.

Church versus State

Rulers in the early civilizations were players in a game that involved competition both within and between state hierarchies. The goal of these struggles was to control individual human and natural resources. By waging successful wars, individual rulers gained power, prestige, and wealth, some of which was passed on to valiant warriors and loyal administrators. Nevertheless, it was a risky game, since rulers could also lose wars and be deposed by their conquerors or have to pay tribute to them. White (1959:324) saw the church playing this game in tandem with the state. Priests participated in mobilizing people for war and often accompanied armies with talismans and images of the gods in order to encourage them. Inevitably, they claimed that victory was a gift of the gods. The wealth and power of religious institutions grew as one state conquered another. Kings had to donate significant portions of tribute, booty, and conquered land to temples as thank offerings (326). They were thus compelled to alienate the spoils of war, whereas religious institutions kept what they received forever. White accepted the supposition that as a result of this process Egyptian priests were able to usurp the power of the kings and take control of Upper

Egypt at the end of the twentieth dynasty, a historical interpretation that has since been discredited (Kitchen 1973:248–50). It is true that in the early civilizations temple institutions often benefited from military success. The leading temples of hegemonic states were transformed into huge and magnificently decorated structures, whereas those of conquered states were often poor and dilapidated for lack of capital (Oppenheim 1964:117).

Yet this analysis fails to consider important aspects of the complex relations between religious institutions and the state. Religious institutions depended on the state to use its force to protect their property and privileges—a clear indication that supernatural sanctions were insufficient even in this highly specific sphere. Crimes committed against these institutions, such as robbery, were generally punished in the same fashion as were crimes against the state, which usually meant that the penalties were much harsher than for the same crimes committed against individuals (Pritchard 1955:166). At the same time, religious institutions had to strive to maintain their rights and privileges in the face of pressure and interference from government officials. Egyptian temples no longer are believed to have been sacrosanct institutions but are seen to have been subjected to much control and supervision by the state. Unless specifically exempted, they could be called on to provide traveling royal officials with food and supplies, in the same fashion as royal storage depots (Lichtheim 1973:27). The pharaohs donated land, slaves, and other wealth to temples as thank offerings, but they could reassign such wealth and use it for nonreligious purposes in time of need. Kemp (1972) has described New Kingdom temples as state banks in which victorious pharaohs deposited the surplus wealth that had fallen into their hands, only to withdraw it again in time of need. In Mesopotamia, victorious kings lavishly adorned and endowed temples of gods to whose support they attributed their success. Yet at the same time they attempted to extend royal control over temple estates, sometimes claiming to do this for the public good (Kramer 1959:45–50).

The possession of wealth, as evolutionary anthropologists are now recognizing (Webb 1975; Webster 1975), is an essential attribute of dynastic power. Wealth is necessary to maintain the army and state bureaucracy, it permits officials to reward loyal retainers, and it is essential to the lavish lifestyle that enhances the status of a king and his officials. The failure of rulers to keep systems for collecting taxes and tribute in efficient working order encourages corruption and a retraction of the economy which, if unchecked, ultimately results in the collapse of the regime (Adams 1981:201; Ibn Khaldun 1969). Successful wars, which enhance the ability of a king to collect tribute and distribute largess, also increase his power, authority, and internal security. The only ultimate check on the geographic expansion of a state is the absence of neighboring peoples with enough surplus wealth to provide a reasonable return over the cost of keeping them in subjection.

Whereas the state exists to maintain law and order in inegalitarian societies, the principal duty of temples and their attendant priests is to perform rituals thought necessary to provide for the welfare of society and individuals. Doing this requires esoteric knowledge, trained personnel, and material resources. All these can be supported on a more elaborate and impressive scale if temples are wealthier; hence, there were probably few priestly corporations in the early civilizations that did not wish to see their gods honored and their own importance enhanced with larger temples and more abundant resources. Yet, because temples were institutions related to specific locations, the incentives for expansion were more restricted for them than they were for a state that could hope to dominate and tax its neighbors. One cult might try to outshine others, but ultimately all were necessary and had to be maintained. It was, therefore, more difficult to merge these separate institutions to form administratively integrated units than was the case for secular administrations. Finally, from a religious point of view, the efficiency of temples was not as seriously curtailed by economic cutbacks as were the power and authority of the state.

Religious institutions aided in the expansion of victorious states and profited from resulting increases in revenue, but they had less power and authority to gain from wars, and perhaps proportionately more to lose from them, than did the secular elite. The vested interests of religious institutions tended to be focused on specific cult centers, together with their personnel and adjacent property. Priests were more concerned with maintaining their institutions intact over long periods than with the risky and often ephemeral expansion of power over increasing territory. Harold Innis (1951) characterized the chief concern of religious institutions as perpetuating themselves and the ideas they stood for over time, that of states as exerting their economic and political control over increasing geographic space. Moreover, for religious institutions, the economic benefits derived as thank offerings from a victorious state were offset to varying degrees by secular officials becoming more autocratic and asserting greater control over temple affairs. For all these reasons, priests were probably less rapacious and less inclined to take risks than were secular officials, whether bureaucratic or military. The former had greater interest in preserving their possessions from the ravages of war and less concern with the material benefits of military success than did their secular counterparts.

Priests therefore generally were more conservative in interstate relations than were the secular elite. They opposed excessive recourse to war and were able to use their connections with religious institutions in other states to help settle disputes and bring wars to an end. It is no accident that in multistate civilizations the broadest formal ties were often religious. Nippur, as a holy city, offered neutral ground where representatives of the various city-states of southern Mesopotamia could meet (Roux 1980:134–35), much as Delphi and Olympia did for the Greeks. The Chou ruler of China continued to perform rituals and his court to provide a symbolic focus for Chinese civilization long after China had become a collection of rivalrous and warring states (Chêng 1963:xxvii–xxix). Religious institutions thus provided an instrument for mediating disputes among states. In this fashion, they were significant in counteracting rulers who imperiled the stability and welfare of their states.

Despite the close links between the state and religious institutions in early civilizations and their common concerns with defending the interests of the upper classes, their functions in regulating the social system were quite different. Religious institutions tended to be more moderate. In particular, they provided a conceptual basis for mediating conflicts between rich and poor and between the state and the individual as well as for moderating interstate conflicts and limiting their destabilizing consequences. Yet the aim of religious institutions, like that of the state, was to stabilize political systems based on inequality and the exploitation of a majority of people by a privileged elite. The religious institutions of the early civilizations were exploitative ones that could not exist without the protection and support of the state. Their universality indicates that, reciprocally and in the long run, the state could not function without the mediation and moderating influences provided by religious institutions.

The Religion of the Oppressed

In general, religious institutions and the state were united by important common interests and worked smoothly together. Divergent interests generated occasional disputes, but these were usually kept under control, since they were of minor importance compared to interests religious institutions and the state shared. Yet the integration of the parts of a system is tested by crises, and in the early civilizations these occurred especially when the rapacity of the state and its personnel failed to be kept within operable limits. Religious cults thrived from the top to the bottom of every society. Those patronized by the state were controlled by upper-class appointees, though the lower echelons of priests and their assistants were sometimes drawn from the lower classes. In New Kingdom Egypt high-ranking priests were recruited from the same classes as were bureaucrats and military officers, whereas lesser ones came from families of soldiers, tenant farmers, and peasants (O'Connor 1983:192–94). Control of formal appointments and of the financial benefits and prestige derived from them gave those in charge a considerable degree of control over the entire hierarchy. Yet perceptions, opinions, and loyalties could vary widely over such a broad spectrum of the priesthood. Many family and local cults also lay beyond the control of the official priesthood. In addition there were shamans, healers, and prophets who were self-proclaimed or whose offices were inherited outside the religious hierarchy. Some of the latter were regarded as dangerous by the authorities and operated in defiance of the state and of religious leaders alike (1 Samuel 28:3).

If the official religious institutions failed to control the rapacity of the state, their power to influence the lower classes was likely to decline also. When this happened, the influence of unofficial religious leaders increased, especially if they began to denounce the rich and powerful. Soon institutionalized religion was challenged by a religion of the oppressed that not only denounced the injustices of state officials but also called into question the ethical status of the religious hierarchy that supported them. As it gained strength, such a movement denied that there was supernatural support for the existing political regime and preached the need to install a more just and humane one.

It is not surprising that there is little record of such popular, largely oral movements in the surviving literature and historical records of Egypt and the Near East. These sources normally express the views of the upper classes. In the Hebrew traditions, which were edited with a pronounced antimonarchical bias, much more evidence survives of popular religious movements. The prophecies of Micah and of the herdsman Amos are filled with denunciations not only of kings who failed to worship God properly but also of the upper classes in general for their mistreatment of ordinary people: "because they sold the righteous for silver, and the poor for a pair of shoes" (Amos 2:6); "they covet fields, and take them by violence; and houses, and take them away: so they oppress a man and his house" (Micah 2:2). The prophet Elijah denounced King Ahab for judicially murdering a man so he could seize his vineyard and prophesied that God would destroy his descendants (1 Kings 21). Later, his disciple Elisha proceeded to annoint the military commander Jehu as king of Israel and to sanction him to murder Ahab's son, King Jehoram, together with his entire family, priests, and followers (2 Kings 9, 10). Many insurrections probably began as religious movements of protest (Shih 1967), as did the Mahdist uprising in the Sudan in the nineteenth century (Holt 1958). To a large degree, the political protests of the oppressed poor tended to be phrased in religious terms and the leaders of such movements were initially religious figures. Rulers were denounced for disobeying divine will, and a call was made for them to be replaced. As a political revolution gained momentum, the official religious hierarchy had either to switch sides or to be replaced. This often produced dissent and divergent behavior among different levels of priests. A major event marking the beginning of the Jewish revolt against Rome in the first century of the Christian era occurred when lesser priests in the Jerusalem temple disobeyed the orders of their superiors and refused to continue offering sacrifices for the well-being of the emperor and the Roman people (Brandon 1971:69).

Religious movements of this sort do not challenge the idea of inequality. The new regime was as hierarchical and despotic as the one it replaced. Its reform consisted of eliminating corruption, which lowered the level of taxation; providing law and order; and carrying out public works. All these activities were conducive to renewed prosperity. Thus the new regime restored a mutually acceptable balance between the demands of the upper classes and the productive capacity of the peasantry (Ibn Khaldun 1969). By assisting in bringing this about, the religion of the oppressed was important in perpetuating a social system based on political and economic inequality. It did so by helping to destroy a corrupt and ineffectual political regime and to replace it with one better able to govern a society. Such a movement was justified ideologically as a return to an older, more just, and more cosmologically valid pattern of government from which recent rulers had deviated.

Early civilizations had social orders that were resilient, enduring, and by comparison with modern complex societies resistant to change. Evidence of richly endowed, hierarchically organized religious institutions is ubiquitous in these societies, and they appear to have controlled a greater proportion of the total productivity than have religious organizations in earlier or more recent societies. Rulers invariably claimed divine sanction, if not quasi-religious status, for their administrations.

While recognizing the importance of religious institutions in the early civilizations, neo-evolutionists have failed to ascertain with sufficient precision their function within these societies. In this essay I reject as simplistic the view that the principal role of religions was to augment the authority of the state as part of a broader system of repressive social control in the early civilizations. I reject even more emphatically the suggestion, reiterated by Service (1975), that fears of supernatural punishment were the most powerful factor supporting the authority of the rulers and officials of these societies. On the contrary, religious institutions had to depend to a considerable degree on the coercive powers of the state to protect their own rights and privileges. To provide a functional explanation of why the equivalent of White's state-church evolved in all these societies, it appears necessary to assign regulatory roles to religious institutions that are both essential and complementary to those performed by the state.

The suggestion that early civilizations could be held together by force alone is no more tenable than the idea that their structures of authority could be maintained solely by fear of supernatural sanctions. The hierarchical and profoundly inegalitarian political structures that governed these societies performed functions vital to the formation and maintenance of their high-density populations. Peasants would have been motivated by self-interest alone to produce and surrender surplus goods in return for these benefits, as long as the demands of the state and the upper classes remained within traditionally acceptable limits. Physical coercion, though essential for the operation of the state, was relied on to curb specific challenges to its authority rather than to maintain the entire social order. Increasing rapacity among the upper classes, declining productivity as a result of unmanagable demographic increases, and environmental deterioration required increasing physical coercion to maintain a stable society.

Marxist analyses of religion are based on the premise that religious ideologies preserve class societies not only by reinforcing the rightfulness of social hierarchies but also by preserving the exploited from experiencing the most damaging psychological ravages of despair and self-contempt. Religion must provide such individuals with acceptable explanations for their social inferiority and convince them that, in spite of their sufferings, they live in a social and supernatural order that is fundamentally just and benevolent. To do this effectively, however, religious institutions must curb at least the worst abuses that can arise from exploitation in an inegalitarian society. Religion had a dual function in sanctioning the power of the central government while at the same time asserting the rights of subordinate regional, ethnic, and occupational groupings and providing an apparently nonpolitical focus for their opposition to state domination. Ideals of just conduct operated to curb the disruptive behavior of the rich and powerful no less than did the latter's fear of rebelliousness among the oppressed poor. By affirming the rights of smaller groups and establishing acceptable norms of conduct between rulers and subordinates, religious institutions helped moderate the exactions of state officials and of the powerful generally. Finally, some cults were able to mediate disputes between states, particularly when these threatened the stability and welfare of all the governments involved.

Unlike the state, which was concerned with controlling and administering large populations, religious institutions focused their interest on specific cult centers and their attendant staff and possessions. Thus they tended to be controlled by administrative hierarchies organized on a different geographic scale from that of the state. Although not averse to economic aggrandizement, religious institutions were more concerned with maintaining themselves over long periods than with seeking an often ephemeral expansion of power over a large territory. A major function of religion was to contain the risk-taking propensities of secular rulers with respect to internal and external policies within safe limits. Such activities helped to establish a balance that served to perpetuate social systems based on inequality and exploitation. In the jargon of general systems theory, the church was an important mechanism of negative feedback which brought a conservative element to the management of hierarchical societies. When formal religious institutions failed to control the extravagance and corruption of the secular elite, grass-roots religious elements began to destabilize the political system and bring about a rebellion or *coup d'état*. The aim of such uprisings was not to eliminate a social system based on inequality but rather to create a regime that would adhere to more traditional and broadly acceptable norms of exploitation and generosity.

Finally, this view of the functional role filled by religion calls into question recent claims that concepts of liberty, justice, human rights, and equity were distinctive of Mesopotamian and later western civilization (Lamberg-Karlovsky 1985) but not of civilizations in other parts of the world (Chang 1984). My arguments do not, however, rule out the likelihood that these concepts became stronger and more explicit as the ancient civilizations themselves grew more complex (Willey 1985).

References

Adams, R. McC.
    1966   *The Evolution of Urban Society*. Chicago: Aldine.
    1981   *Heartland of Cities*. Chicago: University of Chicago Press.
Adams, R. N.
    1975   *Energy and Structure*. Austin: University of Texas Press.
Aldred, Cyril
    1968   *Akhenaton, Pharaoh of Egypt: A New Study*. London: Thames and Hudson.
Bailey, A. M. and J. R. Llobera
    1981   *The Asiatic Mode of Production*. London: Routledge and Kegan Paul.
Baines, John
    1983   Literacy and ancient Egyptian society. *Man* 18:572–99.

Banton, Michael, ed.
- 1966 *Anthropological Approaches to the Study of Religion*. London: Tavistock.

Bevan, Edwyn
- 1968 *The House of Ptolemy*. Rev. ed. Chicago: Argonaut.

Brandon, S. G. F.
- 1971 *The Trial of Jesus of Nazareth*. London: Paladin.

Breasted, J. H.
- 1933 *The Dawn of Conscience*. New York: Scribner's.

Brinkman, J. A.
- 1979 Babylonia under the Assyrian Empire, 745–627 B.C. In M. T. Larsen, ed., *Power and Propaganda: A Symposium on Ancient Empires*, pp. 223–50. Copenhagen: Akademisk Forlag.

Butzer, K. W.
- 1976 *Early Hydraulic Civilization in Egypt*. Chicago: University of Chicago Press.

Calnek, E. E.
- 1976 The internal structure of Tenochtitlan. In E. R. Wolf, ed., *The Valley of Mexico*, pp. 287–302. Albuquerque: University of New Mexico Press.

Chang, K. C.
- 1984 Ancient China and its anthropological significance. *Symbols*, Spring/Fall, pp. 2–4, 20–22.

Chêng, T. K.
- 1963 *Archaeology in China*, vol. 3: *Chou China*. Cambridge: W. Heffer and Sons.

Childe, V. G.
- 1936 *Man Makes Himself*. London: Watts.
- 1942 *What Happened in History*. Harmondsworth: Penguin.
- 1944 *Progress and Archaeology*. London: Watts.
- 1946 *Scotland before the Scots*. London: Methuen.
- 1947 *History*. London: Cobbett.

Coe, M. D.
- 1980 *The Maya*. 2d ed. London: Thames and Hudson.
- 1981 Religion and the rise of Mesoamerican states. In G. D. Jones and R. R. Kautz, eds., *The Transition to Statehood in the New World*, pp. 157–71. Cambridge: Cambridge University Press.

Cohen, Ronald
- 1978 State origins: A reappraisal. In H. J. M. Claessen and Peter Skalnik, eds., *The Early State*, pp. 31–75. The Hague: Mouton.

Cordy, R. H.
- 1981 *A Study of Prehistoric Social Change*. New York: Academic Press.

David, A. R.
- 1973 *Religious Ritual at Abydos (c. 1300 BC)*. Warminster: Aris and Phillips.

1982 *The Ancient Egyptians: Religious Beliefs and Practices.* London: Routledge and Kegan Paul.
Duell, P., et al.
1938 *The Mastaba of Mereruka,* pt. 1. Chicago: University of Chicago Press.
Dunn, S. P.
1982 *The Fall and Rise of the Asiatic Mode of Production.* London: Routledge and Kegan Paul.
Durán, Diego
1964 *The Aztecs: The History of the Indies of New Spain.* Trans. D. Heyden and F. Horcasitas. New York: Orion Press.
Durkheim, Emile
1915 *The Elementary Forms of the Religious Life.* London: Allen and Unwin.
Earle, T. K.
1977 A reappraisal of redistribution: Complex Hawaiian chiefdoms. In T.K. Earle and J. E. Ericson, eds., *Exchange Systems in Prehistory,* pp. 213–29. New York: Academic Press.
1978 *Economic and Social Organization of a Complex Chiefdom.* University of Michigan, Museum of Anthropology, Anthropological Paper, no. 63.
Ekholm, K., and J. Friedman
1979 "Capital," imperialism and exploitation in ancient world systems. In M. T. Larsen, ed., *Power and Propaganda: A Symposium on Ancient Empires,* pp. 41–58. Copenhagen: Akademisk Forlag.
Flannery, K. V.
1972 The cultural evolution of civilizations. *Annual Review of Ecology and Systematics* 3:399–426.
Frankfort, Henri
1948 *Kingship and the Gods.* Chicago: University of Chicago Press.
1961 *Ancient Egyptian Religion.* New York: Harper Torchbook.
Fried, M. H.
1967 *The Evolution of Political Society.* New York: Random House.
Friedman, J. and M. J. Rowlands
1978 Notes towards an epigenetic model of the evolution of 'civilisation'. In J. Friedman and M. J. Rowlands, eds., *The Evolution of Social Systems,* pp. 201–76. Pittsburgh: University of Pittsburgh Press.
Fustel de Coulanges, N. D.
1900 *The Ancient City.* Boston: Lee and Shepard.
Giveon, Raphael
1982 A god who hears. In M. H. van Voss et al., eds., *Studies in Egyptian Religion,* pp. 38–42. Leiden: Brill.
Glock, C. Y., ed.
1973 *Religion in Sociological Perspective.* Belmont, Calif.: Wadsworth.
Gluckman, Max
1940 The kingdom of the Zulu of South Africa. In M. Fortes and E.

Evans-Pritchard, eds., *African Political Systems*, pp. 25–55. London: Oxford University Press.

Godelier, Maurice
1977   *Perspectives in Marxist Anthropology*. Cambridge: Cambridge University Press.

Hallpike, C. R.
1979   *The Foundations of Primitive Thought*. Oxford: Oxford University Press.

Heilbroner, R. L.
1961   *The Worldly Philosophers*. Rev. ed. New York: Simon and Schuster.

Holt, P. M.
1958   *The Mahdist State in the Sudan, 1881–1898*. Oxford: Oxford University Press.

Hooke, S. H., ed.
1958   *Myth, Ritual, and Kingship*. Oxford: Oxford University Press.

Ibn Khaldun, A.
1969   *The Muqaddimah: An Introduction to History*. Trans. F. Rosenthal, ed. N. J. Dawood. Princeton: Princeton University Press.

Innis, H. A.
1951   *The Bias of Communication*. Toronto: University of Toronto Press.

Jacobsen, Thorkild
1976   *The Treasures of Darkness: A History of Mesopotamian Religion*. New Haven, Conn.: Yale University Press.

Kanawati, Naguib
1977   *The Egyptian Administration in the Old Kingdom*. Warminster: Aris and Phillips.

Kemp, B. J.
1972   Temple and town in ancient Egypt. In P. J. Ucko, R. Tringham, and G. W. Dimbleby, eds., *Man, Settlement and Urbanism*, pp. 657–80. London: Duckworth.
1983   Old Kingdom, Middle Kingdom and Second Intermediate Period, c. 2686–1552 B.C. In B. G. Trigger, et al., *Ancient Egypt: A Social History*, pp. 71–182. Cambridge: Cambridge University Press.

Kiernan, V. G.
1983   Religion. In T. Bottomore, ed., *A Dictionary of Marxist Thought*, pp. 413–16. Cambridge: Harvard University Press.

Kitchen, K. A.
1973   *The Third Intermediate Period in Egypt (1100–650 B.C.)*. Warminster: Aris and Phillips.

Krader, Lawrence
1968   *Formation of the State*. Englewood Cliffs: Prentice-Hall.

Kramer, S. N.
1959   *History Begins at Sumer*. Garden City: Doubleday Anchor.

Kus, S. M.
1981   The context of complexity. In S. E. van der Leeuw, ed., *Archaeological*

Approaches to the Study of Complexity, pp. 197–227. Amsterdam: University of Amsterdam.

Lamberg-Karlovsky, C. C.
1985 The Near Eastern "breakout" and the Mesopotamian social contract. *Symbols,* Spring, pp. 8–11, 23–24.

Leach, Edmund
1969 *Genesis as Myth and Other Essays.* London: Cape.

Lévy-Bruhl, Lucien
1910 *Les fonctions mentales dans les sociétés inférieures.* Paris: Alcan.

Lewis, H. S.
1981 Warfare and the origin of the state: Another formulation. In H. J. M. Claessen and P. Skalnik, eds., *The Study of the State,* pp. 201–21. The Hague: Mouton.

Lichtheim, Miriam
1973 *Ancient Egyptian Literature,* vol. 1: *The Old and Middle Kingdoms.* Berkeley: University of California Press.
1976 *Ancient Egyptian Literature,* vol. 2: *The New Kingdom.* Berkeley: University of California Press.

Lloyd, A. B.
1983 The Late Period, 664–323 B.C. In B. G. Trigger et al., *Ancient Egypt: A Social History,* pp. 279–364. Cambridge: Cambridge University Press.

Lumbreras, L. G.
1974 *The Peoples and Cultures of Ancient Peru.* Washington, D.C.: Smithsonian Institution Press.

Marx, K., and F. Engels
1957 *On Religion.* Moscow: Progress Publishers.

Murra, J. V.
1980 [1955] *The Economic Organization of the Inka State.* Greenwich, Conn.: JAI Press.

Oberg, K.
1955 Types of social structure among the lowland tribes of South and Central America. *American Anthropologist* 57:472–87.

O'Connor, David
1983 New Kingdom and Third Intermediate Period, 1552–664 B.C. In B. G. Trigger et al., *Ancient Egypt: A Social History,* pp. 183–278. Cambridge: Cambridge University Press.

Olmstead, A. T.
1948 *History of the Persian Empire.* Chicago: University of Chicago Press.

Oppenheim, A. L.
1964 *Ancient Mesopotamia.* Chicago: University of Chicago Press.

Peebles, C. S., and S. M. Kus
1977 Some archaeological correlates of ranked societies. *American Antiquity* 42:421–48.

Plamenatz, John
1975 *Karl Marx's Philosophy of Man.* Oxford: Oxford University Press.

Polanyi, Karl
  1957   *The Great Transformation*. Boston: Beacon Press.
Pritchard, J. B.
  1955   *Ancient Near Eastern Texts Relating to the Old Testament*. 2d ed. Princeton: Princeton University Press.
Renfrew, A. C.
  1978   Trajectory discontinuity and morphogenesis: The implications of catastrophe theory for archaeology. *American Antiquity* 43:203–22.
Robertson, Roland
  1970   *The Sociological Interpretation of Religion*. New York: Schocken Books.
Roux, Georges
  1980   *Ancient Iraq*. 2d ed. Harmondsworth: Penguin Books.
Rowe, J. H.
  1946   Inca culture at the time of the Spanish conquest. *Handbook of South American Indians*, vol. 2: *The Andean Civilizations*, pp. 183–330. Smithsonian Institution, Bureau of American Ethnology, Bulletin 143.
Sahlins, Marshall
  1968   *Tribesmen*. Englewood Cliffs: Prentice-Hall.
Scharf, B. R.
  1970   *The Sociological Study of Religion*. London: Hutchinson.
Service, E. R.
  1971   *Primitive Social Organization: An Evolutionary Perspective*. 2d ed. New York: Random House.
  1975   *Origins of the State and Civilization*. New York: Norton.
Shih, V. Y.
  1967   *The Taiping Ideology*. Seattle: University of Washington Press.
Silvert, K. H., ed.
  1967   *Churches and States: The Religious Institution and Modernization*. New York: American Universities Field Staff.
Spath, C. D.
  1973   The problem of the calpulli in Classic Nahuatlaca social structure. *Journal of the Steward Anthropological Society* 5(1):25–44.
Steward, Julian
  1949   Cultural causality and law: A trial formulation of the development of early civilizations. *American Anthropologist* 51:1–27.
  1955   *Theory of Culture Change*. Urbana: University of Illinois Press.
Street, B. V.
  1975   *The Savage in Literature*. London: Routledge and Kegan Paul.
Thapar, Romila
  1966   *A History of India*, vol. 1. Harmondsworth: Penguin.
Trigger, B. G.
  1969   *The Huron: Farmers of the North*. New York: Holt, Rinehart and Winston.
  1981   Akhenaton and Durkheim. *Bulletin du Centenaire* (Supplément au

BIFAO 81), pp. 165–84. Cairo: Imprimerie de l'Institut Français d'Archéologie Orientale.

Turner, Ralph
1941 *The Great Cultural Traditions.* New York: McGraw-Hill.

Webb, M. C.
1975 The flag follows trade: An essay on the necessary interaction of military and commercial factors in state formation. In J. A. Sabloff and C. C. Lamberg-Karlovsky, eds., *Ancient Civilization and Trade,* pp. 155–210. Albuquerque: University of New Mexico Press.

Webster, David
1975 Warfare and the evolution of the state: A reconsideration. *American Antiquity* 40:464–70.

Westenholz, Aage
1979 The Old Akkadian empire in contemporary opinion. In M. T. Larsen, ed., *Power and Propaganda: A Symposium on Ancient Empires,* pp. 107–23. Copenhagen: Akademisk Forlag.

Wheatley, Paul
1971 *The Pivot of the Four Quarters.* Edinburgh: Edinburgh University Press.

White, L. A.
1959 *The Evolution of Culture.* New York: McGraw-Hill.

Willey, G. R.
1985 Ancient Chinese—New World and Near Eastern ideological traditions: Some observations. *Symbols,* Spring, pp. 14–17, 22–23.

Willey, G. R., and P. Phillips
1958 *Method and Theory in American Archaeology.* Chicago: University of Chicago Press.

CHAPTER FIVE

Political Power and the Origin of Social Complexity

Elman R. Service

Part of the answer to the question implied in the above title lies in the definition of social complexity. "Complexity" is, of course, a relative term: societies are more or less complex, not absolutely complex. Similarly, a "simple" society is not truly simple, that is, with no differentiated persons or groups whatever in it. So we need to classify primitive societies to distinguish those we usually consider complex from those that are clearly not so complex, or somehow not complex enough to be classified with them. Then we want to see whether the distinguishing characteristics of the more complex are qualitatively emergent in cultural evolution, thus to pinpoint in the definition the apparent causes of the rise of increased social complexity.

There have been many attempts at such a definition, usually in the context of arguing for the salient differences between primitive and civilized societies. Spencer, Maine, Morgan, Marx and Engels, Durkheim, and Weber come readily to mind as examples. All these theorists recognized increased size and complexity as one of the major characteristics of social (or cultural) evolution, although they each held somewhat differing opinions as to the causes of the growth.

We are fortunate today to have available many more ethnological, historical, and archaeological examples of emergent complex societies than did the earlier writers. Rather than discuss their views, let us simply look at a representative sample of kinds of societies arranged in order of complexity. I make no attempt to be exhaustive, but rather to offer a sample that is useful to think about.

We should avoid the "primitive societies" that have been so drastically altered by European diseases, relocation, colonialism, slavery, and the like. The ethnographies I have used refer to the earlier periods of contact; hence, some are ethnohistories rather than modern ethnographies. I have previously found it useful to classify societies as Bands, Tribes, Chiefdoms, and Archaic Civilizations (Service 1971, 1978) or, in a related but more general way, as Egalitarian and Hierarchical (Service 1975); here I follow the same general scheme. My aim is to note the extent to which that ordering would parallel an ordering of simple to complex.

Egalitarian Societies

Bands

The Eskimo. Before European diseases decimated the Eskimo, they numbered about 100,000, spread thinly across the Arctic of North America and Greenland.[1] The size of the settlements varied considerably, however, particularly according to the availability of whales. Hunting methods varied with the nature of the resources, but the majority blended caribou hunting and summer inland fishing with the winter hunting of sea mammals.

There was no law or government of a formal or institutional type; leadership was ephemeral and sporadic, depending on the enterprise being conducted, the personal qualities of the would-be leader, and the esteem in which he was held. Adjudication of quarrels was not done by some kind of public official, but only by the actions of kin groups and public opinion. There were no religious specialists save the curing shaman, nearly universal in primitive society.

The Algonquian and Athabascan Hunters of Canada. These hunters lived to the south of the Eskimo, in a broad band across Canada. The central and western groups were Athabascan speakers, and those to the east and south of Hudson's Bay were Algonkian speakers. These were unrelated language stocks, but the aboriginal cultures were similar. The greatest differences were not from east to west but from the northern tundra or barren grounds, where musk oxen and caribou were the main resource, to the south, where the forests contained deer, small buffalo (in the west), and many kinds of smaller game such as beaver and rabbits. Summer fishing was important in both north and south.

Population was sparse throughout. In summer, large numbers congre-

---

[1] This sample of bands is the subject of a small book, *The Hunters* (Service 1979), to which the reader is referred for fuller description and bibliography.

gated around the lakes where the fishing was good, but in winter people foraged widely in very small communities.

Leadership in aboriginal times was apparently of the same sporadic personal kind as among the Eskimo. Certain influential persons might help adjudicate quarrels, but there was no official filling such a post. The only specialist was the curing shaman, as among the Eskimo. The society was shattered by common European diseases, and most of the remaining people were reduced to working for the European fur traders as professional trappers.

The Basin Shoshone. The Great Basin occupies most of Nevada and parts of adjacent states. Before the use of horses, the area was peopled mostly by speakers of the Shoshonean language. Some of them acquired the horse in the nineteenth century and are now known as Utes; the others are called Paiute and Western Shoshone. The population of the unmounted hunter-gatherers was small and usually scattered in family groups, but larger gatherings were possible, as at the time of the piñon nut harvest.

The closest approach to a specialized leader was the "rabbit boss," who coordinated the activities of participants in a rabbit drive and later distributed the game to the families. But this man was not an "official," and he functioned as a leader only during the drive. The only specialist was the curing shaman. Ceremonial life was simple and mostly recreational. In the 1870s they were placed on reservations, usually in their own territory.

The Ona and Yahgan of Tierra del Fuego. The large island of Tierra del Fuego at the extreme tip of South America offers two contrasting kinds of subsistence. The littoral is rich in shellfish and fish, seals, water birds, and occasionally a beached whale. The inland plains contained herds of guanaco, a species of camelid. Two kinds of Fuegians specialized in exploiting these resources: the Yahgan (or "canoe-Indians") inhabited the coast, and the Ona (or "foot-Indians") hunted the guanaco.

The two groups differed considerably in the technology of subsistence, but they were otherwise similar in the simplicity of their culture. The Yahgan were not forced to be as nomadic as the Ona hunters and could remain within rather constricted territories and support larger communities. Their housing was of conical brush huts, whereas the Ona used only simple lean-tos of guanaco hides.

Both Ona and Yahgan had only simple familial forms of polity and economic exchange. There was no formal way of adjudicating quarrels and no organized warfare. The curing shaman was the only specialist.

Pygmies of the African Congo. In the huge, dense, rainy Ituri forest in the northeast corner of Zaire, almost the exact middle of Africa, ranged small scattered groups of hunters. Some of the game was of monstrous size—elephants, hippopotamus, and buffalo; other game included several kinds of antelope and wild pigs. Of daily importance were the roots, nuts, fruits, grubs, and mushrooms gathered by women. The settlements consisted of at least six or seven families, which supplied the minimal number of males to form a cooperative hunting group.

There were no chiefs or councils. Men of influence might take the lead in a given enterprise, but they had to be ever mindful of public opinion. Ceremonial life featured the usual life-cycle ceremonies of other hunter-gatherer groups, but the boys' initiation ordeals were unusually elaborate and drawn out.

The Bushmen of South Africa. The !Kung of the Kalahari desert have been the most studied of those who had, until recently, maintained their aboriginal culture. They number about 4,000 in total, but those who still practiced the ancient way of life when first studied made up only a few bands.

The male hunting and female gathering division of labor was strictly followed, but otherwise there was no specialization (other than the universal differentiation by age). Even the secret medicine lore, normally a monopoly of shamans, was imparted to all males at their puberty celebrations. The society was extremely egalitarian. Sometimes there arose a "big man," influential in certain contexts, but he had no source of power other than that deriving from his own personality. Such a person must behave modestly, even demurely.

The Australians. Australia, approximately the size of the United States, contained only about 300,000 people before its occupation by Europeans. Some of the tropical coastal areas were rich in edible vegetation, game, and seafoods, with a relatively denser and more sedentary population than the interior deserts, where small bands were widely scattered. Despite these differences in demography and in nomadism, there was a surprising similarity in the cultures of all the Australian aborigines.

Technology was very simple. Spear and spearthrower, clubs, throwing sticks (the boomerang was more a plaything than a weapon), flint knives, and choppers were the main items. The housing was of small domed brush huts. There was no furniture, bed covering, or protective clothing.

There was no economic specialization except for the universal age-sex division of labor. Food was shared according to well-understood principles of reciprocity. Elder men were respected and sometimes sat as a sort of council to adjudicate disputes. Fighting was simply an act of revenge for some insult or injury; it seldom resulted in much bloodshed and never involved taking land or other possessions.

Some aspects of the ideology were rather more elaborated than among other foraging bands, though not differing in kind. The same life-crisis rites obtained, but the boys' initiation was long and complicated. Similarly, the familial social organization contained more named subdivisions than most, including by far the most numerous totems; each social group was believed to be descended from some particular plant or animal kind, and each had the duty of performing the proper rituals to promote the increase of that kind. Thus, in the absence of any important economic division of labor, a ceremonial division of labor promoted social interdependence.

The Semang of the Malay Peninsula. The Semang of former times lived in the lower slopes of the interior mountain ranges of the Malay Peninsula in a tropical jungle of very heavy rainfall.

Only small game was hunted in aboriginal times, and the basis of subsistence was such vegetable foods as wild yams, berries, nuts, roots, shoots, and fruit. Fire-hardened bamboo splinters served as knives and spear and arrow points. The bow and poisoned arrows were the main weapons. Housing was simply a dome-shaped brush hut.

The bands were small, of about twenty or thirty people on the average. One aspect of the economy was noteworthy: the "silent trade" with neighboring Malay villages. The Semang would leave some jungle products at a conventional place, to return later to recover whatever had been left in reciprocity.

There was no political organization above the level of the familial band. There was no formal leadership or authority beyond the respect accorded the oldest man of the band. As usual, the shaman was the most influential person because he was the only person who knew how to exorcise the evil spirits from the body of a sick person.

The Andaman Islanders. The Andamans lie along the eastern side of the Bay of Bengal. The dense tropical forests have a variety of edible roots, fruit, and nuts, reptiles, birds, and wild pigs (the largest animal). Fish, shellfish, dugong (a large aquatic mammal), and turtles were important in the coastal areas. The population is believed to have been about 5,500 before introduced diseases took their toll. Today there are only a few survivors.

Equipment was the bow and arrow, a sharpened digging stick, and dugout canoes. Housing was more substantial than that of the Semang because the village was occupied for several months during the rainy season, then adandoned for the dry season when the people were migrating, to be reoccupied later. The single-family houses were mat-roofed huts, left open at the sides.

Like the other bands in this sample, the Andamanese had no formal governmental institutions; older men were the most influential in community affairs. Relations among the bands were not formalized, but true warfare did not exist, and there was not even much fighting or feuding. The usual shaman was the curer, and he could also cause illness among enemies. There were no other specialists.

In a very general sense, all of the aforementioned societies are small and simple. But the actual size of any of these is variable, and it is also difficult to draw the boundaries of a given society. The Arunta of Australia, for example, were widely scattered in small foraging groups most of the year, but in the rainy season they united into residential groups of several hundred persons. In none of these societies is there institutionalized government or other integrative structures; there is only the integration fostered by shared language and customs, and these tend to shade off rather than separate the peripheral groups from the central core. It is thus difficult to state the "size" of band society, except in a very general sense.

Just as there is no government, as such, there is also a lack of institutionalized groups specializing in economic or technological tasks. The division of labor is based on individual age and sex differences, with the exception of the curing shaman. Exchange of goods is by simple reciprocities. Leadership also is individual, charismatic, and thus changeable in time. Individuals vary in power, prestige, and skills, but the segments of the society (extended families, lineages, moieties) are similar to each other and equal in political power.

All of these bands are foragers of wild food. (Note well, however, that not all foragers are at the band level; some are even complex chiefdoms, like those of the North American northwest coast.) They are perhaps, therefore, "close to nature," but it is interesting to note how distinct are their various habitats, ranging from arctic wastes to tropical jungles, from oceanic coasts to inland deserts. Many tools and weapons, clothing, housing, and so on are variables in the adjustment to these habitats, but the sociopolitical structures remain generally similar in their simplicity.

Tribes

The Iroquois. This large tribe of horticulturalist-hunters were quite representative of the woodland peoples of the northeastern part of what is now the United States.[2] But this area received certain of the sociopolitical consequences of the early arrival of European colonists and traders. The Iroquois survived as middlemen between the Europeans and the fur-trapping groups to the west and north. One of the consequences was the creation of the Iroquoian Confederacy, a voluntary union of five (eventually six) formerly independent tribes of Iroquoian speech. This gave a suggestion of complexity to the sociopolitical organization, but it was not truly an aboriginal organization. Several other tribes besides the Iroquois united to form confederacies, all directly related to the encroachments of the Europeans.

As horticulturalists, the Iroquois were sedentary enough to be able to build wooden and bark lineage houses ("longhouses") and palisaded villages containing several hundred persons. Each community had a council of adult males, who aided the village chief. But these posts were not powerful, and a decision depended on consensus. The Iroquois were known to be very warlike, but this may have been in defense of their control of the fur trade, as a consequence of their intermediate position.

It appears that the Iroquois could be said to be more socially and politically complex than the bands described above. There were more communities in association, more people in each community, and a richer ideological and ceremonial life. Yet the chiefs, council members, and members of the council of the whole confederacy did not hold hereditary offices, so no segments of the society (families, lineages, clans, or tribes) had permanent ascendency over others. Nor were there any religious specialists apart from the curing shaman.

Mounted Buffalo Hunters. The Cheyenne, Arapahoe, Sioux, Crow, and Comanche are well-known tribes typical of the hunters of the Great Plains. They were not fully aboriginal when described, however, for they had acquired the horse through raiding and trading with other tribes who had gotten them from the Spanish in the Southwest. Eventually, too, they acquired firearms from the fur-traders of the northwest borders of the Plains.

But despite the greater affluence due to the acquisition of the horse, the

---

[2]As in the section on bands, I do not burden this section with bibliographic information which, if desired, can be found easily in Service 1971 and or Sahlins 1968.

Plains tribes did not ascend to a level of social complexity above the egalitarian level; all segments of their society were equal in social or political significance. Yet, being immersed in a highly competitive environment with hit-and-run raids endemic, there was a need for leadership in this kind of warfare. The war leaders were, however, simply individuals who rose to the occasion as needed. There was, in other words, no permanent military office or chief, despite the apparent high status of these chiefs.

A Plains buffalo-hunting tribe would meet as an entire entity during the summer for a communal hunt when the buffalo were concentrated in huge herds. There were numerous sodalities—nonresidential clubs or associations—which crosscut the various kinship segments of the tribe. The most important were military clubs, some of them age-graded (a youth passed from one age grade to another as he grew older). These societies had an internal police function as well as being an organized military force, overseeing the complex movements of the tribe and preventing individual groups or persons from unauthorized hunting that might stampede the buffalo herd.

Among many of the tribes, political organization was represented by a tribal council, but these members were chosen for short terms only; the positions were not hereditary, and their decisions were strongly influenced by public opinion. The council was sometimes called on to mediate disputes, but there was no official machinery to punish crimes against individuals.

The only religious specialists were the usual curing shamans. Because of the large number of segments of the tribe assembled in summer, there were at this time a larger number and more kinds of ceremonies than was usually found in band society.

The Guaraní and Others of South America. Throughout the tropical forest of South America were scattered large tribes of horticulturalists, such as the well-known Guaraní, Nambicuara, Bororo, Jívaro, and Yanomamo. These were normally semisedentary, of the slash-and-burn horticultural type, with this basic subsistence supplemented by hunting, fishing, and gathering. Palisaded villages of thatch huts were the norm, but their size varied considerably.

Exchange of goods was in the form of reciprocal gift giving. The segments of the society were egalitarian with respect to economic wealth and political power. Leadership functioned on an ad hoc basis, usually in the hit-and-run raiding types of warfare, and in village relocations after the soil in a region had become depleted. These forms of leadership were sporadic and dependent on the personality of the leader rather than being permanent. Similarly, there was no official priesthood. The curing shaman and sometimes the would-be sorcerer were the only specialized religious practitioners. This is in no way different from what is found in band society.

The Nuer of the Upper Nile. In the region of the Upper Nile River in Africa lived the Nuer, representative of the widely dispersed cattle pastoralists of the great open grasslands of the Sudan. The Nuer (they call themselves *Nath*) totaled about 300,000 people, but they were not politically unified; they considered themselves to be a "people" because their several tribal entities were similar in culture and language, distinct from their neighbors, to whom they were hostile.

The Nuer were seminomadic. In the rainy season they lived in small villages on high ground to cultivate a few crops, mainly millet. In the dry season the villages broke up into family homesteads to search for pasturage and water for the cattle. Each homestead had its own herd of cattle, and prestige accrued to those with the largest, best cared-for herds. But there was no economic differentiation among the homesteads or inherited differences in status. Sharing was so well established that there were no groups of privileged people with respect to consumption of food or goods.

There was no true government or permanent authority, no laws or lawgivers. The position most closely resembling political office was that of the "leopard-skin chief," who wore the skin wrap as a sign of his prestige. He sometimes acted to mediate feuds or quarrels, but his duties were mostly ritual in nature. There was no organized hierarchy of priests. As in other tribes, the shaman was the only religious specialist, but there was a tendency for shamans themselves to specialize: one was good at curing headaches; another might divine not only the causes of illness but also the whereabouts of lost objects.

The Northern Tungus of Siberia. The northern forest border of the arctic tundra of Asia once contained a great arc of reindeer-breeding peoples all the way from Scandanavia to the Bering Sea. The Northern Tungus numbered about 20,000 people, scattered in small independent tribes in northeastern Siberia, the most typical of which lived in northern Transbaikalia.

The reindeer were used primarily for transport and milk. The main day-to-day activity of the men was hunting and trapping. Exchange of goods was simply reciprocal gift giving. The herds of reindeer, though managed by individual families, were not significant property. The size of each herd fluctuated greatly from year to year because of attacks by wolves or epidemics, and each year a clan council redistributed the stock so that each family would have an equal chance to survive the next winter; that is, the family *managed* a herd, but it was really the property of the clan, so there were no important differences in wealth.

The clans (exogamous units of patrilineal relatives) were also equal in wealth. The clan council was composed of respected elders, so its composition was always changing (that is, there were no hereditary authority positions). The shaman (a Tungusic word) was the only religious practitioner and represented the only specialization, aside from the age-sex division of labor.

These are only a small sample of tribes, chosen for diversity in habitat and food production. The technology of food production is of mounted hunting, horticulture, pastoralism, or mixed, and all supplement those basic modes variously by hunting or fishing. Somehow, despite the differences in means of production and in habitat, tribes are alike in having transcended bands in size and certain aspects of complexity.

A good question is whether greater food production is responsible for the increased size and complexity, or whether the greater complexity increases the food supply. It is not feasible to attempt an answer at this point.

The "greater complexity," it should be noted, is that there are more kinds of specialized individuals and groups. The new groups are simply overarching kinship segments such as clans, linked clans (phratries), and new kinds of nonresidential organizations (sodalities). These latter may be of many more kinds and functions than in band society. Nonlocal (that is, dispersed) lineal kin groups become clans, the most characteristic sodality in tribal society. Along with these, we note a rise in frequency of other sodalities such as age-graded associations and of military and ceremonial societies. Exchanges of goods remain reciprocal, not organized by an allocating center.

But this "greater complexity" of more kinds of individuals and groups is not matched by a growing inequality. Individuals, to be sure, are unequal, just as in band society, and inasmuch as there are more people there are more kinds of individuals and specialties, particularly war and ceremonial leaders and craft specialists. But the segments of the society, whether residential groups or sodalities, remain equal to each other; that is, they are not arranged in any permanent hierarchical order. Both bands and tribes remain egalitarian in social structure and neither has instituted hereditary forms of government or priesthood.

Hierarchical Societies

Chiefdoms

The Nootka. The Nootka were centrally representative of the large number of chiefdoms strung along the heavily indented northwest coast of

North America, stretching from what is now northern California to Alaska.[3] The wild food resources of this region were tremendous in their variety. In the forests were big game, such as elk, deer, and bear, as well as waterfowl and berries and edible roots, but far overshadowing these were the coastal resources of shellfish, halibut, herring, cod, aquatic mammals, and above all salmon, whose seasonal spawning runs provided a huge harvest. The northwest coastal peoples had no agriculture or domestic animals other than the dog, but the abundance of resources allowed a population density equal to that of sophisticated agriculturalists.

As in all chiefdoms, and in all hereditary aristocracies for that matter, birth order was the ruling determinant of social and political status. The oldest, or founding, lineage contained a male line of descent by primogeniture which provided the main chief. Other lineages were ranked in terms of their closeness to this main line. Within each lineage, and within each subsidiary family, status was also by birth order, for females as well as males. The social interaction of the segments of the society (families and lineages) were, in contrast to bands and tribes, strongly hierarchical.

The economic functions of the various chiefs was mainly to redistribute goods that had been given to them by the members of their group. In grand feasts, *potlatches,* they gave food, furs, oil, and, particularly striking, large quantities of blankets and copper disks acquired by trade with the Hudson's Bay Company to neighboring chiefs and their constituents. In return, the first group would later be potlatched, and the second would attempt to outperform the first in generosity. But the main aspect of chiefliness was one's stewardship over aspects of production and the channeling of the exchanges. This required authority and planning by a permanent official, a hereditary chief.

The Nootka had the beginnings of a true priesthood in addition to the usual curing shaman. The chief himself performed rituals for the welfare of his people. The most important of these was at the beginning of the seasonal salmon spawning run, at which time the chief was ritually cleansed and then performed a complicated set of rites to ensure a bountiful harvest of fish. Chiefs also served a military role, as planners as well as warriors. They seem not, however, to have been formal adjudicators of crimes or feuds.

The Trobriand Islanders. The natives of Melanesia, except for some Papuan tribes of inland New Guinea, were well represented by the Trobri-

---

[3]The description of chiefdoms, along with analysis and bibliographic information, can be found in Service 1971, 1975, 1978.

and Islanders, so magnificently described by Malinowski. The soil of the islands was very rich, particularly noted for its production of yams; seafood was also plentiful, allowing a dense population of about 8,000 clustered into permanent villages.

The village chief received a proportion of the goods each family produced, which he later redistributed to the villagers at great feasts. Chiefs also conducted the complicated inter-island exchanges known as the *kula* ring. Reciprocal exchanges also occurred among individuals. There was a considerable amount of specialization, not only in food production but in crafts such as canoe building and potting.

Chiefship was hereditary and limited to males, although it descended through the matrilineal line. All persons, male and female, were ranked by birth order and proximity to the main line of descent. Chiefs had no formal mechanism for maintaining their rule, but they did have power to punish anyone indirectly by asking a sorcerer to practice black magic on that person. There was also a sort of priesthood: the hereditary garden magician of each village not only conducted ceremonies but directed the garden workers.

The Tahitians. Tahiti, in the Society Islands, was centrally located and quite typical of Polynesia in general. The most important differences in Polynesia were between the large volcanic "high islands" and the much smaller coral atolls, or "low islands." All the important groups, such as the Society Islands, contain both kinds of islands. Tahiti is a high island, and as in the other Polynesian groups most of the population, as well as the most important chiefs, were located on these rather than on the coral atolls.

Tahiti was rich in domesticated produce such as breadfruit, taro, yams, sweet potatoes, coconuts, pigs, and chickens. It was, however, the sea that provided the most protein, and the Tahitians had a highly specialized fishing technology. Their agriculture was also sophisticated, with terraced hillsides, irrigation, and various fertilizers. Specialists made huge plank vessels as well as smaller dugouts with outriggers. House building was another specialized craft.

Tahitian society was a theocracy; a chief was also a priest and combined political and economic authority with a greater amount of inherited spiritual power (*mana*) than lesser persons. As in other chiefdoms, the ranking of persons was by birth order and inherited proximity to the high chief's line of descent. Economic exchange was by means of gifts from the producers to chiefs, and from lesser chiefs to major chiefs. The chiefs' surplus was in turn was redistributed to their followers. Warfare was often of large scale and involved intricate planning and coordination, but it seems to have had little to do with economic reward.

The Rwala Bedouin. The Rwala were, until recently, fairly typical of the camel-breeding nomads of Saudi Arabia's interior desert. They were pure nomads but not entirely economically self-sufficient, for in the summer they frequently came to the region of settled agriculturalists to trade their surplus animals for grain, cloth, manufactured utensils, and weapons.

The sociopolitical organization was like that of the chiefdoms already described. A person was a member of a local extended family, patrilineal descendants of an aged father or grandfather. This, in turn was a part of a larger patrilineal lineage that could trace its own relationship to others (chiefs of lineages and higher-order paramount chiefs are called sheikhs). In other words, a hierarchy ascended through time to the putative male ancestor of the tribe. Birth order and proximity to the main line of descent were again the signs of ranking statuses.

There were also castelike relationships, by which children of destitute parents from the city were adopted into Arab families to perform drudge household labor. Another caste was that of professional ironsmiths. Like the "slaves," they could not marry into Bedouin society.

Since much of the year the Rwala were widely scattered, warfare was not usually on a large-scale or concerted basis; raids and skirmishes were the normal means, so the military role of the sheikh in planning was somewhat diminished compared to other chiefdoms. The Rwala were a theocracy, but as followers of Islam rather than a local tribal religion.

The Zulu. The present-day "tribe" of Zulu of South Africa were once a group of independent chiefdoms in what is now known as KwaZulu in Natal. After contact with Boers and British colonists of South Africa, and with other Bantu chiefdoms pushed south by the dislocations in central Africa caused by Arab slavers, warfare was continuous in the region. Eventually the famous Zulu warrior Shaka conquered widely and set up a kind of "bully-boy" conquest state over the neighboring chiefdoms. Before this (about 1816), the Zulu were a rather standard chiefdom, representative of a great many others in the region.[4]

Aboriginally, the Zulu were led by priest-warrior-chiefs who were in charge of agricultural ceremonies (like "first fruits" and rainmaking), warfare and redistributional trade, and interpreting customary law in the case

---

[4] I have treated the Zulu, under Shaka, as a "primitive state" (1978: chap. 16), but I now think that it was simply a chiefdom that conquered widely under some unusual circumstances.

of disputes, theft of cattle, and so on. The organization was by hereditary rank by birth order within a hierarchy, with local subchiefs ranked within the whole.

There were several different kinds of shamans and magicians. There was the ordinary curing shaman, as well as a diviner who could "smell out" criminals. Another kind was simply an herbalist. The priest-chief could control thunder and lightning and perform rituals to induce rain. The main chief was also the custodian of sacred fetishes that could keep him in contact with his ancestors, now gods.

Chiefdoms are numerous and widely represented in all quarters of the earth. They also seem to have been found historically in Ireland, Scotland, Germany, and elsewhere in early Europe and evidently in preclassical Greece and Rome.[5]

The transition from egalitarian bands and tribes to hierarchical chiefdoms is essentially the transition toward much greater social complexity. Leadership in chiefdoms has ceased to be charismatic and variable and has become institutionalized and hereditary. In all of our examples, the central governing body undertakes various tasks, which before had been unorganized, in an organized fashion.

The exchange of goods, which had been simple reciprocities, becomes supplemented (not replaced) by redistribution, a movement of goods from producers to the central agency that holds them, to be utilized or dispersed as needed. Long-distance trade can be planned and fostered by this means as well. And the stockpiling of goods, especially of food, makes possible much larger and more elaborate feasts and ceremonies for the members of the society itself and for important visitors. Such ceremonial feasts are an important integrating factor in the society as well as an aid to the leadership in consolidating and enhancing its ability to rule.

An important characteristic of a chiefdom is its religious organization. All chiefdoms are theocratic and thus are ruled by a religious hierarchy, ruling for the gods even when undertaking what today we would consider a secular task, such as building an irrigation canal. Egalitarian societies are religious in the sense of thinking in supernatural terms, behaving ritually, and holding ceremonies, but chiefdoms alter this by creating a priesthood that controls the *society* and creates a religious ideology that helps justify not only the society but the position of the rulers in it.

A centralized permanent leadership can undertake political tasks that the relatively powerless leaders of bands and tribes cannot do, or at least

---

[5] According to Fustel de Coulanges (1964).

not so successfully. Preeminent among these is the waging of war and peace. A chiefdom can plan a military adventure and carry it out and conscript greater numbers of warriors and sustain them in the field much more successfully than the otherwise autonomous families and villages of tribes and bands. Similarly, chiefdoms can make peace with other societies and make such treaties and alliances binding by forcing their own people to respect them and by punishing them for breaking the peace.

An important aspect of the ability to make war and peace more effectively is reflected in the fact that chiefdoms are able to incorporate formerly autonomous districts and villages into the society by assimilating their leaders into the ruling hierarchy as subordinate chiefs. Thus an important aspect of complexity is that formerly free bands and tribes can become parts of a larger entity. This also transforms them, most notably by making permanent and hereditary their own leadership, as it is absorbed into the overall hierarchy. This is probably the most usual way chiefdoms expanded, not so often by conquest as by alliance and because of the evident benefits a helpless, autonomous tribal village could acquire by joining a stronger, more centralized society.[6] This would be coercive, also, in the context of likely warfare with other neighbors.

Archaic Civilization

Teotihuacán of Mesoamerica. Mesoamerica encompasses the complex of related developments of an American Indian civilization that included the huge area from the highlands of central and southern Mexico to the lowlands of Guatemala, Salvador, and Honduras.[7] The two best-known (best researched) examples of the highland and lowland extremes are Teotihuacán (near Mexico City) and the Mayan speakers of Yucatán, Mexico, and the neighboring Petén, in lowland Guatemala.

All the civilizational examples in Mesoamerica had dense, urbanized populations based on water-controlled agriculture (irrigation in the highlands, drainage in the lowlands). But Teotihuacán's urban center was by far the largest (150,000 people) and probably the first. This center dominated large parts of Mesoamerica during the early development of civilization and truly deserves to be called an empire.

One of the characteristics of this empire's complexity was its exploitation

---

[6] Carneiro (1981:38) says that the critical qualitative step in the creation of chiefdoms was this ability to incorporate and transcend local autonomies.

[7] These brief sketches are summaries of the chapters in part 3 of Service, *Origins of the State and Civilization* (1975).

of highly diverse ecological areas, ranging from arid highlands to wet tropical lowlands, and lakes, and rivers. To make such ecological specialization truly symbiotic, a system of planned production and exchange via redistribution centers was created. Redistribution was a common feature of chiefdoms, but in such a huge and variegated area as the Teotihuacán empire the complexity of the attendant bureaucracy and its specialized parts must have been tremendous compared to the chiefdoms. The bureaucratic centers subsidized artists and architects, crafts specialists, and a huge public labor force to build monuments, public buildings, and irrigation canals. All this required record keeping; hence the development of writing and specialized scribes.

Economic relations over a wide area must involve political control over its parts, or at least peacemaking and alliances as well as military force or threat. Standing militia and professional war leaders were necessarily subsidized.

This empire was theocratic, with a highly specialized and bureaucratized priesthood and huge gatherings of the people for many kinds of ceremonies. Much of the art and architecture manifested in the archaeological sites was fostered by the religious aspect of this system.

The Andes. At about the beginning of the Christian era, the Mochica of the north coast of Peru had unified several of the coastal river valleys into a true empire. These valleys had populations ranging from 20,000 to 87,000, with the total polity at over 250,000. The irrigation systems were extensive, systematically coordinated, and elaborate, in keeping with the fact that coastal Peru is a true desert. Cultural evidence from graves and iconography indicates a warrior-priest aristocracy, artisans and artists, and a general population of worker-farmers. This was evidently one of the locations of the origin of civilization in the central Andean region.

The greatest development of complexity in Andean civilization, however, occurred when this coastal culture came into contact with that of the highlands. The tremendous ecological extremes, from intensive irrigation agriculture in the lowland river valleys to extensive herding in the high plateaus, and many variations in between, led to a regional symbiosis that surpassed even that of central Mexico. Great economic redistribution centers arose and extended trade routes were developed, and the power centers of the highlands resulted in such large urban clusters as Huari and Tiahuanaco.

Since it was necessary to control and protect the complicated, far-flung specialized regions and trade routes, a commensurate development of the military specialities occurred. Goods such as pottery were mass-produced, and bronze metallurgy, fine weaving, and sophisticated art styles developed in the hands of subsidized specialists.

As in the case of Teotihuacán, all of the above were cast in the theocratic form of government.

Mesopotamia. The Tigris-Euphrates lowlands did not have sufficient rainfall for dry farming, which evidently developed first in the moister uplands called the Assyrian Steppe. But as population grew and irrigation became more fully utilized, the rich alluvial soils of the lowlands became the basis for a sedentary, intensive agriculture. The river systems also provided an abundance of fish, mollusks, and aquatic birds, as well as the potential for a complex transportation system that could facilitate the exchange of goods and materials over a huge area.

An important difference between this region and those in the New World mentioned above was the greater significance of pastoralism here. As a mixed farming-domesticated animal economy developed and spread over a huge area, different environments could be put to specialized use. The upland grasslands, where agriculture was difficult, could be increasingly turned over to a specialized pastoral economy, with the lowlands trading for meat and hides. As the two kinds of societies became increasingly specialized, they simultaneously became more interdependent; but pastoralists become more mobile and agriculturalists more sedentary as the specialization developed, and a certain kind of military advantage rested with the more mobile, particularly with respect to surprise raids. So raiding as well as trading increased. It is possible that the characteristic walled city-state of the lowlands began out of this need to trade but also to protect against raid.

Sometime early in the third millennium B.C., these urban centers had grown in such number and size that full-scale warfare among the cities, which had earlier only to worry about pastoralists, became a problem. The city-states came to have standing armies and a military bureaucracy.

The cities were theocratic, and the priesthood and temple were as much engaged in economic matters and governance as in religion. The temple was also a redistribution center and storage place. Planned trade was practiced on a huge scale up and down the rivers. Raw materials such as hardwoods and metals (both lacking in Mesopotamia) were brought from distant lands. Meanwhile, notational systems for record keeping developed into true literacy.

As in the other cases reviewed, the population became differentiated into the ruling bureaucracy, or aristocracy, with many specialized parts, and the ruled. Among the ruled were, in addition to simple workers and farmers, a great many artisans whose skill suggests hereditary specialization.

Egypt. The development of civilization in Egypt was nearly contemporaneous with that in Mesopotamia, and the two may have heavily influenced each other. Certain Mesopotamian (Sumerian) inventions—such as the potter's wheel, fired bricks, cylinder seals, some art motifs and stylistic peculiarities, and probably the stimulus, though not the model, of writing and numbering—seem evidence of early contact between Sumer and Lower Egypt. Nevertheless, there are some important differences. The Nile valley was much more isolated from nomadic predators than was Mesopotamia, and it did not develop the series of defensive urban states which in Mesopotamia eventually fought each other so often and developed into so many short-lived military empires. Egypt was remarkably stable politically for well over one thousand years. Another distinction, related to stability, was the line of rulers who functioned as secular kings and as deities: the pharaoh *was* god, not merely head priest.

The great Nile River annually floods its plains; each year new crops could be sown from this natural irrigation. As population grew, eventually canal irrigation was installed, and two crops a year were harvested. Goats, dogs, donkeys, pigs, geese, and ducks were domesticated, but neither horse nor camel was used in the Nile valley. Transportation was by boat, which made economic as well as political integration of the whole valley easier.

The theocracy was a patrilineal bureaucracy, with sons of the pharaoh as principal figures and more distant relatives in minor posts. There were many "departments of state," and of commerce, and of the huge redistribution bureaucracy. There was, however, no permanent military bureaucracy or standing army, at least during the period of the Old Kingdom.

The arts and crafts were highly developed. The architecture and masonry, as demonstrated by the great pyramids and the temples around them, were truly extraordinary. But, in contrast to Mesopotamia, no great urban centers were developed during the formative and classic periods—only the huge, splendid ceremonial centers.

The most distinctive aspect of society in Egypt was its overwhelming size and the complexity of its ruling bureaucracy. The economic system was clearly not based on a division of labor by ecological zones; the specialization was in terms of personnel instead of geographically distinct regions.

The Indus River Valley. For about one thousand years, beginning around 2500 B.C., a civilization of the classic type prevailed over the valley of the Indus River and its tributaries. It had writing and a decimal mathematical notation, specialized skilled crafts including bronze metallurgy, two huge planned cities, water control canals, monumental architecture, vast systems of water transport—all equal to those of Mesopotamia and Egypt but developed about five hundred years later. This, along with other evidence, suggests cultural influences from the earlier centers, especially of trade with Sumer. But, the great uniformity in architecture and decorative styles indicates an overall theocratic unification similar to that of Egypt.

The two large cities, Harappa and Mohenjo-daro, were not walled or otherwise fortified, so a peaceful priestly governance like that of Egypt is suggested, rather than the military empires of Mesopotamia. Maritime and riverine trade were extensive, and the huge granaries suggest highly organized collections and delayed redistributions.

The Bronze Age Civilization of China. Chinese civilization had its beginnings at the middle reaches of the Yellow River in northern China, in the area called the Great Bend. The Shang dynasty (1766–1122 B.C.), the civilizational culmination of a long development out of Neolithic chiefdoms in the region, featured refined arts, particularly the bronzes, writing, the unprecedently large, complex, planned city of An-yang, royal tombs, huge redistribution centers, and widespread trade.

At the apex of Shang government was a grand lineage that was the center of the political, economic, and ceremonial structure—the Shang were a thoroughly hereditary theocracy. The lords who administered the centers of the outlying regions were relatives of the ruler. Individual villages were united into intervillage networks to play specialized roles in the overall redistribution system.

The northern Chinese early civilization was remarkably parallel to the important and better-known cases of Mesoamerica, Peru, Mesopotamia, and Egypt.

All these archaic civilizations seem to have grown out of earlier chiefdoms. All are much larger and commensurately more complex than chiefdoms, but other than that there seems to be no single diagnostic feature in their social and political makeup to set them off qualitatively from the chiefdoms. Both chiefdoms and the civilizations are hierarchical, with a central government, and both are theocratic, redistributional, and capable of legally taxing wealth and conscripting manpower for public works and warfare. The greater complexity is manifested in a greater number of specializations of crafts, bureaucratic offices, and regions. This latter, the regional specialization, is typically an aspect of cultural, or ethnic, differences. The archaic civilizations had grown immensely, but not so much

Political Power and the Origin of Social Complexity 131

by improving birth-over-death ratios as by assimilating other societies, adapting them to the dominant cultural overlay (particularly affecting the local aristocracies) but also evidently retaining many of the local ethnic traits, including hereditary technological specializations. And regions were often ecologically specialized. In other words, the archaic civilizations were empires, incorporating all the cultural diversity the term implies and also all the problems of governance inherent in such diversity. In successfully surmounting these problems, a society creates an ever-larger bureaucracy with specialized offices. This is the epitomization of complexity, and its core, in the preindustrialized societies.

From Political Power to Social Complexity

From this perusal some related generalizations emerge:

A. Simple Societies
  1. A "simple" primitive society ("band," "tribe") is strongly *egalitarian* with respect to the relations of the segments of the society (extended families, lineages, clans, moieties) to each other.
  2. It is *inegalitarian* withrespect to the relations of individuals to each other (manifested by age and sex distinctions, kinship statuses, and relations of charismatic leaders to one another and to their followers).
  3. The degree of *power* of persons is therefore of two kinds:
     (a) that which is fixed (age, sex, and kinship statuses), and
     (b) that which is changeable, created by personalities, skills, and luck of the individuals in contexts of leadership and followership. Let us call the first *familistic* types of power; the second, *charismatic* powers.
B. Complex Societies
  1. A "complex" primitive society (either chiefdom or archaic civilization) is profoundly *inegalitarian* with respect to the relations of the segments of the society. There are "royal" and elite lineages and lesser ones, all arranged hierarchically.
  2. The inegalitarianism of individuals has become, not charismatic, but *hereditary* and thus hierarchical, just as have the social segments.
  3. The degree of *power* of all kinds (familistic and charismatic) has also become fixed by heredity. This is now a power *structure*, capable of creating political solutions to the problems of social

integration that so plagued the simple societies by limiting their size.

How did this great transformation come about? How does a charismatic leader cause his personal status to be passed on to his son (normally the eldest)? It stands to reason that when a charismatic leader is very good, is lucky, and has a son equally good and lucky, the son has a better chance of eventually assuming the father's position than have rival "big men." If subsequent sons can do equally well, the status becomes increasingly an *office*, the dynasty becomes traditional, and finally—supported by new justifying mythologies, rituals, and monuments—a fully theocratic chiefdom emerges.

Such enterprises have probably been tried and have failed innumerably, but some succeeded splendidly in a few places to become the sources of the classical archaic civilizations. This must be because a permanently centralized government is very powerful among less centralized neighbors, and when it finally becomes well established it can continue to grow in size and complexity.

What is it that the centralization of power can accomplish? Our list shows, in varying degrees and combinations, the following: (a) Redistribution (including long-distance trade) and finally true taxation; (b) permanent military leadership and organization (for waging both war and peace); and (c) public works (such as irrigation systems, pyramids, and temples).

Once leadership is strictly inherited it is institutionalized, so to speak, and thus becomes more stable and freer to undertake new tasks. And each new task successfully accomplished, whether a new trade route founded, a war won, an alliance accomplished, an extension of the irrigation system made, a temple built, all help consolidate the society and, in so doing, further secure the government and enable it to grow.

This kind of complexity, as manifested first by the appearance of the segregated "royal" lineage, creates in its wake further social complexity in subsidiary lineages based on hereditary rank, new forms of distinct economic practitioners (particularly related to expanded redistribution systems), new kinds of hereditary craft and regional specializations (subsidized by the government), military and foreign affairs specialists, and, not least, a specialized priesthood in addition to the curing shamans of simple societies. In the development of all these usual aspects of complexity, we see the prior and necessary development of permanent, institutionalized leadership.

A definition of a complex society has finally emerged: *it is a society that has transcended the simple society of similar and politically equal segments* *to institute a permanent hierarchical power center involving both its segments and its individual leadership, and this distinctive characteristic has enabled it to create and govern its parts, which specialize in political, military, economic, and religious practices.*This definition—or conclusion, if you like—is opposed to more current theories of the origins of complexity (or of the state and civilizations). Basically the argument turns on the relationship of distributive (economic) systems to political systems. In our modern society we have become accustomed to a *very* unequal distribution of wealth, and to the result that, directly and indirectly, political power and privilege are also conferred unequally. This, in general, has been the (I think ethnocentric) influence that led Karl Marx and Friedrich Engels, V. Gordon Childe, Leslie White, Morton Fried, and others to share (despite specific differences among them) the general perspectives that economic factors, particularly inequalities, led to, or caused, political institutions to be created to protect the status quo based on inequality. My present version reverses the emphasis.

There *really was* inequality, always. Bands and tribes had unequal persons (but not segments). Chiefdoms and archaic civilizations were profoundly unequal, with regard to both individuals and segments. But the inequality was generated by the theocratic political system, which governed and controlled the economic system. This in turn resulted in gross economic inequalities with respect to consumption, of course, but the question is, which caused which? There were two grossly unequal classes-the governors and the governed—and the power of the governors was total. They were able not only to govern the behavior of their subjects in general but also to settle the question, who gets what, when, and how? In this perspective, political institutions originated the economic system and controlled it, not only the distribution of goods but often the very creation of the supply of goods, as it instituted long-distance trade and subsidized artisans and public works.

Rather than being the mere result of economic causes, the centralized theocratic bureaucracy was itself the creator of many new aspects of culture, in religion, art, literature, economics, technology, and warfare. It seems that this hierarchical apparatus of political power was not particularly the result of forces outside itself; instead, it had undergone an evolutionary development along a causal trajectory that seems to have had its own built-in gyroscope. This does not mean that there was something inexorable about this evolution through its stages. On the contrary, it required just the right balance of several conditions and circumstances, like the growth of a rare and delicate new plant species. But also like a plant, important determinants of the direction of its growth lay within itself.

References

Carneiro, R. L.
   1981   The chiefdom as precursor of the state. In G. Jones and R. Kautz, eds., *The Transition to Statehood in the New World*, pp. 37–79. New York: Cambridge University Press.

Fustel de Coulanges, N. D.
   1964   *The Ancient City*. Trans. William Small. Garden City: Doubleday Anchor Books.

Sahlins, Marshall D.
   1968   *Tribesmen*. Englewood Cliffs: Prentice-Hall.

Service, E. R.
   1971   *Primitive Social Organization*. 2d ed. New York: Random House.
   1975   *Origins of the State and Civilization*. New York: W.W. Norton.
   1978   *Profiles in Ethnology*. 3d ed. Englewood Cliffs: Harper and Row.
   1979   *The Hunters*. 2d ed. Englewood Cliffs: Prentice-Hall.

Part II

POWER, POLITICS, AND HIERARCHY

CHAPTER SIX

Hierarchy and Power in the Tropical Forest

Irving Goldman

The tribes of the Colombian Vaupés live under material conditions of relative simplicity, yet they are organized into social systems that are similar in many fundamental respects to those of larger, more prosperous and more complex societies. In formal structure, if not in cultural content, these systems resemble hierarchical orders of Oceania, North America, Africa, and, closer at hand, the Andes. On the relatively small scale of lowland economy and demography they exhibit, albeit in elementary form, the common modalities of social inequality. One can observe among them the manifestations of genealogical rank, hereditary chiefship, social stratification, economic "exploitation," marriage and occupational castes, leisure class, social pariahness, and, overall, an ideology of dominance and subordination. Although such aspects of inequality are most fully developed among the sedentary horticulturists who are the dominant tribes in this region, they are not altogether alien to the Makuan peoples, the so-called marginal hunter-gatherers of the Vaupés who have only recently learned to farm. As examples of social hierarchy, the Vaupés social systems remind us that social inequalities can coexist with a variety of material circumstances.

It is precisely because they are not associated with states or chiefdoms or highly productive economies that these hierarchical systems are of more than ordinary interest. They merit close study all the more because they can lead in directions other than those conventional theory has been following. Like similar hierarchies among other tribal societies, those of the Vaupés are largely ritualistic. The inequalities and the modes of dependency they impose are those of status and arise from symbolic strengths and weakness. In the Vaupés there is little actual basis for material dependency. Economic self-sufficiency and sentiments of local autonomy are, actually, so strongly established in this region that there is little substantive foundation for a central authority either. Nevertheless, a highly cohesive organization of interdependent sibs has been established largely on the strength, it seems, of religious and metaphysical concepts of unity. Despite appearances of formal resemblance to political hierarchies with their accompanying economic and jural inequalities, those of the Vaupés constitute a distinctive genre. This is not to say that they are unrelated to or are irrelevant to the history of political forms, that would be for systematic comparative and historical analysis to discover.

Since, however, the hierarchical organizations of all tribal societies and of early civilizations also rest on or are integrated with a ritual structure and accompanying conceptual system, they are all to that extent members of a larger family to which the Vaupés and related systems of "simpler" societies also belong. Within such a family the hierarchies of the Vaupés are a preeconomic and prepolitical category of what may be designated "ritual hierarchy"; that is, I am prepared to assume that the Vaupés systems are examples of elementary or undeveloped hierarchical forms. My assumption implies that under proper circumstances they can turn their ritualized inequalities into more material form. There is some evidence for such a development in the Vaupés itself, where some of the dominant horticulturists have begun the commercial and exploitative use of Makuan labor (Silverwood-Cope 1972). I have also presented detailed and systematic evidence for such a development for Polynesian societies (Goldman 1970).

I do not, however, propose to deal in this essay with the larger questions of the origins or courses of development of systems of social inequality. My more immediate purpose is to describe the Vaupés system and, even more specifically, to focus largely on its conceptual foundations. This focus is warranted since this system is, at least as I understand it, conceptual, as though it were an organization of ritual relations. Consequently, since we can never hope to understand the nature of social inequalities and of hierarchical organization without paying close attention to native thinking on these subjects, I hope to introduce into the mainstream of social theory some of these indigenous conceptions. Although these are embedded in religious mysticism, they depend foremost on an intimate knowledge of the surrounding social and natural milieu.

The Vaupés is the seat of a unified cultural tradition that is varied in specifics and in its distinctive emphases on cultural themes but is unified around fundamentals of social organization and key conceptions of cosmological order. Hierarchy is a key concept shared by all. Beyond the range of cultural unities, there is some evidence to suggest that a number of what are now distinct "tribes" with separate languages were once joined into a single social order. Cubeo, for example, consider themselves to have been the "juniors" of the Desana, and the Tukano tribe is still recognized by some as the highest in rank of all. This suggests that a single hierarchical organization once had or in any case is thought to have encompassed a larger social community than it now does.

Four language families share this region: Tukanoan, Arawakan, Cariban, and Makuan. The Tukanoans, represented by more than a dozen languages and dialects, are the dominant ethnic population by virtue of their numbers, the extent of their territory, their control of the major streams, and, more generally, their assertiveness. The Arawakans and the Caribans occupy the periphery of the region and are consequently marginal to the cultural life of the Vaupés. Groups of Arawakan speakers have affiliated as full social segments with Tukanoan tribes, most notably to Cubeo, with whom in relatively recent times they have joined forces as an intermarrying phratry. They adopted the Cubeo language and became part of the tribe. There is not much information on relations with Caribans. The Makú, who are regarded by Tukanoans as intrinsically alien and subhuman residents, are nevertheless enmeshed with them—somewhat in the manner of Mbuti pygmies and village tribes—in intricate and by no means fully understood relations of servitude. Makuan individuals and family groups are still the traditional servitors of Tukanoan masters, in relationships that have persisted for generations (Silverwood-Cope 1972). No Tukanoans intermarry with Makú, none will admit to knowing their language or to having sexual relations with them. Although Tukanoan and Arawakan intermarriages are predicated on social equality, they nevertheless bear a taint of assimilation. In general, the dominant communities do not assimilate to other languages or cultural traditions.

The Tukanoan is by and large a cultural tradition that cherishes distinctions and that finds hierarchical significance in almost all of them. The river systems that flow generally eastward in the Vaupés suggest to their inhabitants a graded topographic order. They associate upriver with weakness, and downstream, in complementary contrast, with strength. Accordingly, those of lower rank normally live toward the river sources and those of higher rank toward the river mouths. For Cubeo, the entire Vaupés river is a chart of the relative rank of all Tukanoans. Being far-upstream dwellers themselves, they concede their social inferiority to Tukanoan tribes that live below them.

Other regional but unofficial hierarchies are those of occupation, style of life, and speech and language. Reichel-Dolmatoff relates that the Desana, whose productive economy is like that of other Tukanoans, nonetheless see themselves, as fully masculine hunters and superior to those whose specialty is fishing and who are therefore feminine and inferior (1971:17). All Tukanoans, however, deride the Makú—by far the best hunters—for being inept at farming, for not building substantial houses and canoes, and, most cutting, for their willingness to till the land and to perform household chores for outsiders. In the face of these disabilities, Makuan hunting skills and their expert knowledge of the forest serves merely to place them among the animals.

Language skills in this region define status differences among persons and among social groups. For social and ritual leadership, rhetorical bravura is a welcome if not essential requirement. Men of rank are eloquent and forceful speakers; shyness and other signs of linguistic ineptness, such as groping for the right expression, are embarrassing signs of inadequacy. Thus the common Tukanoan rule, of language exogamy to which Cubeo and Makuna (Arhem 1981) are the only known exceptions, places a burden of linguistic inadequacy on incoming wives and in-laws, adding an element of inferiority to alliances otherwise deemed to be between status equals.

A single detailed example makes my point clearer. For it, I draw on my field research among the Tukanoan-speaking Cubeo. I began this work in 1939/40, resumed it in 1968, 1969/70, and again briefly in 1979. As a group that is relatively low in status among Tukanoans, the Cubeo may actually underrepresent the full extent of distinctions created by ranking. My published data (Goldman 1963) on the subject of ranking are even more atypical because my early fieldwork was largely with a very low ranking sib. When I returned to the field in 1969, I refocused my studies to include high-rank sibs who were much more involved with the formalities of ranking and had, besides, a deeper knowledge, as they were indeed obliged to, of religious and ritual matters.

Cubeo reasoning about their social order is expressed in the special and esoteric idiom of mythical and ritual images, so its formulations and dicta are often mystifying and seemingly irrelevant. Or else, it seems, they are intent, for reasons unknown to us, on framing their meditations in a secret code that only their savants might understand. In fact, what they have in mind, if mystifying to others, is undoubtedly clear enough to them. It is to represent their social order in its fullness as a complete and living system, not narrow nor dessicated as "social structure," but as an organic entity for which we have no suitable term but which is representative of forces and powers, of human beings, of spirits, animals, and plants, of features of the terrain, of the air, of the sky, and of the gods who worked to bring that order into existence. For such a holistic representation, Cubeo have drawn on their practical knowledge of natural history as well as of what they understand to be the hidden side of nature, which is that of spirits and souls and is magical and religious. They do not fully separate the social order that encompasses their system of ranking from other beings and forces with which they perceive themselves to be related and involved, for their interest in it is not as a system of classification and no more, but as an organization of wide-ranging powers and relationships that concern such vital processes as birth, growth, maturation, and sexual reproduction. It is an organization, in short, of generative forces.

Cubeo reasoning incorporates a concept of historicity that derives the underlying constitution of social institutions from their origins and their subsequent modes of growth and development. For Cubeo, therefore, hierarchies and their powers are not fixed forms; they arise out of natural modes of development. When under certain circumstances they acquire stable and permanent form, this occurs, as I explain below, as part of a ritual process of memorializing formative events. Cubeo acknowledge the principle of historicity when they preface sacred and ritual references to their social order with a recitation of the appropriate origins tradition. The tradition binds the subject to its developmental history, thus giving it its true significance as that which is alive and as that which, having had a history, must be identified with it. To have had a history and not be able to call it to mind in the proper manner is, as Cubeo think, to have lost connections with sources of life. Hierarchies, rooted as they are in traditions of descent, are for Cubeo the quintessential subjects for historical traditions.

The exposition of hierarchy starts, therefore, with traditional accounts of the creation and the subsequent emergence in their home territory of the founding ancestors. The traditions are a genealogical record of sorts. They are simultaneously treatises on the creative powers of gods and human beings, on the stages of their growth and development to maturity, and on the nature of generative and sustaining powers. The traditions attribute human creation to Kúwai, a common culture hero among Arawakans but elevated to creator god by the Cubeo. Among Cubeo, Kúwai is the central figure of a fraternal trinity that in essence controls the origins and subsequent development of the entire social order. In metaphysical terms, the same trinitarian structure that engendered human origins serves as a primordial model for the kin-based and socially ascribed hierarchies that are characteristic of the Vaupés. Such systems rest on the premise that the order of birth within a fraternal line expresses the innately fixed and differentiated functions of the generative powers that are associated with descent. From this premise follows what is, for Cubeo at least, a general maxim of hierarchy: the firstborn initiates an action and the younger brothers complete it.

Kúwai, according to the traditions, conceived of human beings in his mind while seated on a ritual stool that was placed beside a hole leading to the center of the earth. What was at first only the mental image of a human being was later given a material form. Aínyehinkü, the younger brother of Kúwai and the Master of Food and Nourishment, fashioned musical wind instruments from slender palm trunks and from tree bark to represent an original form of the ancestors, their "form soul." Kúwai brought them to a first stage of life by giving them their ancestral names, their life souls, and their voices. It was only then, the traditions say, that people began to be born. The name, the soul, and the voice are the primary forces that sustain life. They exist as a configuration and not as separate entities. The name assigns membership in a line of descent and is the source of rank and accompanying powers. The life soul, a measure of personal vitality, is also an aspect of descent and rank. The voice is still another ancestral power that is expressed through songs and chants, instrumental sound, and rhetorical speech. It is also a power in nature revealed in thunder and other sounds. Cubeo say that is what makes an airplane fly. Later, the third member of the trinity, Mavichikori, deity of sorcery, esoteric knowledge, and death, completed the creation by introducing death.

The concept that the primary act of creation was a mental act assumes special significance in the ritual cycle and in the hierarchical order. At major rituals the senior elders, who, like Kúwai, are seated on ritual stools at the center of the communal longhouse, try to summon up images of their ancestors and the ancestral world. They seek to re-create the scenes of their own creation. The real power of a ceremony, I was told, is to bring images to mind that are so real that they are perceived as being alive. In this manner of bringing to life, they match metaphorically the powers of Kúwai. In earlier times, ritual leadership with the creative powers it implied was the prerogative of a high-ranking sib. Even now, in a more democratic era, these are still the privileges of senior males of the senior lineages. Actually, all males who have passed through a series of initiation rites have an active ritual role that includes visionary experiences and transcendent states induced in part by the full ensemble of ritual events, but mainly by intoxication and the action of coca and hallucinogens. Thus they all have a share in the re-creation, but only as congregants who are directed by their seniors at the center.

In the second stage of their formation, the ancestral spirit beings were ready to be born. They entered a rock house, known as House of People, and were assigned the order of their birth by the ancestral grandmother, Yurédo, who is also midwife and ritual godmother. That basic order of birth and social rank which is the very foundation of social life emerges, however, in a characteristically Cubean manner that always takes cognizance of oppositions and uncertainties. Not all the ancestral spirits are satisfied with their assigned ranks. They turn contentious, and some are able to leave their primordial womb out of turn. Now, when sibs argue about their ranking, they recall that original disorder and draw from it the lesson that even a divinely given order is ultimately subject to the uncertainties of human will and capriciousness. That theme is so common in Cubeo traditions that it must be recognized as a tenet of the faith.

In a succeeding developmental stage, the ancestral spirits enter the transitional sphere of the river, which is their permanent link with origins. Before they became human they must have existed as anacondas and as fish who are progeny of anacondas. There are various opinions on the specifics of transitional states, but common agreement holds that they were "born" as anacondas and were therefore part of the nature of Aínkü (The Devourer), the primordial anaconda. Aínkü is thought by some to be a demon, as though he were an evil counterpart to a beneficent creator. In any case, he is a godlike figure who represents those aspects of existence that were originally absent from the constitution of the creator and from the ancestral spirits he had created. Kúwai and the community over which he presides, known collectively as *kúwaiwa,* are the primary forms of spirit and soul force from which the ancestors were originally created. In their primordial form the *kúwaiwa* were not yet fully developed and were somewhat like the present-day corps of male initiates: not yet sexual, not yet ready for marriage, examples of pure masculinity living in a condition of social isolation. They reproduced themselves as youthful males, like those about to be initiated, in what appears to be the ultimate paradigm of endogamy. This state of developmental immaturity the anaconda corrected. Human beings, the myth implies, cannot proceed with their own development until the gods have advanced their own through marriage with the anacondas. As a lower-ranking deity, Aínkü completes the process of creation Kúwai had begun. The anaconda community included women as wives and daughters and was already complete.

First, however, death was introduced among the *kúwaiwa,* ending their endogamy and personal immortality. The introduction of death was brought about by Mavíchikori, the youngest brother of the Kúwai trinity, who was the first to seek out the anacondas and the first of the *kúwaiwa* to imbibe a fatal dose of the potent anacondan hallucinogen. His death was followed by marriages of *kúwaiwa* with anaconda daughters, in an apt illustration of the evolutionary dictum that personal death follows the appearance of sexual reproduction. The anacondas then gave Kúwai and his *kúwaiwa* the gifts of ritual performance that opened the anaconda world to them and allowed them to participate generally in the life of animals. These ritual gifts—songs, instrumental music, dances, body pigments, and ornaments—are considered to be intrinsic properties of animals like their speech and voices, their body forms, and coloring. Finally, the hallucinogen Cubeo call *mihí* (*Banisteriopsis kaapi*) was the most potent of the anaconda gifts. Through its visions *mihí* revealed the otherwise closed world of anacondas, other animals, and ancestors as though perceived by Aínkü himself. Then—at a later time, after the ancestors had completed their passages through the body of the anaconda and had mystically absorbed the substance of his nature and powers—these properties were given to them for ritual uses by the younger brother of Kúwai, Aínyehinkü. Thus in their own development the ancestors recapitulated a stage in the maturation of the gods.

For the ancestors, the decisive developmental stage was a metamorphosis from anaconda to human form, in essence the familiar transformative passage from one sphere to another. When they had shed the anaconda form and had taken possession of their own sphere of activities, they had also established themselves as a new species that was separate from the animal world of the anaconda. They retained, nevertheless, as part of their descent—that is, as part of their spiritual constitution—qualities from Kúwai and the *kúwaiwa* and those from the anaconda. It is these spiritual links that give potency and effectiveness to the ritual instruments and procedures. In the postmetamorphic state, the ancestors are also trinitarian. That complex makeup consisting of Kúwaian, anacondan, and human traits enters into the structure of the social order they finally establish.

The ancestral transformation is portrayed rather naturalistically in the traditions. It begins as a gradual shedding of anaconda scales and continues with human infants growing up as they travel the rivers from where they first emerged at a rocky rapids to where they will finally live. The rivers and the activity of travel are both represented as agents of their transformation and growth. The intervals of their movements are equated with intervals of transformation and growth. Starting as infants (and as anacondas) they are nourished, as by a mother, on the white spume of the rapids, which they describe as the "milk of the land." After each pause at a particular spot on the river—a beach, a promontory, a lagoon, a place of this or that animal—they develop a new trait. Each pause is also a period during which they observe how much they have grown in number. As they acquire new qualities, the river also matures. It acquires its own character when each twist and turn is given a name. The river, the line that connects the human communities with their origins, is no less than a counterpart form of the primordial anaconda. A clay model of an anaconda lying at the deepest and central part of the river is the heart of Aínkü, and this heart, both of the anaconda and the river, is the source of soul or life force (*umé*) for fish and other river creatures. The anaconda has other hearts in other locations—one of them in the communal longhouse (*maloca*), where it serves to maintain the natal connections and adds its force to all ritual actions. As Master of the River, Aínkü is represented by the piranha, one of his spirit manifestations who acts in the human world as a metaphorical devourer and death bringer. Essentially, the anaconda, in combination with his other forms such as river and piranha, controls the developmental cycle of the human founders of the Cubeo social order from birth to death. But the "death" that comes under this jurisdiction pertains only to ritual events. During hallucinogenic intoxication, when the congregants see visions, they are transported back into the ancestral era.

Finally, the ancestors occupied the rivers in order of their birth. Moving upstream, the first born settled at the mouth, the second born above him, and the last proceeded to the river source. In various Cubeo traditions this order of settlement is described as an action of the anaconda. According to one account, the anaconda entered the river and settled along it with his head at the mouth and his tail at the source. He then split into segments, each of which became a sib. The leading and first-ranking sib was the head and the lowest in rank his tail, and the others lined up in order as intermediate segments of his body. This particular version of the emergence traditions describes the metaphysical constitution of the phratric order of sibs in the strongest possible way. Other versions state the connection with the anaconda more circumspectly. I draw on this strong version so as not to overcomplicate what is intended to be a conceptual model of the hierarchical system. Except for the fact that circumstances inevitably rearranged the order of river settlements to some degree and more or less eliminated one formal system of hierarchy, this model is still real even if it is not fully realized in practice. It is recognized as the way things should be.

Cubeo think of their social structure as a system that developed from the primordial order of birth. Those who emerged from the same rock house were, with some exceptions, brothers. These were the founders of patrilineal, patri-virilocal, and exogamic phratries, each (again with exceptions) a fraternal federation of sibs ranked by a concept of seniority. Originally, there were but two intermarrying phratries—a moiety arrangement--which exchanged brides through bilateral cross-cousin marriages. Since the sibs then married strictly by rank, the phratries were organizations of castes. The Cubeo continue to speak of the phratry as though it were a lineage whose branches and their family lines were genealogically descended from original ancestors. The genealogical conception goes as far as to delineate senior and junior lines on which the basic hierarchy is founded, but it does so without actual genealogical records. The claims to seniority are sustained only by general traditions for which there is a consensus.

This rank order of sibs is the primary reference for all the various modes of hierarchical organization. I refer to it hereafter as "primary rank." This ranking is expressed first as the serial order of the sibs from the "head" sib at the mouth of the river to the "tail" sib at its source. As such, it governs, in principle, the orderly allocation of settlement sites along the river and the orders of precedence in formal salutations at arrival and departure from important ceremonies.

Primary rank has presumably generated such additional modes of ranking of the sibs as (a) a three-class system of seniors, juniors, and servants; (b) a dyadic system of kin relations such as older brother/younger brother, grandfather/grandchild, paternal uncle/paternal nephew, and (c) a serial order of ritual ranks that is no longer operative but is still remembered. This last order consisted of chiefs, ritual leaders, blowing shamans, water-pouring shamans, perhaps warriors, and servants.

Before turning to additional modes of hierarchy, I should emphasize that primary ranking differs markedly from these latter insofar as it alone represents fully the primary events that established the phratries. It is embedded in the mythical era and is the final source of ritual association with the creation and emergence. The order of primary rank is to be understood as though it incorporated the forces from the original birth from the rock house, from the sides of Kúwai and the anaconda, and from the qualities of the river. These circumstances of birth imply that ranking was the prerequisite for emergence. Even though it was Yurédo as midwife who assigned ranks, it was Kúwai who gave the original names whose ranking had been preordained by him. These original ancestral names that were transmitted as name souls to grandchildren are intended to move in accordance with the seniority of sib membership and are the identifiers of original ranking as well as the bearers of its powers. The anaconda and the river convey to the sib still other rank-associated powers, powers that in effect represent them jointly. The head of the anaconda, for example, contains his powers of vision and knowledge as well as his capacity for devouring. The river mouth receives fish who enter and ascend it with the rainy season. Thus, quite literally, the river mouth assumes significance as the nourisher of the phratry. When the upriver sibs attend the ceremonies of the head sib, it is said, "They have come to feed at the mouth."

The three-class system, a fairly flexible categorization of sib ranks, stands for the strictly human standards by which social worth is judged. The criteria of judgment, however, are derived from the basic premises of primary rank, namely, seniority and its accompanying powers. The seniors (*híbuna*), also known as *méana* ("the good people"), commonly include the first three top-ranking sibs. The juniors (*imána*), who are *uménükriwü* ("ordinary souls"), are represented by all lower sibs except for the lowest. The servants (*yebákakúwü*), those who are "under the command," are a group set apart. The distinction between seniors and juniors is equivalent to that between leaders and followers. Educated Cubeo youths have learned to translate this distinction to that between "nobles" and "common people." Older people are concerned for reasons of social decorum to soften these distinctions, but they accept those that exclude the servants. The servants, in fact, are almost always referred to as "makuses," as though they were not merely at the bottom of the social scale but outside and beyond it.

The dyadic system, in effect, converts the primary order of rank into sets of kinship pairs that express what are for Cubeo the most elemental relations of hierarchy, and those are the developmental cycles inherent in kinship. As we gather from the example of Kúwai and his brothers, their unity in hierarchy is responsible for the initial powers of creation: the older initiates, the younger completes; the older is the life-enhancing force the younger the bringer of death. This bond between older and younger brother applies everywhere. It includes all species of life, plants, animals, heavenly bodies. Cubeo kin terms also express the relative seniority of sisters and of brothers and sisters; but it is only the fraternal dyad that has significance as a creative force and that in a system of patrilineal descent carries out the concept of hierarchical structure. In the case of older brother/younger brother, the dyadic hierarchy may also be seen as softening the distinctions of primary rank, since with the aforementioned exceptions each sib is either an older brother or a younger brother to another. Cubeo, generally speaking, are reluctant, even while accepting status differences, to overemphasize the relative worth of brothers. They insist, for example, that the inequalities, such as they may be between older brother and younger brother sibs, are largely ignored within the sib.

The dyad of grandchild/grandparent sibs, however, has the opposite effect of polarizing the order of primary rank. The sib that is called grandfather is at the bottom, equated with "tail" and with servant, and as such is reciprocally bound with the grandson sib that is at the top, as the "head," and in principle the ruling sib, that is, whereas the lowest-ranking sib is grandfather to all other sibs of the phratry, the top-ranking sib is grandson only to the sib at the bottom. Thus, only the lowest is subservient to all, and all others except for the grandfather occupy in this setting a status of dominance. One effect of polarization is to soften in still another way the distinctions of primary rank. Although in this dyadic mode the basic distinctions are relatively harsh in implying the contrasting life styles of master and servant, they are nonetheless derived from the same general principles that define the fraternal dyad. Thus, as to order of emergence, the grandson was first and the grandfather last. The former initiated the postnatal phase of the developmental process, the latter brought it to a close. The grandson who receives a name soul from a deceased member of the line of recent grandfathers is the traditional carrier of the immortality of the sib, and so he represents a state of ascendancy in the life cycle. Grandfathers are, by contrast, the receding generation. They are the old and weak on the way to illness and death. This dyad differs from that of fraternity principally because it deals with a different phase of the life cycle. I have more to say about the grandparent/grandchild pair in connection with the order of functional ranks below

The dyad of paternal uncle/paternal nephew—a reference to the filial relationships, since in Cubeo kinship father and father's brother are close to equivalent—has its place in the order as a courtesy extended to a newly adopted sib who will be addressed as avuncular and accorded the respects owed the father's brothers.

It is unfortunate (for scholars only) that what appears to have been the most elaborate expression of hierarchy—namely, the organization of ritual ranks, or, as they have been called, "specialist roles" (Hugh-Jones 1979)— no longer exists anywhere in the Vaupés. For, unlike primary ranking and that of dyadic kinship, the designation of the ranked sibs by their specialized roles in the ritual order created what was nothing less than a fully integrated system that encompassed the entire tribe as an organic society. Without it, as today, for example, most of the ritual functions have been absorbed by each of the sibs with attendant loss of fully interdependent unity but with a gain in the relative autonomy of the sibs and with an overall reduction in hierarchical powers.

Only a skeletal infrastructure of hierarchical relations now sustains what had been a total system. Cubeo recall the existence of the former system and so do the Barasana of the Río Pirá-paraná. A detailed analysis of that system has been published by Christine Hugh-Jones (1979). My own data and interpretations agree with hers on basic principles, though not on details. The Barasana describe a five-sib organization that consisted of chiefs, dancers/chanters, warriors, shamans, and servants, in that order. Some Cubeo to whom I related the details of a Barasana rank order replied that "we had the same ranks." Others, however, claiming tht there had been no warrior sib "because all young men were raised to fight," provided a somewhat different list of sibs, such as chiefs, dance/song leaders, blowing shamans, water-pouring shamans, and servants. Since this order calibrates with primary rank and with dyadic kinship, it follows that chiefs are the grandsons of the servants and that they are the older brothers of the dance/song leaders (ritual leaders). The latter are, in turn, the older brothers of the water-pouring shamans. The father's brothers as adopted sibs were not in this picture. I am uncertain about a warrior sib, and so I do not include them either within the order. I comment on warriors separately.

Neither the Cubeo nor the Barasana authorities could describe in substantial detail how the older system worked. But we can reconstruct it from proffered recollections, from the remaining forms of these ranks as they are today, and ultimately from our perception of the whole structure of rank that originally contained these ranks. Even as we may make allowances for the distortions that accompany ancient and revered memories of an esteemed past, there is still good cause to accept that recalled history as reasonably reliable. Most difficult to reconstruct, however, is the nature of the ranks of special interest, namely, those of chiefs and of servants. Yet even these types continue to exist, though much modified, to provide guidelines for reconstructing their past.

Chiefs

Cubeo describe the earlier chiefs as commanding authorities over the entire phratry and contrast them admiringly with those of today whose leadership does not extend beyond their own sib. The general nature of this authority, though narrower in scope, is essentially the same. Local chiefs or headmen today still have the most prestigious voice in deliberations; they have much to say about the ritual cycle and the economic preparations it requires; they are the formal representatives of their sib community in important relations with outsiders. They give the word for war or settlement; they engage in the most distant trade, traveling well into neighboring territories. Formerly, as phratric leaders, they helped resolve disputes among sibs. And in the old days the chiefs were the acknowledged masters of the servant sib and thus enjoyed a style of daily life that has long since gone.

We can understand the traditional Cubeo concept of chiefship best by comparing it with another order of leadership that has always existed yet need not be related to descent. The traditional or hereditary chief is still remembered as the *hŭbükü*, The Senior Man, and also as the *hipóbü*, literally the Head Man. This early chief incarnated the founding ancestor of the phratry usually by bearing his name, but in any case by representing him ritually and by appearing metaphorically as the head of the anaconda, the mouth of the river, and the grandson who carries forward the immortality of the sib and phratry. Coming from the mythical sphere of founders and formative spirits, the sources of his authority are spiritual. In the familiar sense of the term, he is a charismatic leader. By contrast, another order of leadership is associated with the *habókü*, more like the familiar headman who deals with the practicalities of everyday life and is often chosen for the variety of his useful skills and his helpfulness. To set forth for the moment a useful but crude distinction, the *hŭbükü* or *hipóbü* stands for sacred leadership and the *habókü* for its secular side. Today, as in the past, each sib has its *habókü*, who is the local leader. In sibs of high rank the position is inherited through the senior line.

The distinction between sacred and secular cannot be stretched too far, for *habókü*, a term Cubeo translate as *dueño* in its Spanish meanings as "owner" and "person in command," has mystical and religious connotations as well. The stem *habó-* is difficult to translate, but it implies "that which supports." The earth is *habóno*, for example. More meaningfully, the term applies to the leadership of spheres of the nonhuman order as well. Each species of life has its own *habókü*, who is, as Reichel-Dolmatoff (1971) has termed him, its Master. Kúwai is *habókü* of the Cubeo and not their "chief," since he does not head their senior lines.

In each sphere the *habókü* is the most masterful figure. Among animal families he is the largest or most aggressive member of the family. The anaconda is Master of fish, but in his special manifestation as a piranha. The coca plant is *habókü* of the manioc gardens; Single-Breasted Woman, the mother of the principal demon of sorcery, is Mistress of the animals of the forest. The *habókü* is always at the center of his or her sphere, commonly enough a circle. There he or she exists as its heart (*uméndü*), which is the source of soul stuff that nurtures all within it. The concept of *habókü* is centric, a simple relationship of direct control; that of chief is cephalic, linear and hierarchical. The heart at the center sustains life and nurtures the growth of entities that are thought of as though each were a single organism. The head that Cubeo conceive of as the source of knowledge, vision, and the powers of devouring in its opposing capacities of life giving and death dealing commands the line of growth, of developmental cycles, and of historical continuity.

In its fully hierarchical form, chiefship is a historical office with the special historical mission of caring for the continuity of descent. Such chiefs are not caretakers. It is they who are the nurtured, cared for by their grandparent, "tail" and servant sib. Like early Caduveo (Lévi-Strauss 1964:160) they existed as a leisure class. In an evidently deliberate act of being set apart from *habókü* leadership, they were expected to do nothing. Their servants hunted, fished, cultivated the soil, drew water, gathered firewood, tended the fires, prepared chicha, and even lighted the ceremonial cigars of the exalted "seniors" and "heads." We can understand this extraordinary inversion of ordinary Cubeo standards of virtue only as kind of sanctification of office, a stripping away of the fully human traits of productive labor so that chiefs would resemble and remind the community of their ancestors in emergence before they had settled down to be truly Cubeo. The inversion of standards is carried to the point where, in fact, it is the grandfathers who by caring for the chiefs become the nurturers of the entire phratry, "feeding them at the mouth."

This special character of chiefs as persons removed from the ordinary rules of labor and made to live an unreal existence as though they were forever grandchildren compels us to see the phratry in a special light as well. In the ordinary sense, the phratry as a largely fraternal union of sibs maintains a collective order along a stretch of river and serves as the defining structure of the social system. But in an extraordinary sense it exists as a replica of the conditions that brought Cubeo society into existence. In a formal sense, too, the hierarchical structure of the phratry is a monument, a memorial to events of creation, a permanent structure of social relations expressly designed to arrest the passages and transformations of time by fixing them firmly in place like figures in stone.

It may well be that all formal structures memorialize their beginnings. That of Cubeo is noteworthy for its explicitness. It has fixed once and for all the order of emergence, the patterns of movement and settlement. It has enclosed the variety of human interests and capabilities within such unalterable forms as rivers and serpents. It has converted patterns of fraternity and kinship from their natural and generational cycles to still lifes in which older brothers are never younger brothers and grandchildren are never grandparents. In conformity with the same deliberate pattern, it has locked chiefs and servants, ritual leaders and shamans into species-like categories. Only the *habókü*, the practical man, remains as a symbolic heart that supplies soul force to everyday life. We should not, however, think of the monumental social structure as something dead. On the contrary, it exists to bring to life, in Cubeo memory, a complete, indeed a total, picture of themselves as beings who are connected to their sources. The imaginative re-creation of beings and events is in ritual life analogous to the original human creation by Kúwai. In this most vital respect, therefore, the phratry is a constituent of a total ritual effort to bring the ancestors to life.

As a constituent of what appears to be a comprehensive ritual structure, the hierarchical phratry has a complementary function of representing the historical continuities of present communities with ancestral beginnings by its constant presence as the permanent representation of Cubeo as an ethnic entity. The other constituent, that which we normally recognize as *the* ritual structure, confines itself almost exclusively to the more parochial interests of the community. It is concerned with the developmental cycles of persons: the local events of birth, maturation, marriage, death, and the celebration of natural periodicities of seasonal harvest and abundance.

The phratry, nevertheless, has a dual character; it is mythic and social, commemorating and incorporating the ancestral sphere and serving, at the same time, as the framework of social existence in the human era. Accordingly, chiefs and all others of its specialized sibs exist as double figures. In one guise the chiefs are ritual figures. But since they are palpably of "this world," as Cubeo say, they are shadowed by what can only be a calculated ambiguity. I say calculated because they and all others are perceived as living permanently on the margins of both spheres. From the mythical and ritual side, the powers of chiefs and their corresponding status are incorporated within biological and mystical forms and processes that are essentially free of evaluation as "high" or "low," "good" or "bad." The placing of value is a human responsibility as Cubeo understand it. The human side places social value on strength over weakness, health over sickness, assertiveness over passivity, and, understandably, life enhancing over death dealing. Whereas the mythical and ritual side is dominated by stable and dependable forces, the human side, which is after all a unique configuration, is forever willful and contentious and is therefore capable of transforming itself, but within boundaries set by the religious system. Cubeo speak of chiefs who used their powers for active and aggressive wars against close neighbors, of sorcerers without restraints, and of servants who were subdued beyond the measured protocol of the grandparent/grandchild relationship. When they took to referring to that lowest-ranking sib as "our Makuses," they had begun to think of them as outsiders and of their servitude as menial and degrading. Whether this was a gradual development or was always the practice, no one could say, but real Máku, who were truly despised as born originally of rats, became in Cubeo eyes a servile labor force removed from the constraints of kinship and subject, therefore, to the rule of utility. When one side found the company of the other burdensome, relations were broken off (see Silverwood-Cope 1972).

Ritual Leaders

Chiefship within the phratric hierarchy is linked with the second-ranking sib in the dyadic relationship of older brother/younger brother. The ritual leaders, a priesthood, are the "younger brothers" whose powers are those of completing an initiative. If the initiator is representative of the forward edge of the ancestors, the completors organize the ritual means that actively associate the phratry with its ancestors. On the plane of myth the chief is analogous to Kúwai, and the ritual leaders are on the secondary plane represented by the anaconda. There are four principal ritual functions within the priestly province that may be mastered either separately or in various combinations: singing, dancing, chanting, and recitation of ancestral narratives. Currently each of these is a responsibility of elders of senior lineages in each of the sibs. When the phratry was a truly organic entity, the elder males of the second-ranking sib were its active religious functionaries who controlled the means generating images of the ancestral past.

Each element of a Cubeo ritual is artfully planned to contribute to a transcendent setting that places the congregation close to or within the nonhuman setting of gods and spirits. Mind- and mood-altering substances such as *chicha*, coca, tobacco, and *mihí* are perhaps the decisive agents of visionary transcendence. But the ritual setting as a whole—with its dances, its music, its colors and ornamental objects—creates the evocative atmosphere, while the chants and ancestral recitatives add their cognitive content to the visionary state. These priestly powers may be thought of as confined to the sphere of ritual only from a narrow view of the relations between the ritual and social spheres. Ritual serves to focus and to intensify the Cubeo experience of their ethnicity. They say of dance, which expresses for them the full structure, "It is our life," that is, the collective existence. The priestly powers are considerable. What is more, they are tangible and unambiguous because, unlike those of chiefs, they are fully located within the sphere of ritual. Particularly because priests are religious leaders, they command the sensitive centers of ethnic feeling and are ultimately a potent force for social cohesion. Nevertheless, in their dyadic relationships with chiefs they are the junior element.

In one sense this is a positive side that represents the younger brother as a completor of actions and therefore, as Cubeo are always pleased to point out, the wiser one. In still another respect, the junior has a dangerous and evil side, which surfaces in ordinary social life in the commonplaces of sibling jealousies and rivalries that are not to be taken too seriously. Cubeo prefer to suppress manifestations of inequality within the nuclear family and at least to restrain it within the sib. The counterplay between good and evil, as between senior and junior, takes place in the more elevated realm of metaphysical thinking on the nature of death. It most assuredly begins with the implied antagonism between brothers and pursues the broader implications of such rivalry. Cubeo seem to understand that the completion of an action applies to the life cycle as a whole. Accordingly, death completes what was begun at birth. They also understand the occult connection between knowledge, on the one side, and death and death's companions—sorcery and illness—on the other. That connection is portrayed in the creation traditions dealing with the origins of death. In one such tradition, Mavíchikori, a younger brother of Kúwai who is both Master of Death and the first to gain knowledge of hallucinogens and visions, is carried off by the anaconda just as he has begun his initiation into maturity. The anaconda swallows him and is forced to vomit him up. Because of ritual errors, his resurrection is aborted and Mavíchikori, passing quickly from the onset of maturity to his final death, brings death into the world. Male initiation rites recapitulate this theme. Cubeo call the rites *anchíndowaino*, "knowing." The initiate acquires knowledge of ritual meanings and with it an understanding of death and its origins in the afflictions of sorcery. The hallucinogenic vision that is the source of deep knowledge of ancestral origins is rendered by Cubeo as a form of death, and the hallucinogen itself is known by a sacred term that means "death substance." In these respects the caste of ritual leaders is, in effect, a priesthood of the anaconda who guides the community back to its beginnings—into a deathlike regression. This negative association joins them with what Cubeo consider an evil direction and enhances the popular perception of their powers.

The Shamans

On the scale of basic ranking, chiefs and ritual leaders belong to the class of seniors, the elite representatives of the first ancestors. The shamans are a middle group of juniors, the ordinary people, even though their powers are very highly regarded whether as healers and dealers of soul stuff or as deeply feared sorcerers. They are ordinary only in the special terms of traditional ranking that place the highest value on proper descent. In that special respect, the shamans are indeed the proverbial outsiders. They have the connections that all have with Kúwai and anaconda, but their patron spirit is the double being who is both Thunder and Jaguar. As professionals they are therefore a class apart. Their visionary powers and their knowledge of spells and chants notwithstanding, they are not the leading figures within the common congregation of orthodox visionaries and imagistic reconstructors of the original primal scenes. Their role in collective ritual is secondary to their primary interest in the fate and welfare of individuals. The nature of their expertise with respect to souls shows how they differ from ritual leaders or priests. The latter deal with soul on a large and collective scale, with *umé* that belongs to the descent lines. The shaman has no access to the original sources of soul; hence, he scavenges for lost souls and for fragments of soul for those of his clients who suffer from soul loss and weakness.

On the dyadic scale, both types of shaman are, collectively, the younger brothers of the ritual elders. Insofar as collective ritual can be said to initiate processes on behalf of the general welfare of the community, the private rituals of shamans bring these to completion by attending to the unfinished business of persons and their families. On the same scale of older brother/younger brother, the blowing shamans occupy a higher status for specializing in soul. The soul, *umé*, is thought to be like the air or wind, a breath that can be moved and directed by blowing it. Cubeo traditions refer to a magical whistle, *po'oye*, that contained all the souls of the tribe. When Kúwai blew the whistle, the souls flew out and populated the earth. Song, voice, and instrumental sound are all associated with soul. The blowing of soul is a professional skill. The blower has learned dozens of chants, each a lengthy text that calls on the powers of ancestors, animals, plant and other substances for assistance. Equally important to this specific and substantive knowledge is the shaman's general knowledge and personal demeanor, also cultivated, a demeanor of authoritative calm that is appropriate for an official spokesman for a human community that seeks rapport with nonhuman spirits. He chants the spell and blows tobacco smoke. Ritual leaders among Cubeo also blow chants in the same manner, but ordinarily in the course of collective ceremonies.

The blowing shaman specializes in blowing and chanting for illnesses. A step below the priestly ritual elders, he is the equivalent of older brother to the water pourer who completes a cure by washing the illness out of the patient's body. The water pourer, a diagnostician as well as a healer, discovers the specific nature of the illness so as to place the blame and accept a commission to avenge the victim. His specialty identifies him most closely with the origins of illness, sorcery, and death, in themselves the incarnations of evil. Cubeo, however, are inclined to place the blame for the appearance among them of such disturbances on some manifestation of social failure or disorder. In the traditions that justify the *anchíndowaino* rites, the claim is made that it is disobedience to ritual rules, in substance, a lack of respect for traditional authority, that introduces illness and sorcery. In corresponding traditions that deal with the initiation of shaman novices, it is the same disregard for ritual rules that is shown as responsible for turning healing shamans into sorcerers.

Warriors

I cannot place warriors within the order of sib ranks because of the uncertainty of Cubeo opinion on this matter. Even though there were some who thought there had been a warrior caste in the past, I am inclined to accept the contrary opinion that all youths were warriors because it would have been otherwise difficult for Cubeo to have defended themselves in this warlike region. Even so, a discussion of the characteristics of Cubeo warriors as a generalized status is pertinent for the light it might cast on the nature of warrior sibs elsewhere in the Vaupés, or on Cubeo themselves if they did indeed have such a sib.

The warrior is, in any case, the youth who has emerged from his initiation rites as a full-fledged adult with broad and unspecialized knowledge of practical and esoteric matters and with all the other attributes of manliness, chiefly those of hardness and fierceness. In the ordinary sense, the warrior youth is no less than the exemplar of masculine strength and assertiveness. He is the forward edge of the display of forcefulness by which each community faces the outer world. The warrior youth is, however, a combatant in two spheres. In the social world, he faces real enemies. In the metaphysical sphere—where weakness, decay, illness, and death are the permanent antagonists—he is, shaman-like, a projection of the durable strengths and procreative vigor of the descent lines. His initiation rites have converted him from an immature youth to a complete man. They have joined him with the original ancestral beings, the *bükűpwanwa*, who are the immortal prototypes of the sibs; and they have taught him the essential unities of existence. Since the rank order is a system of metaphysical values, the strengths of the initiate elevate him to a high status. He is reborn as an ancestral prototype—not as a weak infant, but as a youth at a physical peak. The Barasana system, in which a warrior sib ranked above that of shamans, is consistent with this view. But there is a Cubeo position that democratically elevates all youths to a distinguished status, transient as that may be.

Women

As though it were part of a calculated symmetry of oppositions, the social and ritual position of the newly adolescent girl is set as a general model for female virtues and values that remain, however, outside the spheres of the hierarchical order. The male is cultivated to mature as an insider, within the phratric system as a whole. His age-mated sister arrives at her sexual maturity to become, if not wholly an outsider to the life of the phratry, at least peripheral to its hierarchical functions. When she marries, shortly after menarche, she enters the generative cycle of her husband's sib and phratry and is ultimately, except for some specialized ritual duties, alienated from her own. The system of exchange marriages softens but cannot overcome this essential estrangement. Yet the conditions of postmarital residence would not in themselves bar women from an active role in a hierarchical order. Other primitive aristocracies readily honor women of senior lines equally with men. In the Cubeo system, however, gender outclassed hereditary rank. Women were neither chiefs, ritual leaders, shamans, warriors, nor *habókü*. For that matter, even ritual servitude was conceived to be a special masculine condition. Within their respective sibs they shared in the respects (negative and positive) that were owed to male functionaries. Thus women of the sib of chiefs enjoyed not only the prestige of membership in it but the servitude of the lowest rank as true servants and menials, although they themselves were not in the class of ancestral representations. Similar menial services, it is said, were available to the wives of ritual leaders who were not, in that ritual capacity, privileged as a leisure class. Beyond such rights, women of that sib were chosen for special ritual functions that required a symbolic female presence. As for the wives of shamans, they were subject mainly to the restrictions on sexual contacts that were laid on their husbands. In the order of sibling dyads, women of older brother sibs were, of course, older sister to the others, also a position of respect but peripheral in this sib, as in the others, to the main principle of hierarchy.

This peripheral, if not quite fully negative, appearance of women in the formal order of hierarchy follows from its specialized character as a memorial to the era of mythical origins, to the time, that is, when even ancestral women did not exist. In Cubeo development theory, the masculine side, representing one set of forces, emerges first and then arrives at its maturity through sexual relations and marriage. Through women human development is completed. On this grand scale the Cubeo see a balanced rather than a hierarchical process, and on this process they pass no judgment. Although there is the merit of priority on the masculine side as an initial and initiating force, that merit does not weigh against that of the female, who is the means of completion. If, then, the hierarchical order is indeed the field of action of men, mainly, it was the female presence of Yurédo as midwife that presided over its formation.

What we have observed in the Vaupés is no simple rank order but a complex organization of hierarchy that combines several modes of ranking within a coherent set of general principles. These principles, in substance a metaphysics of social existence, form the ideological bases for social and ritual relations. A useful distinction may be drawn between those modes of order that govern the internal life of the sibs and those that organize them in the phratric relations. The sib, the true community of kinship, as it is of subsistence production and of practical authority, is essentially self-sufficient. Except for what are the close-to-universal social inequalities of generation, order of birth, and gender, the sib is not, in the traditional system I have described, a hierarchical organization. Only after the older order had itself changed did it acquire a subdued and simplified hierarchy. In the latter form, the sib is governed by a social mode of order in its conventional meaning, as against that of ritual. The ritual mode simultaneously characterizes the relations of phratry and of hierarchy. It is in this light that the Vaupés hierarchies appear as ritual systems and differ from hierarchical organizations elsewhere that have more clearly defined political and economic functions.

Ritual hierarchies may drift into political and economic areas, but their powers are derived from mythical and ancestral spheres and are manifested ritually, their hierarchical structures memorials to ancestral origins. Mystical as these powers and structures may seem, they are perceived as substantial and essential to virtually every aspect of everyday life, and in these respects they are real and functional. Within their own frame of reference, their powers are as far-reaching and diversified as those of more pragmatic systems, and in at least one fundamental respect they are even more formidable because they are perceived as underlying the sources of collective existence.

Ultimately, the hierarchical organization seems to be a manifestation of descent, by which Cubeo and probably all Vaupés peoples mean far more than Western societies do. Descent in their manner of thinking implies the entire process of creation and formation of the ancestral lines. In the manner of genetic reasoning, they impute to the ancestral heritage all the varied influences that have contributed to their formation and endowed them with assorted powers that promote their growth, their development and differentiation, and their capacities to deal with one another and with the spheres of animals and spirits.

One may ask, finally, what the native peoples of the Vaupés are truly concerned with. Is it with the nature of social inequalities, the structures of hierarchy, or is it with the more fundamental issues of descent? To ask the question in this form is to imply the answer. Although Cubeo and their neighbors are not naive about the moral significance of hierarchy, their intellectual concerns are more comprehensive. It is not inequalities the ritual elders choose to talk about, but their ancestors.

References

Arhem, Kaj
 1981 *Makuna Social Organization: A Study in Descent, Alliance and the Formation of Corporate Groups in the North-Western Amazon*, Uppsala Studies in Cultural Anthropology, no. 4.

Goldman, Irving
 1963 *The Cubeo: Indians of the Northwest Amazon*, Urbana: University of Illinois Press.
 1970 *Ancient Polynesian Society*. Chicago: University of Chicago Press.

Hugh-Jones, Christine
 1979 *From the Milk River: Spatial and Temporal Processes in Northwest Amazonia*. Cambridge: Cambridge University Press.

Lévi-Strauss, Claude
 1964 *Tristes Tropiques: An Anthropological Study of Primitive Societies in Brazil*. Trans. John Russell. New York: Atheneum.

Reichel-Dolmatoff, Gerardo
 1971 *Amazonian Cosmos: The Sexual and Religious Symbolism of the Tukano Indians*. Chicago: University of Chicago Press.

Silverwood-Cope, Peter
 1972 A contribution to the ethnography of the Colombian Maku. Ph.D. Diss. University of Cambridge.

Chapter Seven

State and Household Crops among the Jola (Diola) of Senegal

Olga F. Linares

That different crops can have separate histories and also vary markedly in their political and social impacts was elegantly demonstrated by Murra in his seminal article "Rite and Crop in the Inca State" (1960). Murra argued that root crops played a subsistence role in the economy of the Tawantinsuyu whereas maize played a political and ritual role. Root crops, especially potatoes, were the hardy, native staples of Andean peasants. In contrast, maize was of foreign introduction. Its cultivation on a large scale was possible only after the Inka state appropriated the labor of the population through *mit'a* labor services. Murra concluded that each crop represented not only a different agricultural technique but also a different cultural and social system. Furthermore, this reflected duality in crop function is a situation in which a dominant system—"the power-wielding Inca state—was in the process of incorporating and transforming the other [system]" (Murra 1960:401).

In this essay I explore, in the context of contemporary West African farmers, the ideas put forth by Murra concerning the divergent significance of state and of peasant crops. My purpose is to show that Murra's model

---

This paper is based on several years of fieldwork among the Jola of Senegal, beginning in 1964 and continuing to date. I thank the National Science Foundation, the Wenner-Gren Foundation for Anthropological Research, the Smithsonian Institution, and the Smithsonian Tropical Research Institute in Panama for financial assistance. Their grants have enabled me to experience firsthand the important changes taking place during the last decades in Jola society. I also thank Martin H. Moynihan, my husband, for his help and encouragement while he was doing fieldwork on *Caraciiformes* birds in Senegal. My deepest gratitude goes to many good Jola friends; if only the rest of the world were half as hard-working. To them, "Emitei kati kasumai."

has wide applicability to other peoples in other lands. The appropriation of revenue crops by a nascent bureaucracy may well be intrinsic to the process of state formation. Many West African colonial and postcolonial states have monopolized the production or marketing of introduced crops, leaving control over the older indigenous crops in the hands of the peasantry. The "dominated" crops are often cash crops of New World origin the export of which brings revenues to the state. One need only think of cocoa in Ghana, rubber in Liberia, or groundnuts in Senegal. Precisely because they were introduced into West Africa by foreign colonial powers and are now appropriated by emergent African states, cash crops have become symbols of social and economic domination. In many respects they are the modern-day equivalents of state crops in the Tawantinsuyu.

Local crops still being controlled by peasants, in contrast, tend to be indigenous West African domesticates with a long history of cultivation—plants such as finger millet, sorghum (Guinea corn), yams, and African rice. They have not been the subject of local state appropriation and export for one of several reasons: low yields, lack of industrial use, poor preservation, "exotic" taste (to Western palates), and so forth. With them production for use has remained more important than production for exchange. Thus a dual agricultural economy has developed with the overall effect of reinforcing state bureaucracies while maintaining the peasantry self-sufficient in food yet dependent on state government for services and consumer goods.

But revenue crops may well have profound effects that go beyond the political economy of states and governments. State patronage of crops often has serious consequences for the local, domestic economy (Linares 1985). It may transform family land tenure patterns, affect the sexual division of labor within the household, change patterns of labor reciprocity, alter practices of storage and consumption, substitute some local ritual uses for others, and introduce new forms for commerce. How these processes unfolded in the households of Inka farmers was touched on by Murra in his discussion of labor service obligations to the state (Murra 1961, 1975a, 1975b, 1978). Here I concentrate to a greater degree than Murra did on processes of change at the village and conjugal family level.

The following discussion involves a comparison of the role of rice with the role of groundnuts (peanuts in American English) in the organization of production and consumption among the Jola of southern Senegal.[1] Rice

---

[1] Jola appear in the literature as, for example, "Diola," "Joola," and "Djola." Previously, I have used "Diola." Here I have switched to Jola, using the orthography recommended by CLAD for writing the Senegalese languages. The term "Joola" seems absurd to me; the long "o" is inappropriate. At any rate, Jola is a Wolof name for various subgroups who call themselves by different terms: Kujamaat, Esudadu, Banjal, and so forth.

is the ancient, culturally elaborated, and basic subsistence crop; groundnuts are a recent foreign introduction of limited ritual use. The purpose of this comparison is to show that groundnut cultivation has had a profound effect on political processes and on the social division of labor. It has created a dual agricultural economy. Being a stateless people (Colson 1975), the Jola offer a nice contrast to the centralized government and hierarchical society of the Tawantinsuyu.

A Historical Sketch

The Jola are a coterie of about 300,000 cultivators occupying the marshy terrain known as Lower Casamance. This region covers 7,340 square kilometers of the southwestern corner of Senegal, on both sides of the Casamance River (Linares 1992:5–7). It is bounded on the north by Gambia, on the south by Guinea Bissau, and on the west by the sea. On the east, the Soungrougrou River separates the Jola from the Manding peoples, who occupy the Middle Casamance. Early Portuguese and French explorers referred to the whole area from Senegambia to Liberia as the Southern Rivers (Rodney 1970:1–38). At least seventeen major rivers flow through this area from the Fouta Djalon mountains on their way to the sea, creating an aquatic landscape marked by numerous tributaries, tidal channels (*marigots*), and islands.

Lower Casamance itself was once a secondary center of diversification of the indigenous species of African rice, *Oryza glaberrima*. According to Portères (1950, 1962), this species was cultivated more than two thousand years ago along the Niger River in the present state of Mali. At some later time, it was taken across the Fouta Djalon into the deltas of the Southern Rivers. In the process, *O. glaberrima* lost its primitive floating character and developed new salt-resistant qualities. According to this theory, the cultivation originally practiced in the Casamance and adjacent rivers entailed management of water. Fast-maturing upland varieties were a secondary specialization (Harris 1976). By implication, Portères's theory reverses the widely held idea, first proposed coherently by Boserup (1965), that intensive systems of irrigated agriculture based on maximum use of labor and land resources evolved later than more extensive systems.

The Jola were important in the precolonial cultivation of *O. glaberrima*. The oldest account we have of a Portuguese voyage to the region already mentions rice being grown there. Written in the 1450s, Zurara's account describes large fields planted in rice: "all that country looked to them [the Portuguese] as having the aspects of a *marais* [pond]" (Zurara 1960:246).

Although Zurara may have been referring to the mouth of the Gambia and not to the Casamance, both areas were inhabited by Falupos. Falupos (Felupes, and others) was the general term given by the Portuguese explorers to the Jola. A bare fity years after Zurara, Pacheco Pereira (1956) and Valentim Fernandes (1951) referred to the Falupos of the coast as having lots of rice. That this rice was probably wet rice grown in standing water can be inferred from Almada's visit to the area about 1570 (Mark 1985:14–15). In making their rice fields, he says, the blacks construct dikes of earth for fear of the tides. Once "the rice has sprouted, they pull it out and transplant it in land that is less inundated, where the rice yields" (Almada 1964:57). Almada seems to have been confused about the reasons for transplanting rice, which should be put into more, rather than less, flooded land. But this may be because rice was not grown in Cabo Verde, where Almada was born, until several centuries later. It was simply imported into these islands from the nearby African coast (Lauer 1969).

In 1685, de la Courbe again described the land occupied by Falupos as covered with "fields of rice located all along the river; they are divided by small walkways from space to space that prevent the running out of the water; after it rains, one sees the rice, which grows in the water" (1913: 208–9). This amounts, of course, to a classical description of diked paddy fields.

The rice being grown at this time was almost certainly O. glaberrima. Asian rice, O. sativa, was not introduced until later. It was brought to the Southern Rivers, probably from the Portuguese possessions in India, Goa and Cochin, by the end of the sixteenth century. Although O. sativa was certainly grown in medieval Spain as early as the tenth century, it does not seem to have been grown as a major crop. This, plus the fact that O glaberrima was the sole rice species widely cultivated in West Africa until recently, argues against a pre-1500 introduction of Asian rice. Be that as it may, Asian rice was successfully introduced precisely into those areas where there was already a flourishing rice economy (Lauer 1969; Portères 1962). The substitution of one rice species for another seems to have caused little if any immediate social or ecological disruption. Despite obvious morphological differences, the technical and ecological requirements for the planting of the two species are similar. Furthermore, no special circumstances seem to have surrounded the introduction of Asian rice. The new cultivar diffused gradually and imperceptibly, being neither promoted nor discouraged by the Europeans. Had Asian rice been encouraged in order, let us say, to increase production for provision to the slave ships, a different pattern might have emerged.

Today, most West African peoples practice extensive bush-fallow cultivation of introduced *O. sativa*. Though still grown in many places, *O. glaberrima* is becoming a relict crop. It is more hardy than, and under some conditions as productive as the Asian species. But it is more difficult to pound manually with a standard mortar and pestle. In any case, among the Jola, *O. glaberrima* varieties were dominant within the memory of living elders and are still grown today.

The groundnut or peanut (*Arachis hypogaea*) is a lowland South American cultivar (see Pickersgill and Heiser 1977). It was brought into West Africa perhaps as early as the sixteenth century by the Portuguese, probably via Brazil. Prior to the 1830s, groundnut cultivation in the whole of the Southern Rivers was negligible (Brooks 1975). After this date, Gambia took the lead in producing and exporting it to Britain. In England, as well as later in the United States and France, the oil and fat from the groundnut were used in the manufacture of soap and candles. It may also have served as a substitute for olive oil in some places.

Within the Casamance, groundnuts were first cultivated in the lands occupied by the Manding. By the 1860s, the town of Sedhiou in the Middle Casamance had become a major exporter of groundnuts under French commercial control. The Jola of Lower Casamance did not adopt the groundnut until the beginning of the twentieth century, at the same time as they were being converted to Islam by Manding clerics. In fact, the spread of Islam and groundnuts went hand in hand. Thus the Jola entered the cash economy later than many neighboring peoples (Mark 1978:1). Once the Jola and the Manding stopped fighting in the 1890s, they started trading with each other. After failing to dominate the Jola by force, the Manding began to influence them in religious and commercial ways.

Groundnut cultivation, according to Mark, was initially taught to the Jola by Manding traders. There were, and still are, important differences between Manding and Jola society (Linares 1981, 1984, 1992). Briefly, the Manding of Gambia and Middle or Upper Casamance are a complex society. They are characterized by formal social classes, including agrarian slaves in the past, by a legacy of centralized states managed by ruling elites, by the Central role played by Islam in their social and political organization, and by their attempts to subjugate coastal peoples like the Jola (Quinn 1972; Schaffer and Cooper 1980; Wright 1977). The Jola are a stateless people; they have acephalous polities. Their villages are dispersed, and their society is organized along territorial and kinship ties, not hierarchically. Thus the Jola's first exposure to groundnuts came from an expansionist and stratified society bent on spreading the Muslim faith. As late as the end of the nineteenth century, the Manding had actually used Jola slaves to grow groundnuts as a cash crop.

State and Household Crops among the Jola   165

The French colonial government also encouraged groundnut production among the Jola after 1910. Not only was groundnut oil needed in France, but also the colonial administration wanted Casamance to be self-supporting, and local merchants agitated for new markets. These were standard arguments for pushing cash crops. The Jola themselves saw groundnut cultivation as a way of getting cash to purchase European goods. But the fact remains that groundnuts would not have had such an impact were it not for the French colonial policy of increasing taxation and actively promoting the new crop. Between 1918 and 1920 the head tax was increased from 5 to 10 francs, and collection became more vigorous (Mark 1985:105). Thus the French policy involved creating needs for new goods, providing actual incentives in the form of seed, storage facilities, and loans, and backing the whole thing with taxation enforced by the military. Roads were built to connect trading and administrative centers such as Bignona and Ziguinchor. It is interesting to note that (as in Tawantinsuyu) many of these roads were built by corveé labor. Even in the worst years of the depression, groundnut production continued to mount. This trend is still going on, with obvious and often negative consequences.

In 1964 I was able to interview elders from the village of Jipalom, located in one of the mixed rice and groundnut Jola sub-regions north of the river known as the Kajamutay. The Kujamaat (the singular form is Ajamaat), still remembered when groundnuts were first planted around the turn of the century. At that time, some Jipalom men belonging to one of the *eluup* ("house," or agnatic group) decided to clear and cultivate a small plot which they then owned in common. The idea came to them while traveling in Gambia and seeing the Manding. When the groundnuts were ripe and ready to harvest, however, nobody knew what to do. At first the entire plants were pulled out and brought home in bunches; the nuts were then detached from the roots by hand. The crop was then winnowed in special baskets, like rice. Thus groundnuts were initially processed like rice, and like rice they were brought into the domestic domain. But, unlike rice, groundnuts were planted in communal fields. Nowadays groundnuts are processed directly in the fields, and from there they are sold to oil processing factories. Yet their cultivation still involves more group effort than does rice.

The expansion of groundnut cultivation in Jipalom was due to a particularly enterprising mature man we will call Fofana. Born in Jipalom, Fofana had been raised by matrilateral kin in the nearby village of Balandine. Balandine had in 1907 been declared a French administrative post, and a garrison had been established there to enforce the payment of the head tax. As late as the beginning of World War I (1914–15), the Kujamaat were still to be completely "pacified"; there were pockets of resistance to payment of the head tax (Roche 1976:336–54). By 1916, the Balandine post was presumed to have forty soldiers lodged in twenty roundhouses. In Balandine, the young Fofana had started to work jointly with a French trader, helping him sell merchandise among the Jola of the region. Fofana eventually moved back to Jipalom when the Europeans gave him the prestigious post of *chef de village;* but he continued to work with the French trader. Sometime around the 1920s, Fofana hired several Manjaku from Guinea Bissau, where groundnuts had been grown since the 1840s, and brought them up to Jipalom. The Manjaku were set to cutting large tracts of forest. The transformation of the plateau lands had begun in earnest.

Essentially, then, groundnut cultivation north of the Casamance River was deliberately encouraged by outsiders: colonial officers, Manding middlemen, Manjaku tree cutters, and Jola entrepreneurs like Fofana. Hesitant as the first stage of groundnut cultivation may have been, it was soon to become a dominant cash crop, produced on land owned and worked in very different ways than was paddy land.

Ownership and Usufruct in the Kajamutay

A bird's-eye view of the lands extending north from the Casamance River immediately reveals a striking contrast. An irregular mosaic of bunded paddy fields dominates the low-lying alluvial lands; a symmetrical pattern of larger, more open fields dominates the sandy, lightly forested plateaus. This contrast corresponds to two agricultural systems, one permanent and intensive, the other shifting and extensive. Because both systems have been described in some detail before (Linares 1970, 1981, 1985, 1992; Pélissier 1966), I simply point out the main features of land tenure and technology.

The rice fields are collectively known as *biit*. They are finely differentiated into several categories: nurseries (*kuyolen*), paddies lightly inundated by rainwater (the *biit* proper), paddies that receive a great deal of runoff (the *kuyelen*), paddies that are on slightly raised ground (the *sibaaf*), and, finally, a whole category of fields once recovered from the mangrove (the *weng*). When I first visited the Jola in the 1960s, all these lands were being intensively cultivated. With years of drought in the late 1960s, the 1970s, and 1980s, however, large sections of the *biit* and *sibaaf,* all of the *weng,* and a great number of nurseries have been abandoned. During the worst years of the drought only the *kuyelen* fields yielded anything. Whether Jipalom's rice system will ever return to its earlier condition is open to question. Nonetheless, the productive process remains, at least in principle, the same.

When a young man marries he is given an adequate number of parcels in each of the aforementioned categories by his closest male kin (father, father's brother, and so on). Immediately, the young man assigns most of the fields to his new wife for her to work. He keeps only a few for himself to feed strangers, pay for social obligations, and in the old days exchange for cattle. As his needs increase during the developmental cycle of his domestic group, he is given more parcels. In some regions, Jola women have rights of disposition as well as rights of usufruct over land, but in the Kajamutay region they do not. A widow can, however, remarry within her deceased husband's agnatic group and retain usufruct rights to the same land she worked. An elderly woman can also stay and live with her sons, continuing to work the same parcels she had always cultivated. At her death, it is her sons, and not her co-wife's sons, who inherit these parcels (this is *per stirpes* inheritance). In addition, a divorced woman may borrow land from distant agnates living in her own natal village. And, finally, all sons have the right to borrow extra fields from their mother's real or classificatory brothers. Within paddy cultivation, then, women have important rights to use or gain access to land and to dispose of its product.

Men of all generations have permanent rights to paddy land. Adult married men are the most secure, especially when their children are of working age (in Chayanov's terms, when they have low dependency ratios). But even old men are never alienated from the means of production. Only when totally disabled by age or disease do they actually stop working in the rice fields. Everyone in Jola society has access to land and labor. There are no landless or dispossessed members of society. Such differences in landed wealth as exist among individuals are due to differential inheritance, not to the appropriation of the productive forces by a privileged class or group of rulers, as in hierarchically organized societies such as the Inka.

For groundnuts, the land tenure system is quite different. Women have no rights of usufruct. Men cultivate on bush-fallow fields (see Boserup 1965:15). Both the fallow and the cultivation periods are short, two to six years. The general term for the groundnut field is *karamba*, the same term used for a forest. Although there is a way to describe land that is resting, there are no special terms for old and young fallow. This lack of semantic differentiation contrasts with the elaborate categorization of rice fields. Within the village, every man owns two to four sizable *karamba* fields; one or two he inherited from his father, the rest he cleared himself. It should be noted, however, that land close at hand is seldom sufficient to tide a person over the complete fallow cycle. Individuals frequently must borrow parcels elsewhere. They do this mostly from friends, seldom relatives, living in one of the villages to the north where the land is drier and people cultivate only groundnuts and millet. The friends are usually Manding, or Jola who have acquired Manding ways. Land is not rented but lent in exchange for gifts and the obligation to reciprocate at some future date. This system is possible because Islamic values stressing hospitality and generosity have helped create wide networks of friendship which the Kujamaat use to their own advantage. As we see below, the introduction of groundnuts and the process of Islamization went hand in hand. Yet the connection between groundnuts and Islam is not ritual but social, not direct but indirect: a historical by-product of other forces.

Production

Rice production in the Kajamutay is based on a balanced gender division of labor within the household. With rice, the division of labor is task specific, but it is not crop specific as for groundnuts. Briefly, men build up the bunds, ridge and fallow the land repeatedly, control the water flowing in and out of paddies, and pasture cattle on the land after it is harvested. Women weed the nurseries, pull out the plants and transplant them into inundated fields, and harvest and take home the product. Male and female members of the household coordinate their tasks carefully, always keeping in close communication. When the household needs extra help, especially at harvest time, it calls on larger teams (the *sikáf*). There are different *sikáf* membership rules for men and women. The most common female group is made up of in-married women (*kuseek*) who work for each other in rotation. The out-married women (*kuríimen*) seldom go back to their natal villages to cultivate for a male relative, except during special ritual occasions. Male groups consist of loose age classes; often, though not always, these are individuals who were initiated together.

Labor arrangements are really quite different when it comes to growing groundnuts. To begin with, production has been taken completely out of home and courtyard, and even out of the village, and placed in the fields. Further, the productive unit has changed from being centered on the conjugal pair to being centered on a pair of adult men, usually brothers, less frequently father and son. When asked to explain this, men often say that groundnut cultivation is more difficult than rice because there are more steps involved; hence work must be done in pairs. The real reason, however, seems to lie in an overall shift away from egalitarian relations toward more pronounced gender and status asymmetries as a result of Islamization,

Manding contact, and cash cropping (Linares 1992:172–203). In fact, work in the rice fields is harder; groundnut soils are usually light and easy to work.

In Table 7.1 I have listed labor inputs by gender in the cultivation of rice and groundnuts. As one can see at a glance, female labor is considerably more important in rice work. From a task-specific and complementary division of labor in rice cultivation, the Jipalom Jola have developed a more crop-specific and segregated system in groundnut cultivation. This situation has been accelerated by the adoption of the plow.

The use of the plow for work in groundnut fields began in earnest in Jipalom in the 1980s. In 1981 there were only three complete plow teams (with oxen and carts to transport the harvest) for a village with 115 male household heads. The teams cost about 100,000 francs CFA ($400.00), nearly two years of groundnut earnings. The owners were considered rich; much of their money came from remittances from their sons working in Dakar. They lent their plows, their oxen, or their carts to a few selected men. This was part of an emergent patronage system based on differences in wealth. By 1985, there were eleven complete plow teams. In addition to the whole team, some individuals owned only oxen, or only plows, or only carts. For the wives of those lucky individuals who owned oxen, however, there was more, rather than less, work in stock. Oxen were fed special diets of sorghum, which women must pound for hours every day—this is in addition to working in the fields, cooking, and caring for children. Whoever says plows make work lighter is only thinking of men.

It is calculated that what a man can accomplish in one month ridging and furrowing manually with the *kajandu,* or fulcrum shovel, he can do in four days with oxen and plow. As a consequence of the plow, agricultural work is transforming. Plows are replacing the men's work groups or *sikáf.* In 1964–66 a great deal of field preparation was done by large workbees, sometimes composed of all the men in the cluster of *eluup* that make up each of the Jipalom wards. They would work each other's groundnut fields,

Table 7.1. Jipalom labor inputs (adult days/ha) by gender

	1981, Women	1981, Men[a]	1964, Men[b]
Wet rice	85	—	42
Groundnuts	16	24	71

Sources: From Berger Report 1981. Additional information from my field notes of 1981.
[a]Field preparation using the ox-plow. Note that animal traction is only used in the groundnut fields.
[b]Field preparation using the long-handled fulcrum shovel or *kajandu.*

in rotation, for a feast and abundant millet beer. By 1981, however, few fields were being prepared this way. Individuals either did their own fields with the help of their sons or borrowed a plow in exchange, let us say, for the loan of a team of oxen. Once the few who had access to plows abandoned their reciprocal labor obligations, the whole system fell apart.

Exposed to new attitudes, new technologies and skills, in schools and cities, teenage boys have the self-confidence it takes to drive the oxen team and guide the plow. Their fathers, lost in admiration, often assured me that they themselves could never learn. Whether the new skills help to make the young men more independent of their fathers is questionable, however. Until he marries, and in the "Mandingized" areas for much longer, a young man is subordinate to his father. Subtle as it may be, this kind of subordination is being expressed in groundnut cultivation in other ways as well. One often sees a young man cultivating for a *marabout* (Islamic cleric) as part of his religious obligation, and to pay his respect. In addition, younger brothers often cultivate for older brothers, sons cultivate for their fathers, wage workers for absentee owners, and so forth.

Storage, Consumption, and the Circulation of Rice

There is much truth to the often-repeated assertion that the Jola do not sell their rice. This is not to deny that an active trade in rice existed during the nineteenth century. Especially in the Banjal area south of the Casamance River, the Jola were selling their rice to the Portuguese residing in Ziguinchor (Snyder 1981:115–18). When one lives in a village for a long time, one notes a constant informal exchange of rice among households. But this is only in times of plenty. For two decades at least, most Kujamaat have had to buy supplementary quantities of rice.

Nonetheless, in line with other values emphasizing frugality, self-sufficiency, and wealth, Jola attitudes toward the granary and the storage of rice are still very traditional, however one may want to define this fuzzy notion. After the rice is harvested and tied into bundles, it is taken home and stored in the granaries. Each wife has her own separate granary, or *buntuŋ*, a small structure with the kitchen underneath and a closed storage area on top. From her stores she feeds the family. The husband may also have a separate *buntuŋ* where he keeps the harvest from his special fields; this rice goes to feed strangers, to send out cultivators, and to save up for funerals and the *futamp* (initiation ceremony). Granaries are very secret places. Their contents are rarely shown to people outside the immediate household. It is thought that the grain will magically disappear if shown to strangers; the expression is that "the rice will run away." In a typical granary the rice harvests of different years are stored separately. No other crop but rice should be stored in bundled form. It is considered dangerous for grains of rice and other cereals (such as millet and sorghum) to get mixed up accidentally and be cooked together in the same pot. If millet is to be stored in the granary, it should be pounded and bagged beforehand. The general rule is against mixing the produce of the *biit* with the more recent products of the *karamba*.

The general word for a meal, *sinang*, also glosses as cooked rice. A Jola cannot conceive of a meal without rice, to which a sauce of palm oil, or occasionally fish or meat, is added. As noted above, it is absolutely taboo to cook rice with other grains in the same pot. If rice is accidentally mixed in cooking with other grains, a special spirit (*enáati*, sing.) "traps" the person that eats the food, making him or her swell up. Once a person has been trapped, the only way to undo the damage is to cook rice and tabooed grains in the same pot, mixed with a special neutralizing medicine. Rice can, however, be mixed with groundnuts and safely eaten. In fact, groundnuts are not considered *furiaf* (food), but *bakoloŋ* (condiments).

The inauspiciousness of mixing crop categories involves eating as well as cooking. Parents and their married children are prohibited from eating out of the same bowl lest the parents be trapped by a spirit called *Kujaama*, which brings severe stomach upsets (Sapir 1970). As with other Jola prohibitions, *Kujaama* guards the young couple, the newly founded household, from encroachment on its privacy and its resources by the elder generation. In general, older folks in the parental category can cook for the younger generation, but not the reverse. The usual procedure is for a woman to eat with her own young children, from the same bowl. When boys reach six to eight years of age, they eat with their fathers. In Jipalom a man eats together with his unmarried male children, sundry "nephews," younger brothers, and so on. Women often eat with their co-wives and their unmarried daughters. In the fields, men frequently share the same bowl, as long as they stand in the relation of brothers, or fathers and unmarried sons, to each other. The same, again, applies to women. Thus a great number of attitudes and prohibitions pervade the cooking and consumption of rice, whereas groundnuts are simply not considered to be food.

Traditionally millet was a minor crop. For many reasons, including drought, the Kujamaat Jola have been forced in the last two decades to eat more millet than they like. Millet requires less rainfall than rice and is also easier to grow. When I was first in the Casamance in 1961, people would often boast that they had never tasted millet. It was commonly recounted of the old man Fofana that when he visited Manding, or Mandingized Jola, and was offered millet for a meal, he would pretend to eat it but would discreetly drop it on the ground with the polite remark, "I am full." Nowadays it is still said that, in porridge or beer, millet is good tasting; but as food it is awful. During the worst years of drought it was served day after day until people grew so tired of it they would refuse to eat it. Some groups outside the Kajamutay have adopted millet as a staple more or less voluntarily; but even they identify rice with being Jola. Two other crops that have become increasingly important are manioc and maize, both of which are also more tolerant of drought conditions. Neither of them, however, are considered to be staple food.

Secular and Sacred Rituals

The Kujamaat have several festivities, such as hospitality, individual gift giving, or even marriage, at which rice is usually cooked and served, but the food preparation itself is not thought of as particularly sacred. In fact, like the potato in the economy of the Inka, rice among the Kujamaat Jola is a predominantly secular crop; its production is not surrounded by any special ceremonies, nor is it used to propitiate the shrines (*sináati*, pl.). Yet, as Bourdieu (1977) has pointed out, there is always a legitimating function to secular rituals. They help structure the principles of social reality by creating acceptance for rules or standards, such as the sexual division of labor and respect for elders. Secular rituals make the established order appear natural through constant and daily repetition of small routines of greeting, gift giving, and sharing. For these sorts of occasions, the Jola use cooked rice. Thus, a visiting stranger is given an overflowing bowl of rice to eat, an elder is taken an extra bowl with a special sauce, a husband is never given old rice, a child is fed rice porridge, considered special baby food. These individual acts of status recognition are voluntary; they involve relatives as well as persons who do not stand in kin relation to each other. Much more "marked" than these customary routines are the rice exchanges that take place at important life crises. These involve obligatory prestations in raw (uncooked) rice among different categories of kin. The two most important occasions are funerals and the *futamp*.

Essentially, the Kujamaat Jola recognize two categories of formal prestation. In the *kamaiñjor* (glossed as "getting to know each other") rice and cattle are brought in during a funeral and given to the immediate agnatic kin of the deceased to help with funeral expenses. The givers are the matrilateral kin: the collectivity of mother's brothers or (*sipaay*) and mother's sisters or (*siñaay*). They give to each of the deceased's sons individually.

In addition, the husbands of the out-married female agnates (*kuríimen*)—in effect the sons-in-law of the deceased—often contribute also. The *kamaiñor* prestations involve live animals, usually bulls, and many kilograms of unpounded raw rice. The *kamaiñor* really involves two recipient groups: the actual sons of the deceased, who receive help from their matrilateral kin, and the collectivity of agnates from the *eluup*, who are usually real or classificatory brothers of the dead person.

The second category of prestations is called the *kawol*, which can be glossed as "birth rights." It involves everything that goes out at a funeral, that is, what the sons and brothers of the deceased give to the matrilateral kin of the deceased. Again the amount given depends on the closeness of the relationship. *Kawol* is conceived of as a continuation of bridewealth payments. Marriage engenders this obligation, it is said, but in reality this happens two generations down: the sons of the deceased are helping to pay for the mother of the deceased, that is, for their grandmother. *Kawol* also involves prestations of live cattle and uncooked rice. In the Kajamutay the *kawol* prestations are fast disappearing with the coming of Islam. Nowadays, payments go out only to the *sipaay*, the deceased's immediate mother's brothers. Apparently *kawol* is now considered a pagan practice. Raw food seems to be less hospitable than cooked food: the former is taken away, the latter never is. At Muslim funerals the cattle are killed and the meat is distributed to visitors during the ceremony itself, or at the memorial services that take place six and forty days later. On all these occasions, cooked rice flour is mixed with sugar and distributed in lumps, together with kola nuts.

The *kamaiñor* and *kawol* also occur at the boys' initiation (*futamp*), which is supposed to take place every fifteen years or so. Because rice has been scarce due to the drought that lasted all through the 1970s and into the 1980s, Jipalom has had to postpone its *futamp* repeatedly; the last one was in 1958. Among the things expected to come in (*kamaiñor*) at a *futamp* are, again, animals, this time goats and chickens added to cattle; these are usually contributed by the *sipaay*. Pounded rice in great quantities is contributed by the *siñaay*. These same two groups, in turn, get some of the *kawol* prestations, including bulls for the *sipaay* and goats and unpounded rice for the *siñaay*. Thus, categories of kin who give also receive, in more or less balanced amounts. At a *futamp*, each head of household with more than one son being initiated may in the end contribute, raw and cooked, more than ten bulls and 500 kilograms of rice. Taking the whole village together, hundreds of bulls and many tons of rice may be consumed or given away.

Groundnuts do not enter the sphere of prestations. The connection that exists between groundnuts and Islamization is historical and indirect. There is a more direct connection between Islam and consumption of millet in the form of beer. It seems that in every society some particular product is used for making fermented beverages, to lubricate social relations. In fact, Murra (1960:397–99) mentions that this was one of the important uses to which maize was put by the Inka, to make *chicha* for the gods and the people. The non-Islamized Jola drink enormous amounts of palm wine and also use it to libate their spirits (Linares, in press). The Kujamaat Jola who have converted to Islam have had to give up palm wine; they have taken to millet beer (*bunkay*) instead. Although they claim that it is not alcoholic, it is obviously intoxicating. In Jipalom large amounts of millet beer are consumed in the sundry celebrations leading to the *futamp*. But on all these occasions it is served as a drink for guests, not as a sacred beverage.

Commerce

It is too early to predict exactly how groundnuts will ultimately change Jola society. Their greatest potential as an agent of change lies in their linkage to the "modern" commercial sector.

Until a decade ago, groundnut cooperatives bought the product, distributed seed, and provided credit for buying and also renting plows, oxen, and carts. The relationship with the state-owned cooperatives was problematic, however. Before 1961 the groundnut harvest was handled by a few local Jola middlemen. They bought from independent farmers and shipped the product to the Casamance regional capital of Ziguinchor. Then, in 1961, cooperatives were organized. Participation was at first voluntary. In 1967, ONCAD (Office National de Cooperation et d'Assistance au Developpement) took over and began managing the buying and selling processes authoritatively (Direction de l'Aide au Developpement 1973). For many years ONCAD controlled all aspects of the internal marketing of groundnuts, siphoning resources from rural areas to the cities by paying relatively low prices to the farmers (Gellar 1982:56). After years of corruption, neglect, and chaos, ONCAD was abolished in 1980 by the Senegalese National Assembly. After that date, the residents of Jipalom joined with residents of a neighboring village to form a "private" cooperative that sold groundnuts directly to the oil refinery in Ziguinchor. Regardless of the locus of control, private marketing groups are obviously a new and potentially revolutionary institution.

In this essay I have invoked Murra's (1960; 1978:36–48) contrast between an indigenous peasant crop and a foreign, state-dominated crop in order to explain some past and present realities among the Kujamaat Jola of Senegal. The point of the comparison is to show that cash crops not only are appropriated by the state but also often lead to the restructuring of social relations at the household as well as the state level.

Partly because of their isolation, their self-sufficiency, and their opposition to authority, the Kujamaat Jola were late to enter the Senegalese groundnut trade. Circumstances surrounding the introduction of groundnuts into the Kajamutay are complex. The Jola learned to cultivate groundnuts from the Manding, a stratified people. The French colonial administration also promoted groundnut cultivation through coercion, including raising the head tax so that the Jola would have to earn cash and enforcing payment by direct military force (Roche 1976). Then, in the 1920s and 1930s, the government introduced forced labor to build roads and bridges, which facilitated the transport of groundnuts to commercial centers. Exactly how this *corvée* worked at the village level is not at all clear, but we do know that compulsory labor was enforced by administrative sanctions and the penal code (Snyder 1981:128–29).

In the Kajamutay, the cultivation of groundnuts has proceeded at a fast pace despite increasing ecological problems (Loquay 1979, 1988). Links with the national government, and ultimately the French metropolis, have grown (Fatton 1987). Though no longer the only "critical resource of the Senegalese economy and the most important tax base of the Senegalese State" (Cruise O'Brien 1979:212), groundnuts are still extremely important. Because the Senegalese state is an immense urban bureaucracy—functionaries are almost half of all employees in the nation—the groundnut trade ultimately finances a civil service elite residing in the cities. Without forcing the comparison too far, there are obvious parallels with the efforts of the Tawantinsuyu to appropriate the cultivation of maize.

These parallels are even more marked in areas of Senegal north of Casamance controlled by the Mourides, a uniquely Senegalese, Muslim brotherhood. Here groundnuts are cultivated almost exclusively by disciples under the close supervision of a saintly leadership of charismatic officers (Copans 1980; Cruise O'Brien 1979). Thus groundnut cultivation *is* a religious obligation among the Mourides. It contributes directly to the prestige and power the leadership wields at the national level. In Casamance, groundnuts are a strictly secular crop. But they are the only form of ready cash available (besides wage labor) to the Jola of the Kajamutay. And cash doubtless brings prestige. Individuals who are wealthy, like Fofana, whose case was discussed earlier, have power.

In detail, however, there are many and basic differences between the case Murra discusses and the one I have described. The Jola who were sold to the Manding to work the groundnut field were agrarian slaves. The *yana* captives described by Murra (1975b) were mostly herders rather than farmers. Similarly, one should not confuse the corvée duties imposed by a culturally alien French administration on the Jola with the all-pervasive system of *mit'a* labor service in the Tawantinsuyu (Murra 1978:135–75). Third, unlike the Quechua peasantry who labored periodically in the lands of the state growing maize, the Jola peasantry cultivates its groundnuts on its own private land. The day may come, however, when the Senegalese state enforces its new "eminent domain" laws (Van der Klei 1978), or when groundnut land becomes scarce and the Jola need to borrow forest land owned by the state.

Groundnut cultivation has already produced marked changes among the Jola at the village and household level. Thus it is important to summarize the traditional wet-rice growing system and show what other systems of production emerged later on.

Wet rice is the ancient and basic food staple of the Jola. Like root crops in the Andes, African rice permitted colonization—in this case, of the deltas of the Southern Rivers. By the time the first Portuguese made contact in the middle of the fifteenth century, *O. glaberrima* was being cultivated in Lower Casamance with the same tools and techniques found there today. Despite the ravages of the slave trade, the continuous wars with the Manding, and conflicts first with the Portuguese and then with the French, the Jola on both sides of the Casamance River continue to grow wet rice by intensive techniques. The introduction of the Asian species, *O. sativa*, apparently had very little effect on the land tenure system. Agriculture continues to be based on individual male ownership of parcels in different land categories, with important usufructuary rights being extended to women. Production depends on a balanced division of labor within the household; men and women perform different but complementary tasks. Nobody in Kujamaat society is dispossessed of land or the right to work it. Although there are marked differences in the size of different people's estates, they are based as much on the vagaries of *per stirpes* inheritance as they are on an individual's capacity to accumulate fields during his lifetime through pledging and other forms of exchange.

In contrast, groundnuts are grown by shifting, bush-fallow cultivation. Beyond the fields a man owns in his natal village, he has access to extra fields through the manipulation of friendship ties based on the wide community of Islam. Groundnut cultivation is gender-specific; women have no usufructuary rights to groundnut lands and few duties with the system. Increasingly, the plow is contributing to accentuate the sexual division of labor and to eliminate traditional forms of male cooperation in agricultural work.

It is not only the system of production, but also those of consumption and circulation, which differ between the two crops. Rice is consumed as the daily food; it is culturally elaborated with respect to patterns of hospitality and status recognition. It enters the sphere of circulation through its use in rituals that mark important rites of passage. Together with cattle, rice is the basis of all reciprocity between categories of kin, thus legitimating the social structure. In contrast, groundnuts do not enter the domestic domain, nor are they used in ritual functions. They are an alien crop; their association is with the world outside the village, be it French or Manding.

To conclude, the introduction of a prestige, state-dominated crop led to the creation of a dual agricultural economy among both the Inka and the Jola. A subsistence sector grows a traditional crop by long-established methods of labor reciprocity. A "foreign sector" produces crops for the state under a different system of land tenure, labor organization, and technology. Despite enormous differences in political organization, both the Senegalese and Tawantinsuyu governments decided not to interfere with the peasantry's capacity to feed itself. In both instances the state also assumed the functions of a market. It may well be a strategy of most nascent bureaucracies to appropriate the production or marketing of export crops while relying on the peasants to feed themselves from their own harvests (see also Meillassoux 1981:95).

References

Almada, André Álvares de
    1964   *Tratado Breve dos Rios de Guiné do Cabo Verde*. Ed. A. Brásio.
    [1594] Lisbon: Editorial L.I.A.M.

Berger Report
    1981   Program for the Development of the Baila *Marigot* in Casamance. Report prepared for Ministry of Rural Development (Senegal) and U.S.A.I.D.

Boserup, Ester
    1965   *The Conditions of Agricultural Growth: The Economics of Agrarian Change under Population Pressure*. Chicago: Aldine.

Bourdieu, Pierre
    1977   *Outline of a Theory of Practice*. Cambridge: Cambridge University Press.

Brooks, George E.
    1975   Peanuts and colonialism: Consequences of the commercialization of peanuts in West Africa, 1830–1870. *Journal of African History* 16(1):29–54.

Cheneau-Loquay, Annie
  1988 Les relations entre l'espace el l'énergie en Casamance. In *Energie et Espace au Sénégal,* Ph. Grenier and Chaneau-Loquay, eds., tome 2, pp. 109–243. Travaux et Documents de Géographie Tropicale, no. 62. Bordeaux: CEGET-CNRS.
Colson, Elizabeth
  1975 *Tradition and Contract: The Problem of Order.* London: Heinemann Educational Books.
Copans, Jean
  1980 *Les Marabouts de l'Arachide: La confrérie Mouride et les paysans du Sénégal.* Paris: Le Sycomore.
Courbe, Sieur de la [Jajolet de la Courbe]
  1913 *Premier Voyage du Sieur de la Courbe fait à la coste d'Afrique en*
  [1685] *1685.* Ed. P. Cultru. Paris: Champion, Larose.
Cruise O'Brien, Donald B.
  1979 Ruling class and peasantry in Senegal, 1960–1976: The politics of a monocrop economy. In *The Political Economy of Underdevelopment: Dependence in Senegal,* pp. 209–27. London: Sage.
Direction de l'Aide au Developpement
  1973 *Sénégal 1971–1972.* Dossier d'Information Economique. Paris.
Fatton, Jr., Robert
  1987 *The Making of a Liberal Democracy: Senegal's Passive Revolution, 1975–1985.* Boulder: Lynne Rienner Publishers, Inc.
Fernandes, Valentim
  1951 *Déscription de la Côte Occidentale d'Afrique (Sénégal au Cap de*
  [1519] *Monte).* Th. Monod, A. Teixeira da Mota, and R. Mauny, eds. Centro de Estudos da Guiné Portuguesa, no. 11. Bissau.
Gellar, Sheldon
  1982 *Senegal: An African Nation between Islam and the West.* Boulder, Colo.: Westview Press.
Harris, David
  1976 Traditional systems of plant food production and the origins of agriculture in West Africa. In J. R. Harlan, J. M. J. DeWet, and A. B. L. Stemmler, eds., *Origins of African Plant Domestication,* pp. 311–56. The Hague: Mouton.
Lauer, Joseph J.
  1969 Rice in the history of the lower Gambia-Geba area. M. A. thesis, Department of History, University of Wisconsin, Madison.
Linares, Olga F.
  1970 Agriculture and Diola society. In Peter R. M. McLoughlin, ed., *African Food Production Systems: Cases and Theory,* pp. 195–227. Baltimore: Johns Hopkins University Press.
  1981 From tidal swamp to inland valley: On the social organization of wet rice cultivation among the Diola of Senegal. *Africa* 5(2): 557–95.
  1984 Households among the Diola of Senegal: Should norms enter by the front or back doors? In R. Netting and R. Wilk, eds., *Household*

     Changes in Space and Time, pp. 405–45. Berkeley: University of California Press.
1985 Cash crops and gender constructs: The Jola of Senegal, *Ethnology* 24(2):83–93.
1992 *Power, Prayer and Production: The Jola of Casamance, Senegal.* Cambridge: Cambridge University Press.
(in press) Palm oil versus palm wine: Symbolic and economic dimensions. For Papers from the Symposium, Food and Nutrition in the Tropical Forest, Paris 1991.

Loquay, Annie
1979 Thionck-Essyl en Basse Casamance: Evolution recente de la gestion des resources renouvables. Thèse, CEGET, Université de Bordeaux III. (see also Cheneau-Loquay)

Mark, Peter
1978 Urban migration, cash cropping, and calamity: The spread of Islam among the Diola of Boulouf (Senegal), 1900–1940. *African Studies Review* 21(2):1–14.
1985 *A Cultural, Economic, and Religious History of the Basse Casamance since 1500.* Studien zur Kulturkunde, no. 78. Franz Steiner Verlag Wiesbaden GMBH, Stuttgart.

Meillassoux, Claude
1981 *Maidens, Meal and Money: Capitalism and the Domestic Community.* Cambridge: Cambridge University Press.

Murra, John V.
1960 Rite and crop in the Inca state. In Stanley Diamond, ed., *Culture in History: Essays in Honor of Paul Radin*, pp. 393–407. New York: Columbia University Press.
1961 Guaman Poma de Ayala: A seventeenth-century Indian's account of Andean civilization. *Natural History*, pts. 1 and 2 (Sept. and Oct.): 35–47, 53–63.
1975a En torno a la estructura política de los inka. In *Formaciones económicas y políticas del mundo andino*, pp. 23–43. Lima: Instituto de Estudios Peruanos.
1975b Nueva información sobre las poblaciones yana. In *Formaciones Económicas y políticas del mundo andino*, pp. 225–42. Lima: Instituto de Estudios Peruanos.
1978 *La Organización Económica del Estado Inca.* Mexico: siglo XXI editores, s.a.

Pacheco Pereira, Duarte
1956 Esmeraldo de Situ Orbis. Ed. R. Mauny. Centro de Estudos da Guiné
[1506–8] Portuguesa, no. 19. Bissau.

Pélissier, Paul
1966 *Les paysans du Sénégal: Les civilisations agraires du Cayor à la Casamance.* Saint-Yrieix, France: Imprimerie Fabrègue.

Pickersgill, B., and C. B. Heiser
1977 Origin and distribution of plants domesticated in the New World

tropics. In Charles A. Reed, ed., *Origins of Agriculture,* pp. 803–35. The Hague: Mouton.

Portères, Roland
- 1950 Vieilles agricultures de l'Afrique "intertropicale." *Agronomie Tropicale* 5(9–10):489–507.
- 1962 Berceaux agricoles primaires sur le continent africain. *Journal of African History* 3(2):195–210.

Quinn, Charlotte A.
- 1972 *Mandingo Kingdoms of the Senegambia.* Evanston: Northwestern University Press.

Roche, Christian
- 1976 *Conqûete et Résistance des Peuples de Casamance (1850–1920).* Dakar and Abidjan: Les Nouvelles Editions Africaines.

Rodney, Walter
- 1970 *A History of the Upper Guinea Coast, 1545–1800.* Oxford: Oxford University Press.

Sapir, J. David
- 1970 Kujaama: Symbolic separation among the Diola-Fogny. *American Anthropologist* 72(6):1330–48.

Schaffer, M., and C. Cooper
- 1980 *Mandinko: The Ethnography of a West African Holy Land.* New York: Holt, Rinehart and Winston.

Snyder, Francis G.
- 1981 *Capitalism and Legal Change: An African Transformation.* New York: Academic Press.

Van der Klei, Jos
- 1978 Customary land tenure and land reform: The rise of new inequalities among the Diola of Senegal. *African Perspectives* 2:35–44.

Wright, Donald R.
- 1977 *The Early History of Niumi: Settlement and Foundation of a Mandinka State on the Gambia River.* Athens: Ohio University, African Series, no. 32.

Zurara, Gomes Eanes de
- 1960 *Chronique de Guinée.* Trans. L. Bourdon. Institut Français d'Afrique
- [1453?] Noire, Memoires no. 60. Dakar, Senegal.

CHAPTER EIGHT

Women, Status, and High Office in African Polities

Ronald Cohen

There has been a burgeoning of interest in women's roles and their changing statuses since the 1970s by anthropologists (see, for example, Rosaldo 1974; Schlegel 1972; Whyte 1978). These works and efforts by many others have turned the topic of gender roles into a subspecialty, with its own beliefs, assumptions, favorite citations and recitations, as well as issues and possibly even its most favored answers. In this regard, it is no different than other well-known approaches whose questions and answers are often forecast by the paradigm.

The issues I discuss here are, first, the validity of arguments for and against widespread male dominance in human cultural traditions; second, the related division of male and female spheres into private and public domains; and finally, the related issues of women holding high political offices in early African states. To do this I examine the concepts of authority and gender relations, then utilize these ideas to analyze the division of human activities into private and public spheres. The materials are African because I have worked in West Africa for *many* years; I utilize data on other regions much less often and with less familiarity.

I theorize, first, that male dominance in authority relations is the most widespread form of evolved cultural tradition governing the sexes as actors in African precolonial sociopolitical contexts. And, second, that I argue in the public sphere African cultures, especially the more complex systems,

---

I collected material for this essay from both library and field research, including a 1983–84 review of ethnographic sources on women's private and public roles in a sample of African societies. I am grateful to Christopher Rippel for helping with this review.

used female gender to symbolize a wide assortment of constitutional principles essential to the unity and continuity of the political order and the proper exercise of leadership.

Male Authority

Several writers (Lamphere 1974; Rosaldo 1974) accept in whole or in part the proposition that, for all human societies, authority resides more in male roles than in female ones, that is, when we compare activities, actions, and control over scarce resources, more are given over to men's control than to women's. Furthermore, men's activities seem to be more highly valued when overall comparisons of gender domains are made within any one cultural tradition. As Michelle Rosaldo puts it,

> male as opposed to female activities are *always* recognized as predominantly important, and cultural systems give authority and value to the roles and activities of men.... there is little reason to believe that there are, or once were, societies of primitive matriarchs, societies in which women predominated in the same way that men predominate in the societies we actually know. An asymmetry assigned to women and men appears to be universal. (1974:19, emphasis added)

It is important to insert the caveat here that Rosaldo is referring to societies lacking in active, effective movements for female emancipation. Industrialized societies are changing rapidly to achieve more equal status for men and women, in such a way that gender is not considered morally relevant in terms of status, authority, power, and the division of labor.

No one, including Rosaldo (1974), taking this position is so naive as to assume congruency between power and authority. Given evidence of male authority and its extremely widespread occurrence, all writers accept and even highlight the capacity of women to seek power, to influence, even to trivialize male authority: women usurping male authority has been a well-documented feature of social life even in the most overtly male-dominant cultural traditions. And such observations are not new. Hearne (1958), the early traveler in the Canadian Arctic, observed that Chipeweyan women claim to have menstruated several times a month. Since they are enjoined to remain out of camp, and away from male authority during such periods, we can easily interpret these events as female attempts to manipulate cultural directions and undermine or subvert male authority. Major Denham (1826:231) comments that in Africa of the the 1820s a Kanuri bride's girlfriends placed her shoe above the bridal chamber so that the groom might pass under her foot, giving superior power in the marriage to this wife. Grooms were warned, he says, to watch out for the shoe and remove it (see also Cohen 1971).[1]

For present purposes, however, I wish to avoid the topic of women's power seeking and the successes they have achieved in all human societies in subverting male authority. The well-documented and unsurprising fact that some women are successful power seekers is important for understanding how men and women react to their roles in real-world situations. But it is outside the more fundamental question of authority itself and its division among persons and sex roles in society. Authority relations emerge from social evolution—from constellations of recurrent activities and incremental changes that are produced and reproduced when humans interact with a living tradition. In Africa male authority in both public and private spheres is an extremely widespread phenomenon. Why this should be so, indeed whether it is so, is at issue.

In recent writings on this topic, especially in the African literature, a tendency has developed to deny male authority and to interpret differences as complementary rather than authoritative. In this view, many traditional African societies practiced interdependence and parity in male and female roles, especially economic activities. As Sudarkasa puts it for traditional African materials,

> there does not seem to be a basis for holding that women's occupations were usually thought to be "inferior" to those of men, although such occupations were usually thought to be inappropriate for men, just as men's occupations were normally consi- dered inappropriate for women. The point here is that the maintenance of separate occupational domains for the two sexes did not automatically imply a hierarchical relationship. . . . if one were to apply the "beast of burden" stereotypes to women, one should apply it also to men. (1982:280)

This passage should be compared to Rosaldo's (1974:20–21), which concludes that some or all male activities are generally considered more important than those carried out by women. Concomitantly, there are always arenas of activities deemed important for society as a whole from which women are barred by authoritative rules of exclusion.

Using cross-cultural survey data, Whyte (1978:167) concludes that for

---

[1] Wherever possible I use observations of male–female relations made before the colonial period. Although the observers were mostly men and their interpretations were often biased and invalid, I assume that reported behaviors and customary actions are accurate.

a large sample of societies there are *none* in which women are reported as generally dominant over males. Instead, the data show a variation from widespread male dominance to broadly based equality and circumscribed female dominance for specific activities. He suggests, therefore, that we cannot assume universal male authority over women, nor should we look for a universal explanation of this widely various phenomenon. Nevertheless, it is significant and inescapable that some logical possibilities, such as generalized female dominance across a wide spectrum of activities, do not occur. Human sexual differentiation, then is nonrandom; it displays regularity and constraints, such that not all of the logically possible outcomes can be observed in real-world situations. Why? Questioning nonrandom distribution and attempting to explain why patterns exist is the job of science. To suggest that such occurrences do not exist or that their identification is based on mistaken assumptions is counterfactual. Worse still, to suggest that these regularities have no explanation is to eschew the scholar's responsibility to search for explanations.

Having gone this far, I wish to make clear my position on patterned regularity. It is impossible in my view to support any assertion or conclusion of universal male dominance. Goldberg's (1973) rather sensationalistic writing on this topic is clearly invalidated by Whyte's (1978) more careful empirical testing. In a significant minority of societies, men-women relations are relatively equal in dyadic and family-relation terms (Whyte 1978:92). Still, men tend to monopolize or predominate in the realm of politics. In 98 percent of Whyte's (1978:5) world sample of societies, non-kin political leaders were men only or from both sexes with men more numerous and more powerful. The twenty seven societies in which this was not the case clearly indicate that Goldberg's (1973) thesis of universal male dominance cannot be upheld. Still, there is a very strong association between male gender and non-kin political roles in human society that cannot readily be brushed aside.

My interpretation of these data parallels those of Rosaldo (1974). I theorize that division of labor in early hominid societies had survival value that favored biosocial factors supporting the differentiation of the sexes. The interaction was in all likelihood a cybernetic one. Biological capacities to differentiate helped to support and develop social differentiation; political-economic differences helped in turn to select for more biological differences. The question of which came first is both irrelevant for present purposes and outside my competence to discuss. Nevertheless, once in place such distinctions helped to determine further differentiation of public and private spheres. These include males wandering farther from camps and male public-arena socialization that ejects men (more often than women) from the nurturant private home into more public competition with one another (see Chodorow 1974; Rosaldo 1974). Given such differences as a starting baseline, further evolution of society associated with agriculture involved increased fertility and more nurturance, along with the increased value of women's labor in the household and the fields, and an increased frequency of polygyny and bridewealth. In other terms, this led to an increased tendency to view women as scarce resources for labor and the production of new descent group members as well as a more elaborate and hierarchical set of relations in the public life of communities with men coming to predominate in the authority structures of family, descent groups, households, and community.

Recent work on polygyny tends to support these generalizations. Reitz and Burton (1983) have found a significant and close relationship among polygyny, technology, and the sexual division of labor. Where women are a significant factor in agricultural production and technology is simple, polygyny is predictably more frequent in a society's traditions. Increased use of the plow decreases the incidence of polygyny. In other words, where women are valuable resources for farm labor there is a tendency for the society to evolve rules allowing men to be married to more than one woman and to control women as a labor force on their husband's farm. The material basis for simple agricultural production is therefore a selective pressure in the direction of polygyny and a hierarchical relation between wives as laborers and husbands as managers.

This does not mean that we can always predict women's status from a few easily observed indicators. Whyte's conclusions are too well supported to allow us that privilege. In effect, we now know (Whyte 1978:173) that there is no such thing as "women's status." As a group, women hold a variety of statuses and positions across societies, and these are not easily classified into a single category or indicated by one predictor. It is therefore wise to speak of women's statuses and to envisage these as variable in terms of the importance accorded them, the activities included, and the degree of hierarchy involved in male–female relations.

Public and Private Relations

Private Sphere

In general, African men as either husbands or compound heads have the final authority in the private sphere. They have greater degrees of power delivered into their hands by the legally binding rules of the community. Women can be controlled, inherited, and remarried by the decisions of their husband's lineage and even given to male friends as part of household hospitality. They can be divorced for no reason, whereas women must give reasons. Women must prepare and deliver food to the men of the household, often using servile body postures as part of the formal etiquette of relationships. A male household head must be respected and obeyed. He can adjudicate disputes, mete out punishments, and make agreements for the household and its members to the wider community, obligating all household members (male as well as female). In traditional Ashanti it is a capital offense for a wife to call a husband a fool (but not vice versa), since he is viewed as her protector and, at least to some extent, her provider. In Nupe and the western Sahel in general, wives are required by custom to report to, and discuss, or even request permission of the husband and household head to leave the household for legitimate purposes. In the private sphere, where much has been made of women's capacity to subvert male authority and exert or achieve power, there is a clearly and easily coded general tendency for authority to rest in men's roles across a wide spectrum of activities.

Bridewealth is ubiquitous in Africa. No matter how one argues the case, bridewealth involves the exchange of resources for valued objects or services. A woman may refuse to be involved, although actual instances of refusal at first marriage are rarely reported. Still, the very notion of bridewealth involves an assumption that a man or his lineage obtains rights in the woman concerned. Those rights include control, that is, authority, over the woman's future activities (work and child rearing) which in effect the prestation indemnifies. Bridewealth is an indemnity—reparation for damage or loss to those losing the services and company of the bride. This is made dramatically clear in societies in which normal sexual divisions of labor are abrogated as part of bride service such that a prospective groom must perform woman's work for his in-laws for a stipulated or negotiated period before the wedding can take place (Allen and Thompson 1848:2.196). Such an institution is impossible to understand unless we assume authority by the household and its head man over a woman's services lost to her own family and gained by her husband and his family. If it is she herself, in later marriages, who receives the prestations, then she is giving up full control over her own services and capacities and must therefore be compensated by the man gaining such authority.

No amount of discussion and reporting of women's successful influence within the household can overturn these major domains of activity which signify male authority in vital arenas. In constitutional terms, my reading of the record suggests that African men as husbands and household heads hold final authority by traditional rule in clear-cut arenas. In a very real sense it is a "residual powers" status. Unless clearly and consensually spelled out as rules governing behavior within specified realms, domestic authority is in the male domain.

Women universally have rights to their own huts and the goods within; often they have their own fields and keep the proceeds. They own or rent market stalls in their own names and keep the proceeds of their trading activities. Women are supposed to agree to a marriage, although this seems more pro forma than real for their first unions. Women can also under special circumstances abrogate a man's authority. Thus, Igbo wives can, by rule, cohabit with other men if they are accused of being barren and wished to prove it was their husband's fault. The husband is, however, pater to all children resulting from such unions. In some of African societies (for example, Ashanti, Yoruba, Kanuri) women can become household heads, take up male occupations, and sometimes even marry and have their wives produce children for them through approved sexual liaisons.

The authority of the mother-in-law is commented on widely. In the case of Lovedu, mothers help their sons to manage and control the household organization. By supplying cattle for bridewealth, the mother obtains rights in the marriage; should a conflict arise between her and a particular wife, she can request the return of the cattle, thereby dissolving the marriage. Given the high rate of divorce which is widespread in Africa, a significant number of women tend to end their lives as single, postmenopausal residents in a son's compound. As women they live and work with their sons' wives, but, unlike the wives, they are closely linked to their sons by descent and therefore represent male authority in a woman's world.

I conclude that men predominate in many African households but that women have final authority over specific activities and realms of behavior with regard to wifely duties. In several cases they are successful traders outside the household, protected by laws and rules of local usage. When Sudarkasa (1982) describes the relationship as complementary, she is correct. Men's and women's activities constitute a whole to which each contributes vital portions. But complementarity and authority vary independently. Equals may complement each other; so too may unequals. Complementarity creates interdependency and therefore empowers each side that has need of the other. Authority, however, apportions rights and powers constitutionally, and in the latter instance traditional African societies give the major share of private authority to husbands as household heads—a role generally associated with a male occupant.

The Public Sphere

The most widely held position concerning women and the public sphere tends to emphasize lack of representation and even exclusion from this domain. As Rosaldo notes, "Few women in history have achieved a dominant position in the working world, and even fewer have competed with male politicians and become political leaders" (1974:37). Many public organizations in traditional Africa are banned to women, as well as to immature preadults of both sexes. African societies use these organizations to link adult male status with authority and public order. Supernatural sanctions are applied to wrongdoers. In status terms, these "secret" organizations place women and minors together in one category, adult men in another, with men in the position of enforcers and judges. In Islamic Africa the ideal for women is seclusion within the household and lack of participation in the public sphere. Women often have special male appointees to speak for them in public or in the courts (Cohen 1971). Women in the public sphere, in trade, or living as single unmarried persons are by definition loose in their morals, enjoyable as sexual partners but not quite respectable as moral actors. This status can be changed once they marry and come under male control. Until that event they are, however, less than proper because, I contend, they are in the public sphere as free agents. In traditional, mostly male-centered, African society this is an anomaly.

Many commentators also note that in centralized African societies it was common for women, at least a few privileged and elite ones, to hold high political offices. For many writers, this fact gives the lie to the proposition that women do not exert authority in the public sphere in non-Western cultures. This leads to an important issue which some writings avoid but which seems to me central to these apparent contradictions. If we accept male authority as a firm and central feature of African political cultures, how can we explain its opposite, a widespread acceptance of high political office (that is, authority) for women? Why do male-centered political orders evolve positions of high office for women?

Women's Offices in African Polities

The Royal Household

In the more complex kingdoms of West Africa, the households of officials were large-scale organizations involving hundreds—sometimes, as in Dahomey, even thousands—of people. Under such circumstances the ordinary tasks of cooking and running the woman's side of a household become a managerial project involving the planning and direction of a large labor force. Possibly the most formalized of these managerial positions was that of the Kotoko to the south of Lake Chad. The royal women were under the general direction of the *magir*, or queen mother, who lived in her own separate residence near the palace. Through intermediaries (women and eunuchs) the *magir,* directed the activities of the *imma* (royal wives), who were in turn divided into four official wives, each with her own title (*gumsu, bendangum, manduma, marba*) and an unlimited number of slave concubines, or *kilime.* The queen mother was responsible for planning and producing the food for the palace, especially during festivals, educating the young children, especially the girls, and overseeing the repair of palace walls. She was barred from formal decision making in the royal court, but she had many private audiences with the king. People saw her as an avenue to influence because of her proximity to the royal person. If, however, she overstepped her authority, the common people could request the King to exile her from the capital (Lebeuf 1969:131).

This same function was reflected in varying degree in the role of senior wife or queen mother in many of the Sudanic states and chieftancies: Kanuri, Hausa, Pabir, Jukun, Bolewa, and Hadejia to name only a few. The organization was repeated at lower levels in the political hierarchy in such a way that subchiefs, nobility, and local village heads could utilize these titles for similar or related purposes in their own household organizations.

In these respects, the African kingdoms were no different from those in other parts of the world. The normal division of labor between the sexes interacted with the evolution of social stratification to produce greater complexity of female tasks at the higher levels of society. Thus, noble women did jobs similar to those of other women but for larger numbers and more elaborately because of the aristocratic lifestyle of their husbands.

The Head of the Unmarried Women

Where divorce rates were high, as in the Muslim emirates of the Sudan, most women occupied two roles during their adult lives: married woman and divorced or free woman (Cohen 1971). Behavior during marriage was ideally submissive and nurturant. Once divorced, however, a woman is much freer with her favors and could even have several men compete for her affections. She could travel when and where she pleased and even walked differently—less sedately, more provocatively. The bifurcation of these roles was traditional and was observed in the early nineteenth century by the first European travelers in the area (Denham and Clapperton 1826).

Traditionally in Bornu, and possibly elsewhere as well, such women were organized under a titled female relative of the monarch—the *maram.* Each town and village had its own *maram* as well. This official could be appealed to by women over court cases, especially divorced women, to try to get a particular case heard by a (male) political or judicial leader. Her most important duty, however, was to organize the divorced women for public dances and the entertainment of strangers to the royal court. Since such women were free of male constraints in their private lives, it was assumed that sexual favors accompanied or could accompany the entertainment. The *maram* also organized the divorced women to cook for military call-ups when large numbers of men assembled in the capital. Such duties were repeated by the local *maram* in each town and village.

Frequent divorce and a more public and freer role for divorced women thus combined with the needs of the state to create an office of head organizer of the free women. In effect, once the condition of family life created a large population of divorced women, the preindustrial African state tended to mobilize these women under a female official appointed for that purpose.

In locally autonomous societies to the south of the emirates, an elected female leader organized unmarried girls for women's dances in the village. The village head among the Bura called on this woman to lead the girls to a festival or communal work project where their dancing and singing served to excite and stimulate competition among the participating men. In this case, age grading and nonmarital status were structurally analogous to the way such activities were carried out in the state societies. In keeping with political ideology in general, however, the female leader in these societies was more democratically chosen. The leader of the unmarried women and the leader of the young men were viewed among the Bura to be senior officials in the village organization under the final leadership of the village head.

Public life in a village or the more widely organized state societies often required collective action by women. Married women were less available for free participation in such open display. Thus the society utilized unmarried women, either divorced or not yet married, to fulfill such functions. The need for these collective actions stimulated the emergence of female leaders to coordinate and organize participation by women in the public life of the community.

Ritual and Symbolic Functions

Continuity and survival were both enacted and expressed by sexual activity. Thus, even though political authority was most often in the hands of men, completeness, harmony, and fertility tended to be expressed in the roles and rituals carried out by leading women in African polities. Just as the family and the lineage required women for their procreative powers, so too the polity was seen as needing both men and women leaders to survive and flourish.

The idea that male and female together represented completeness and harmony was best expressed in the well-known Mawu-Lisa cosmology of Dahomey (Argyle 1966:63). The world began with the pair of twins (Lisa-male, Mawu-female). They were the leaders of the sky gods, seen sometimes as one self-fertilizing being, or a Janus-like figure with one side of its body male and the other female. The male side was the sun, the day, power, toughness, bellicosity, heat, strength, hard labor, all things difficult to achieve. The female side was the moon, the night, motherhood, gentleness, forgiveness, rest, joy, freshness, nurturance, peace. The harmony and wholeness of the world required all these qualities and therefore an equilibrium and harmonious representation of male and female qualities in the organization of life, including the political realm.

In organizational and constitutional terms, this meant that the state was conceived as the outside (male) and inside (female) sectors, looking at it from the king's household. The women of the royal household were divided into queen mother, those who had given birth to a king or those appointed to represent the queens after their deaths, as well as the mother of the reigning queen; royal wives; and finally royal women who cooked the palace food and acted as a warrior bodyguard for the palace. Each of these senior women in the palace was appointed as "mother" to a number of male officials in the administration outside the palace. And for each noble at court (inside the palace) there was a mother of the palace. In other words, to be complete every administrative position must have a male and female representative (Argyle 1966:63–64). To be whole and complete the kingdom must embody all the metaphysical qualities symbolized by male and female and the relations between them. In this sense gender was a major constitutional principle defining African statehood. Its analogue in our culture was not gender but checks and balances.

In Asante the queen mother is said to symbolize the female side of the king's power. She is the "whisper behind the throne." She must admonish the king when he rules badly. When a new capital was built, there were two sections, one for the king and one for the queen mother. Even though a council of men was primarily responsible for choosing the new king, the queen mother proclaimed the name of the ruler to the public: she "delivered" (as a woman should) the new king to his people (Rattray 1956:143, 215, 216).

This notion of completeness or wholeness expressed in a sexual idiom was present as well in Barotseland. There the two capitals were seen as a great and primary one in the north under the king and a lesser one in the south under a queen. The southern center was said to be a sanctuary from the authority of the north, but the two acted in unison to carry out public policy. When one went to war, the other had to assist; when the king sacrificed at the royal graves, the queen had to be present and participate (Gluckman 1959:24–27).

Again, wholeness and completeness symbolized as male plus female, embodied in an official role for a queen, or more often a queen mother, who represented in her person the feminine side of social and cultural reality. In effect, this conception of authority was a metaphorical expression of social and political integration. Human existence at its most fundamental levels required man and woman, husband and wife, father and mother, to be complete. So too political systems had to embody all human qualities to complete and order social life. The various pieces must fit together: the authority structure must coordinate and represent all interests as well as the range of possible responses leadership can make to those under its control. There must be mercy with justice, peace with war, consultation with decisiveness, and nurturance with exploitation; in other words, femininity with masculinity.

Fertility

The most common qualities of femininity are those of fertility, continuity, and procreativeness. And certainly these are represented in the role of many official women, especially that of the queen mother. In the Kotoko kingdoms the four official wives, especially the senior one (*gumsu*), could not have children, and abortive plants were eaten if pregnancy occurred. According to Lebeuf (1969:127–29) these women had to relinquish their personal fertility "to become like the earth, a universal mother," whose fertility and nurturance was not bestowed on their own children but on the nation as a whole. The Jukun queen mother planted the royal seeds each year, and once appointed she could never marry or have sexual intercourse. A breach of this rule was believed to bring disaster to the crops of the kingdom (Meek 1931:340). This idea possibly reached its ultimate development in Lovedu, where sometime in the not too distant past kingship was changed to queenship. The queen transformed clouds into rain for her people and withheld it from her enemies. She symbolized the fertility of nature and something more. Through her, human beings intervened in nature to wrest from it control over their own welfare (Krige and Krige 1943:271).

Fertility, however, was also a form of power and control and in this sense was often embodied in the role of a king or chief. In the triannual royal rituals of Ha-Kobe Zaghawa, the king went to the sacred mountain of Kobe to ask former kings for rain and productivity for his people. A pregnant camel was sacrificed. At the climax of the ceremony the fetus is thrown into a deep hole at the back of a sacred cave on the mountain. Tubiana (1964:47) interpreted this to mean that the king gave to the womb of the earth one of the most prized of human possessions, the increase potential of a herd of camels. He did this as intermediary between his people and the forces that provided fertility and sustenance. In a much less elaborate manner, kings and local chiefs throughout the western Sudan made annual sacrifices at the tomb of the ancestors, the purpose quite manifestly being the welfare and productivity of the land and people.

Possibly the most dramatic male fertility rite was that of the famous Swazi *incwala* ceremony of the new year. Here the king, after being vitalized for a number of days, walked naked among the masses, except for an ivory penis-cap. Later he entered his marriage consummation hut. Inside he took a special medicine for sexual potency; it contained materials symbolizing greenness, toughness, rapid growth, and renewal. He then spit to east and west through apertures in the hut as the elders cry, "He stabs it!" His spitting was said to go "right through" his people to vitalize them (Biedleman 1966:398; Kuper 1947:214–15). Although many aspects of kingship were symbolized here (Biedleman 1966), clearly the king was ritually fertilizing the people and the land, renewing the power of those under him to reproduce.

Manliness is generally associated with authority; therefore, women in authority express their legitimate power by taking on manlike qualities. In Dahomey women warriors referred to themselves as men. Cowardly soldiers of either sex were referred to pejoratively as "women" (Argyle 1966:88). In the Chad basin, women title holders wore men's robes when they appeared in court or on occasions of public festivals. In Barotseland, the queen of the southern Lozi capital changed when she met with her royal council. On such occasions she was viewed as a man, not a woman (Gluckman 1959:22). A woman in authority therefore had the social and cultural attributes of a man.

Added to this idea is the quintessentially human capacity to abstract and generalize, that is, to eliminate dissimilarities across very different phenomena and express similarities in metaphorical and taxonomic terms. Gender is possibly the most ubiquitous category for conceptualizing and generalizing across nongender entities and activities, although other features such as the changes in the seasons, siblingship, parenthood, and childhood are universal experiences easily culturized to express similar qualities in quite different contexts. All cultures abstract sexual identities and assign these features to nongender phenomena; one of the most important targets for such idiomatic expression is political office and the normally appropriate exercise of authority.

The Lovedu case, extraordinary though it was, shows how gender and political office can in effect vary independently. The Lovedu society utilized the idiom of gender to express political ideology, mixing gender in novel ways because of the high value placed on femininity as a necessary ingredient for successful enactment of political skills and the exercise of authority. The polity was led by a woman during the last three reigns dating back one hundred and forty years from the time the ethnography was carried out (Krige and Krige 1943). The rule that the queen could not marry a man emphasizes by negation the authority that husbands have over wives. Logically the queen could not have a consort whose household authority would abrogate her constitutional responsibility to rule or, worse, give her husband illegitimate powers in the polity. As ruler, that is, as a manlike entity, the queen married a series of virgin wives from the noble lineages of the realm. As previously unmarried women, they had never come under another husband's authority and were thus unsullied (i.e., previously subordinated) linkages between the nobles and the throne. When and if these wives became pregnant by private lovers, they were reallocated by the queen as wives to district chiefs called "mothers" of the district. These "female" chiefs were, however, 86 percent men and 14 percent women at the time of the study. Ostensibly both male and female chiefs received these gift wives. Husband-as-head-of-the-family-and-the-compound can be male or female. All paters need not be the same sex.

The leitmotif of Lovedu public life was the practice of varying the gender of political actors for ideological reasons. Whereas men tended to dominate and predominate as actors in the public sphere, the most essential features of leadership and political skills were seen as feminine, not masculine, qualities. These were embodied in the belief that compromise, caring, welfare, order, and nurturance of the land and its people were womanly. In contrast, differences of opinion, competition, conflict, coercion, and violence, along with blustering formality and argumentation, were seen as manly. Politics that works was feminine, politics that leads to disparate or even violent conclusions was masculine.

Krige and Krige describe a typical court scene that exemplifies this ideology. Women, usually older ones, speaking audibly but to no one in particular, often comment on "the tortuous ways of men when such and such is the simple solution" to the problem (1943:198). Invariably this woman's way of doing things is "jumped upon" and forms the basis for a solution. At least this is what people believe. Men coerce, argue, strut, and command;

women compromise and seek solutions, not prestige. In effect, men compete, women seek order. No wonder, then, that the society sees woman's qualities as the most highly valued political skills, and no wonder Lovedu society is led by a queen. The Lovedu case is instructive because womanly qualities are the cardinal virtues associated with political skills even when, as they usually are, the practitioners are men.

Women's Offices as Symbols and Mechanism of Integration

All political systems up to the inception and development of the state have fissiparous tendencies as part of their ordinary political process. To segment, split, and send off buds is not civil war but rather an expected result of population growth, land shortages, competition for leadership, and other factors that become more and more likely as a locally autonomous polity develops (Middleton and Tait 1958). Chieftancies have some supralocal authority but have not developed enough centralized force or a functioning centrally coordinated bureaucracy to ensure continuity. Such systems develop subsections that eventually hive off to become separate polities. Barnes (1954) calls them snowball states because they expand to the breaking point and break, and then each segment begins again, expanding toward its own inevitable breaking point. True states, however, have developed sufficient control of the center through an organized bureaucracy and the use of force to overcome these tendencies. In this way disparate ethnic elements can remain as citizens under one authority, a territory can be held, controlled, expanded, and exploited, and the emerging bureaucracy can ensure continuity of centralized control even when a ruler or high official dies or retires from office. In my view, then, statehood involves among other things the evolution of organizational strategies for overcoming the fissiparous qualities inherent in all nonstate systems (Cohen 1976, 1978, 1981).

Continuity is not, therefore, simply a functionalistic fallacy in which a sociologist "explains" an institution by claiming in an unprovable way that it contributes to the maintenance of the system. Prestate political systems split up normally. They are by nature noncontinuous; therefore, continuity is for them an intrinsic structural problem. This brittleness is enhanced by the fact that almost all preindustrial political systems judge political strength to be a function of the number of the followers any particular leader or set of them can muster and maintain. Splitting not only proliferates a set of locally autonomous systems across the landscape, it also seriously weakens them at the time of the split. In this sense it is viewed as a danger and a threat, and even though its occurrence is inevitable in prestate polities it is generally considered an unhappy and unwanted outcome of normal patterns of growth.

In previous work (Cohen 1977) I have examined case material from the Pabir kingdom of Nigeria to show how the queen mother's office evolved as a counterforce to pre-state fissiparous processes. Here I review those materials briefly and look at comparable data to indicate how the pattern elaborated in the region and beyond.

In the Pabir state the queen mother was usually the senior living daughter of a previous monarch—the same rule of eligibility as that for a male monarch. Her father and that of the monarch could never be the same person, that is, she represented a separate royal lineage segment from that of the king. The choice was made from a recently deroyalized segment or from a segment that recently lost out in a succession struggle. Her brothers, having been members of their father's royal court; now took on titled roles in the queen's court, and simultaneously renounced any claims to the throne when they moved to the queen's village a mile from the capital town. The queen herself gave up her husband if she was married, and officially she remained chaste for the rest of her life.

At her installation the queen was given a special man-robe and hat. She spent a night in the monarch's mother's house and the next day received the sacred regalia of the realm. These she took to her own town to keep in a special house guarded by two men with the same title, one appointed by her, the other by the king. Only the queen could touch the objects; they were sacred, secret, and the talismans of the state and its power. Her duties were to keep the objects safe and to visit the capital twice a year to discuss affairs of state. Her cemetery was the burial ground for all of royal blood who were not monarchs. The royal burial ground was elsewhere and served as a national shrine.

Her other major duty was to help install a new king. The heir apparent went to her village for seven days. During that period he was made to interact with the sacred objects and to have a topknot of hair from the founder of the royal dynasty sewn into his own hair. After the seven-day period he emerged from the queen's village as a person who had obtained kingliness and returned to the capital.

One other point is important. All towns and villages of the area had annual hunts in which men gathered, sometimes with men of other villages and hunted for wild game. The queen's village had no hunt. Informants said it was "a woman's place"; therefore, its men hunted with men of the capital or other towns.

There is much more detail, ceremonial and symbolic, that could be elaborated on. But this summary has provided the basis for my interpretation. The queen symbolized continuity, subordination, unity, and the integration of potentially fissiparous segments of the state. The queen created—gave symbolic birth to—the new king. She provided a link to the mystical founding of the dynasty and linked the heir palpably to that line of monarchs. Power, the people said, passed through her, and in a very real sense it did.

In Pabir constitutional theory the sacred objects could not empower her or her male courtiers *because she was a woman.* Informants repeated this point until they were sure I understood. A womann could not be a king, so the sacred basis of royal power was safe in her hands; a man would have used it to make himself king. The male guardians were twofold: one the king's, one the queen's loyal appointment. A system of checks and balances was in use, but again it reflected gender as the two halves of a whole—the state. To enhance the sacred inviolability of power, the guardians protected but did not touch the objects; only the queen could handle them and allow their power to pass to the heir apparent, empowering his enthronement.

The retreat and symbolic rebirth of the king-to-be had another adaptive result. The death and burial of the previous monarch brought people from the entire countryside. Passions ran high. By cultural definition it was a time for weeping and anxiety, for considering what hopes had been dashed or raised by the change of regimes. All this time the *kadalla,* or king-to-be, was in retreat at the queen's village. The inevitable jealousies that could create conflict, even violence, could not touch him. His symbolic rebirth was also a means of keeping him safe. Continuity meant that the institutional nexus surrounding succession enabled him to become king safely without engendering conflicts that could have prevented the succession procedures from operating smoothly. The queen mother in her separate residence provided a sanctuary for nurturing the new king-to-be when he was so vulnerable. In this sense she was a metaphorical mother and provided real protection for the royal dynasty and its constitutional means for continuing the monarchy and the state.

But in Pabir political theory she was the daughter of a king and could never be biological mother to an actual king, for she was mother to the people and to the state itself and had to keep these interests as well as the king's in mind. Furthermore, and more important, she was chosen from a segment of the royal line whose male members lost their claim to the throne when she was appointed. In nonstate chieftaincy systems, these were the very people who tended to split the state, to revolt. Cleavage lines in chieftaincies such as Nguni (Barnes 1954) occurred along lines of segmentation in the royal lineage. Lack of access to leadership, plus followers who hoped for position and office as a return on their loyalty, created strong fissiparous tension along these lines. The newly appointed queen mother represented just such a group. Her appointed officials included leading members of her father's administration. They were also members of a royal lineage segment that lost out in the succession competition and who therefore became deroyalized. Not only were they experienced at statecraft, but they were also the very group most likely to instigate insurrection or succession conflict. Just as with nonstate systems throughout Africa there was a split, but using gender ideology the split was institutionalized within an integrated polity with a woman heading the potentially fissiparous segment joined to the original as two parts of a whole. The separated group had its own hierarchy and ran many of its own affairs, but it was an integral and vital part of the continuing state.

To emphasize these integrative functions, the queen mother's town had no walls. I have noted elsewhere (Cohen 1976, 1978) that the use of walls among the Pabir for protection against outside raiders was one of the most important requirements of their interpolity relations. The queen's town also stood at the center of a cluster of forces creating their centralized institutions. Informants say of Kogu—the queen's town—that there was no need for walls, each house had a wall to protect it against thieves, and besides it is a "woman's town" so why should it have walls around it? In case of attack against Kogu, the king at Biu sent troops to defend the town. Thus the means for total political independence, walled fortification and armed forces, were by constitutional arrangement not part of the queen mother's administration. This fact emphasized the dependence of the potentially fissionable parts and provided assurance that this dangerous royal faction remained an integral part of the state.

This integration was reflected again in the concept of the queen mother's household. Each new queen mother built a new house. To help, the king ordered out workers, dancers, drummers, and provided beer for a communal work force from the capital and all the surrounding villages of the realm. Representatives from the entire kingdom contributed their work, while the king contributed and redistributed wealth for the occasion.

Informants constantly emphasized conflict avoidance in the relation of the queen mother to the king. They had to live in separate towns; they could quarrel if they were together. They could not be children of the same father because they would compete and "she would not want to go back" (to her own town of Kogu), that is, she and her main male officials—all members of the royal family—could seek to overthrow the throne. The separate residence not only created integration among possible competing segments of the royal line but structured an avoidance between the two groups that decreased the opportunity for conflict and fission. The concept of the queen mother in the Pabir kingdom embodied a multiple set of forces all directed at creating continuity and integration among predictably contentious parts of the state.

Directly to the north of the Pabir are the Kanuri of Bornu. For over a century outsiders have known of Gambaru, the ruin of a burned brick palace of the queen mother situated several miles from the royal capital. It is said in the oral traditions that the mother of Idris Alooma, the great sixteenth-century monarch, built the palace as a refuge for him to grow up in because so many of his rivals wished to harm him and prevent his accession to the throne. The area around the palace is covered in all directions with sherds indicating a town site of respectable size associated with the palace. Barth (1857–58:2.687) also speaks of the *munni*, or bundle of sacred objects, of ancient Kanem, the kingdom or chieftaincy of which Bornu was the successor state. It is said that the bundle was opened and because of this sacrilege the monarch-chief and his followers lost their power, because it "called forth and provoked every powerful man to ambition and intrigues in the government and in high charges" (2.687). A cadet branch of the royal family (the Bulala) revolted at this time, forcing the royal clan (the Magumi Sefuw) to migrate into Bornu southwest of Lake Chad from the Kanem area to the northeast.

Assuming that many of the pre-Islamic ideas and practices of this open country are widespread, these hitherto obscure aspects of Bornu political history can now be reinterpreted. The sacred bundle represented royal power, handled only in a restricted manner if at all. "Opening it" was therefore the breaking of rules dealing with the legitimate recruitment to high political office. The Bulala usurpers could thus not be contained. They or some other as yet unknown faction tried to grasp power and to do so broke the mystical rules associated with succession to the chief position in the "state." This loss of Magumi Sefuwa ascendancy to nonlegitimate contenders was enshrined in the oral traditions as the desecration of the sacred objects that symbolized the power of the ruling lineage and the operation of constitutional rules of succession. The Kanem state was not strong enough structurally to withstand normal fissionable forces. Only later in Bornu under conditions of conquest were they able to create a new constitution and state system that could contain such problems.

The queen mother in all likelihood represented one of these newer institutions. According to tradition, the Pabir copied many of their constitutional ideas from the Kanuri of Bornu. Certainly, her separate unwalled town and palace near the capital were almost identical concepts to those of the Pabir. Her palace was seen as a refuge for royal heirs. It is at least plausible to suggest that her office represented a similar constitutional principle to that more recently practiced in the Pabir state. Indeed, I suggest that the idea of such a role being used to safeguard succession and maintain the continuity of the state, not only symbolically but in clear-cut political terms, was probably a widespread one in the pre-Islamic Sudan and beyond.

What I am proposing is a concept of African constitutionalism that uses women in high office to represent and carry out essential duties connected with (a) the passage of power during succession and (b) the maintenance of sociopolitical integration in potentially fissionable polities.

The idea of a queen mother or female ruler as the symbol of continuity and the creator of kings was widespread in Africa. The Swazi conceived of political power as inherited from men, but always through women. Therefore the rank of the mother of a king-to-be was the chief criterion for royal succession (Kuper 1947:91). As we have seen, the Asante queen mother named the new chief because "power passes through her" (Rattray 1956:143). Possibly the most revealing rituals in this regard were those of the Jukun. Although not the most important of the titled women, the *wakuku* symbolized continuity and legitimized the passage of power. On his way back from the royal installation ceremony, a new Jukun king was met by a widow of the late chief, afterward known as the *wakuku*. She helped him down from his horse and took him to a specially removed enclosure where she disrobed him and gave him a loincloth. He slept with her that night and possibly the next as well (Meek 1931:138,341), but never again. This act makes the *wakuku* the organizing head of the royal women although she must live at the house of a male relative and not the palace. The king has now ritually replaced his predecessor by sleeping with the queen, thus providing them both with high office and legitimizing the continuity of these offices.

The difficulty with this idea of women officials as legitimizers of succession and vessels for continuity was that at times just the opposite was true. As we have seen, Kotoko royal wives were supposed to use abortive techniques to prevent themselves from having children. In effect, only sons of the royal concubines (non-free women) could become kings. Furthermore, it was said in the oral traditions that, before Islamization, the Kotoko ruler had to kill his mother and sacrifice her to the welfare of the people. Later, with Islamization, this rule changed so that on enthronement the mother was made to move to a separate residence and never meet her son again (Lebeuf 1969:130–131). The clue to the meaning of this practice can be seen in the Swazi constitution that forbade a queen mother from bearing sons after she had given birth to the royal heir. She was removed from contact with the king and all wifely relations to him. Furthermore, she was always a specially appointed wife, married to the monarch when he was well on in years (Kuper 1947:31). Generally she outlived him, and her son then came of age just when a successor was needed. Thus a queen's capacity to pass on power was often carefully controlled or interdicted altogether.

In a more fundamental sense, however, these negative practices emphasize the same point. Power *does* pass through women. In giving birth to members of the royal line, they produce contenders. Therefore, to control this process was to gain some control over the disruption caused by competition for the throne. The Kotoko took this idea much further, showing us the link between continuity and integration. Kotoko constitutionalism developed an avoidance of matrifiliation as a possible source of weakness to the throne and the kingdom. The royal heir must be from among the royal female slave concubines. In legal terms this means that the king's mother had no politically active kin. Just in case she tries to use *her* kin as a faction, and possibly to stop her from having any more sons, she is said to have been killed at the time of her son's installation. The matrifiliation link to the ruler was cut. Less obvious, but just as important, was the constitutionally ordained infertility of the titled free wives. The senior wife of the king by rule had to be the daughter of the *iba,* or chief official, of the king's administration (Lebeuf 1969:127, 223). The other wives also came from leading families of titled officials. If this woman were to bear a possible heir, the chief minister would then be the maternal grandfather, and his lineage would have direct access to the throne. Since these leading men decided on the succession, it would involve too great a conflict of interest if they were also deciding on their own versus another noble's relative for the kingship. The Kotoko solution, then, was to continue having noble lines supply wives to the king, but to obtain royal heirs from elsewhere (from union with slave concubines). In other words, we again can see that the fundamental adaptation reflected in the political offices devoted to women in African societies is that of integration of potentially fissioning parts.

The Pabir data are clear on this point. In effect, the queen mother takes a deroyalizing segment and its leading members away to her village. They have a separate village headed by a woman but subordinate to the capital. Kanuri data are unclear as to the details, although oral traditions suggest that in both the first (Magumi Sefuwa) and second (Kanembu) dynasties the queen mother held many chief towns under her control. She was, therefore, an active member of the state administration, even though she traditionally lived in a separate residence away from the capital. The Kotoko emphasized the point negatively. By making sure that no free wives bore heirs, using a concubine instead and possibly killing the king's mother at the time of installation, they minimized possible rivals even though noble lines gave daughters as wives to the king.

The integrative utility of the royal women of Dahomey is quite remarkable. Heirs to the throne were limited to sons of wives given to a ruler when he was heir presumptive. Such women (*kposi,* wives of the panther) were always of commoner origins. No son of a royal princess could be nominated or heir to the throne. The princesses took commoner husbands whose children belonged to their mother's royal descent group and were under the authority of the palace. These princes and princesses were married to commoner spouses, linking royalty to the people (Argyle 1966:57–58).

The royal women, queen mothers, or those appointed to represent a deceased one for all previous kings, queen wives, and other wives were appointed to offices that paralleled those of the kingdom at large. As already noted, each noble official outside the palace had his female counterpart inside. When such officials visited the palace, they came first to their "mother." She arranged for an audience; she remembered all negotiations and business between the king and her outside counterpart. She also obtained information from outside the palace to check on the validity of her outside counterpart's report (Argyle 1966:54–55). Mercier (cited in Argyle 1966:65) called these women the king's memory or record-keepers and his inspectorate.

But there was more here than bureaucratic efficiency. Whenever the king and his women officials appeared in public, "they are separated by a bamboo palm laid end to end on the ground" (Argyle 1966:67). To cross this line was a capital crime for any man except eunuch officials of the king. These were the king's women; they were also his top-line secretariat. They could not usurp power since constitutionally no woman could be king. He had authority over them as a husband over a wife. For anyone to interfere with such authority was akin to adultery with the king's wife. By acting as "mothers" to his administration they integrated the various sections of the state structure into the central government. Dahomean political philosophy and constitutional theory used males and females to make a single system of authority in which the royal household related the government to the people through the royal women. To tamper with the bureaucracy was equivalent to adultery.

Although data are not totally clear for Jukun, it is evident that they evolved structural ideas similar to those of the Pabir kingdom. We have already noted the symbolic continuity of authority obtained through a sexual connection to the previous king's wife, who then became the *wakuku* of the new regime. Jukun had other titled roles for royal women, the most important of which was the *angwu tsi*. She was chosen from among the widows of a former king. Meek made it clear that she was not necessarily from among the predecessors wives; she could be from a more distant and therefore deroyalized segment. This woman lived separately, had her own officials and court, observed daily rituals similar to those of the king, and was addressed with the same honorifics ("Our Corn," "Our Beans"). She was head of all women of the kingdom; her house was an asylum for those who incurred royal displeasure; she planted the royal seeds to ensure crops for the people; and she was considered the "door," or the founding head of several important towns of the realm. She abstained from marriage and sex as long as she held her title (Meek 1931:340–41).

Like the Pabir *magira,* or queen mother, the Jukun *angwu tsi* clearly represented a deroyalized segment of the royal lineage. By making her a central part of the administration—using a woman to head up this faction—the Jukun were counteracting the tendency of subparts of the royal lineage to break off and form their own polity. This was reflected most clearly in the fact that the queen was viewed as a "door" to several towns.

The word "door" in many Chadic languages also means lineage segment that has split off from a larger set within a major segment of a clan. It is derived from the notion of the door to a wife's hut. Multiple wives produce half-brothers who ultimately form their own lineages. Thus to be the "door" is to be the link between potentially fragmented factions (royal lineage segments and their followers) of the Jukun polity. The fissiparous nature of simpler lineage-based systems was therefore still recognized but counteracted by the queen's role.

I interpret the traditional Lozi system in the same way. The capital in the north is mirrored by one in the south under a woman. Her court is a sanctuary for dissidents from the king's capital. She is said to have full rights as a ruler, but she and her administration are always subordinate to the northern capital. In other words, she represents the tendency to break away and even serves as a refuge for those who might do so. Still, her sector remains within the realm. Her ritual duties at the royal graves are necessary for the welfare of the realm; she must help in war. In other words, the strength of the state depends on cooperation from her and those she leads. Again, a queen represents and contains the tendency to fission.

The Swazi material may be interpreted in a similar manner. Kuper (1947:54–56) reports that at the peak of the political system are the king (Lion) and his own mother (Lady Elephant). He succeeds as a son of the previous ruler. His mother's cattle bridewealth is paid for by the nation, making her the "Mother of the People" and her son "Child of the People":

> The king and his mother hold positions of unique privilege and authority. . . . They preside over the highest courts; they summon national gatherings, control the age classes, allocate land, disburse national wealth, take precedence in ritual, and help to organize important social events. . . . The monarchs receive complaints, discuss matters of national importance, interview local authorities, listen to major cases, represent the people in negotiations with foreign diplomats and supervise ceremonies. Their ritual duties sometimes keep them intensively occupied for weeks on end. (54)

But the power is delicately and interestingly balanced between mother and son. The king's court is the highest, but his mother's comes second and her counselors argue cases in the king's court. Like the Lozi queen mother's, her separate residence is a sanctuary for dissidents and even those sentenced to death. The king controls the army, but the commander-in-chief has his household in the queen mother's village.

The meaning of these practices is the use of gender as a symbol and a constitutional principle of integration. If this is so, we can expect that, even if all parties to a political interaction are men, one means for containing conflict and maintaining integration could be through the use of gender in the political culture of the group. Such indeed is the case with the Borana Galla of southern Ethiopia. Borana leadership is derived from two sources, one elected and the other inherited. The elected leaders come from the warrior age group and are elected by men because of their leadership capabilities. They are temporal decision makers who control access to vital resources, especially water, and who lead in warfare. They are always referred to in terms of male images, male activities, and they are judged in terms of adult masculine role requirements.

The inherited clan leaders are sacred heads of a complex of lineage segments whose connection to the ancestors provides ritual duties the object of which is the welfare of the people. The installation ceremonies of a clan leader are instructive. The occasion is believed to create his sacred power—it is also referred to in *female* terms and the rituals are enactments of *female* activities. As with many other installations this one involves a retreat symbolizing the new role. The retreat is not, however, seen as a rebirth but a confinement. On coming out, the new chief goes through a series of rituals modeled on those of the exit and release of women who have undergone confinement and postpartum taboos. Legesse (personal communication) sees these rituals as a means of organizing political polarities and oppositions without having the group actually split up. In Borana political discussions, the majority who back up the decisions of the temporally elected leaders form one group. The minority who for various reasons oppose the majority go to the sacred inherited "female" leader. The sacred leader must aggregate this opposition and speak to the temporal leaders about the unresolved conflicts occasioned by their decision as expressed to him by the dissidents.

The Borana do eventually split and segment, but this male–female leadership that contains opposition is said (Legesse, personal communication) to inhibit the process from occurring as rapidly as it could if such an institution were not present. The result, therefore, is to create integration and, more obvious for the Borana themselves, numerical strength.

The material presented here tends to support the generalization that African precolonial societies were male-dominant in their beliefs and practices and in the private sphere, where household heads, usually men, were leader/managers of complex units of local organization. Women could head households, own their own land, and carry on their own economic activities, but in matters of political and administrative importance they related to the public sphere through the household head or their husbands (the latter could, on occasion, be women).

In the public sphere, I have concentrated on women in high office. Here two major point are significant: first, women and men as gender actors lived within traditional roles and statuses that tended, in the main, to tilt authority relations into the realm of male activity. Even when women acted with authority in the public sphere, they did so by adding male qualities such as men's clothing; or, in their private spheres, they married women, making themselves household heads and paters in relation to household members.

In the realm of high political office, African centralized societies utilized gender imagery in many instances to symbolize the utility of hierarchical relations that are necessary if complex political systems are to thrive and not revert to the normal fissioning of uncentralized segmentary societies. Gender is in this sense an instantly recognizable symbol of complementarity, interdependency, and superior-subordinate relationships. Sexual imagery and the relations of the sexes to one another become the expressive, ritual, and structural metaphor for the relations between the ruler and the ruled.

Gender is also a means of expressing fertility, reproduction, and the continuing welfare of a people whose rulers take on these responsibilities as part of the ritual duties of high office. In this domain of meaning and expression, both male and female qualities are important; sexual imagery requires both male and female for continuity and welfare. It is not surprising, therefore, that at least in one case—Lovedu—female qualities were selected as the most valuable for the political culture of the realm. Even so, and even though the highest office was that of a queen—as it should be if womanly skills were so important—still many, if not most, important political actors were men, not women. Gender and gender ideology are independently variable. Men may find feminine qualities valuable and use this ideology as part of their political culture.

In one sense, Africa was ahead of Western societies. Its people evolved systems of thought and expression in which gender became a means of expressing the need for integration within the state. Gender was also a constitutional principle that counteracted fission and signified continuity of state authority through the generations. Mead was right: sex and temperament are not the same thing, and African societies developed this potential much further than is generally realized.

References

Allen, William (Capt.), and T. R. H. Thompson
    1848   *A Narrative of the Expedition Sent by Her Majesty's Government to the River Niger in 1841*. London: Richard Bentley.

Argyle, William Johnson
    1966   *The Fon of Dahomey: A History and Ethnography of the Old Kingdom*. London: Oxford University Press.

Barnes, John Anundal
    1954   *Politics in a Changing Society: A Political History of the Fort Jameson Ngoni*. London: Oxford University Press.

Barth, Heinrich
    1857–58   *Travels and Discoveries in North and Central Africa: Being a Journal of an Expedition Undertaken under the Auspices of H.B.M.'s Government in the Years 1849–1855*. 5 vols. London: Longman, Brown, Green, Longmans and Roberts.

Biedleman, Thomas O.
    1966   Swazi royal ritual. *Africa* 36:373–405.

Chodorow, Nancy
    1974   Family structure and feminine personality. In Michelle Zimbalist Rosaldo and Louise Lamphere, eds., *Women, Culture and Society*, pp. 43–66. Stanford: Stanford University Press.

Cohen, Ronald
    1971   *Dominance and Defiance: A Study of Marital Instability in an Islamic African Society*. Washington, D.C.: American Anthropological Association.
    1976   The natural history of hierarchy: A case study. In Tom R. Burns and Walter Buckley, eds., *Power and Control: Social Structures and Their Transformation*, pp. 185–214. Beverly Hills, Calif.: Sage.

1977 Oepidus, rex, and regina: The queen mother in Africa. *Africa* 47(1):14–30.
1978 State foundations: A controlled comparison. In Ronald Cohen and Elman R. Service, eds., *Origins of the State: The Anthropology of Political Evolution,* pp. 141–60. Philadelphia: Institute for the Study of Human Issues.
1981 Evolution, fission and the early state. In Henri J. M. Claessen and Peter Skalnik, eds., *The Early Study of the State,* pp. 87- 116. The Hague: Mouton.

Denham, Dixon, and Capt. Hugh Clapperton (with W. Oudney)
1826 *Narrative of Travels and Discoveries in Northern and Central Africa, in the Years 1822, 1823, and 1824.* London: J. Murray.

Gluckman, Max
1959 The Lozi of Barotseland in northwestern Rhodesia. In Elizabeth Colson and Max Gluckman, eds., *Seven Tribes of British Central Africa,* pp. 1–94. Manchester: Manchester University Press.

Goldberg, Steven
1973 *The Inevitability of Patriarchy.* New York: William Morrow.

Hearne, Samuel
1958 *A Journey from Prince of Wales' Fort in Hudson's Bay to the North-*
[1813] *ern Ocean, 1769, 1770, 1771, 1772.* Edited with an introduction by Richard Glover. Toronto: Macmillan.

Krige, Eileen Jensen, and Jacob Daniel Krige
1943 *The Realm of a Rain-Queen: A Study of the Pattern of Lovedu Society.* London: Oxford University Press.

Kuper, Hilda
1947 *An African Aristocracy: Rank among the Swazi.* London: Oxford University Press.

Lamphere, Louise
1974 Strategies, cooperation, and conflict among women in domestic groups. In Michelle Zimbalist Rosaldo and Louise Lamphere, eds., *Women, Culture and Society,* pp. 97–112. Stanford: Stanford University Press.

Lebeuf, Annie
1969 *Les principautes Kotoko.* Paris: Centre National de la Recherche Scientifique.

Meek, Charles Kingsley
1931 *A Sudanese Kingdom: An Ethnographical Study of the Jukun- speaking Peoples of Nigeria.* London: Kegan Paul, Trench, Trubner.

Middleton, John, and David Tait, (eds.)
1958 *Tribes without Rulers.* London: Routledge and Kegan Paul.

Rattray, Robert Southerland
1956 *Ashanti Law and Constitution.* London: Oxford University Press.

Reitz, K. P., and M. L. Burton
1983 A multivariate model of polygyny. Paper presented at the Annual Meeting of the American Anthropological Association, Chicago.

Rosaldo, Michelle Zimbalist
  1974   Women, culture, and society: A theoretical overview. In Michelle Zimbalist Rosaldo and Louise Lamphere, eds., *Women, Culture and Society,* pp. 17–42. Stanford: Stanford University Press.
Schlegel, Alice
  1972   *Male Dominance and Female Autonomy: Domestic Authority in Matrilineal Societies.* New Haven: Human Relations Area Files Press.
Sudarkasa, N.
  1982   Sex roles, education, and development in Africa. *Anthropology and Education* 7:279–89.
Tubiana, Marie Jose
  1964   *Survivances pre-Islamiques en pays Zaghawa.* Paris: Université de Paris, Institut d'Ethnologie.
Whyte, Martin King
  1978   *The Status of Women in Preindustrial Societies.* Princeton: Princeton University Press.

CHAPTER NINE

Women's Writing in Heian Japan: Expressions of Power

Denise O'Brien

During roughly a hundred years in Heian Japan, from about A.D. 950 to 1060, five women lived and wrote about their lives. Their writings, though little known in the Western world, became an integral part of Japanese culture, models for centuries of later writers; they are still read in schools today. Women, no matter what their time and place, rarely write, and when they do their writing is often suppressed (Russ 1983).[1] How were Heian women, the five whose memoirs are examined here and many others, able to write, and what do their writings tell us about power in a state society?

Heian Japan

The Heian period began in A.D. 794 with the establishment of a capital at Heian-kyo, the city known today as Kyoto, and ended in 1185 with the

---

I wrote this essay while I was a visitor at the Humanities Research Centre of the Australian National University in 1983–84. I am grateful to Professor Ian Donaldson, director of the HRC, and to its staff for providing a hospitable and stimulating place to work, and to Temple University and the W. K. Kellogg Foundation for financial support. I thank Catherine Broderick, Richard Bowring, John Docker, and Thomas Harper for their help and suggestions and absolve them of any responsibility for my interpretations and conclusions. I am grateful too for guidance from Robert J. Smith and skillful editing by Patricia J. Netherly.

[1] The statement that women rarely write is based on a comprehensive cross cultural and historical perspective that does not ignore women's publications in the past two hundred years but considers as equally important the barriers toward women becoming literate reflected, for example, in European history and in the percentages of illiteracy by gender existing through the world today (Hunter College Women's Studies Collective 1983:398–421).

emergence of the Kamakura military government (Hall 1974:7; Varley 1973:64). By mid-Heian times, when women writers were flourishing, Kyoto had a population of over 100,000 (Hall 1974) and was the center of political, social, and religious activity for the aristocratic class, estimated at about 20,000 persons (Hurst 1974:45). Since the women whose writings are central to this essay were all from the ruling class, the background material presented here pertains primarily to that class.[2]

At first glance, Heian culture seems uncannily familiar to an ethnographer schooled in the prestate societies of Melanesia and Africa. There are, for example, patrilineal clans, polygyny, menstrual seclusion, competition among males for ceremonial titles, and reliance on divination. Yet significant differences mark Heian Japan as a state society, among them a centralized bureaucracy, class stratification, an emphasis on literacy, codification of laws, and a tax system. Indeed, by the sixth century the pre-Heian court can be classified as an emergent state (Hurst 1974:41).

The imperial court and the aristocracy depended on an economic base of wet-rice agriculture. Rice, cloth, and other goods produced in rural provinces were transported to Kyoto and allocated to individuals according to rank (Hall 1974; McCullough and McCullough 1980:827–31; Sato 1974). Before the Heian period the nobility had maintained provincial households as well as residences in the shifting capital city, but with the building of Kyoto the aristocracy gathered there on a permanent basis. They could afford to maintain permanent residences in the capital because the rural estates from which their incomes derived had local resident managers. There was an effective tax system and the nobility became absentee landlords (Hall 1974; Sato 1974). Aristocrats wanted to live in Kyoto because it was the hub of their world, and Heian women's writings are full of commiserations about the misfortune of male relatives and friends who must leave Kyoto because they have been assigned posts at the provincial government level.

The most inclusive kinship unit was the *uji*, identified by modern scholars as a clan (Fox 1967; Hurst 1974; McCullough 1967:141, 165). Before and

---

[2]*The World of the Shining Prince* (Morris 1964), a social history of the mid-Heian period, makes court life seem very accessible to one who is not a specialist in Japanese history and literature. I have not relied on it, however, given criticisms of Morris' historical (McCullough 1967) and linguistic (Cranston 1967) accuracy and apparent discrepancies between women's behavior as stated in their own writings and as interpreted by Morris (see below for references to these discrepancies). The most useful sources in English on the history and culture of Heian Japan, aside from translated literature of the period, are Hall and Mass 1974, McCullough 1967, and McCullough and McCullough 1980.

during the Heian period, the patrilineal clan lost its territorial, land-owning character, and segmentation into lineages and sublineages proliferated (Hurst 1974:40–44). At the Kyoto court, members of eight clans held the most important political positions, and one sublineage from the northern branch of the Fujiwara clan dominated the government (Hurst 1974:44–45). The emperor's power was overshadowed by that of the Fujiwara regent (McCullough and McCullough 1980:794–96).

The *ie*, variously termed "extended family," "coresidential family," and "household" (Hurst 1974:45; McCullough 1967:141), was the social unit most significant to an individual's daily life. Postmarital residence among the Kyoto nobility was uxorilocal or duolocal, with a move toward neolocal residence during the eleventh and twelfth centuries. Usually a woman owned the family residence. Thus a typical household consisted of a married couple, their married daughters and daughters' children, their daughters' husbands (who would, however, in cases of duolocal residence remain at their mothers' homes), and their unmarried sons. Maternal grandparents were the most important agents of children's nurturance and education.

Religion was a blend of Buddhism, Shinto, Confucianism, and divination based on a Chinese model (Seidensticker 1964:17; Varley 1973). Heian literature is replete with descriptions of curing ceremonies, purification ceremonies, pilgrimages to shrines and temples outside Kyoto, priestly interpretations of dreams, recitation of the sutras, and taboos governing the direction one could go on any given day. Many women and men became nuns and monks, particularly in old age, or younger if they had suffered economic or political decline.

Education was deemed necessary for both boys and girls, and instruction in literature, calligraphy, and music was emphasized. Men studied Chinese literature and history, while women learned Japanese poetry (McCullough 1980:160), though this division was not absolute, since women alluded to Chinese poems in their own writing and men knew Japanese poetry. Everyone was expected to be able to produce a poem at a moment's notice, as part of a letter of thanks, to celebrate someone's good fortune, to cheer a friend stuck out in the provinces, to woo a lover, or simply to take note of the latest flowers in one's garden. Poetry was very much a social art and poems were written to be exchanged. Men were also to excel at mixing perfume and incense, and women at dyeing fabric. An educated woman was valued, the deathbed statement of a Fujiwara noble lamented that his daughters were still unmarried since his motivation in taking "the greatest pains" with their education was to ensure that they made excellent marriages (McCullough and McCullough 1980:302).

212 Denise O'Brien

Heian Women's Writing

Women of the mid-Heian period, writing during the ascendancy of the Fujiwara regency around the year 1000, were enabled to write partly because they existed in a community of women who wrote, a community that extended back in time for several centuries. A tradition of women poets whose work appeared in imperial and private anthologies includes, the empress Kōgyoku, who died in 661 (Keene 1981:26); Lady Kasa, whose poems appeared in an eighth-century anthology (Keene 1981:27); the famous ninth-century Ono no Komachi (Keene 1981:30; Waley 1928:160; Walker 1977:139); Otsubune, who lived in the early tenth century (Cranston 1969:283); Hon'in no Jijū, whose work dates from about 950 (Harries 1980b:314; McCullough and McCullough 1980:330), and Koōgimi, active in the late tenth century and known as "one of the Thirty-Six Poetic Geniuses" (Harries 1980b:314; McCullough and McCullough 1980:179). Some women writers were invited to join the household of the empress or dowager empress as ladies-in-waiting, a custom sufficiently popular to allow twentieth-century sources to speak of the literary "salon" at the early eleventh-century imperial court (Keene 1981:38; McCullough and McCullough 1980:288–89).[3]

The five women whose autobiographical writings are central to this essay are Lady Kagerō, author of *Kagerō nikki* (ca. 975), translated as *The Gossamer Years* (Seidensticker 1964); Sei Shōnagon, author of *Makura no Sōshi* (ca. 994), translated as *The Pillow Book* (Morris 1967, 1971; Waley 1928); Izumi Shikibu, author of *Izumi Shikibu nikki* (ca. 1010), translated as *The Izumi Shikibu Diary* (Cranston 1969; Miner 1969:95–153); Murasaki Shikibu, author of a diary (*Murasaki Shikibu nikki*, ca. 1010) and poetic memoirs (*Murasaki Shikibu shu*, ca. 1020) (Bowring 1982), though best known for her novel *The Tale of Genji* (Seidensticker 1976); and Lady Sarashina, author of *Sarashina nikki* (ca. 1060), translated as *As I Crossed a Bridge of Dreams* (Morris 1975). Other contemporary women writers included Ise no Tayū, poet and member of the imperial salon (Bowring 1982:11, 13, 181; McCullough and McCullough 1980:288–89); Sagami (McCullough and McCullough 1980:47); and Akazome Emon, renowned by her peers for her poetry. Akazome is valued today as the author of a

---

[3]Implicit in the term "salon" is a reference to French culture; it would be interesting to compare Heian women writers with women writers in seventeenth-century France, through sources such as Lougee 1976. McCullough and McCullough (1980:372, 824) note that, although similarities are sometimes said to exist between the Heian court and the court of Louis XIV, they believe that in terms of ceremonial offices greater similarities exist with the late eighteenth century court of Louis XVI.

lengthy description (*Eiga monogatari*) of the Fujiwara rise to power.[4] Though obviously partisan toward the Fujiwara and particularly toward Fujiwara no Michinaga (966–1027), the most renowned regent of the period, Akazome's narrative is a wonderful source for deciphering mid-Heian culture.

The social world of the Heian court was small and dense, its members closely related by kinship and marriage. Figure 9.1 shows how, with the exception of Izumi, the autobiographical authors—Kagerō, Sei Shōnagon, Murasaki, and Sarashina—and some of those they wrote about were related.[5] We can see, for example, that Lady Saishō, one of Murasaki's friends at the imperial court, was Kagerō's granddaughter and that Sarashina was her niece. Michinaga, the most powerful Fujiwara regent, Murasaki's patron and perhaps her lover (Bowring 1982:11–12), was the son of Kagerō's husband, Fujiwara Kaneie, by another wife. Figure 9.1 also illustrates the uncertainty surrounding the exact birth and death dates of women

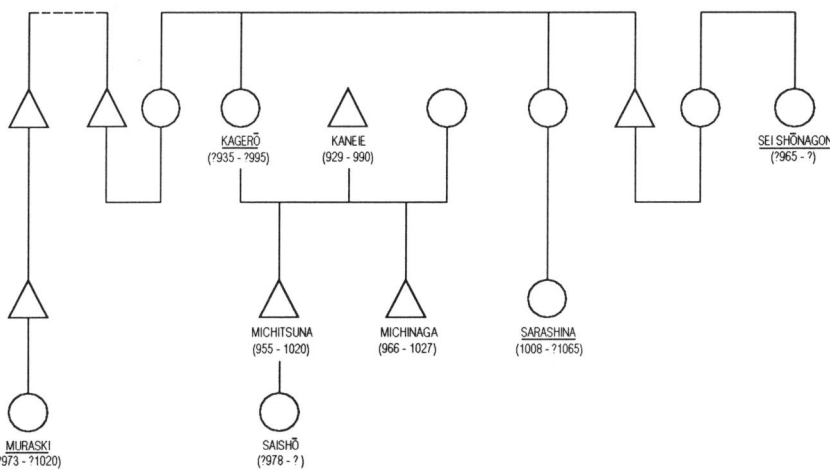

Figure 9.1. Genealogical relationships among Heian women writers.

[4] Akazome's putative authorship is discussed at length in the authoritative and thoroughly annotated translation of *Eiga monogatari* by McCullough and McCullough (1980:37–50) and in Brown (1979:374–79).

[5] This illustration is based on information in Seidensticker (1964:9–13), McCullough and McCullough (1980:367), and Bowring (1982:45, 91–147, 153, 171–81) and is meant to indicate only certain relationships, not a complete genealogy. The dotted line linking Murasaki's father's father and Kagerō's sister's husband is my interpretation of Seidensticker's statement (1964:9) that one of Kagerō's sisters was married to a great uncle of Murasaki Shikibu. It is, of course, possible that Murasaki's great uncle was a kinsman other than her father's father's brother.

writers. Except for Sarashina, whose birth is pinned at 1008 (Morris 1975:4), the life spans of the other authors can only be estimated. Their writings, however, can be more positively dated.

The names of Heian women writers are more tags or titles applied by their peers or posterity than actual personal names. Though Japanese scholars may wince, I refuse to call the author of *The Gossamer Years* (*Kagerō nikki*) "the mother of Michitsuna" (Figure 9.1), as is usual (Bowring 1982:36; Keene 1968:94; McCullough 1980:14; Morris 1975:4; Seidensticker 1964:7; Waley 1928:160) Not only is this cumbersome, it is sexist in identifying her only in relationship to a male and minimizing her autonomous identity. Instead, I propose to call her Lady Kagerō, or simply, Kagerō. The precedents for this nomenclature are many. No one is sure of the personal names of most Heian women (Seidensticker 1981:199), and Kagerō has sometimes been called Lady Gossamer on the basis of a disputed gloss of *kagerō* as "gossamer" (Seidensticker 1964:8, 27, 29). Though Sarashina, too, is sometimes known by a male nominal, "Takasue's daughter," I have followed her translator in calling her Lady Sarashina, or Sarashina (Morris 1975:2). Sarashina is the name of a mountainous district in central Japan and was applied to Sarashina's autobiography by later Japanese scholars (Morris 1975:13). Murasaki's name derives from the heroine of *The Tale of Genji* and from one of her father's titles, Shikibu (Bowring 1982:12). Sei Shōnagon's name signifies her clan and her rank at court, "Minor Counsellor" (Morris 1971:2). Izumi Shikibu's name derives from her marriage to the governor of Izumi province and a court nickname that probably refers to one of her father's bureaucratic positions (Cranston 1969:6–7).

The autobiographical writings of Kagerō, Sei Shōnagon, Izumi, Murasaki, and Sarashina cover the years between 954 and 1060. Kagerō and Sarashina, chronologically the first and last writers, produced sustained narratives that cover long periods in their authors' lives. Sei Shōnagon, Izumi, and Murasaki, writing close to the turn of the century, wrote autobiographical pieces that are quite different from each other but, in comparison to the work of Kagerō and Sarashina, are more episodic, with less sustained narrative structure; in the case of Murasaki and Izumi, the prose is more heavily interspersed with poems.

The Gossamer Years (Seidensticker 1964) is an account of twenty years (954–74) in Kagerō's life, during which she was a secondary wife of Fujiwara no Kaneie. Kaneie was one of the most politically powerful men of his day and became both chancellor and regent. The emphasis in Kagerō's writing is on her relationship, or lack of relationship, with Kaneie. She was jealous of Kaneie's attention toward his other wives and enraged at his numerous casual affairs. References to "counting the nights" (35, 132) indicate that, as is usual in polygynous societies, a husband was supposed to divide his time among his wives, but Kaneie neglected both Kagerō and his principal wife, Tokihime (39, 41). Early in her marriage Kagerō bore a son, and almost twenty years later, in 972, she adopted a girl said to be Kaneie's daughter by another woman (126–29). Household affairs occupy little space in Kagerō's writing, though there is evidence that she oversees a garden and does some gardening herself (85, 96–98, 112). She "watches" her house being cleaned, does some sewing, and supervises sewing and dyeing done by her servants (94–95, 121–22, 141). Kagerō also paints pictures (140), writes many letters and poems (to Kaneie, to his sister, to one of her co-wives, to her father), helps her adolescent son compose courtship poems (143), describes her dreams (98, 125, 139), and goes on many journeys. Most of these trips occur and are written about toward the end of the narrative, and many have a religious character, enabling Kagerō and a friend (e.g., 132) or Kagerō and her son, Michitsuna (e.g., 99ff.), to visit a shrine or temple. Kagerō's narrative breaks off on the eve of a new year. In the final section she expresses pride over her son's performance in a court festival and interest in his marriage plans and sends poems to Kaneie, who has failed to visit her for some time (165–66, 200).

The Pillow Book (Morris 1971) is not a sustained narrative about Sei Shōnagon's life, though there are many short narratives embedded in it. Rather, it is a great mix of observations, poems, lists of things, gossip, and stories about incidents at the imperial court. Because of its episodic and disjointed nature, the *Pillow Book* is much harder to analyze or to summarize than the writings of Kagerō, Izumi, Murasaki, and Sarashina, but Sei Shōnagon gives the modern reader more insight into life in Heian Japan than do the other authors. Sei Shōnagon was a lady-in-waiting to the empress Sadako from about 990 to 1000, but other details of her life, including whether she was married or had children, are vague (9).

Sei Shōnagon presents herself as a person with strong feelings and opinions that she expresses forthrightly. To give just a sample, she hates rain (238), thinks the inside of a cat's ear is squalid (170), envies people who have nice children (172), regards pear blossoms as vulgar and prosaic (63), is moved by a "thin wisp of cloud across a very bright moon" (210), loves going up to a mountain village in the spring (199), and takes great pleasure in writing poems that are praised (89–93, 103, 154–55), though she sometimes feigns embarrassment at the praise (91) or refuses to write a poem on request (122–24). From her writings one gets a vivid sense of her likes and dislikes, and of how she acts in certain situations, but little knowledge about the total shape of her life.

Many details about the life of Izumi Shikibu are disputed, so much so that the suggested dates for her birth range from 966 to 979 and when she died is unknown (Cranston 1969:4,17). Izumi was brought up at the court of Grand Empress Dowager Masako, where her parents were household officials; she was a lady-in-waiting to Masako around the year 1000 (Cranston 1969:5–6, 198, 200; McCullough and McCullough 1980:219–20). Her diary covers about nine months during 1003, when she begins a relationship with Prince Atsumichi (born 981), the brother of a former lover who died in 1002 (McCullough and McCullough 1980:116). The diary is replete with poems—poems written by Izumi reflecting her emotions and poems written by Izumi and Atsumichi to each other. Atsumichi, at least as reported by Izumi, is attracted not only by her charm and beauty but even more by her verbal skill and intelligence as demonstrated in her poems and conversations (Cranston 1969:161–69). Izumi's narrative, the story of one relationship, not of her whole life, ends with Atsumichi convincing a somewhat reluctant Izumi to move to his home. Emperors and imperial princes were the only Heian men who practiced virilocal residence (McCullough 1967:106, 147). As an emperor's son, Atsumichi had his own mansion. After Izumi went to live with Atsumichi, his principal wife decided to leave and moved back to her childhood home to live with her sister and her sister's children (1969:189–91, 202, 294). After Prince Atsumichi died in 1007, Izumi "joined the coterie of literary ladies" at the court of the empress Shōshi (McCullough and McCullough 1980:249; cf. Bowring 1982:13) and may have been a lady-in-waiting to Grand Empress Dowager Akiho as late as 1026 (Cranston 1969:4, 198).

Murasaki Shikibu, as author of *The Tale of Genji,* is unquestionably the most famous of these five women. Murasaki came from a literary family: her father, grandfather, and great-grandfather were scholars and poets (Bowring 1982:7). There is no evidence that her mother or any of her female ancestors were writers. In 996 she accompanied her father to Echizen province, where he had been appointed governor. Murasaki probably remained there until 998, when she returned to Kyoto to marry an older man who already had several wives. Murasaki apparently was happy with her marriage; she had a daughter in 999 and grieved when her husband died in 1001 (8–10). She became a "cultural companion-cum-tutor" to the empress Shōshi, probably in 1006 (1982:11). Murasaki's prose diary (43–155) covers only two years of her service at court, from 1008 to 1010, and moves between descriptions of court life and introspective musings. Early in the diary, for example, Murasaki describes at length (51–73) the birth of a son to the empress, emphasizing the ceremonies surrounding the birth and extending for some time after. She continues to write about the imperial infant, including a moment when the baby urinates on his delighted grandfather, the regent Michinaga (73), but mixed with scenes from court life are passages about growing old (73, 75), how her *Tale* [*Genji*] is being received (95), how she is ignoring her music and her Chinese books (133), and how women should behave (135–37).

Murasaki's poetic memoirs are a collection of poems, most accompanied by short prose prefaces, which Bowring (1982:210) emphasizes must be viewed as a fictionalized life portrait. The poems deal with love (e.g., 232–33, 245) and observations of nature (e.g., 242), among other themes. Without the distilled annotations of generations of scholars, the autobiographical nature of the poetic memoirs would be difficult to grasp. Even with this aid, Murasaki's poetic memoirs are complex and have none of the neat symmetry of Izumi's account of her relationship with Prince Atsumichi.

The latest of the mid-Heian autobiographical women writers is Sarashina. Her diary, like Kagerō's, is a narrative account of her life, from about 1020 to 1060. Unlike any of the other writers, Sarashina begins with her childhood; in the opening passage she describes her love for *Tales* and her desire to read them rather than merely hear them told (Morris 1975:31). Most of her diary (31–110) is devoted to describing her feelings and experiences, focusing on nature, death, friendships with other women, relationships with her parents and sisters, dreams, religions, journeys, and animals. Sarashina is interested in narrative, for in addition to writing her own story and reading many *Tales* (52, 54, 64, 80, 93, 106) she embeds the stories of others in her memoirs. Sometimes these stories are dreams (50–51, 70–71), sometimes legends (36–38), sometimes experiential accounts (41, 85–86). In her early thirties, Sarashina becomes a lady-in-waiting to an infant imperial princess (75–88, 101, 104–5, 132), but she does not enjoy life at court. Marriage and motherhood do not loom large in Sarashina's narrative, though she does marry in her late thirties and has a son.[6] She goes on pilgrimages when health permits, at least once because her marriage was going badly (100, 105). Although Sarashina says virtually nothing about her feelings for her husband while he is alive, she grieves at his death with what seems to be deeply felt and sustained sorrow (106–10). The narrative following her husband's death is quite short, though it covers "many years" according to the final section (107, 109, 110).

---

[6]Sarashina had two sons and a daughter (Morris 1975:138), but only one son, presumably her firstborn, is mentioned in the diary.

Throughout her diary Sarashina presents herself as a person rather than as a wife, a mother, a lover, or a court lady. The social role that receives most attention is Sarashina as daughter.

I have designated the writings of Kagerō, Sei Shōnagon, Izumi, Murasaki [excluding *Genji*], and Sarashina as autobiographical and as diaries or memoirs. There is a substantial literature in Japanese and in English (e.g., Bowring 1982; Cranston 1969:90–125; Harries 1980a, 1980b; McCullough and McCullough 1980:9–37; Miner 1969, 1981; Walker 1977) on what genres and subgenres are applicable to Heian women's writing. None of the works discussed here can be considered a diary in the sense of a day-by-day record of the writer's experiences. But the Japanese term *nikki*, which is consistently applied to the writings of Kagerō, Murasaki, Izumi, and Sarashina, is routinely glossed as "diary." The term *nikki* has never been part of the Japanese title of Sei Shōnagon's *Pillow Book*, as it is of all the other works considered here except for the *Murasaki Shikibu shū*, or "poetic memoir." The *Pillow Book*, though, is described as having numerous resemblances (Miner 1969:16) to the *nikki* or diary form.

There is also a question of whether these works are fiction and thus should be interpreted as romances or novels rather than as autobiographies. The possibility of Izumi's work—to which both the title *nikki* (diary) and *monogatari* tale have been applied in its Japanese textual history—being fiction, perhaps even written by someone other than Izumi, has been strongly debated. No one contests that the narrative about Izumi and Atsumichi was based on a relationship that actually occurred in 1003; rather, debate centers on attribution of authorship and on the degree to which the author created a romance, a roman à clef. Bowring (1982:31), for example, thinks that Izumi's work is clearly fictional, as does Walker (1977), who notes the tensions between realism and idealized love in the narrative. Cranston, translator of Izumi's work, presents evidence on authorship and genre but leaves it to the reader to decide the degree of fiction in Izumi's narrative (1969:44–89, 90–125). When specialists disagree, the reader must choose. From reading the translation and following Miner (1981:86), it is reasonable to think that Izumi is the author and that the work is autobiographical. One difficulty in making any definitive judgments about genres is that no one is sure that modern readers are reading complete texts as written by the authors. The earliest extant manuscript of any of these mid-Heian works dates from a century or so after its composition, and the textual pedigree of each work is exceedingly complex.

There are almost as many definitions of autobiography (Gunn 1982; Olney 1980; Spengemann 1980) as there are of power, but a common denominator is that autobiography involves a consciously shaped version of an individual's life, written by that individual. In that sense Sei Shōnagon's *Pillow Book* is not an autobiography, though there are autobiographical sequences embedded in it, but the works of Kagerō and Sarashina are certainly autobiographies; so too are the works of Izumi and Murasaki, if we agree that an autobiography can deal with part of an individual's life rather than with its totality.

Expressions of Power

Heian women's autobiographical writings are expressions of power in three senses: writing an autobiography is one way of defining the self, discovering an identity, and becoming an autonomous person; examples of Heian women acting autonomously are numerous in their autobiographical writings; and the work of these five women and their contemporaries in the imperial salons shaped Japanese literary traditions for centuries after the Heian period. The last expression of power is widely accepted; what is interesting is the reason women's writings rather than men's should have determined the canon. Heian women are not, however, regarded by modern scholars as autonomous beings, and an analysis of power in their writings must begin by dispelling that misreading of their work.

Reviewing a modern translation (Harries 1980a) of Lady Daibu's poetic memoirs, which were written at the very end of the Heian period—150–200 years after Kagerō, Murasaki, and Sarashina lived—Richard states that this autobiography is written "within the personalized framework of the emotional paradigm universal among Heian women: the lover rarely met, yet on whose signposts a lady ties her strings of self-recognition" (1981:341). Such a paradigm may be valid for Daibu and for some mid-Heian writers such as Kagerō, but it is certainly not universal in Heian women's writing. Izumi's diary focuses on a love affair, but the meetings between herself and Prince Atsumichi are frequent, not rare. Neither Murasaki's diary nor her poetic memoirs is constructed around longing for a lover. In his introduction, Bowring (1982:209–16) emphasizes the inner strength and force of character Murasaki displays in her memoirs. The man most central in Sarashina's writing is neither a lover nor a husband but her father. Sei Shōnagon writes amusingly and eloquently about how lovers should behave and describes some of her amorous encounters, but nowhere in her variegated work is there a suggestion that her self-recognition depends on a lover.

Richard's far from universal paradigm is an example of the purdah complex that characterizes modern discussions of Heian women. Translators and other literary scholars depict these women as delicate ladies living in psychological and social isolation, shrouded within dark homes, immobilized by heavy layers of clothing (Keene 1981; Morris 1964:34, 205, 210; Seidensticker 1964:14–15, 19, 21–22). In one memorable instance, Seidensticker says that the Heian lady "rarely ventured beyond the veranda" unless she was appointed to a post at the imperial court (1964:21). The phrase appears in the introduction to Kagerō's work, despite many descriptions of times when Kagerō, not a court lady, left her veranda. Not only did Kagerō leave the veranda, she sometimes left against her husband's wishes (Seidensticker 1964:65, 100). Once she went to meditate at a mountain temple (100) and remained there for several weeks despite Kaneie's attempts to bring her home (101, 105–10). Kaneie was an important political leader, but he could not control his wife's behavior. As a court lady, Shōnagon was expected to leave her home, and she clearly like to travel, even in winter (Morris 1971:139–43). Sarashina, described as "timorous" and "solitary" by her translator (Morris 1975:10), was a frequent traveler. Much of the early part of her autobiography is taken up with the account of a three-month journey made when she was twelve. Other trips and pilgrimages recur throughout her life story and, like Kagerō, Sarashina sometimes leaves her veranda no matter what men may say. In one instance, "having firmly made up my mind," Sarashina chooses to leave Kyoto at the time of a major imperial festival and go on a pilgrimage, alone except for servants (90–94). Her decision is supported by her husband, but her brother is outraged. Her servants do not want to go; they are ridiculed by crowds in the street and imperial attendants and spend the first night in a rough cottage—where they are scared while Sarashina is merely amused. If Sarashina is a timid, immobile Heian lady, what would a bold, mobile one do?

Other kinds of autonomy are represented in the autobiographies as well. Since women owned their own homes, changes in men's careers did not necessarily disrupt their lives. Potential disruption occurred when one's husband or father was unlucky enough to be appointed to a government post in the provinces, far from Kyoto. Some women accompanied their male kin to remote outposts, but others did not. Sarashina was bitterly disappointed when her husband was appointed Governor of Shinano (Morris, 1971:105, 144–45) and remained in Kyoto. Kagerō seems to fit Richard's (1981) model of a lovesick lady whose selfhood depends on her lover better than the other writers, since so much of her autobiography revolves around her husband, Kaneie, and the frequency of his visits to her home. Yet even Kagerō asserts herself against Kaneie. She leaves her veranda despite his protests and occasionally refuses to do his laundry and sewing or to have intercourse with him (Seidensticker 1964:95).

Women appear from their autobiographies to function as household heads, directing the activities of servants and taking responsibility for others, adults as well as children. Kagerō, for example, says that "all the children in the place . . . were dependent on me" (Seidensticker 1964:118–19). Izumi worries about leaving her home to live with Prince Atsumichi because she looks after her parents, sisters, and child (Cranston 1969:175). This acceptance of responsibility indicates another dimension of Heian women's autonomy.

In a literate society, works that are both written and read come to define the canon for future literary production and thus have a powerful influence on ideology and values. Clearly Murasaki and her contemporaries had that kind of effect on subsequent Japanese literature (see Brazell 1983: xiv, xxii; Danly 1981:19–20, 60–61, 65; Keene 1981:38–39; Miner 1969:3–39; Morris 1971:1; Seidensticker 1964:10). In the state societies of Europe and North America, women writers have been muted (Showalter 1982:33–34) and have had minimal effect on the literary canon (see, e.g., Fiedler and Baker 1981; Waley 1928:157). How could a group of women a thousand years ago in Japan, writing mainly about themselves, be so influential?

Heian women have been read for centuries in Japan because they were the first Japanese authors to write a recognizably Japanese prose. Writing began in Japan about the fourth century with the use of Chinese characters to represent Japanese syllables. Chinese and Japanese are markedly different phonetically, and gradually there emerged a simplified version of the Chinese characters, called *kana*, that more adequately and precisely represented Japanese sounds. By the time Murasaki and Sei Shōnagon were writing, a cursive syllabary had developed, known today as *hiragana*. During the Heian period these syllable symbols were called *onna-de* ("women's/ladies' hand"), even though both men and women wrote poems and letters in the flowing *hiragana* characters (Hadamitzky and Spahn 1981:19; Miller 1967:121). In contrast, official prose records continued to be inscribed by men in the more formal and angular Chinese script, a script that most Heian men also used for their diaries.[7] There was great prestige attached to writing the "difficult classical Chinese" (Keene 1968:17), and

---

[7] There were a few Heian men who wrote in Japanese (Keene 1968:21). The most important is Tsurayuki (869–945), whose *Tosa Diary* is "the parent of all Japanese prose fiction" (Miner 1969:20). In the *Tosa Diary*, written in 935, Tsurayuki pretends to be a woman, opening his narrative with: "It is said that diaries are kept by men, but I shall see if a woman cannot also keep one" (1969:59).

for a Heian man to write Japanese prose has been compared to a modern Englishman appearing publicly as a transvestite (Waley 1928:158). The diaries written by Kagerō, Sarashina, and their female contemporaries were among the first sustained narratives in Japanese prose (Kato 1979; Keene 1981). Gradually men began writing prose in Japanese, and the prose of Heian women became important as models.

Thus it seems clear that Heian women's writing became central to Japanese culture because they wrote prose in Japanese at a time when no one else did. But this is only part of what their writings tell us about the relationship between gender and power in a state society.

Power, like truth or beauty, is one of our more slippery notions, and there are many definitions of this complex concept. Here I propose a definition couched in everyday discourse, one that fits the scope of this essay: power is the ability to act or to cause others to act. The choice not to act and the ability to withstand another person's acts constitute autonomy, an important kind of power for the individual. Writing is an expression of power that depends on access to education, a carefully regulated resource in state societies often closed to persons in certain categories. Writing also depends on time free from other productive and reproductive activities. Although individuals can live without writing, it is necessary for the existence of the state. Whether we agree with Lévi-Strauss (1973:299) that writing has been used in state societies primarily to facilitate slavery, writing consolidates power in the state through laws, history, propaganda, literature, and education.

Heian women wrote about their lives because they lived in a society that valued writing and because they were free to engage in socially valued action. Davis describes the attitude toward language expressed in Richardson's *Pamela:* "There is . . . a meticulous care for the material aspects of language—the fetishization of style and penmanship, the concern with the minutiae of sending and receiving, intercepting, forging, and the logophilia that demands every event be obsessively incarnated into the word" (1980:143). Just such an obsessive attitude toward writing—in the value placed on calligraphy, in the careful attention to the color and texture of paper used for letters and poems, in the demand that events and emotions be inscribed—is a marked characteristic of Heian Japan. Miner (1969:11) has noted the striking resemblance between the growth of the English novel from an epistolary tradition, as is represented in *Pamela,* and the growth of prose fiction in Japan from diaries. It may well be that the valorization of language in eighteenth-century British novels and in Heian prose and poems represents a belief that reality can be transcribed into language, a belief necessary for the creation of fiction or autobiography.

The freedom Heian women had to engage in the socially valued action of writing and their choice of writing autobiographies are not simply consequences of abundant leisure and membership in the ruling class. Heian women's autonomy had an economic and legal basis in residence rules and inheritance codes. Women's ownership of property, particularly of family residences and rural income-producing estates, gave them economic independence.[8] Uxorilocal or duolocal residence created households with a stable core of female members—a community of women at the family level mirrored in a larger community, the salon, at the imperial court.

The hypothesis that there are causal relationships between residence rules, household structure, inheritance patterns, and women's writing is strengthened by historical evidence from the post-Heian period. Neolocal residence gradually replaced uxorilocal and duolocal residence during the late Heian period, and by the Kamakura period (1200–1333) virilocal residence was normative. At the same time, inheritance of the marital residence shifted to the patrilineal line (McCullough 1967:118, 123). Thus, women moved from a situation in which they owned homes where they lived with their children, their sisters, and their sisters' children to one in which homes were owned by men and a wife lived in her husband's home. This shift in household structure and decrease in women's economic independence occurred at the same time as a decline in women's writing or, at least, an absence of writing entering the public canon.[9] Scholars agree that there were no women writers of any note in Japan from the fourteenth to the nineteenth century (Danly 1981; Keene 1981:26; Miner 1969:12; Waley 1928:159–60).

To return to our central topic, how were Heian women able to write and what do their writings tell us about power in a state society? Because of a particular intersection among class structure, family structure, and language use, women in Heian Japan were able to exercise power in their individual lives and through their writing to shape aspects of Japanese culture from their

---

[8] In the United States the largest number of women's diaries and autobiographies were written during two periods marked by increased access to education, more legal rights, and greater economic independence for women: 1890 to World War I, and in the late 1960s and 1970s. The historical pattern of autobiographical productivity for American males is quite different (Jelinek 1980:5–6).

[9] The Mundurucú of Brazil provide a parallel example of historical change from a prestate, nonliterate society. Formerly a culture marked by patrilinial descent and uxorilocal residence in which there was a high degree of residential and economic solidarity among women, the Mundurucú moved to a neolocal or virilocal residence pattern and women lost some degree of autonomy (Murphy and Murphy 1974).

own time to the present. The raw material for these conclusions has been available to scholars not fluent in Japanese since 1920, when the first extended English translations of three Heian diaries—those by Murasaki, Sarashina, and Izumi—were published (Omori and Doi 1920). In her introduction to this edition, Amy Lowell, an imagist poet known for her appreciation of Japanese culture, mentions that Heian women wrote in Japanese, while men wrote in Chinese, and she recognizes the historically rare advantages of education, inheritance of property, and ownership of domiciles enjoyed by these women. Lacking in 1920 were three elements necessary for one to understand the autonomy of Heian women and how they expressed their power in literature that retained a power of its own: adequate historical data, good translations, and new paradigms from anthropology and literary criticism. Required for the argument advanced here were authoritative historical research on Heian social, political, and economic life; linguistically sound and well-annotated translations of the Japanese texts; and models created by combining anthropological research on gender with literary scholarship that emphasizes the cultural context of all writing, the importance of gender, and autobiography as a genre. The coexistence of these three factors permits a new interpretation of the Heian material that answers the recurrent question of why so many women writers of distinction and genius existed in tenth- and eleventh-century Japan and provides a new perspective on what their works signify for our understanding of gender and power. Of course, changes in scholarship since 1920 and this conclusion also say something about power in our own state society.

References

Bowring, Richard, trans.
   1982   *Murasaki Shikibu: Her Diary and Poetic Memoirs.* Princeton: Princeton University Press.
Brazell, Karen, trans.
   1983   *The Confessions of Lady Nijō.* Feltham: Zenith (Hamlyn) Paperbacks.
Brown, Delmer H.
   1979   Pre-*Gukanshō* historical writing. In Delmer H. Brown and Ishida Ichiro, trans., *The Future and the Past: A Translation and Study of the Gukanshō, an Interpretive History of Japan written in 1219*, pp. 353–401. Berkeley: University of California Press.
Cranston, Edwin A.
   1967   Review of Ivan Morris, *Dictionary of Selected Forms in Classical Japanese Literature. Harvard Journal of Asiatic Studies* 17:261–66.

Cranston, Edwin A., trans.
1969   *The Izumi Shikibu Diary: A Romance of the Heian Court.* Cambridge: Harvard University Press.
Danly, Robert Lyons
1981   *In the Shade of Spring Leaves: The Life and Writings of Higuchi Ichiyō, a Woman of Letters in Meiji Japan.* New Haven: Yale University Press.
Davis, Lennard J.
1980   A social history of fact and fiction: Authorial disavowal in the early English novel. In Edward W. Said, ed., *Literature and Society,* pp. 120–48. Baltimore: Johns Hopkins University Press.
Fiedler, Leslie A., and Houston A. Baker, Jr., eds.
1981   *English Literature: Opening up the Canon.* Baltimore: Johns Hopkins University Press.
Fox, Robin
1967   *Kinship and Marriage.* Harmondsworth: Penguin.
Gunn, Janet Varner
1982   *Autobiography: Toward a Poetics of Experience.* Philadelphia: University of Pennsylvania Press.
Hadamitzky, Wolfgang, and Mark Spahn
1981   *Kanji and Kana: A Handbook and Dictionary of the Japanese Writing System.* Rutland: Charles E. Tuttle.
Hall, John W.
1974   Kyoto as historical background. In John W. Hall and Jeffrey P. Mass, eds., *Medieval Japan: Essays in Institutional History,* pp. 3–38. New Haven: Yale University Press.
Hall, John W., and Jeffrey P. Mass, eds.
1974   *Medieval Japan: Essays in Institutional History.* New Haven: Yale University Press.
Harries, Phillip T., trans.
1980a   *The Poetic Memoirs of Lady Daibu.* Stanford: Stanford University Press.
1980b   Personal poetry collections: Their origin and development through the Heian period. *Monumenta Nipponica* 35:299–317.
Hunter College Women's Studies Collective
1983   *Women's Realities, Women's Choices: An Introduction to Women's Studies.* New York: Oxford University Press.
Hurst, G. Cameron, III
1974   The structure of the Heian court: Some thoughts on the nature of "familial authority" in Heian Japan. In John W. Hall and Jeffrey P. Mass, eds., *Medieval Japan: Essays in Institutional History,* pp. 39–59. New Haven: Yale University Press.
Jelinek, Estelle C.
1980   Introduction: Women's autobiography and the male tradition. In *Women's Autobiography: Essays in Criticism,* pp. 1–20. Bloomington: Indiana University Press.

Kato, Shuichi
 1979 *A History of Japanese Literature: The First Thousand years*. Tokyo: Kodansha International.
Keene, Donald
 1981 *Appreciations of Japanese Culture*. Tokyo: Kodansha International.
Keene, Donald, ed.
 1968 *Anthology of Japanese Literature to the Nineteenth Century*. Harmondsworth: Penguin.
Lévi-Strauss, Claude
 1973 *Tristes Tropiques*. Trans. by John and Doreen Weightman. New York: Atheneum.
Lougee, Carolyn C.
 1976 *Le Paradis des Femmes: Women, Salons, and Social Stratification in Seventeenth-Century France*. Princeton: Princeton University Press.
McCullough, Helen Craig
 1980 *Ōkagami, The Great Mirror: Fujiwara Michinaga (966–1027) and His Times*. Princeton: Princeton University Press.
McCullough, William H.
 1967 Japanese marriage institutions in the Heian period. *Harvard Journal of Asiatic Studies* 27:103–67.
McCullough, William H., and Helen Craig McCullough, trans.
 1980 *A Tale of Flowering Fortunes: Annals of Japanese Aristocratic Life in the Heian Period*. 2 vols. Stanford: Stanford University Press.
Miller, Roy Andrew
 1967 *The Japanese Language*. Chicago: University of Chicago Press.
Miner, Earl
 1969 *Japanese Poetic Diaries*. Berkeley: University of California Press.
 1981 On distinctions, functions, and hard works to translate. *Monumenta Nipponica* 36:85–92.
Morris, Ivan
 1964 *The World of the Shining Prince: Court Life in Ancient Japan*. London: Oxford University Press.
Morris, Ivan, trans.
 1967 *The Pillow Book of Sei Shōnagon*. 2 vols. London: Oxford University Press.
 1971 *The Pillow Book of Sei Shōnagon*. Harmondsworth: Penguin.
 1975 *As I Crossed a Bridge of Dreams: Recollections of a Woman in Eleventh-Century Japan*. Harmondsworth: Penguin.
Murphy, Yolanda, and Robert Murphy
 1974 *Women of the Forest*. New York: Columbia University Press.
Olney, James
 1980 *Autobiography: Essays Theoretical and Critical*. Princeton: Princeton University Press.

Omori, Annie Shepley, and Kochi Doi, trans.
  1920   *Diaries of Court Ladies of Old Japan.* Introduction by Amy Lowell. Boston: Houghton Mifflin.
Richard, Kenneth L.
  1981   Review of Phillip Tudor Harries, trans., *The Poetic Memoirs of Lady Daibu. Monumenta Nipponica* 36:341–43.
Russ, Joanna
  1983   *How to Suppress Women's Writing.* Austin: University of Texas Press.
Sato, Elizabeth
  1974   The early development of the *shōen.* In John W. Hall and Jeffrey P. Mass, eds., *Medieval Japan: Essays in Institutional History,* pp. 91–108. New Haven: Yale University Press.
Seidensticker, Edward
  1981   A splendor of scholarship. *Monumenta Nipponica* 36:195–200.
Seidensticker, Edward, trans.
  1964   *The Gossamer Years: The Diary of a Noblewoman of Heian Japan.* Rutland: Charles E. Tuttle.
  1976   *The Tale of Genji.* New York: Knopf.
Showalter, Elaine
  1982   Feminist criticism in the wilderness. In Elizabeth Abel, ed., *Writing and Sexual Difference,* pp. 9–35. Chicago: University of Chicago Press.
Spengemann, William C.
  1980   *The Forms of Autobiography: Episodes in the History of a Literary Genre.* New Haven: Yale University Press.
Varley, H. Paul
  1973   *Japanese Culture: A Short History.* New York: Praeger.
Waley, Arthur, trans.
  1928   *The Pillow-Book of Sei Shōnagon.* London: George Allen and Unwin.
Walker, Janet A.
  1977   Poetic Ideal and Fictional Reality in the *Izumi Shikibu nikki. Harvard Journal of Asiatic Studies* 37:135–82.

Chapter Ten

Keeping Up with the Stuyvesants: House Size and Status in Seventeenth-Century New Amsterdam

Nan A. Rothschild

Anthropologists have long been interested in the relationship between social structural characteristics and the use of space. This relationship can be expressed in several ways. At the level of community organization, for example, the use of space may be seen to reflect underlying structure (e.g., dual organization; Lévi-Strauss 1963), kin affiliations (Douglas 1963; Léroi-Gourhan 1964–65; Turner 1957), or a symbolic ordering of the universe based on cosmological symbols (Frigout 1966). At the level of house layout, the same kinds of principles may be reflected, but there are also particularly good data showing the structuring of space to reflect age, sex, and culturally specific symbolic differences (Deetz 1977; Freeman 1958; Glassie 1975; Hayden 1976; Kent 1983; Needham 1960). Economic variations may also be reflected spatially, providing relatively direct access to social structure in complex societies.

The research described here considers the relationship between one spatial and one social variable, namely, that existing between house size and the control of economically important resources, abbreviated here as wealth. Archaeologists frequently assume a correlation between these variables. I

I owe a large measure of appreciation to those who helped with this research. Denise Avicolli, Barbara Balliet, and Georgia Frank did considerable tedious work; Barbara, David Cohen, and Charles Gehring were invaluable guides to historic documents or sources for architectural information. Bob Bettinger, Bill MacDonald, and especially Ed Rothschild helped me clarify and quantify appropriately; Anne-Marie Cantwell, Don Grayson, Keith Kintigh, and Carol Kramer offered extremely useful comments; and Barnard College provided several kinds of support. I am also grateful to The New York City Landmarks Preservation Commission and Swig, Weiler and Arnow for sponsoring and financing the work at 7 Hanover Square which provided the initial idea for this research.

suggest here that this relationship takes a specific form. As a society becomes increasingly stratified, higher-ranking individuals use the structures in which they live as symbols of their own status, wealth, and power. Stratified systems offer some contrast to egalitarian systems, in which houses often do not vary in size, due partly perhaps to a social norm that dampens the display of status differences (Beaudry 1983; Root 1983). Even in egalitarian systems, however, individuals or families may manipulate space, using the positioning of houses to reflect status and social relationships (Turnbull 1965).

I chose house size (used here to mean the area of the ground floor) as a focus because archaeologists often retrieve information on this spatial element, whereas dimensions of land holdings (another spatial measure of interest) are not likely to be recoverable archaeologically. Although I use data from the historic, or Euro-American, period in North America, I hope to provide information on the relationship between house size and wealth that is broadly applicable to other times and places. The society in question is seventeenth-century New Amsterdam, a Dutch colony that existed in Manhattan, New York, from 1624 to 1664. New Amsterdam began as a temporary trading outpost and, during the period of Dutch rule, underwent a rapid transition to a town, or at least a central place (in the sense of being more densely settled and serving more functions than surrounding, more rural areas; Berry 1967). This transition was accompanied by an increase in stratification, resulting in a society characterized by the existence of three or four ranked groups. It is my expectation that, as the transition progressed, house size came to reflect wealth and status, although I recognize that other factors may affect this relationship (Ember 1973; Naroll 1962; Netting 1982). Kramer (1979, 1982a), in particular, has discussed the complexity of the relationship among these variables and has indicated which aspects of house size do and do not reflect wealth and status.

Data Types and Sources

The data from this research derive from a ten-year period from 1655 to 1665; their collection was stimulated by the excavation of the 7 Hanover Square block in lower Manhattan (Figure 10.1), which I codirected with Arnold Pickman and Diana Wall (Rockman) of New York University in 1981. These excavations uncovered the foundations of a series of houses built between 1687 and 1697. These foundations (Figure 10.2) did differ in size; the large foundation was for a house owned by Robert Livingston, a wealthy Scots merchant, whereas the smaller ones were built on land

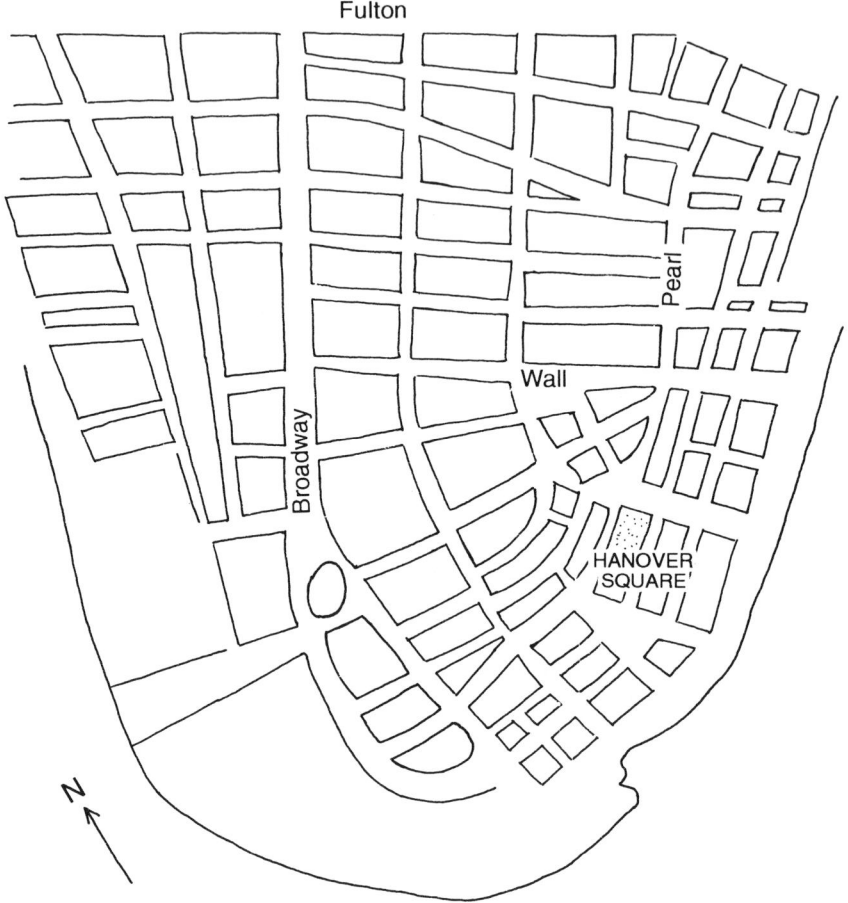

SITE LOCATIONS

Figure 10.1. Location of Hanover Square house sites.

owned by Dutch families. Thus, differences in both wealth and ethnicity existed among these families. I propose here to investigate the reasons for these observed differences in size and to try to determine the relative effects of each of these factors on house size.

Additional data come from documentary sources: a variety of early tax records and, especially, the 1660 Castello Plan, a bird's eye-view of the

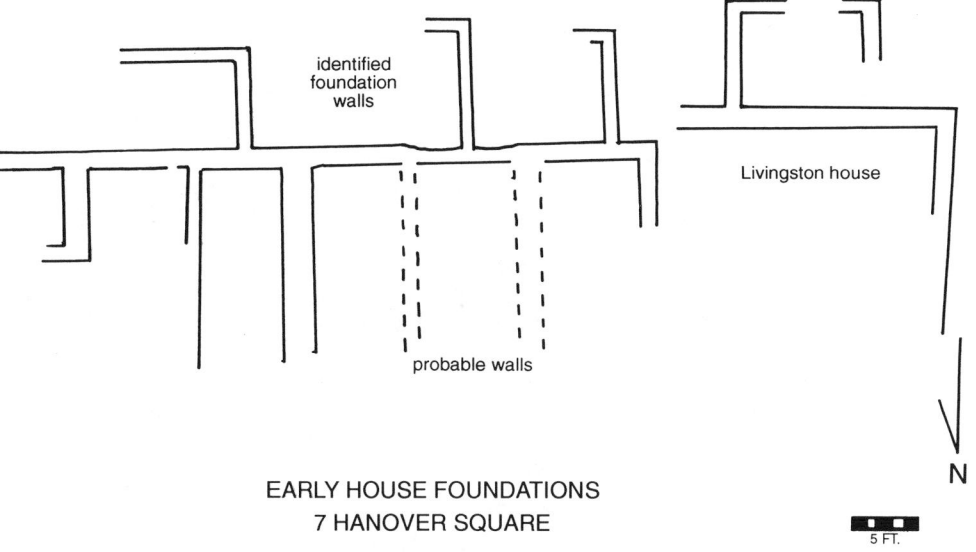

Figure 10.2. Early house foundations at 7 Hanover Square.

town of New Amsterdam based on an original survey by Jacques Cortelyou (Stokes 1909:2.209) which was drawn in such detail that building sizes can be measured. Using an enlarged copy of the Castello Plan (Figure 10.3) available in the New York City Public Library, I measured and tabulated the dimensions of more than three hundred houses (length, width, and number of stories). I used Stokes's *Iconography of Manhattan Island, 1498–1909* (1909), a compendium of maps and documentary information, to identify the owner of each building and, where possible, the function of the building. It should be noted that in the seventeenth century most people lived and worked in the same building.

To assess wealth, I examined documentary sources for lists of taxes paid by citizens, as recorded in the minutes of the Common Council (Fernow 1897). I selected tax lists over other measures of wealth—such as information from wills (Pelletreau 1894), a list of house owners (Valentine 1853:319), and a list of the most affluent inhabitants of the city (Brodhead 1856:23.699)—because either these latter sources included only a small sample of the total number of citizens or else the basis for the estimation of wealth was extremely vague. The tax lists chosen, one from 1655 and one from 1665, were selected because they came from a primary source (minutes of the Common Council), they were the closest in time to the Castello Plan, both were extensive, and both were in Dutch currency. Although it is true that the 1665 list was assessed under English rather than

Figure 10.3. Castello Plan of New Amsterdam (1660).

Dutch rule, neither the currency nor the names of those responsible for setting taxes seem to have changed in this first year of English rule. The 1655 list included forty-seven people noted as house owners on the Castello Plan; the latter list included sixty-nine, of whom twenty-two were listed on both lists and the Plan. Taxes are, for the moment, assumed to be a reliable measure of wealth. These data are biased, of course, toward the more affluent members of society who were landowners and had enough property to be assessed in time of community need.

Both taxes were "special purpose" taxes. The first tax was needed to strengthen the wall, now Wall Street (see Figure 10.1), making a curtain of planks "against an assault of the barbarous Indians" (Stokes 1909:4.159). The second tax was needed to pay for the quartering of soldiers, presumably British soldiers who had successfully taken over New Amsterdam the year before, because none of the Dutch wanted the soldiers in their homes (4.254). The seventeenth century Dutch system of revenue collection did not include regular, income-based taxes (Price 1974:77). It is therefore difficult to get a consistent picture of the basis on which taxes were assessed in this period. For one thing, the basis of assessment is not always stated; for another, the stated bases vary. In 1654 a levy on real estate was noted (Stokes 1909:4.158); in 1655 (the list used herein) a tax on houses, lots, and real estate was levied (6.619); and in the same year, land, cattle, and rent were taxed (Stokes 1909:4.158). Liquors and other spirits were also taxed regularly, as were weights and measures, but these were business rather than personal taxes. The basis of the 1665 list is unknown and may or may not be similar to that of the 1655 list.

Using the tax data and house measurements derived from the Castello Plan, I calculated correlation coefficients on taxes and ground floor area and on taxes and total floor space (ground floor area times the number of stories or floors) in a structure. The two sets of correlations yielded similar results, but I discuss only the former correlations here because I think that the cost of land was the limiting variable. Estimation of a series of maps of Manhattan (the 1639 Manatus map, the 1660 Castello Plan, the 1661 Duke's Plan, and the 1728 Bradford Map or Lyne Survey) shows that land, and especially desirable land, was becoming increasingly covered with buildings and therefore increasingly scarce. The early practice of making land, beginning in 1687, also implies a perceived scarcity of land. It should be noted further that the likelihood of archaeologically recovering information on the number of floors in a structure is quite small, and from this point of view correlations between taxes and total floor space are less useful to other archaeological situations.

Before examining the results, I discuss three predicted outcomes, symbolized by possible relationships between tax data and ground floor space. These are schematized in Figure 10.4.

1. The dashed line in Figure 10.4 represents a hypothetical perfect linear relationship between wealth and house size. Such a correlation could reflect one of three situations: (a) house size is the basis of taxation, and all other wealth is excluded; (b) house size is perfectly correlated with total or other wealth, and that is the basis of taxation; or (c) house size and total other wealth are perfectly related and both form the basis of taxation.

2. Group A, which does not fall on the path of the majority of the data points, represent cases in which house size is larger than taxes would predict (or, alternatively, taxes are less than house size would predict). This could be the result of (a) a graduated tax with the wealthy taxed at a lower rate than the rest of society, or with taxes levied only up to a limit (similar to FICA today); (b) tax relief offered to wealthy or important individuals for reasons other than their wealth; (c) variation in tax rates in different areas; (d) some individuals being house or land poor, or having suffered a recent decline in their fortunes; or (e) some people having larger houses for sociocultural reasons than would be predicted by their wealth alone.

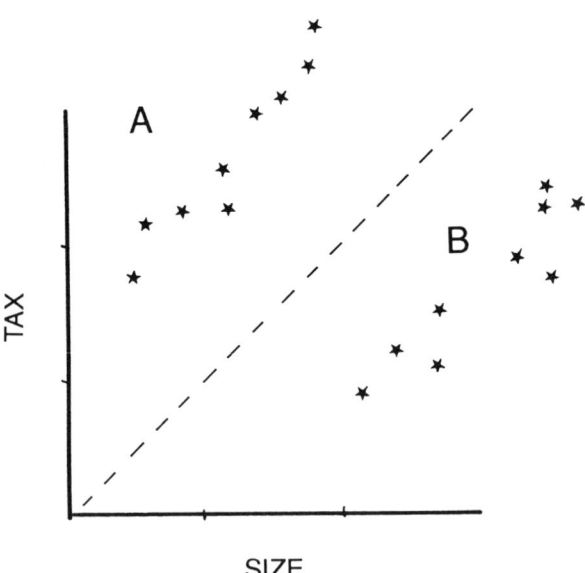

Figure 10.4. House size and taxes.

3. Group B again does not conform to the relationship between taxes and house size that characterizes the major group. This group has houses smaller than their taxes would predict (or again, taxes higher than predicted by house size). This could result from (a) a differentiated tax rate for different segments of society, in this case a higher rate for the rich; (b) variation in tax rates in different areas; (c) the inclusion of other wealth as the basis for taxes; (d) a recent improvement in economic position not (yet) matched by the acquisition of a larger house.

Analysis of Results

Examination of correlation coefficients (Figures 10.5, 10.6) shows that for both tax lists there is a statistically significant relationship between tax rate and house size. It should be noted, however, that the relationship between house size and taxes is closer for the 1655 list ($r = +.66, p \leq .02$) than the 1665 list ($r = +.39, p \leq .02$). This is due in part to the nature of the 1665 tax, which assessed individuals at one of four levels (6, 12, 18, or 24 florins), whereas the 1655 tax was more continuous. Thus it can be concluded that, for a large sample of individuals for whom tax data and house size measurements exist in the period examined, richer people (assumed to be those paying higher taxes) did, in fact, live in larger houses.

For each of the tax lists and house size measures used, there are individuals who fit the A and B situations noted above and who therefore can be considered atypical. I discuss only the 1655 situation (and the ground floor area variable) in detail, but the conclusions apply to each tax list and to total floor space as well. The A group—those who are outside the line representing one standard error of estimate (Downie and Heath 1970:139) and who pay at least 30 florins less than the mean suggested by the regression line (Figure 10.7)—includes several prominent individuals: Peter Stuyvesant; van Dyck, the military commander of the Dutch West India Company; Philipse of Philipse Manor; Domine Megapolensis, one of the earliest ministers in New Amsterdam; and van Couwenhoven, the brewer. The 1665 graph shows an A group that includes Stuyvesant; Jacobus Kip, the treasurer of the Common Council; Cregier, the captain of the burgher guard; van der Grift and Bedfloo, schepens or aldermen; and Kierstede, the first physician in town.

More research is needed to specify which of the suggested situations noted earlier actually explains the composition of this group; in fact, it is probable that more than one of the suggested considerations obtains, with different individuals fitting different possibilities. It is clear, however, that

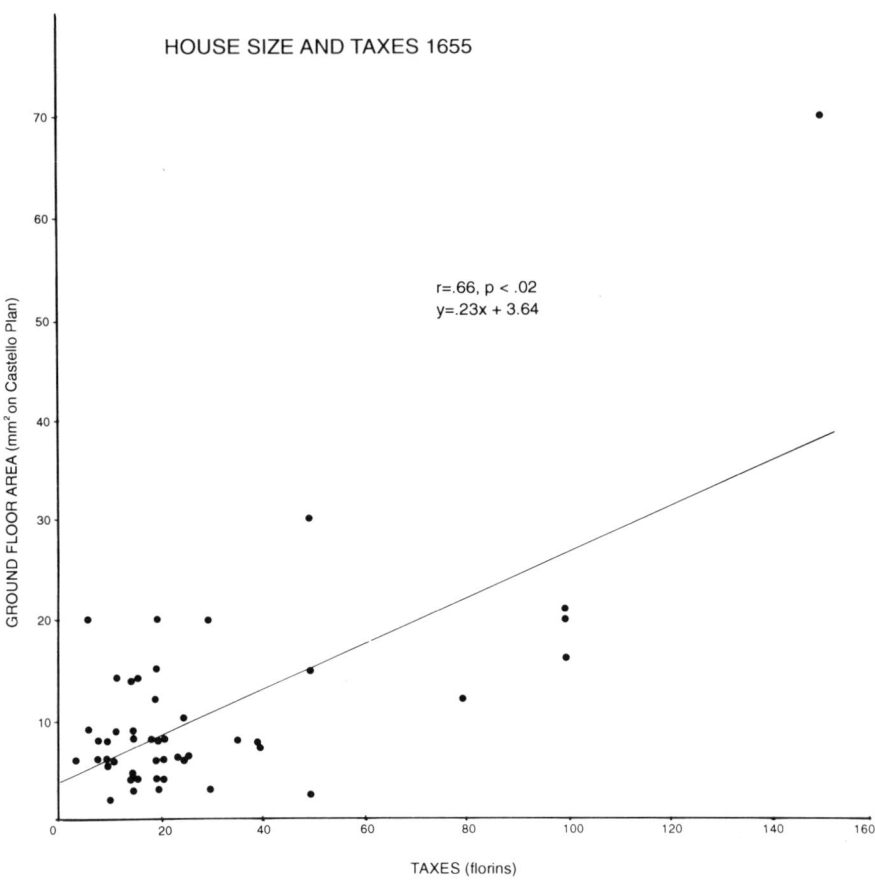

Figure 10.5. House size and taxes, 1655.

most of these individuals performed some sort of public service. A cynic might suggest that corruption existed in the seventeenth-century tax structure as it does today; a more charitable explanation is that tax relief was granted for public service. It also seems likely that the extreme size of Peter Stuyvesant's house (twice as large as the next largest house in the community) was the result of symbolic considerations rather than personal needs.

The B group includes individuals beyond the line representing one standard error of estimate who pay at least 30 florins more than the regression line suggests. Their apparently high taxes may be based on other land or other forms of property. Inventories found with wills often describe paintings, furniture, clothing, jewels, and other items that could have been

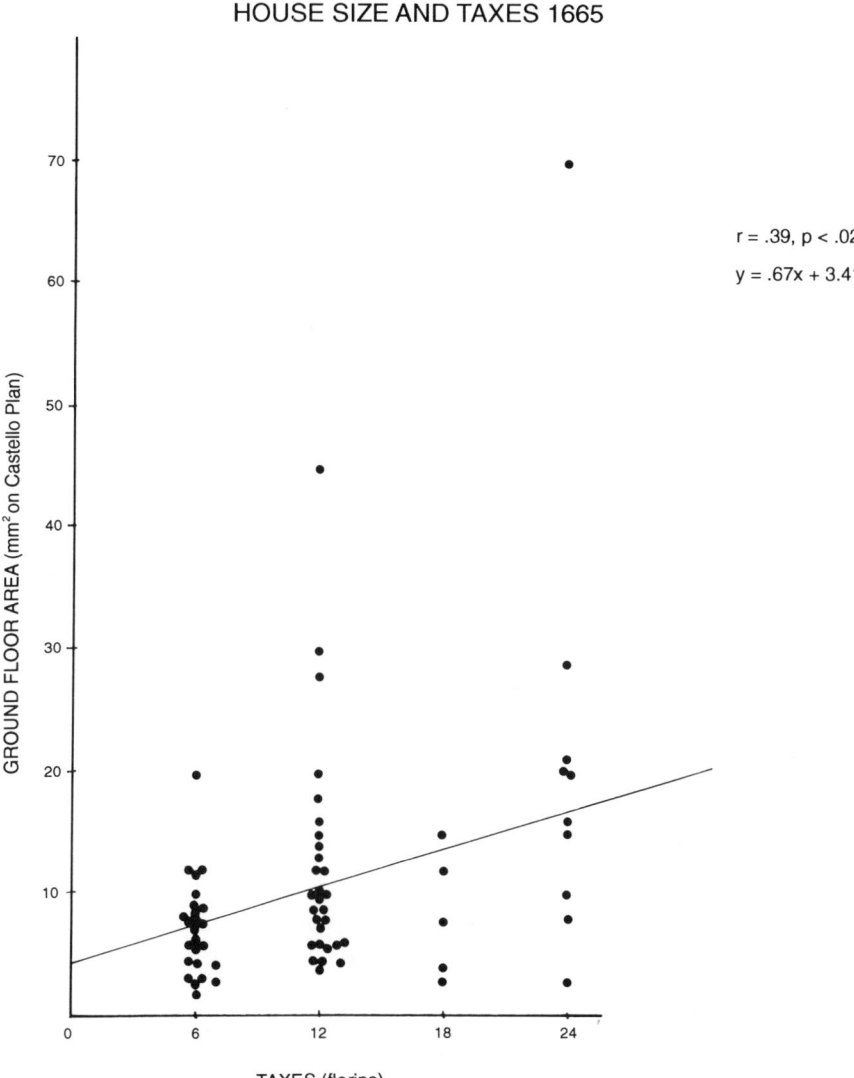

Figure 10.6. House size and taxes, 1665.

taxable, as they are today. But another interesting fact about many of those in group B is the location of their houses, more than half of which are on or near the water (either on one of the canals built by the Dutch into the interior of New Amsterdam or on the shore). Waterfront property may have been taxed at a higher rate than non-waterfront property, or there may

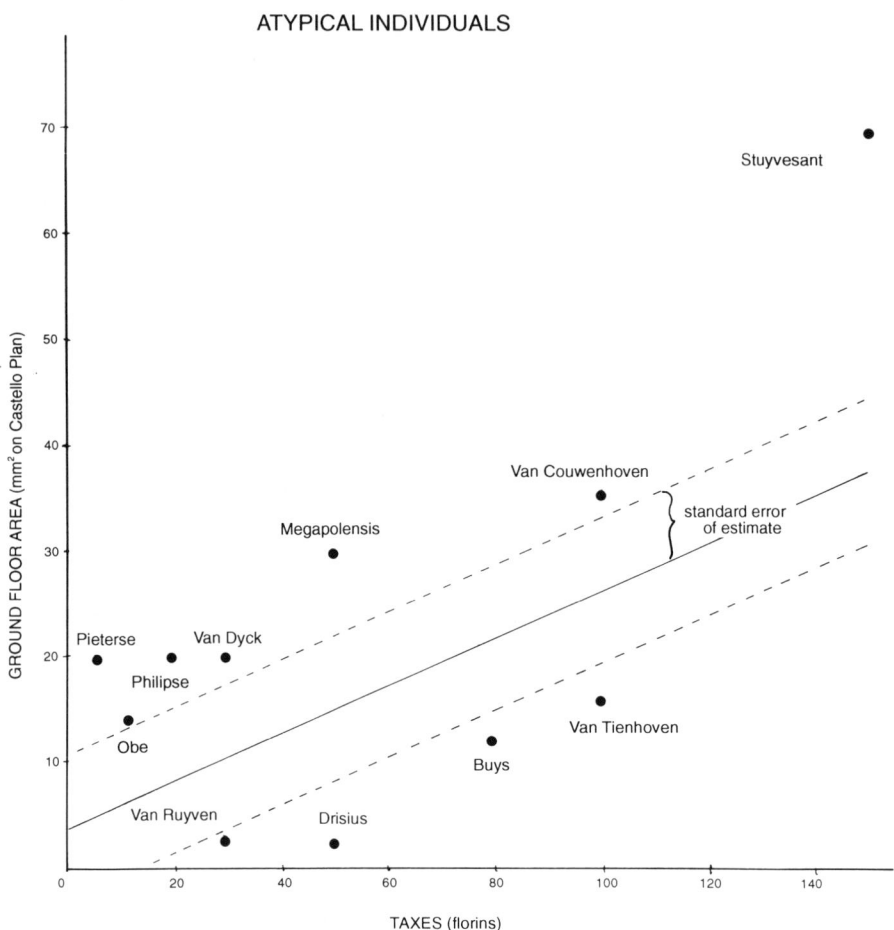

Figure 10.7. House size and taxes for atypical individuals.

simply be a close relationship between wealthy individuals and desirable locations for house sites. It would not be surprising to find that such people had preferential access to these locations. New Amsterdam in the seventeenth century was a community that faced across the water and depended on water transport for trade, its major raison d'être. The seventeenth-century section of its mother city, Amsterdam, is also threaded with canals that allowed movement of people and goods throughout it. The Castello Plan shows denser settlement along all waterfronts than elsewhere. Waterfront houses are, in fact, on the average 150 square feet larger than non-waterfront ones, when mean sizes are compared (583.7 versus 435.6 square feet, based on the enlarged Plan).

The variation in house location is an example of a broader phenomenon in which control of an important resource is maintained by placement of residential or other structures (such as burial mounds) on or adjacent to the resource. This is seen most typically in agricultural systems where desirable land is retained by the location of houses and the burial of ancestors on the land (e.g., Goody 1962).

Other Constraints on House Size

A brief consideration of the possible effect of other factors on house size is in order. It is clear that a substantial proportion of the variance is not related to taxes paid. The function of a structure could influence its size. An examination of the mean size of three types of structures—warehouses, taverns, and residences—in 1660 (Stokes 1909:2.209–43) shows surprisingly little difference in size (taverns, 444.3 square feet, warehouses, 531.4 square feet, residences, 509.6 square feet). Another possible influence on house size is national origin (Glassie 1975; Merwick 1980; Wacker 1979; Zentkuyl, personal communication). Merwick in particular has suggested that the Dutch did not invest their money in larger houses at Fort Orange/Albany because they came from an already crowded environment and retained the habit (or cognitive pattern) of building small houses. Mean sizes of Dutch and English houses (lumped for the earlier analysis) on the Castello Plan do not appear to differ (English, 505.3 square feet; Dutch, 514.0 square feet) although the English sample is very small (6).

The research results described here appear to contradict Merwick's findings; any of several factors could explain the difference. Fort Orange was a more isolated community than New Amsterdam, deeper in the heart of presumably hostile territory. The constraint of building within a fort could certainly act to limit house size. Furthermore, it was not as urban (in the sense of a large, densely settled community, with specialized institutions) or as ethnically heterogenous as New Amsterdam. The latter is said to have been a place in which eighteen languages were spoken (van der Zee and van der Zee 1978:97), even though most of the house owners identified on the Castello Plan were Dutch. In this international setting, the building of a house that displayed one's wealth may have taken on a nationalistic or chauvinistic function as well as having been used to identify group membership (Wobst 1977) by means of architectural stylistic details.

House size could also obviously be affected by household size, which both Kramer (1979, 1982b) and Netting (1982) indicate as varying in relation to wealth. A full discussion of this possibility is beyond the scope of this essay, but I suggest that the cost of land would act to extend buildings upward rather than outward in an increasingly densely settled community. It also seems that large families would not be as adaptive in a nonagrarian economy as in an agrarian one, although households (or "housefuls" in Laslett's terms, cited in Kramer 1982b:666) often included servants or other non-kin members of the unit of production.

Finally, the length of the period during which houses are constructed may affect house size. The sizes and locations of houses built early in a community's history are theoretically less constrained than those of later houses. Although we cannot be certain how much time elapsed between construction of the first and the last of the houses depicted on the Castello Plan, it must have been a relatively short period. New Amsterdam was settled in 1624 (van der Zee and van der Zee 1978). The first houses constructed there were those built by the Dutch West India Company and some crude, probably bark-lined huts built by individuals (Brodhead 1856:1.368). The construction of permanent houses may have been going on for a twenty-five-year period when the Castello Plan was drawn, but the existence of open space on the plan indicates that, although some of the open space was already owned, there was probably still freedom to build a house of one's choosing, at least in reference to size, if not location.

Thus none of these factors—building function, ethnicity of builder, household size, or timing of construction in the history of the city—had obvious major effects on house size.

In conclusion, it is not surprising to observe that wealthy people manipulated the apportionment of space in seventeenth-century New Amsterdam.

I have used data from the historical period to examine the relationship between wealth and house size. The positive correlation of these factors can in theory be extended to other times and places and should be useful to archaeologists working with prehistoric data. One note of caution must be added, however. The modern Euro-American notion of space is dominated by geometric concepts; space is seen as continuous, isotopic, and homogeneous and easily divisible by arbitrary units whose points and intervals are fixed and identical. This concept of space lends itself to the imposition of economic criteria to create valued spaces that can be treated as commodities. Other societies have more personal, less abstract views of space, size, and distance (Evans-Pritchard 1940; Littlejohn 1967). Thus one should exercise caution in formulating hypotheses about which aspect of space would most likely be related to status differentiations in a specific setting.

The conclusions reached here may therefore not be applicable in nonmarket economies, nor in nonhierarchically arranged social systems. For colonial Dutch New Amsterdam, however, a preliminary analysis has confirmed the familiar archaeological assumption that wealth and house size are directly related. Furthermore, the relationship is a complex one in which certain groups had lower than typical taxes, or higher than typical taxes, for a variety of political and economic reasons. Further research will, I hope, allow the extension of these findings to other sociocultural contexts.

References

Beaudry, Mary
- 1983 Yeomen and gentlemen: An archaeological perspective on social rank in seventeenth-century Massachusetts. Paper presented at the Annual Meeting of the Society for American Archaeology, Pittsburgh.

Berry, Brian J. L.
- 1967 *Geography of Market Centers and Retail Distribution.* Englewood Cliffs: Prentice Hall.

Brodhead, J. R.
- 1856 *Documents Relative to the Colonial History of the State of New York.* 80 vols. Albany: Weed, Parsons.

Deetz, James
- 1977 *In Small Things Forgotten.* Garden City: Anchor Books.

Douglas, Mary
- 1963 *The Lele of the Kasai.* London: Oxford University Press.

Downie, M. M., and R. W. Heath
- 1970 *Basic Statistical Methods.* 3d ed. New York: Harper and Row.

Ember, Melvin
- 1973 An archaeological indicator of matrilocal vs. patrilocal residence. *American Antiquity* 38:177–82.

Evans-Pritchard, E. E.
- 1940 *The Nuer.* Oxford: Clarendon Press.

Fernow, Berthold, ed.
- 1897 *The Records of New Amsterdam from 1653–1674 AD.* New York: Knickerbocker Press.

Freeman, Derek
- 1958 The family system of the Iban of Borneo. In Jack Goody, ed., *The Development Cycle in Domestic Groups,* Cambridge Papers in Social Anthropology, no. 1. Cambridge: Cambridge University Press.

Frigout, Arlette
- 1966 L'espace ceremoniel des Indiens Hopi. *XXXVI Congreso Internacional de Americanistas, Actas y Memorias,* vol. 3. Seville.

Glassie, Henry
- 1975 *Folk Housing in Middle Virginia.* Knoxville: University of Tennessee Press.

Goody, J. R.
   1962   *Death, Property and the Ancestors*. Stanford: Stanford University Press.

Hayden, Dolores
   1976   *Seven American Utopias: The Architecture of Communitarian Socialism 1790–1975*. Cambridge: MIT Press.

Kent, Susan
   1983   The differentiation of Navajo culture, behavior, and material culture: A comparative study in culture change. *Ethnology* 22:81–91.

Kramer, Carol
   1979   Architecture, household size and wealth. In *Ethnoarchaeology*, pp. 139–63. New York: Columbia University Press.
   1982a   *Village Ethnoarchaeology: Rural Iran in Archaeological Perspective*. New York: Academic Press.
   1982b   Ethnographic households and archaeological interpretation. *American Behavioral Scientist* 25:663–75.

Léroi-Gourhan, André
   1964–65   *Le geste et la parole*, vol. 2. Paris: Editions Albin Michel.

Lévi-Strauss, Claude
   1963   *Structural Anthropology*. Trans. C. Jacobson and B. G. Schoepf. New York: Basic Books.

Littlejohn, James
   1967   The Temne House. In John Middleton, ed., *Myth and Cosmos*, pp. 331–47. American Museum Sourcebooks in Anthropology. Garden City: Natural History Press.

Merwick, Donna
   1980   Dutch townsmen and land use: A spatial perspective on seventeenth-century Albany, New York. *William and Mary Quarterly* 37:53–78.

Naroll, Raoul
   1962   Floor area and settlement population. *American Antiquity* 27: 587–80.

Needham, Rodney
   1960   Alliance and classification among the Lamet. *Sociologicus* 10:97-119.

Netting, Robert McC.
   1982   Some home truths about household size and wealth. *American Behavioral Scientist* 25:641–62.

Pelletreau, W. S., ed.
   1894   *Abstracts of Wills on File in the 1894 Surrogate's Office*. New York: Publication Find Service.

Price, J. L.
   1974   *Culture and Society in the Dutch Republic during the Seventeenth Century*. New York: Charles Scribner's Sons.

Root, Dolores
   1983   Material culture and strategies of social inequality in non-stratified societies. Paper presented at the Annual Meeting of the Society for American Archaeology, Pittsburgh.

Stokes, I. N. Phelps
   1909   *The Iconography of Manhattan Island, 1498–1909*. 6 vols. New York: R.H. Dodd.
Turnbull, Colin
   1965   *Wayward Servants*. Garden City: Natural History Press.
Turner, Victor
   1957   *Schism and Continuity in an African Society: A Study of Ndembu Village Life*. Manchester: Manchester University Press.
Valentine, David T.
   1853   *History of the City of New York*. New York: G.P. Putnam.
van der Zee, Henri, and Barbara van der Zee
   1978   *A Sweet and Alien Land*. New York: Viking Press.
Wacker, Peter O.
   1979   Relations between cultural origins, relative wealth, and the size, form and materials of construction of rural dwellings in New Jersey during the eighteenth century. In *Geographie historique de village et de la maison rurale*. Bordeaux: Centre Nacional de la Recherche Sientifique.
Wobst, H. Martin
   1977   Stylistic behavior and information exchange. *University of Michigan, Museum of Anthropology, Anthropological Papers* 61: 317–42.

CHAPTER ELEVEN

Technologies of Power: The Andean Case

Heather Lechtman

Painting anything more than a superficial picture of the relations between state politics and state technologies within *Tawantinsuyu*, the Inka empire, is not an easy matter. The task is compounded by (a) the generally mistaken appreciation of Andean technologies as simple, which translates as unsophisticated; (b) the paucity of detailed technical data based on analysis of individual technological complexes that were crucial to maintenance of state power, such as the technologies of cloth and metal production; (c) the tendency on the part of scholars of the Andes to relegate to the realm of economics what properly belongs to the realm of technology; and (d) the overall lack of interest within the profession of anthropology, including archaeology, in technology as an arena of social life whose study is capable of providing broad insight into the phenomenon of culture or of furnishing a fruitful perspective on those areas of anthropological inquiry that continue to receive primary attention—for example, social organization, economics, politics, symbolic systems. Discerning discussion of the technological realm within complex society has come more often from historians and philosophers—William McNeill, Lewis Mumford, David Noble, Lynn White, to name a few—than from anthropologists, though Robert Merrill (1968) and, more recently, Pierre Lemonnier (1986, 1989) and Tim Ingold (1988, 1990) are notable exceptions.

In a comparison of the political economies of the Aztec and Inka states, Pedro Carrasco describes the subsistence and industrial technologies fundamental to both:

As in all archaic civilizations, intensive agriculture was the material basis of Mesoamerican and Andean societies. . . . Agriculture was carried on with only rudimentary tools, and an intensive investment of labor was of greater importance than the complexity of the tools employed. . . . Industry was at a technical level similar to that of agriculture. The most highly developed were characterized by intensive and highly skilled human effort using simple tools. The slight utilitarian use of metal and the absence of the wheel and of work animals make clear the technical limitations of both industry and agriculture. (1982:25–26)

Although he gives due consideration to the wide variety of cultigens raised through a range of intensive farming techniques, including terracing and raised or sunken fields, recognizing that "these techniques make cultivated land itself partly a product of human effort" (26), nevertheless Carrasco's rendering of the situation is the traditional and stereotyped one that leaves the impression of a labor- or energy-rich, simple or technically poor technological condition. This view never entertains technology as knowledge or as the social organization and coordination of that knowledge. The emphasis on apparent technical limitations—such as the lack of the wheel or the preponderantly nonutilitarian use of metal—ignores the elegant and highly complex set of technologies developed by Andean societies on which the Inka state ultimately rested. This ignorance of the extraordinary performance of Andean systems of technology stems, in part, from the equation of technology with technique and, in part, from a real lack of information about the technical characteristics of the systems in question. For example, although Andean metallurgy stressed the nonutilitarian quality of its products, it was among the most sophisticated of prehistoric metallurgical traditions in the Old World and the New, and it was through the very technologies involved in their manufacture that those same nonutilitarian metal objects provided the Inka with an important means for perpetuating their normative power (Lechtman 1984). Somehow the wheel and utilitarian objects of metal have come to represent the hallmark of technological maturity in prehistory. It is time we abandoned that technologically illiterate stance.

Contemporary Western thought defines hardware—tools and machines—as the heart of technology. Major technological events have to do with bringing such physical entities into existence. But one cannot appreciate or understand Andean technology in terms of hardware. In the Andes, the tools and machines of technology were never at the forefront. The invention of labor-saving devices for agriculture, construction, or war was not at issue. Material tools were traditional and mechanically straightforward. The nonmaterial tools of technology were human energy and intelligence and the organization of that energy and intelligence. From this perspective, abandoning the overemphasis on sophisticated hardware, Andean systems of technology emerge as mature and complex. They were also heavily weighted on the side of management, in two senses: management of the physical environment, an environment that was and is the dramatically dominant feature of the Andean zone of South America; and management of the social units of production, whether at the community or state level.

As John Murra (1974) is fond of insisting, the Andean zone is the only place in the world where a grand civilization proceeded through the efforts of peoples residing at 4,000 meters and above. The vertical environment is unique: at once richly varied and hostile, extreme and unpredictable, bountiful and unforgiving. The overriding technological concern in the Andes has always been the management of that special landscape, and the evolution of social and political systems had to be consistent with that concern. The style of such environmental management was traditionally nonmechanistic, totally consonant with the nonhardware bias of the technology. Andean peoples coped with one of the most complex and varied environmental systems in the world. It was a disparate system, uncoordinated spatially and temporally. Solutions to its productive management had to be solutions of articulation and integration, solutions activated through skilled engineering, design, and labor orchestration rather than through tools, artifacts, or machines. The environment was transformed, but not through its mechanical manipulation. The technology emphasized accommodation rather than alteration, reciprocity rather than invasion.

It is disappointing, though not surprising, that no one has seen Murra's (1972) model of vertical complementarity as the quintessential Andean form of technological system, based on the articulation of disparate, noncontiguous entities, emphasizing integrity in variety. In his interpretation, Andean wealth lay in management of a highly heterogeneous and vertical landscape: in securing access to and control of many narrow, vertically arranged ecological floors, each with its characteristic food and raw material resources. An individual community dispatched settlers to colonize distant ecological zones; the products of those zones were exchanged internally among these "islands" of kinfolk. Each community functioned as a "vertical archipelago," combining people and resources into one political and economic macrosystem with exchanges based on traditional forms of reciprocity. The Inka state relied heavily on the use of this system for maintaining subsistence viability among the peoples it conquered. "The strength and versatility of Murra's model lies not simply in its explanatory function of the social organization and control of resources but in its usefulness as an indicator of the organization of a vast technological system.

The organization of the system, the management of the technology, is part of the technology itself. After all, the claim is not that the Andes is the unique instance of civilization arising among peoples who lived at 4,000 meters but that it occurred and could be sustained by people who exploited, managed, controlled an ecosystem that included all resources from sea level to 5,000 meters. The technological sophistication at the heart of *Tawantinsuyu* was extraordinary" (Lechtman 1981a:17; translation from the Spanish).

Technology reflects the political environment in which it evolves. The relations of power inform not only the uses of technology but what is conceived of as technologically possible and appropriate. The relations of power inform the design of the technology itself (David Noble, personal communication, May 1982). Is it not remarkable, then, that Andean technology has attracted so little scholarly attention, given its obvious political dimensions? The splendid book edited by Collier, Rosaldo, and Wirth (1982) on the Inka and Aztec states has not one article on the technologies that laid the groundwork for and that were employed by those states. The absence is particularly remarkable in the Andean case, because an "Andean world" was a political reality during Tawantinsuyu, because the enterprise itself as well as the landscape in which it proceeded was so dramatic, and because the success of it all relied on the complex organization and integration of a variety of technological systems that were crucial to the functioning of the empire. One can only imagine that Andean scholars consider there was no technology, at least in the sense of something special or complex. I suspect that, apart from a general lack of interest in technology among anthropologists, we are accustomed to thinking about the technology of empire as machine-oriented, a technology that can be characterized first and foremost by its physical inventory—weapons, wheeled vehicles, and the like. What sort of corresponding inventory could we draw for the Andes? Modest, at best. Even freeze-drying (Mamani 1981) and the other impressive food preparation and storage regimes crucial to Andean life and to the functioning of the Inka state are rarely discussed as high technological achievements (but see Morris 1981). They are always couched or buried in what seems the larger picture: redistribution, reciprocity, compliance systems.

The Inka achievement in the realm of technology, as in many other realms (Collier 1982; Murra 1980a), was fully grounded in the Andean developments that preceded it and which it tailored to the purposes of state. Although the landscape was physically altered for the first time on a monumental scale with the "grooming of the hillsides" (Murra 1980b) in thousands of miles of state agricultural terraces, nevertheless the predominant tone of accommodation to the environment rather than its mechanical alteration remained at the core of Inka technological perceptions. What we do see with the formation of the empire is systematic attention to the highly organized management of labor. Inka technology resembled modern engineering management in the sense that the state engineered people through its organization of them and their energies. Large scale movements of *mitmaq* colonists were designed to carry out state agricultural projects (Wachtel 1982), and teams of corvée workers traveled to distant sites for duty on state public works enterprises. The articulation of the landscape was still at the forefront of the Andean design, but it was an articulation motivated and executed from political considerations that, ultimately, had to cope with more than 3,000 miles of empire.

Of course, in any other sense Inka social engineering, if we can even call it that, was a far remove from anything we experience in contemporary Western society. Within the design of Tawantinsuyu, power resided in the ability of the Inka to maintain compatibility between the technological changes required by the state to achieve its goals of production and those fundamental institutions of Andean life that remained primary to state and community alike. What was organized in the Andes was the human activity of production. Unlike modern engineering management—which in its attempt to rationalize and systematize industrial production deliberately attempts the appropriation of the intelligence of production (Noble 1979), "gathering in . . . all the great mass of traditional knowledge, which in the past has been in the heads of the workmen, and in the physical skill and knack of the workman" (Taylor, cited in Noble 1979:267)—the Inka state relied totally on the intelligence of the system it managed. The state restructured the labor force to achieve necessary changes in production, but the techniques of production, the technical aspect of the technology, had already been long in place and formed the shared experience of the Andean public. Most of the technical changes initiated by the Inka were changes in scale, not in kind, changes that never alienated or expropriated from the populace its technical knowledge and skills.

Furthermore, in Andean society—even at the level of the Inka state—technological knowledge was not esoteric knowledge, nor did it reside among the elite. As Tawantinsuyu expanded and new forms of political communication and control of information were instituted or developed, some concentration of specialized systematic knowledge occurred in the hands of experts. The *quipu* system of accounting is a clear example. In fact, Zuidema argues persuasively that "the development of an Andean interest in exact and systematic knowledge was not motivated by an involvement in measurements . . . but by moral and abstract concepts. . . .

[It was the latter] that led the Incas to explore the boundaries of knowledge. The abstract system that they developed then helped them in the solution of practical problems" (1982:425). There was a trend toward the incorporation of the technological realm into the realm of systematic knowledge, an attempt to control technological events through a framework of rational and, to a certain extent, predictive systems that allowed coordination in planning time and space. Thus the use of *quipus* and the elaborate accounting system they enabled, the establishment of a state calendar and the long-range planning of agricultural production cycles, the laying out of *ceques* and the siting and planning of administrative centers (Hyslop 1990; Morris 1984; Zuidema 1977, 1982) must all have been in the hands of small and specialized groups of people within the state administration. But generally the Inka state depended on systems of technology that the Inka themselves had practiced and on which the subimperial life of many of the central and south Andean polities was built. As an aside, it is also interesting to note that most of the major "bursts" of technical invention and change in the Andes occurred not during the horizon periods—the periods of religious or political hegemony when concern was for the intellectual or political handling of large, new groups of people—but during the so-called intermediate periods when attention turned to local affairs and energies were directed toward the solution of different kinds of problems (Willey 1991).

Although the emphasis of this discussion has been largely on agricultural production and on the need of the state to manage a rich but recalcitrant environment to yield the huge surpluses it required, the production of goods such as cloth and metal that functioned in the remunerative and normative spheres of political life (Etzioni 1961) was equally essential and grew in importance as the empire grew. Such production involved elaborate technological enterprise.

As Collier (1982) states: "Under the Inca, compliance appears to have increasingly shifted through time from coercive to remunerative and finally to normative integration. This trend makes sense for an imperial system that was expanding militarily while striving to overcome alienation in its hinterlands and to generate full commitment at its core" (16).

This plot of the change in Inka political mechanisms of compliance ought to suggest where to look for corresponding imaginative concentrations of technological activity as the state became consolidated. Inka effort went into organization of agricultural production on the one hand and into ideological invention on the other. Andean technology may not impress some of us as innovative in the sense of the invention of means for transforming the natural world into objects that work through mechanical advantage, but it was extraordinarily innovative in transforming the natural world into objects that imparted ideological advantage. It was precisely in the normative realm that innovation resided, and it is to normative technologies that we should look for an appreciation of the power behind the technological enterprise (Lechtman 1984).

William McNeill argues that, in the prehistoric situation or among archaic civilizations,

> getting enough to eat was the central task of life and presented a perpetual problem for most persons. Everything else took second place. The industrial basis of large-scale enterprises though real enough—public works required tools as much as armies required weapons—was a trivial element in the sense that access to tools and weapons was seldom felt to be a real limit upon what human beings could or did undertake. (1982:23)

The technology of power for the Inka was not primarily or exclusively a military technology. Their strength resided in a carefully orchestrated balance between the technologies of food getting, storage, and distribution on the one hand and the technologies of ideology on the other. The balance was shifted and maintained through Inka skills at management, organization, coordination of the various technological activities that had to be consonant for the system to work: storing agricultural surpluses needed for reciprocal obligations to corvée parties; producing fine cloth essential for redistribution and continual reaffirmation of political ties between the state and local leaders; mining and metal manufacture to feed the house of the sun and to reiterate the link between the sun and the emperor, the human seat of secular and spiritual power. The imaginative use and orchestration of elegant and widely available technologies within Andean society was the foundation on which state power was built. These technologies were used to cement and eventually to reinforce the changing relationships of power.

Inka Normative Technologies: Metallurgy and the Production of Cloth

Two technologies operating in the normative realm were of outstanding importance in conferring and maintaining power among the rulers of Tawantinsuyu: metallurgy and cloth production. Neither system of technology was simple; both were complex and sophisticated, and both were highly elaborated long before their utilization by the Inka. Yet in assessing Inka imperial technologies, there is never mention of metallurgy as a technology of power. Cloth production fares better, because Andean scholars have long appreciated the central role of cloth as the item through which the state recognized, validated, and cemented relations with the polities it subdued and later ruled (Morris 1974, 1978; Murra 1962). In this sense, the state's political investment in cloth is clear, and the role of cloth in state reciprocity has attracted scholarly attention. Although cloth was the most important item of material culture throughout Andean prehistory, serving as the prime visual medium for the expression of ideas and with religious and ceremonial functions as important as its economic and military roles, nevertheless the technology behind cloth production is rarely the subject of study. Why have we persisted in overlooking technological enterprises so fundamental to the realization and maintenance of Inka political control?

In the case of metallurgy, the reasons seem obvious. Until the 1970s, the substantive literature devoted to Andean metallurgical technologies was extremely sparse (Bergsøe 1938; Caley and Easby 1959; Easby 1955; Mathewson 1915; Root 1949, 1951, 1964). We did not have the technical data with which to assess and interpret metallurgy as a technological endeavor, much less as a dynamic part of Andean social life and social change. That scholars have not been interested in obtaining those data stems largely from the ways in which we, today, think about metals, from models that have been put forward to account for the rise and development of serious metallurgies in prehistory, and from a comparison of New World metallurgy with its counterpart in the Old World.

The properties we normally ascribe to metal as a general class of material are strength, hardness, sharpness, malleability. These are mechanical properties that impart to metals considerable durability and the ability to withstand great stress. We recognize them because they are the properties industrial societies value most in metals, properties engineers use and seek to enhance in construction and in the manufacture of all classes of commodities. They are also properties that we associate with masculinity and with serious, utilitarian activities. When Carrasco argues that in the Inka world "the slight utilitarian use of metal and the absence of the wheel and of work animals make clear the technical limitations of both industry and agriculture," he is alluding to the fact that Andean metallurgy was not oriented primarily around the development and utilization of the mechanical properties of metals in the same way as were the metallurgies of the ancient civilizations of Europe and the Near East. There the manufacture of bronze and iron tools of war, agricultural tools, and wheeled conveyences provided avenues of utility enabling the metallurgical revolutions of the Bronze and Iron Ages. The dramatic impact of Old World technologies of metal manufacture and metal use reinforces our notions of the appropriate arenas for the performance of metals and our estimation of what "metalness" is all about: metals are utilitarian; they provide a wide range of mechanical properties that few other materials possess; they can be fashioned into tools that operate on other natural organic and inorganic materials; they are primarily made and used by men in the serious activities of life. Metallurgy is a "hard" technology.

Andean metallurgies focused elsewhere. Color was the single property of metal whose achievement and manipulation stimulated the most innovative and sophisticated developments of Andean metallurgical technologies. Except for iron, which was not manufactured in the prehistoric era, Andean metalworkers produced and used most of the same metals and alloys we associate with the Old World: copper, copper-arsenic bronze and copper-tin bronze, silver, lead, and gold (Lechtman 1980, 1988). In addition, copper-silver and copper-gold alloys were uniquely developed for their ability to confer the colors of silver and gold on objects made from them. The mechanical properties of metals were not neglected by Andean smiths. No craftspeople seriously and consistently involved in the production of metal over long periods of time fail to recognize and use the salient properties of the materials they intimately know. Copper-silver, for example, was one of the earliest alloys invented in the central Andes. Its combined properties of malleability and toughness when hammered made it an alloy of choice for the production of sheet metal, and these properties were as important to the forming and shape retention of sheet metal objects as were the enriched silver surfaces that objects made of this alloy displayed. Agricultural tools, needles, and spindle whorls of copper-arsenic bronze were common in the northern Andes after the Middle Horizon (Lechtman 1981b), and the Inka disseminated tools and weapons of copper-tin bronze throughout their vast empire. But if we look for the locus of attention of the metallurgy, for that arena in which both the expectations of metal performance and the realization of such performance were highest, we find it not in the realm of utility but in the realm of the symbolic.[1] In the Andes, metals carried and displayed the content or message of status, wealth, and political power and reinforced the affective power of religious objects (Lechtman 1984a). Andean metallurgy received its greatest stimulus in the arena dominated by status and political display. An underlying cultural value system that strongly influenced the visual manifestation of status and power was a color symbolism oriented about the colors of silver and of

---

[1] This notion of technological locus having to do with areas where expectations and realizations of performance meet was stimulated by Jacques Maquet's (1971) concept of aesthetic locus.

gold (Lechtman 1979b). Thus a concern for the color of metals rather than for their mechanical properties became a central and an early concern in Andean metallurgical developments.

Since all of the important models that have sought to account for the beginnings, growth, and elaboration of metallurgy in prehistory are based entirely on data from the Old World (Childe 1944; Renfrew 1973; Wertime 1973), it is not surprising that the development of metallurgical technologies in other areas of the ancient world do not match the expectations. Certainly the course described by Andean metallurgies does not correspond to or even parallel those offered for European and Near Eastern sequences (Lechtman 1980). Old World models of metallurgical development do not stand the test of cross-cultural comparison; nor, in the opinions of some (Heskel and Lamberg-Karlovsky 1980; Lechtman 1980), do they even account for Old World events. Yet we are so impressed by Old World metallurgy—and it was impressive—that we continue to use it as a yardstick when considering other systems. For example, whereas Andean smiths invented both copper-arsenic and copper-tin bronze, those alloys came late in the sequence of alloy developments—not early as in the Near East—following many centuries of experience in the manufacture of other alloys used for soldering, welding, gilding, and silvering (Lechtman 1980, 1988). And, as a superficial glance shows, peoples of the Old World developed the principal properties for which we value metals today because they used metals in utilitarian modes: for tools, for weapons, for transport. In such contexts, bronze and iron became the metals of power, and the technologies of their production were sophisticated. New World metallurgy cannot boast a Bronze or an Iron Age. In the Andes, gold and silver appear to have dominated the metallurgical scene.

New World metallurgy was never taken seriously by scholars because its presumed focus was on two precious metals the technologies of which are not normally of special note. Andean objects made from gold and silver were decorative, ceremonial, even charismatic, but not technically useful and not perceived as within the sphere of masculine endeavors. This was a "soft" technology—soft in the metals it treated, soft in the properties for which those metals were developed.

Thus, in the late 1960s, when I suggested to an eminent scholar of Andean prehistory that we take a serious and careful look at Andean metallurgy, he rejoined, "But there wasn't any." Andean metallurgy simply did not exist for most of us because we were looking for it in the wrong place, seeing it always against the backdrop of an ancient European and Near Eastern stage. Today, with many more technical studies on hand and with a focus on the technology from within an Andean cultural framework, we can appreciate it as one among the great traditions of ancient metallurgy (Caley 1973; Epstein and Shimada 1983; Gonzalez 1979; Gordon 1985; Gordon and Rutledge 1987; Hosler, Lechtman, and Holm 1990; Lechtman 1971, 1973, 1976, 1979a, 1979b, 1980, 1981b, 1984a, 1984b, 1986, 1988, 1991; Lechtman, Erlij, and Barry 1982; Newman, Hill, and Wang 1991; Rodriguez 1981; Scott 1983, 1986a, 1986b; Scott and Bray 1980; Scott and Doehne 1990; Shimada 1985; Shimada and Merkel 1991). It was through the technology itself that power was conferred on those who managed and controlled it. That power, as we see it functioning in the Inka state, lay within the normative realm, based on the allocation and manipulation of esteem, prestige, and ritual symbols.

What of cloth? Why consider together two sets of technologies, two classes of materials, two universes of objects so apparently disparate as metal and cloth? Because in Andean society both technologies received great stimulus and cultural support within the normative realm, and both served to enhance the normative power of the state; because both were information-bearing technologies, the purpose of whose products was in large measure the communication of message, so that the very design of the technologies, the styles of technological performance, had to be consonant with those purposes; and because some of the "classical" avenues along which metallurgy might have developed in the Andes had already been preempted by cloth (Lechtman 1984a). Finally, we might cast cloth production together with metallurgy because of its neglect among scholars as a technology of consequence, in spite of the obvious centrality of cloth in Andean community, religious, and political life.

It is harder in the case of cloth production than in that of metallurgy to account for the lack of interest in the technology behind that production since the fundamentality of cloth within Andean society has long been recognized. As early as 1962 John Murra, in one of his most perceptive and provocative articles, called attention to the exceptional role played by cloth among Andean peoples throughout their prehistory. By Inka times, he argued, the state reckoned cloth and agriculture as dual forms of wealth. In Andean society, cloth performed importantly in virtually all aspects of life: it had religious and ceremonial functions, political and military functions; it was the commodity that carried with it the highest status and, for the Inka, was the item most valued by the state and individual alike. Textiles were the primary visual medium for the expression of ideas, the fundamental art form of Andean peoples. At the height of Inka hegemony, textile manufacture was a technology with some 4,000 years of development behind it.

Yet, in spite of the primacy of cloth in Andean life, twenty one years after publication of the 1962 article, Murra (1983) still had to ask the question, Why has progress in our understanding of the use of pre-European cloth been so slow? He suggested several reasons: because archaeologists treat Andean cloth as they would any other artifact, and it has been only since art historians began to work closely with archaeologists that another dimension was added to this static perception of cloth; because the religious, social, and economic contexts that surrounded cloth are still accessible only through scrutiny of sixteenth-century ethnohistoric documents, and there has been no systematic examination of such documents to provide these contexts; and because most scholars who study Andean cloth are "foreigners" who rarely "acknowledge [Andean] priorities felt in the region." Murra was not asking abour our lack of progress in understanding the technologies behind cloth production; he was asking about the products of those technologies. My discussion and my queries here are about process, not product.

It cannot be argued, as in the case of metallurgy, that the products of cloth technology were largely nonutilitarian. Quite the contrary. In fact, it makes sense to see cloth as just one aspect—albeit the most highly elaborated aspect—of a pervasive technological environment oriented around the manipulation of fibers. Andean peoples were fiber-producing and fiber-using. Cotton and camelid wool were their domesticated staples for cloth manufacture, but they processed and managed a much larger range of fibrous materials. Andean solutions to the most fundamental physical and mechanical problems of daily life, as well as to that of the communication of ideology, were sought, conceived, and executed through recourse to technologies based on the engineering of fibers.

Cloth for clothing; for the blankets, tents, and apparel that the Inka imperial armies drew on, stockpiled in large warehouse complexes throughout Tawantinsuyu; for sacks and other packaging and carrying arrangements vital to human portage in an environment lacking draft animals—these are some of the utilitarian fiber products that were fundamental to community and state alike. Andean peoples also built suspension bridges constructed wholly of fibrous materials. Vines, twigs, branches, and cordage were twisted, plaited, and knotted into cables of requisite strength (Gade 1972; Hyslop 1984). The prehistoric tradition of bridge building and bridge maintenance through fiber manipulation continues in some highland areas today (Palomino 1978). House roofs, both on the coast and in the sierra, were made of thatched vegetable fibers. The *quipu,* the mnemonic device that was key to the elaborate Inka census and accounting system and already in use by the Middle Horizon (Conklin 1982), was an instrument designed to record information on sets of coded and knotted strings.

Finally, one of the reasons metal was not readily incorporated into Andean technologies of warfare was its chief competitor on the field of battle: cloth, used both offensively and defensively (Lechtman 1984a). Slings, made by weaving, braiding, and plaiting animal and vegetable fibers, were among the most important weapons used throughout Andean prehistory. They are, essentially, tools of cloth. In the line drawings Felipe Guaman Poma (1936) rendered to illustrate his 1,200-page letter to King Philip III of Spain in 1613, the Inka emperors and the captains of their armies are depicted as great warriors. The weapon Poma chose above all as the attribute of their military strength is the sling. For body armor, soldiers wore quilted cotton tunics or wound layers of cloth around their bodies. Most of the Spanish soldiers adopted quilted armor from the Inka, regarding it as superior to European steel breastplates (Montell 1929). Inka troops used quilted or wooden helmets, and sometimes individuals wrapped cloth around one arm, using it as a shield to ward off the blows of offending clubs. But cloth competed with metal as a war material for other, deeper, culturally symbolic reasons. It had a magico-military significance of its own, embodying the conditions of strength and force. Thus an enemy stripped of his garments was an enemy without retaliatory capacity. His force and his energy lay in his clothing. Such Andean attitudes, reflected in the Spanish chronicles (Murra 1962), had deep roots and were clearly current among the Moche peoples of north coastal Peru at least 1,000 years before the Inka expansion. A Moche battle scene—painted on the flaring inner lip of a pottery vase in the Museum für Völkerkunde, Berlin—shows a group of Moche warriors in full battle regalia leading their bound captives who march, naked, stripped of their garments (Lechtman 1984a; Murra 1962). Murra (1962) reports that, according to Zarate, during the European occupation of Xauxa, an important Inka administrative center in the Peruvian highlands, the Inka general Quizquiz retreated suddenly, leaving behind 15,000 llamas and 4,000 prisoners but burning all the cloth he could not carry. And there are numerous other accounts in the same vein.

Cloth production must be seen as part of a wider Andean commitment to the use of fibers, and fiber technologies were paramount in the Andean culture area. At the same time, the specific technologies associated with cloth manufacture developed the pervasiveness and the virtuosity they had because they were elaborated around that category of material culture of greatest significance to the individual, the community, and the state. Aside from its many and crucial utilitarian functions, cloth served as the aesthetic locus of Andean society. It was the most important carrier of status, the material of choice for the communication of message, whether religious, political, or scientific. Zuidema (1977, 1982) describes Middle Horizon (Huari) and Late Horizon (Inka) textiles as calendars representing both sidereal lunar and solar years. The Inka relied heavily on the use of cloth for their military, diplomatic, and ideological success. The special and technically elegant *cumbi* cloth, woven by state retainers—the female *aclla* and male *cumbi camayocs*—was distributed by the state as gifts to outstanding army officers and administrative officials, as grants to the leaders (*curacas*) of vanquished polities to cement their political allegiance, and as diplomatic exchanges. Or it was ritually sacrificed, in great quantity, according to the requirements of the state ceremonial calendar (Morris 1974; Murra 1962). As the state expanded and consolidated, the mechanisms of political control practiced by its rulers shifted toward increasingly ideological, symbolic, and prestige manipulating forms in which cloth, in larger and larger quantities, played the major and remarkable role.

Why do we hear so little, then, about the technology of Andean cloth manufacture, the technology that lay behind "the artifact of greatest prestige and thus the most useful in power relations" (Murra 1962:721)? Andean weavers of the prehistoric period have been credited with the manufacture of virtually every type of preindustrial cloth except satin weave, and "almost every known technique of modern weaving was used as well as a number which are either impossible or impractical for mechanical looms" (Bennett and Bird 1960:257–58). The exhilaration and technical virtuosity of the technology account for such unusual and complex forms of weaving as triple and quadruple cloth, or patchwork based on discontinuous warps (Bennett and Bird 1960; Stone-Miller 1992). Weft counts on archaeological textiles executed in tapestry technique frequently register over 250 wefts per inch on the average, and some exceed 500 wefts per inch in areas of detail (Bennett and Bird 1960; Gayton 1961), documenting the extraordinary fineness and regularity of the diameter of the yarn and the paramount control of the tension on the fibers during spinning. Spanish accounts of Inka textiles describe the finest as silk-like (Rowe 1946). The machinery of production was straightforward, the inventory of equipment modest. Spindles and spindle whorls of many sizes and weights were used for spinning yarn of cotton and wool. Loom types known through the ethnohistoric and archaeological record, whether depicted on pottery or textiles or available as preserved artifacts, include variations of the backstrap loom, the horizontal loom, the A-frame loom, and the vertical loom (Skinner 1974).

What made possible the impressive industry of cloth production at the scale required by the Inka state were two features of the technology unrelated to its hardware: the availability of the technology—the knowledge, the skills, the cultural commitment—at all levels of society and to virtually all its members, regardless of age and sex, and the organization of this "intelligence of production" into the state enterprise.

Apparently, virtually all members of Andean society spun, and all women and some men wove. This is still the case in some of the more isolated communities in the central highlands. Studies of such contemporary communities (Bird 1968; Franquemont and Franquemont 1987; Goodell 1968;) show that between the ages of about six and ten years girls have become accomplished spinners, and the finest yarn is often spun by nimble-fingered girls at this age level. It comes as no surprise, then, that the Inka recruited their *aclla* spinners from such a pool of practitioners. The girls left their communities fully trained—mistresses of their craft. The state had essentially an inexhaustible supply of such specialists, who must have received subsequent instruction in the design and execution of garments made exclusively for the crown and church (Murra 1980a), either in Cusco or in the special weaving establishments located in administrative cities throughout the realm (Morris 1978). It is more difficult to document the careers of the *cumbi camayocs*, the male retainers whose woven products constituted the prestige items distributed by the state. The Spanish chroniclers paid much more attention to the phenomenon of the "weaving nuns" than to their male counterparts. Nevertheless, in many Andean communities then, as now, men as well as women wove, and Murra's impression (1962) from the ethnohistoric literature is that it was the men who, at the community level, produced the specialized fabrics. It was from among such men—particularly those physically infirm who were less likely to engage in agriculture and set up households (Murra 1962)—that the state drew individuals to become skilled *cumbi camayocs*. Certainly there were centers known for the quality of their weaving in pre-Inka times, and it is equally certain that specialists in the production of fine cloth from throughout the empire were incorporated into the state manufacturing system (Murra 1962). But the fundamentals of the technology—the "bodies of skills, knowledge, and procedures" that constitute any technology (Merrill 1968:576)—were universal. They were more than a mere resource for the state. They were the technological backbone which, in quintessentially Andean fashion, impelled the expression of state power through a medium—cloth—to which Andean society was irrevocably committed.

The Inka achievement lay in the organization and management of this Andean technological spine. The obligation of adult women to the state was realized through a weaving corvée, the annual household production of a certain quantity of *awasqa,* plain cloth, destined primarily for use by the army. This responsibility was carried out at the community level with issues of raw cotton and wool supplied by the state from its vast storehouse reserves. Thus the machinery of production was skillfully orchestrated: annual supplies of plain cloth for military ends were in the hands of community women whose citizenship in Tawantinsuyu was cemented through their weaving obligation. At the same time, the increasing needs of the Inka for fine cloth, which served their political ends in the normative realm, were met by specialists who wove solely and in great quantity for the state.

The cloth industry of the Inka was impressive, but its production technology remains uncelebrated. Murra himself provides a partial explanation when he remarks, "There is nothing strange in the political use of prestige objects; the novelty consists in discovering that, in the Andean area, the artifact of greatest prestige and thus the most useful in power relations was cloth" (1962:721). Is this the stuff of which empires are built? In the Inka case, clearly it was. But can an army wielding woolen slings and cotton armor be taken as seriously—by us, not by their adversaries—as one armed with bronze or iron weapons? What is "hard" about a technology whose resource base is fibers—soft, impermanent, needing frequent renewal, and certainly not the material of which tools and machines are made. From our perspective, Andean textile technology was "low tech", hardware poor, a technology with feminine overtones. All the nonspecialized production took place in households and was in the hands of women, as was the cloistered manufacture of *cumbi* for the royal person, his *ayllu* (lineage), and his clergy. The feminine bias of the technology, the "softness" of the activity and its product, its tool-poor status all mark it as unnoteworthy. But, in a larger sense, we have lacked interest because we have failed to recognize in the state's impressive coordination and management of the rich technological base it inherited the aspect of the technology that was key to its industrial success.

Metallurgy, Values, and Power

Metallurgy developed quite differently in the Old World and in the New during the prehistoric era.[2] The metallurgical technologies of the Bronze

---

[2] The substance of the following discussion appears in Lechtman 1984a. The reader is referred to that publication for a detailed explanation of the metallurgical processes involved in electrochemical replacement plating and depletion gilding, which have been omitted here.

and Iron Ages received their greatest stimulus in the domains of warfare, transportation, and agriculture.

In Europe and the Near East, both in the hand-to-hand combat of the foot soldier and in equestrian battle, the effectiveness of weapons was based largely on their piercing and cutting action. Knives, daggers, long and short swords, lance heads, spears, javelins, and battle axes of bronze and later of iron became the new arsenal replacing stone, wood, and bone weapons, which could not compare in strength and durability. The manufacture of such offensive weapons was accompanied by the equally important production of their defensive counterparts—body armor, manufactured in both bronze and iron. Iron armor scales have been found that date to the eleventh century B.C., accompanying the early use of iron for offensive weaponry in the Near East and the Aegean.

Although few examples remain of metal-rimmed wheels from chariots, wagons, carts, and other such vehicles, it is clear that the availability of bronze, and more especially of iron, for the manufacture of animal-drawn wheeled conveyances had a profound effect on long distance-travel and the movement of goods. By the end of the fifth century B.C., complex iron bridge bits and wheel pegs, linch pins, nave fittings, and tires for chariots were in common use in Europe and the Near East (Pleiner 1980; Snodgrass 1980, Waldbaum 1980). By Roman times, the effectiveness of military legions in their movements throughout Europe in particular was dependent on ease of transport of the gear and provisions that accompanied them, much of it conveyed on wagons of wood and iron.

The agricultural use of both bronze and iron was important in the Old World, although it was not primarily through the manufacture of metal tools for farming that the technology of metal production received its greatest impetus. The Early Iron Age (ca. 1200–900 B.C.) was a period of transition from the use of bronze for all weapons and implements made of metal to the introduction of iron onto the scene. We see a change from the exclusive use of bronze for ploughshares, axes, adzes, and hoes at twelfth-century B.C. habitation sites in Cyprus and Palestine, for example, to the preferred use of iron for those same agricultural tools, including sickles, by the tenth century (Waldbaum 1980). Iron approached something akin to common use throughout the eastern Mediterranean, both for weapons and tools, by the end of the tenth century.

Turning to the Andes, we find that in neither war nor transport did metals play an extraordinary part. Cavalry did not exist in South America before the introduction of the horse by the invading Spaniards. All combat was on foot. Hand-to-hand fighting involved the use of clubs of various kinds that depended on the crushing action of the blow delivered rather than on the cutting or piercing action of the weapons; mace heads of stone and bronze were equally effective. Of equal importance, however, were long-distance missile weapons. Spears and spear throwers, slings and sling shot were crucial to Andean styles of battle. Clearly, whether an adversary was hit by shot of stone or of metal could not have made any great difference. We have already recognized the central and competitive role of cloth in Andean military operations, both for offensive and defensive tactics, relegating metal to a marginal status for certain military uses. By the period of Inka domination, the panoply of Andean highland weapons included the sling, the star-headed mace, the spear with tip of fire-hardened wood or bronze, the long, sword-shaped double-edged club made of hard chonta palm wood, and the halberd with bronze head (Rowe 1946). Given the style of warfare in the Andes among both coastal and highland peoples, with weapons that depended on strength at impact rather than on a cutting edge, metal weapons did not confer great advantage either on the aggressor or the defender.

Those who have traveled in Andean South America will have been impressed by the topography of that great land mass, a topography entirely dominated by the rugged and almost impassable Andes mountain chain. The Pacific coast of the central Andean zone consists of a narrow strip of barren, sandy desert from which the precipitous mountain slopes rise abruptly to the east. The wheel was not invented and could not have been utilized in this part of the world. Local fauna provided no draft animals or beasts of burden. The largest domesticated animals of the Andes are the camelids, the llama and alpaca. An adult llama typically carries only about 60 pounds. Movement, including the long-distance travel of the Inka armies, was entirely on foot along narrow roads, often hewn out of the living rock, which covered the entire length of the 3,000-odd mile expanse of the empire (Hyslop 1984). There was, in essence, no transport technology into which metals could be incorporated.

The combination of a steep, vertical terrain on which to cultivate and the unavailability of local fauna large and strong enough to be suitable as draft animals resulted in highland agricultural technologies based on terracing. Where terraces were not used, long periods of fallow were combined with the most conservative amounts of soil movement in tillage to minimize erosion and the ever-present threat of downslope loss of soil by gravity. Thus the *chaqui taclla*, the Andean footplough—a tool that functions as both hoe and digging stick—became the most important implement for planting, and in many highland areas it remains so. The blades of such tools were typically of stone, though bronze blades are known from the Peruvian north coast that date to about A.D. 1000, and modern blades are forged from iron (Lechtman 1981b). The animal-drawn plough was introduced by the Spaniards in the sixteenth century.

Metals performed at a totally different level in the New World from that in the Old. Their locus was in the realm of the symbolic. Andean domains of life in which metals were most important were those domains associated with political power, status display, and religious affective force. That is not to say that Andean societies lacked tools or even weapons of metal. They had and used both. What differed markedly in the Andean culture area was the emphasis in metal production, the kinds of objects at the center of metallurgical attention because they were at the center of social attention. Such objects—the attributes of rank and power in both life and death—included elaborate ear spools (a form of earring) and nose rings, death masks fitted onto mummy bundles, religious cult objects, and, as an example of Inka royal investment in the symbolic power of metals, entire gardens within the imperial palaces filled with plants, flowers, and birds all fabricated of gold and silver.

Status among Andean peoples, as in many societies, was instantly conveyed by what one wore in life and at death. Ear spools, for example, were appurtenances of men and sometimes women (Donnan 1993) of high rank, perhaps kings or priests. Some of the earliest and most splendid examples are of Moche origin. Although we have spools of wood and others covered with feathers or inlaid with precious stones and shells, the finest are often made from metal (Jones 1979). Their importance as conveyors of status and worldly or spiritual power was formally institutionalized by the Inka who alone were permitted to wear them. Guaman Poma's (1936) drawings of the Inka emperors show them wearing such ear spools. In Poma's illustrations, we can distinguish between members of the royal lineage and other individuals on the basis of their garments and whether or not they wear ear spools. In fact, Spanish references to the Inka as *orejones* (big ears) reflect this practice.

At death, it was the custom in many parts of the Andes to inter the deceased in the form of a mummy, the body wrapped with cloth of a quality that denoted the individual's position within the community during his or her lifetime. In addition, those of highest status were sometimes also provided with masks of metal sewn onto or lying just beneath the outermost layers of cloth. The finest and usually the largest mummy masks are golden, though originally they were painted and decorated with plaques of copper and other materials. Those most often exhibited by museums are attributed to the Sicán culture (Carcedo and Shimada 1985) and, at a later time, to the Chimu kingdom, which dominated the north coast of present-day Peru from about A.D. 1200 until its conquest by the Inka in 1470.

The thrust of Andean metallurgy lay in the development of metals, alloys, and fabrication procedures that would realize specific properties essential to the proper cultural performance of objects that functioned in the secular and religious realms. The property, above all others, that metalworkers sought to control was color. The focus of Andean metallurgy on the production and manipulation of color in metal reflected and reinforced a value system deeply embedded in Andean society, a system that equated the visual manifestation of status and power with the colors, textures, and reflectivity of metallic gold and silver. A glance at the inventory of surviving precolumbian metal objects that functioned as symbols of rank and of political and religious power indicates that it was their color—as much as, if not more than, their form—which acted as the carrier of such symbolic information. From the earliest involvement of Andean peoples with metal up to the time of the Spanish conquest of the Inka empire, the two colors that were paramount in the metallurgical spectrum were those of gold and silver.

Indeed, gold and silver had special ritual and political significance throughout Andean prehistory, from their first important use as carriers of religious iconographic motifs associated with the Chavín cult that swept through the central Andes about 800 B.C. until their use by the Inka royal dynasty as symbols of political power used solely by the emperor. All the vast mineral wealth of the Andean empire belonged to the Inka, and among the metals he controlled gold and silver were prominent. They were his birthright, for the Inka dynasty began with the offspring of the sun and the moon. The first Inka was the son of the sun. In Inka cosmology, gold represented the sun, silver the moon. Thus, these two metals were intimately associated with the origin myth of the ruling dynasty and were second only to cloth as visible indices of its wealth and power. Everyone is familiar with the stories recounted by invading Spaniards of Inka palaces whose walls were covered with sheets of silver and gold, of special rooms with miniature gardens that sprouted golden plants through whose leaves flew gold and silver birds. Of course, little of this wealth remains, for it was converted to bullion in the European melting pot.

Once color becomes the focus of property development, we are dealing with the metallurgy of surfaces, because the color of a metal object resides at its surface. The object may have one color at the surface and a totally different color underneath, corresponding to differences in metal or alloy composition at the surface and in the underlying material. Because Andean metallurgy was color-oriented, it was also surface-oriented.

The most innovative and interesting aspects of Andean metallurgy arose as a response of the technology to an overriding system of visual communication, as smiths attempted to produce metallic gold or silver surfaces on objects that were made of other metals. These efforts resulted in the purposeful manufacture of binary and ternary alloys of copper, silver, and gold and in a remarkable set of metallurgical and electrochemical procedures for gilding and silvering objects made of copper.

The two most sophisticated Andean gilding procedures—electrochemical replacement plating and depletion gilding—can now be credited to the metalsmiths of Moche society, which flourished along the north coast of present-day Peru from about 100 B.C. to A.D. 800. In many respects, Moche metallurgy epitomizes the central Andean tradition of metal manufacture. The virtuosity of its technology and the quality of its products were unequaled by those of succeeding cultures, including the Inka. A large group of objects of Moche style was found at the site of Loma Negra, on the far north coast of Peru, near the Ecuadorian border (Lechtman, Erlij, and Barry 1982). Most are made of hammered sheet copper, individual, shaped pieces of which were often joined to produce three-dimensional forms. The outside, and occasionally the inside, surfaces of the copper sheet were covered with extremely thin coatings of gold or silver so that the objects appeared to be made of those metals.

Laboratory study of the Loma Negra artifacts together with experiments designed to reproduce the gross characteristics and microstructures of these remarkably thin (0.5–2 μm) and uniform gold and silver coatings revealed that the copper had been plated (gilt or silvered) by some system of electrochemical deposition (Lechtman 1979a). In other words, Moche smiths were able to deposit gold or silver onto copper without the use of modern chemicals, such as cyanide or aqua regia for dissolving the gold, and without the use of an external source of current. They apparently dissolved gold and silver in mixtures of corrosive minerals—such as common salt, potassium nitrate, and potassium aluminum sulphate—which were readily available in the coastal desert environment and which earlier studies have shown were probably used by the Moche (Lechtman 1973). Once in solution, the gold or silver plated directly onto the surface of copper objects dipped into the solution, providing those surfaces with infinitesimally thin and regular coatings of the precious metals.

Plating by electrochemical replacement occurs when a metal, such as copper, high in the electromotive series (at the negative, or base, end of the series) is placed in an electrolyte containing ions of a metal, such as gold, lower in the series (at the positive, or noble, end). Chemically, a simple replacement reaction occurs, such as:

$$2AuCl_3 + 3Cu \rightarrow 2Au + 3CuCl_2$$

But such an equation does not reveal the mechanism, which is identical with that in the simple cells used by the first electroplaters. It is necessary to have anode and cathode areas, both of which must be in contact with an electrolyte, and a complete circuit for electrons to flow from the anode through the metal to the cathode area, balanced by the return flow of ions through the electrolyte.

In replacement plating, different parts of the same metal surface provide both the anode and the cathode. In the case of the Loma Negra objects, small pits or irregularities on the surface of the copper sheet initially acted as anodes and continued their anodic activity until they were completely blocked or protected from the electrolyte by the deposit—the gold—which plated onto adjacent cathodic surfaces (Lechtman 1979a).

Moche metalsmiths were not limited solely to gilding and silvering objects made of copper. Their desire to achieve culturally valued color effects was played out in the alloy systems they developed, some of which have come to be considered the hallmark of Andean prehistoric metallurgy.

One of the most interesting and exciting aspects of any indigenous metallurgy is the way alloys develop—the reasons for which particular alloy systems emerge from the range of possible choices, and the relations between those alloy systems and other aspects of culture. In the Andes there is at least one trend we can follow from its earliest, circumscribed appearance to its ultimate, far-flung dispersion from present-day Peru to Mexico: the development of a series of alloys whose primary use was the creation of a silver or gold color on the surface of metal objects made of the alloys.

The earliest of these alloys to be identified archaeologically is that of copper and silver (Lechtman 1979b). Copper-silver alloys have two properties that were of primary importance to Andean craftspeople: their toughness when hammered and their development of enriched silver surfaces when hammered and annealed. The central Andean tradition of metal manufacture was a sheet metal tradition based on the working of metal (Lechtman 1988), in contrast to the casting tradition of Colombian and other Central American peoples. The large majority of metal objects manufactured in the Andes were made of hammered metal, often in the form of sheet. The malleability of copper-silver allowed it to be hammered and shaped; its toughness and hardness ensured that, once formed, the metal would retain its shape. It was thus an excellent material for metalworkers whose forte was the production of items—often complex three-dimensional sculptures—from elaborately hammered and joined pieces of preformed metal sheet.

In addition, copper-silver alloys display marked surface enrichment when they are worked and annealed in air. When a piece of metal is hammered cold, as in the production of sheet, it becomes hard and increasingly difficult to work. Heating the metal to a dull red enables it to recrystallize; its malleability is restored, and hammering can proceed. When a copper-silver alloy is heated in air, however, the copper reacts preferentially to form a superficial layer of scale. The removal of this oxide scale by mechanical or chemical means exposes the underlying layer of metal, enriched in silver through loss of copper. Repeated sequences of hammering, annealing with attendant oxidation of surface copper, and removal of the copper oxide scale results in the gradual depletion of copper at the surface. After a few such anneals, the surface of the sheet looks like, indeed is, nearly pure silver (Lechtman 1971; Root 1949).

Thus, metal made from such alloys, of a mottled copper color when cast, is bright silver in color after having been hammered into sheet. The formation of silvered surfaces on objects hammered from these alloys is an inescapable consequence of annealing in air and of the attendant loss of surface copper through oxidation. There is, essentially, no way of preventing it. We have called the process depletion silvering.

Although a few objects of copper-silver alloy are known long before the period of Moche florescence, the Moche developed the alloy and used it over a wide range of silver concentration: from a few percent to over 30 percent silver, by weight. They manufactured objects from it that were hard and tough and that looked like silver. In later periods, these alloys continued to be used for the same reasons.

By far the most important alloy system developed by the Moche was that of copper-gold, often referred to as *tumbaga*. Copper and gold, when melted, mix together in all proportions and remain mixed in the solid state, forming a complete solid solution series throughout the entire range of possible alloy compositions. Precolumbian objects of *tumbaga* vary widely in their relative proportions of copper and gold, some containing as little as 12–15 percent gold, by weight. Silver is also often found in these alloys, either because the gold used contained some silver, as Andean placer gold usually does, or because the ternary alloy was produced by adding gold to a binary copper-silver alloy.

Copper-gold alloys, like copper-silver alloys, become hard on hammering but retain their flexibility. They were, therefore, well suited to the sheet metal tradition already characteristic of north Peruvian metalworking. But these alloys were used and subsequently highly developed primarily for another property: the gold color that articles made from them can be given by chemical treatment. An ingot of copper-gold alloy may be coppery red or pink or gold in color, depending on the amount of gold it contains.

When such an ingot is hammered to produce thin sheet metal, copper is lost from the surfaces of the alloy through oxidation on annealing, just as in the case of coper-silver alloys. Objects made from reddish, copper-rich *tumbagas* soon develop golden surfaces as increasing amounts of copper are lost.

Many of the large golden mummy masks from Peru familiar to museum goers are of Sicán and Chimu origin. The largest known example of these, in the collection of the Metropolitan Museum of Art in New York City, measures 29 inches wide by 16 inches high. Its golden surface is dazzling, yet the mask is made of a ternary alloy containing only 39 percent gold, the remainder being silver (49 percent) and copper (12 percent) (Lechtman 1973).

In manufacturing the sheet metal for a mummy mask, periodic annealing keeps the alloy malleable and formable. On each anneal, a brown to black copper oxide scale coats the surface and must be removed before hammering can continue. Andean smiths could have used certain acid plant juices or stale urine, which degrades to ammonia, to pickle off the copper oxide scale. After many sequences of hammering, annealing, and pickling, the resulting thin metal sheet loses enough surface copper to enrich the surfaces in silver and gold. A mummy mask at this stage of manufacture would appear as if made of silver, since the binary silver-gold alloy remaining at the surface is usually silvery white in color.

But the mummy masks are brightly golden. Sicán and Chimu smiths, approaching the task of gilding from the same point of view as that of silvering, were faced with the problem of removing the silver in the surface silver-gold binary alloy in order to leave only the gold in place. A modern chemist might use various cyanide solutions or distilled nitric acid to part silver from gold, but we can assume that such distilled acids were not available to Andean smiths. Laboratory studies suggest (Lechtman 1973) that what they did have at hand and apparently used were combinations of naturally occurring acid minerals—such as ferric sulphate and sodium chloride (common table salt)—which in aqueous solution, effectively remove silver from a silver-gold alloy, leaving the gold behind. This discovery had already been made by the Moche, though it was most widely adopted by the later Sicán and Chimu.

Depletion gilding—the term used to denote this set of procedures—relies on the removal from the surface of an alloy of its baser metal constituents to leave the noblest metal in place. It was used effectively by the Chimu to gild sheet metal objects that contained as little as 12 percent gold by weight.

The *tumbaga* alloys with their inherent gold-enrichment properties swept through the Americas from Peru to Mexico and were in common use in that entire region when the Spaniards invaded Mexico and Central and South America in the sixteenth century. They constitute the most significant contribution of the New World to the repertoire of alloy systems developed among ancient societies.

In the central Andes, copper-rich *tumbagas* were used primarily to produce gold-colored objects of sheet metal. In Colombia, Central America, and Mexico, they were used in lost wax castings (Bray 1978; Root 1964). Once cast, objects made of *tumbaga* can be gilt directly by dissolving the surface copper with a corrosive solution. If the alloy contains very little gold, such castings can be annealed and pickled several times to enrich the gold at the surface.

Electrochemical replacement and depletion silvering or gilding represent two opposite approaches to the production of a colored metal surface on a metal substrate. Both involve sophisticated chemistry, and precolumbian surface metallurgy is surely as much chemistry as it is metallurgy. But replacement plating achieves color change by covering one metal with another, hiding what is underneath. Depletion systems, in contrast, transform surfaces by selectively developing at the surface certain properties of the material that lies beneath. One system covers and hides. The other system develops and enhances.

It is significant that of the various surface covering or coating systems identified thus far in a general inventory of Andean objects—electrochemical replacement plating, the use of gold foil, the flushing on of molten gold—none had more than a local and brief impact on the development of precolumbian metallurgical technologies. Depletion surface metallurgy, however, dominated the metallurgical scene in the New World for between one and two millennia.

There has been considerable discussion about why *tumbaga* had the impact it had, why it spread so far, accommodating to the metalworking traditions of the various cultures that adopted it. Traditions of artisans from the Andes and the Intermediate area were almost polar opposites: the former were exquisite forgers of metal, the latter were superb founders. Each tradition tailored the concept of depletion and enrichment to its own techniques. Explanations have invoked the economy of the system, that is, that one can spread one's gold much farther if objects are made of *tumbaga* rather than of pure gold. But if one argues for the economizing of gold, one has also to bear in mind that in alloys of *tumbaga* all the gold inside the alloy is "wasted." Only that at the surface is functional in the sense that it is visible. Using gold leaf or other external plating systems would be much more economical. The ternary copper-silver-gold *tumbagas* were also used, at least in parts of Colombia, in the manufacture of tools such as awls and axes, which were cast and selectively work-hardened to rival the best Inka products in copper-tin bronze. Thus it was a serviceable alloy for tool production, though it was used much less frequently for making tools than for almost every other variety of object produced by the Colombians—nose rings, *tunjos,* vessels, ornaments, and so forth. Root (1951) argued that, although *tumbaga* might have been used because it made casting easier, because it made objects harder, and because it made a small amount of gold go farther, the most likely reason for its employ was that the people who made and used it preferred the color of gold to that of copper; or, to put it another way, they liked the color of *tumbaga* more than that of gold or copper.

Although all these considerations presumably enter into the technology of *tumbaga,* there is another factor that lies more in the realm of attitudes—attitudes of artisans toward the materials they used and attitudes of societies toward the nature of technological events themselves. We are really seeking explanations, not for the use of the particular copper-gold alloy called *tumbaga,* but for the development, geographical spread, and persistence for over two millennia of systems of surface enrichment that stimulated the invention of a variety of alloys and that were adapted to quite different traditions of handling metals.

The force behind this unusual metallurgical tradition, or what we may certainly call a technological style, was ideological. The basis of Andean enrichment systems is the incorporation of the essential ingredient—the gold or silver—into the very body of the object. The essence of the object, that which appears superficially to be true of it, must also be inside it. In fact, the object is not that object unless it contains within it the essential quality, even if the essence is only minimally present. Translated into metallurgical terms, the alloy of which an object is made must contain the metal—gold or silver—which is later to be developed and enhanced at its surface and which becomes the visual hallmark of the object.

The metallurgy of surfaces was important in the New World because precolumbian metallurgy was color-oriented. The increasing attention of craftspeople to surface phenomena and their sophistication in developing systems to transform metal surfaces reflects the importance of the surface as the visible manifestation of an inner state or property. The surface became the location where aspects of the inner state were realized and enhanced. Surfaces are, after all, boundaries between an inner condition and an external reality or environment. The surface is where the two meet. It is the place of communication, the seat of greatest information content. When information is conveyed visually, the surface assumes special importance.

Reichel-Dolmatoff's (1981) ethnographic research among the Desana and other Tukanoan peoples of the northwest Amazon—in what is today the nation of Colombia—is telling in lending strength to the development of these interpretations provoked by the technical analyses of Andean metals. Desana wear ornaments—some made by them, others heirlooms that have been handed down for generations—such as necklaces and ear pendants made of silver, but they say that in former times these adornments were also made of gold. Ear pendants are often of copper. A Desana tale (Reichel-Dolmatoff 1981: 20–21) that describes the tradition of metallurgy in the rainforests of the northwest Amazon speaks of two metals: white and yellow. Reichel learned from his informants that what the tale designates "as 'white and yellow' does not refer to actual metallic colors, but to abstract qualities, to an invisible 'white' crative force, and to a visible and material yellow potential." The Desana explained that "these two forces met and mingled in different proportions. The basic material state was the visible sun, associated with gold and with human semen, while the 'whiteness' was a modifying abstract cosmic force which heightened or diminished the quality of the golden component" (21).

Yellow is symbolically the most important color for Desana, who distinguish some thirty different hues, intensities, and values that range from a pale yellowish to a deep orange color. In Tukanoan color symbolism, white and yellow are associated with male potency. Complementary to this male color symbolism of white/yellow is a color range of reddish hues. Red is said to be a female color. The color combination of yellow/red stands, therefore, for male/female fertility and fecundity:

> In Tukanoan mythology and cosmology the sun represents a male-fertilizing principle associated with the yellow color range, while the moon is female. Her colors are variable because they depend entirely upon the influence of the sun; they range from yellow-green to a dark red-orange and to blue-violet. ... Both Sun and Moon are imagined as human prototypes, as a heavenly couple that exemplifies male/female relationships, be they between husband and wife, father and daughter, or brother and sister.
>
> Ideally, the sun fertilizes a brilliant New Moon which [then] passes through a sequence of yellowish, reddish, and copper-colored phases which are compared to ... the process of embryonic development. (Reichel-Dolmatoff 1981:21)

Copper, in this thought system, is considered a material of transformation. Thus the process of fertilization, of transformation, and of birth—in other words, Desana concepts of potency, generation, and growth—is held to be a model of metallurgical combinations (Reichel-Dolmatoff 1981: 21). For the purposes of our discussion here, it is a model for alloying, for combining copper, silver, and gold in the preparation of the alloys of *tumbaga*. To quote Reichel-Dolmatoff, "the main importance of personal metal adornments [among present-day Tukanoan peoples] lies in their symbolic associations expressed in their alloys, coloring, shape, and odor" (22).

It is in every way reasonable to consider that the Inka insistence on the colors of silver and gold and the deep-seated Andean commitment to the alloy *tumbaga* and to the procedures that transform the copper of that alloy to silver or gold—a commitment prevalent for millennia throughout the entire Andean culture area and, as we have seen, still persisting in the Amazon lowlands today—expressed an equation, the equation of power with the control of certain metals—metals which, when alloyed and transformed, embodied and communicated the continuity of the royal lineage and therefore of the state. The laboratory-analytical data are congruent with the ethnographic and ethnohistoric data.

Although enrichment systems—whether of silver or gold—have been used by metalworkers in other areas of the world, their position in the Andes is unique. Almost from the earliest appearance of metallurgy there, depletion and enrichment processes assumed a special place that persisted throughout the entire course of Andean metallurgical development; they were responsible for stimulating some of its most interesting achievements. Although ideological considerations may have had little to do with the initial working out of these procedures, it seems certain that the way Andean peoples perceived such processes (or at least the objects that resulted from their use) had a great deal to do with the way the technology emerged and matured. Belief systems and attitudes toward materials supported the technology and gave rise to further developments along similar lines.

Technologies of Ideology, Technologies of Power

On another occasion, I suggested that one of the ways to test hypotheses concerning incorporation of essences as an ideological motif underlying the elaboration of Andean metal-gilding technologies and its possible involvement in a general style of technological behavior within Andean society would be to examine those technologies that surround what is unequivocally the most important arena of Andean material culture: cloth production (Lechtman 1977). Do similar concerns appear to have operated in the elaborate weaving techniques utilized by Andean specialists in the prehistoric period?

No other item of manufacture in the Andes assumed the importance of cloth. Although from quite early periods of Andean prehistory it is clear that groups of specialists were involved in the production of elite textiles, it is equally evident that the technology was a pervasive, universal element of Andean life. This intense involvement in the technology, in conjunction with the social-ideational significance of cloth, led to the elaboration of an extremely wide range of highly sophisticated weaving techniques. All scholars agree that Andean textiles rank among the finest preindustrial cloth.

One of the most impressive aspects of Andean weaving results from the preponderant use of "structural" as opposed to "suprastructural" techniques for realizing the patterns carried by the finished cloth. When a design or pattern is achieved through suprastructural means, the design is added to a completed web. Its removal from that web would in no way affect the integrity of the woven cloth, which acts as a support for the design but is otherwise structurally unchanged by it. Embroidered designs fall in this category, as do brocading and painted cloth; dyed textiles, achieved by tie-dye or, in a sense, *ikat,* are also included in this group. Such techniques were used by Andean weavers. In contrast, designs achieved by structural means are realized through the manipulation of warp and weft yarns during the process of weaving so that the design emerges from the structural rendering of the web. To remove the design would be to destroy, literally to unweave, the cloth. Tapestry techniques; double, triple, and quadruple cloth; gauze weaves; discontinuous warp or scaffold weaves; and warp patterned weaves as well as plain weaves are only some of the Andean cloth types whose characteristics are achieved through manipulation of the structural elements of the fabric. There is no question that the primary creative direction of Andean weaving lay in the rich elaboration of structural techniques, in the playing out of a structural technological style. As Anna Gayton observed when discussing ancient Peruvian textiles, "this potency of structure, sufficient to enhance or mar the qualities of yarns, colors, and designs, was a major motivation for developing the different methods of interlacing warps and wefts which distinguish one weaving technique from another" (1961:117).

Comparing Andean weaving with any of the other great traditions of cloth manufacture, whether Asian or European, nowhere else do we find such an elaboration of and commitment to a broad range of weaving techniques based on loom yarn manipulation. It is not simply that Andean cloth production greatly emphasized and relied on patterns structurally rendered, but that the complexity of such structural manipulations—as in quadruple cloth—went far beyond mere virtuosity. William Conklin (personal communication, September 1982) argues persuasively that the reason behind such a rich field of structural invention in Andean weaving lies in the role of textiles as the chief carrier of cultural message in conjunction with the availability of the technology at all levels of the society.

What we must ask is whether the visual message carried by Andean cloth, to the extent that that message was borne by the design motifs, had to be contained in and generated by the very structure of the fabric itself; that is, just as in the case of the depletion gilding of metal, does there come a point at which the technology itself becomes the medium for the expression of message? In the case of Andean highland weaving, intricate manipulations of many warp planes and myriad weft yarns were, strictly speaking, unnecessary to the accomplishment of the designs. Simpler techniques could have achieved the same patterns. But Andean weaving seems to have responded to notions of the visual, surface message as emerging from underlying, invisible structural relations. Andean weaving insists that message be embodied in and expressed by structure.[3]

It is clear that key technologies associated with cloth and metal production shared stylistic modes, perhaps because those modes are expressions of cultural ideals, incorporating ideological concerns of the society at large. Lexicographic and ethnographic studies of Andean metallurgical and weaving vocabularies should certainly help to integrate the realm of technical process with that of cosmic ideas about universal processes. Ethnohistoric research on craft production and on Andean cosmologies is absolutely essential in this regard. For example, both Regina Harrison (1982) and Gerald Taylor (1974–76) call attention to the use in late sixteenth- and early seventeenth-century Quechua religious texts of the term *camay,* the act of infusing life spirit into an inanimate object. In various ritual poems that refer to the acts of creation by Viracocha, the creator, the term *camay* is used expressly to denote Viracocha's animating or breathing a spirit into an object. *Camay* refers to the domain of the material, to the domain of people and the natural and cultural objects they fashion and use. Perhaps the notion of "technological essence," of the visually apprehended aspect of an object as revealing its inner structure, is related to these fundamental Andean concepts of the divine animation of all material things.[4]

---

[3]In thinking about the similarities underlying aspects of Andean prehistoric metallurgical and cloth technologies, I have benefited greatly from discussions with two scholars of Andean cloth production, William Conklin and Edward Franquemont.

[4]I am most grateful to the Andean ethnologist Tristan Platt for calling my attention to the Harrison (1982) article and to the possible relevance of the concept *camay* to the technology of essences. In a personal communication of June 1982, while discussing Andean metallurgy, Platt speculated that the notion of a divine force animating a particular object *could* be equivalent to a divine metal giving life to an alloy.

Andean peoples engineered metal and fibers so that objects that functioned within the aesthetic and power loci of Andean society were there by virtue of their rendering. The styles of Andean technologies strongly influenced the spheres of cultural activity and perceptions in which such objects functioned. The technologies themselves conferred power and maintained the relations of power because process and product were culturally indivisible and, therefore, manipulable to the ends of ideology.

References

Bennett, Wendell C., and Junius B. Bird
    1960   *Andean Culture History.* Handbook Series, no. 15. New York: American Museum of Natural History.

Bergsøe, Paul
    1938   The gilding process and the metallurgy of copper and lead among the pre-columbian Indians. *Ingeniorvidenskabelige Skrifter* A46:1–56.

Bird, Junius B.
    1968   Handspun yarn production rates in the Cuzco region of Peru. *Textile Museum Journal* 2(3):9–16.

Bray, Warwick
    1978   *The Gold of El Dorado.* London: Times Newspapers.

Caley, Earle R.
    1973   Chemical composition of ancient copper objects of South America. In William J. Young, ed., *Application of Science to Examination of Works of Art,* pp. 53–61. Boston: Museum of Fine Arts.

Caley, Earle R., and Dudley T. Easby, Jr.
    1959   The smelting of sulfide ores of copper in preconquest Peru. *American Antiquity* 25:59–65.

Carcedo M., Paloma, and Izumi Shimada
    1985   Behind the golden mask: The Sican gold artifacts from Batan Grande, Peru. In Julie Jones, ed., *The Art of Precolumbian Gold,* pp. 60–75. New York: The Metropolitan Museum of Art.

Carrasco, Pedro
    1982   The political economy of the Aztec and Inca states. In George A. Collier, Renato I. Rosaldo, and John D. Wirth, eds., *The Inca and Aztec States, 1400–1800,* pp. 23–40. New York: Academic Press.

Childe, V. Gordon
    1944   Archaeological ages as technological stages. *Journal of the Royal Anthropological Institute of Great Britain and Ireland* 74:7–24.

Collier, George A.
    1982   In the shadow of empire: New directions in Mesoamerican and Andean ethnohistory. In George A. Collier, Renato I. Rosaldo, and John D. Wirth, eds., *The Inca and Aztec States, 1400–1800,* pp. 1–20. New York: Academic Press.

Collier, George A., Renato I. Rosaldo, and John D. Wirth, eds.
1982   *The Inca and Aztec States, 1400–1800*. New York: Academic Press.
Conklin, William J.
1982   The information system of Middle Horizon quipus. In Anthony F. Aveni and Gary Urton, eds., *Ethnoastronomy and Archaeoastronomy in the American Tropics*. Annals of the New York Academy of Sciences, no. 385, pp. 261–81.
Donnan, Christopher B.
1993   The Moche royal tombs of Peru. Paper presented at the colloquium on Andean Royal Tombs, Works of Art in Metal. The Metropolitan Museum of Art, New York.
Easby, Jr., Dudley T.
1955   Los vasos retratos de metal del Peru. *Revista del Museo Nacional* (Lima) 24:137–53.
Epstein, Stephen M., and Izumi Shimada
1983   Una reconstruccion de la produccion de la aleacion de cobre en el Cerro de los Cementerios, Peru. *AVA-Beitrage* (Munich) 5:379–430.
Etzioni, Amatai
1961   *A Comparative Analysis of Complex Organizations: On Power, Involvement, and Their Correlates*. New York: Free Press.
Franquemont, Christine, and Edward Franquemont
1987   Learning to weave in Chinchero. The Textile Museum Journal 26:55–78.
Gade, Daniel
1972   Bridge types in the central Andes. *Annals of the Association of American Geographers* 62(1):94–109.
Gayton, Anna H.
1961   The cultural significance of Peruvian textiles: Production, function, aesthetics. *Kroeber Anthropological Society Papers* 25:111–28.
Gonzalez, Alberto Rex
1979   Precolumbian metallurgy of northwest Argentina: Historical development and cultural process. In Elizabeth P. Benson, ed., *Pre-Columbian Metallurgy of South America*, pp. 133–202. Washington, D.C.: Dumbarton Oaks.
Goodell, Grace
1968   A study of Andean spinning in the Cuzco region. *Textile Museum Journal* 2(3):2–8.
Gordon, Robert B.
1985   Laboratory evidence of the use of metal tools at Machu Picchu (Peru) and environs. *Journal of Archaeological Science* 12:311–27.
Gordon, Robert B., and J. W. Rutledge
1987   The work of metallurgical artificers at Machu Picchu, Peru. *American Antiquity* 52:578–94.
Guaman Poma de Ayala, Felipe
1936   *Nueva coronica y buen gobierno*. Facsimile ed. Université de Paris,
[1613] Travaux et Memoires de l'Institut d'Ethnologie, XXIII.

Harrison, Regina
    1982   Modes of discourse: The relacion de antiguedades deste reyno del Piru by Joan de Santacruz Pachacuti Yamqui Salcamaygua. In Rolena Adorno, ed., *From Oral to Written Expression: Native Andean Chronicles of the Early Colonial Periad,* pp. 65–99. Syracuse: Maxwell School of Citizenship and Public Affairs, Syracuse University.

Heskel, Dennis, and Carl Clifford Lamberg-Karlovsky
    1980   An alternative sequence for the development of metallurgy: Tepe Yahya, Iran. In Theodore A. Wertime and James D. Muhly, eds., *The Coming of the Age of Iron,* pp. 229–65. New Haven: Yale University Press.

Hosler, Dorothy, Heather Lechtman, and Olaf Holm
    1990   *Axe-monies and Their Relatives.* Studies in Pre-Columbian Art & Archaeology 30. Washington, D.C.: Dumbarton Oaks.

Hyslop, John
    1984   *The Inka Road System.* New York: Academic Press.
    1990   *Inka Settlement Planning.* Austin: University of Texas Press.

Ingold, Tim
    1988   Tools, minds and machines: An excursion in the philosophy of technology. *Techniques et Culture* 12:151–76.
    1990   Society, nature and the concept of technology. *Archaeological Review from Cambridge* 9(1):5–17.

Jones, Julie
    1979   Mochica works of art in metal: A review. In Elizabeth P. Benson, ed., *Pre-Columbian Metallurgy of South America,* pp. 53–104. Washington, D.C.: Dumbarton Oaks.

Lechtman, Heather
    1971   Ancient methods of gilding silver: Examples from the Old and the New Worlds. In Robert H. Brill, ed., *Science and Archaeology,* pp. 2–30. Cambridge: MIT Press.
    1973   The gilding of metals in pre-columbian Peru. In William J. Young, ed., *Application of Science in Examination of Works of Art,* pp. 38–52. Boston: Museum of Fine Arts.
    1976   A metallurgical site survey in the Peruvian Andes. *Journal of Field Archaeology* 3:1–42.
    1977   Style in technology: Some early thoughts. In Heather Lechtman and Robert S. Merrill, eds., *Material Culture: Styles, Organization, and Dynamics of Technology,* pp. 3–20. St. Paul, Minn.: West.
    1979a   A precolumbian technique for electrochemical replacement plating of gold and silver on objects of copper. *Journal of Metals* 31:154–60.
    1979b   Issues in Andean metallurgy. In Elizabeth P. Benson, ed., *Pre-Columbian Metallurgy of South America,* pp. 1–40. Washington, D.C.: Dumbarton Oaks.
    1980   The central Andes: Metallurgy without iron. In Theodore A. Wertime and James D. Muhly, eds., *The Coming of the Age of Iron,* pp. 267–334. New Haven: Yale University Press.

1981a	Introduccion. In Heather Lechtman and AnaMaria Soldi, eds., *Runakunap kawsayninkupaq rurasqankunaqa: La tecnología en el mundo andino*, pp. 11–22. Mexico: Universidad Nacional Autónoma de México.
1981b	Copper-arsenic bronzes from the north coast of Peru. In Anne-Marie Cantwell, James B. Griffin, and Nan A. Rothschild, eds., *The Research Potential of Anthropological Museum Collections*. Annals of the New York Academy of Sciences, no. 376. pp. 77–121.
1984a	Andean value systems and the development of prehistoric metallurgy. *Technology and Culture* 25(1):1–36.
1984b	PreColumbian surface metallurgy. *Scientific American* 250(6):56–63.
1986	Perspectives on the precolumbian metallurgy of the Americas. In Clemencia Plazas, ed., *Metalurgia de America Precolombina*, pp. 20–36. Bogota: Banco de la Republica.
1988	Traditions and styles in central Andean metalworking. In Robert Maddin, ed., *The Beginning of the Use of Metals and Alloys*, pp. 344–78. Cambridge, Mass.: MIT Press.
1991	The production of copper-arsenic alloys in the central Andean culture area: highland ores and coastal smelters? *Journal of Field Archaeology* 18(1):43–76.

Lechtman, Heather, Antonieta Erlij, and Edward J. Barry, Jr.
1982	New perspectives on Moche metallurgy: Techniques of gilding copper at Loma Negra, northern Peru. *American Antiquity* 47(1):3–30.

Lemonnier, Pierre
1986	The study of material culture today: Toward an anthropology of technical systems. *Journal of Anthropological Archaeology* 5(2):147–86.
1989	Bark capes, arrowheads, and Concorde: On social representations of technology. In Ian Hodder, ed., *The Meanings of Things*, pp. 156–71. London: Unwin Hyman.

McNeill, William
1982	*The Pursuit of Power: Technology, Armed Force, and Society since A.D. 1000*. Chicago: University of Chicago Press.

Mamani, Mauricio
1981	El *chuño*: Preparación, uso, almacenamiento. In Heather Lechtman and AnaMaria Soldi, eds., *Runakunap kawsayninkupaq rurasqankunaqa: La tecnología en el mundo andino*, pp. 235–46. Mexico: Universidad Nacional Autónoma de México.

Maquet, Jacques
1971	Introduction to aesthetic anthropology. *Current Topics in Anthropology* 1(4):1–38.

Mathewson, C. H.
1915	A metallographic description of some ancient Peruvian bronzes from Machu Picchu. *American Journal of Science* 40:526–616.

Merrill, Robert S.
1968	The study of technology. In David L. Sills, ed., *International Encyclo-*

pedia of the Social Sciences, vol. 15, pp. 576–89. New York: Macmillan.

Montell, Gösta
   1929   Dress and Ornaments in Ancient Peru: Archaeological and Historical Studies. Goteborg: Elanders Boktryckeri Aktiebolag.

Morris, Craig
   1974   Reconstructing patterns of non-agricultural production in the Inca economy: Archaeology and documents in institutional analysis. In Charlotte Moore, ed., Reconstructing Complex Societies, pp. 49–60. Cambridge: American Schools of Oriental Research.
   1978   The archaeological study of Andean exchange systems. In C. L. Redman et al., eds. Social Archaeology: Beyond Subsistence and Dating, pp. 315–27. New York: Academic Press.
   1981   Tecnología y organización inca del almacenamiento de viveres en la sierra. In Heather Lechtman and AnaMaria Soldi, eds., *Runakunap kawsayninkupaq rurasqankunaqa: La tecnología en el mundo andino*, pp. 327–75. Mexico: Universidad Nacional Autónoma de México.
   1984   Architecture and the structure of space at Huanuco Pampa. In Graziano Gasparini and Luise Margolies, eds., *Tecnología, urbanismo, y arquitectura de los Incas*. Caracas: Ediciones Venezolanas de Antropología.

Murra, John V.
   1962   Cloth and its functions in the Inca state. *American Anthropologist* 64:710–28.
   1972   El 'control vertical' de un máximo de pisos ecológicos en la economía de las sociedades andinas. In *Visita de la provincia de León de Huánuco (1562)*, vol. 2. pp. 429–76. Huánuco: Universidad Nacional Hermilio Valdizán.
   1974   Andean cultures. *Encyclopaedia Britannica*, 15th ed., pp. 854–55. Chicago: Helen Hemingway Benton.
   1980a   *The Economic Organization of the Inka State*. Greenwich, Conn.:
   [1956] JAI Press.
   1980b   The Incas. Program in the Odyssey TV series. Boston: Public Broadcasting Associates.
   1983   The role of cloth in Andean civilization. Paper presented at the Wenner-Gren International Symposium No. 93: Cloth and the organization of human experience. Amenia, New York.

Newman, Richard, Claudia Hill, and Dana Wang
   1991   Pre-Columbian Muisca tunjos: A technical re-examination. *Archeomaterials* 5(2):209–29.

Noble, David
   1979   *America by Design*. New York: Knopf.

Palomino, Salvador
   1978   El puente colgante de Sarhua. In Rogger Ravines, ed., *Tecnología andina*, pp. 653–58. Lima: Instituto de Estudios Andinos.

Pleiner, Radomír
   1980   Early iron metallurgy in Europe. In Theodore A. Wertime and James D. Muhly, eds., *The Coming of the Age of Iron*, pp. 375–415. New Haven: Yale University Press.

Reichel-Dolmatoff, Gerardo
   1981   Things of beauty replete with meaning—Metals and crystals in Colombian Indian cosmology. In Sweat of the Sun, Tears of the Moon. Exhibition catalog, pp. 17–33. Los Angeles: Natural History Museum of Los Angeles County.

Renfrew, Colin
   1973   *Before Civilization*. New York: Knopf.

Rodriguez Orrego, Luis
   1981   La production metallurgique dans les societes precolombiennes des andes meridionales. PhD diss., Ecole des Hautes Etudes en Sciences Sociales, Paris.

Root, William C.
   1949   The metallurgy of the southern coast of Peru. *American Antiquity* 15:10–37.
   1951   Gold-copper alloys in ancient America. *Journal of Chemical Education* 28:76–8.
   1964   Pre-columbian metalwork of Colombia and its neighbors. In Samuel K. Lothrop, ed., *Essays in Pre-Columbian Art and Archaeology*, pp. 242–57. Cambridge: Harvard University Press.

Rowe, John H.
   1946   Inca culture at the time of the Spanish conquest. In Julian H. Steward, ed., *Handbook of South American Indians*, vol. 2: *The Andean Civilizations*, pp. 183–330. Smithsonian Institution, Bureau of American Ethnology, Bulletin 143.

Scott, David A.
   1983   Depletion gilding and surface treatment of gold alloys from the Narino area of ancient Colombia. *Historical Metallurgy* 17(2):99–115.
   1986a   Gold and silver alloy coatings over copper: An examination of some artifacts from Ecuador and Colombia. *Archaeometry* 28(1):33–50.
   1986b   Fusion gilding and foil gilding in pre-hispanic Colombia and Ecuador. In Clemencia Plazas, ed., *Metalurgia de America Precolombina*, pp. 281–306. Bogota: Banco de la Republica.

Scott, David A., and Warwick Bray
   1980   Ancient platinum technology in South America. *Platinum Metals Review* 24(4):147–57.

Scott, David A., and Eric Doehne
   1990   Soldering with gold alloys in ancient South America: examination of two small gold studs from Ecuador. *Archaeometry* 32(2):183–90.

Shimada, Izumi
   1985   Perception, procurement, and management of resources: Archaeological perspective. In Shozo Masuda, Izumi Shimada, and Craig Morris,

eds., *Andean Ecology and Civilization*, pp. 357–99. Tokyo: University of Tokyo Press.

Shimada, Izumi, and John F. Merkel
- 1991 Copper-alloy metallurgy in Ancient Peru. *Scientific American* 265(1):80–6.

Skinner, Milicia D.
- 1974 The archaeological looms from Peru in the American Museum of Natural History collection. In Patricia L. Fiske, ed., *Archaeological Textiles: Irene Emery Roundtable on Museum Textiles*, pp. 67–76. Washington, D.C.: Textile Museum.

Snodgrass, Anthony M.
- 1980 Iron and early metallurgy in the Mediterranean. In Theodore A. Wertime and James D. Muhly, eds., *The Coming of the Age of Iron*, pp. 335–74. New Haven: Yale University Press.

Stone-Miller, Rebecca
- 1992 To weave for the sun: an introduction to the fiber arts of the ancient Andes. In Rebecca Stone-Miller, ed., *To Weave for the Sun*, pp. 11–24. Boston: Museum of Fine Arts.

Taylor, Gerald
- 1974–76 *Camay, camac, et camasca* dans le manuscrit quechua de Huarochirí. *Journal de la Société des Américanistes* 63:231–44.

Wachtel, Nathan
- 1982 The *mitimas* of the Cochabamba Valley: The colonization policy of Huayna Capac. In George A. Collier, Renato I. Rosaldo, and John D. Wirth, eds., *The Inca and Aztec States, 1400–1800*, pp. 199–235. New York: Academic Press.

Waldbaum, Jane C.
- 1980 The first archaeological appearance of iron and the transition to the Iron Age. In Theodore A. Wertime and James D. Muhly, eds., *The Coming of the Age of Iron*, pp. 69–98. New Haven: Yale University Press.

Wertime, Theodore A.
- 1973 The beginnings of metallurgy: A new look. *Science* 182:875–87.

Willey, Gordon R.
- 1991 Horizontal integration and regional diversity: An alternating process in the rise of civilizations. *American Antiquity* 56:(2)197–215.

Zuidema, R. Tom
- 1977 The Inca calendar. In Anthony F. Aveni, ed., *Native American Astronomy*, pp. 219–59. Austin: University of Texas Press.
- 1982 Bureaucracy and systematic knowledge in Andean civilization. In George A. Collier, Renato I. Rosaldo, and John D. Wirth, eds., *The Inca and Aztec States, 1400–1800*, pp. 419–58. New York: Academic Press.

CHAPTER TWELVE

Pancho Villa and the United States

Friedrich Katz

No figure in the history of Latin America has ever roused more interest or provoked more controversy in the United States than the Mexican revolutionary leader Francisco (Pancho) Villa. In 1912 the U. S. ambassador in Mexico, Henry Lane Wilson (1927:293–94), asked Mexican president Francisco Madero to have Villa arrested because of acts of pillage he and his troops had allegedly committed against American properties. Only two years later in a conversation with the British ambassador in Washington, U. S. Secretary of State William Jennings Bryan called Villa "Sir Galahad" (Cline 1953:190). In December 1913, President Woodrow Wilson remarked to the French military attaché in Washington, "Perhaps this man today represents the only instrument of civilization in Mexico. His firm authority allows him to create order and to educate the turbulent mass of peons so prone to pillage."[1] Two and a half years later Wilson sent an army of nearly 10,000 men to pursue Villa across the vastnesses of his stronghold, the northern Mexican state of Chihuahua, to capture the "notorious bandit leader" who in March 1916 had attacked the town of Columbus, New Mexico. Today the main park of that town is called Pancho Villa Park, and in nearby Tucson, Arizona, a statue of Villa has been erected.

These contradictory American attitudes toward Villa are also reflected in Hollywood. There is no Latin American personality about whom Hollywood has made more films, and they in turn reflect the variety of northern opinions of Villa. Actors ranging from Wallace Beery to Yul Brynner have

---

[1]Archives du Ministère de la Guerre, Vincennes, France 7n 1716, French military attaché in U.S. Bertrand to Deuxième Bureau, Dec. 30, 1914.

portrayed Villa as either a well-meaning but ignorant revolutionary peon or a bloodthirsty bandit.

Some of the reasons for both American interest and ambivalence toward Villa are obvious, some perhaps less so. Villa was the kind of figure about whom legends naturally spring up. He was the only revolutionary leader to rise from the lowest stratum of Mexican society, the peons on the haciendas, to become a national leader. He had become a charismatic personality whose popularity was unequaled during the stormy years of the Mexican Revolution. Many aspects of his personality certainly lend themselves to the making of a legend: his many wives, his alternating generosity and cruelty, his skills in leadership and organization which contrasted with his almost complete lack of formal education. Yet all these traits would not have awakened the kind of interest they did in the United States if more profound motives had not been at work.

The Villa movement was the only revolutionary upheaval ever to occur along the borders of the United States. Villa was the only foreign military leader to attack the mainland territory of the United States since the War of 1812. The fact that he got away with it and that U.S. troops were never able to capture him, in spite of the huge amounts of men and materiel destined for this purpose, only enhanced the American interest in him.

Scholars have been fascinated and puzzled by Villa's elusiveness. Neither he nor his movement seems to fit conventional categories of analysis. Villismo cannot be classified neatly either as a bourgeois revolutionary movement, a working class movement, or a "pure" peasant movement like its southern ally, the peasant movement headed by Emiliano Zapata in Morelos. The ideological ambivalence of Villa's movement is perhaps best characterized by the fact that in the 1930s the Mexican volunteers to the International Brigades in Spain named their combat unit after Pancho Villa. At the same time in Mexico, a native fascist movement called itself Los Dorados (The Golden Ones), which was the name of Villa's elite fighting unit.

To thoughtful scholars, Villa presents a puzzle of a special kind. His movement was perhaps the only revolution in Latin America genuinely allied with the United States, both with the U.S. government and with a large number of American corporations. The reasons why this alliance finally broke down may be seen in many respects as symptomatic of larger problems in relations between the United States and Latin America.

As scholarship on the great social upheaval known as the Mexican Revolution of 1910–20 proceeds, it becomes ever clearer that this movement was in many ways quite different from other major revolutions in the twentieth century. Its diversity was far greater, particularly in terms of the importance of regional and local upheavals. One of these local revolts was the great uprising in the northern Mexican state of Chihuahua which Villa eventually came to lead. Its social base was constituted by a kind of peasantry that could be found in few other places in Mexico. The Chihuahuan peasants were descendants of military colonists who had been sent to the northern frontier of Mexico in the eighteenth century, when Mexico was still part of the Spanish colonial empire, and in the nineteenth century after it achieved independence, to fight off Apache marauders. In return for their military contributions to the defense of the northern settlements, these men were awarded privileges their counterparts in southern and central Mexico did not enjoy. They received large allotments of land and paid few taxes. They not only had the right to bear arms but were required to do so. During the Spanish colonial period, unlike the Indian peasants of southern and central Mexico, they were full-fledged citizens and not wards of the crown. Both their legal status and their isolation from the rest of the country allowed them to enjoy an exceptional degree of autonomy and self-government.

After 1884 the situation of the former military colonists changed rapidly and dramatically. In that year the last major Apache leader, Geronimo, was captured by U.S. troops, and the first railway line linking Chihuahua to both central Mexico and the United States was inaugurated. As a result Chihuahua was absorbed economically by the southwest of the United States and politically by the newly emerging dictatorial government of central Mexico headed by Porfirio Díaz. For most of the former military colonists, this brought an unmitigated disaster. As foreign investment increased and railways crisscrossed the state, land values sharply increased and there was a strong incentive for both the landowners and the state bureaucracy to expropriate the lands of these military colonists. Appeals to the courts or to Porfirio Díaz himself proved to be of no avail. "We are deeply concerned that lands we consider our own since we have received them from our fathers and worked them with our own hands are now passing into other hands," the inhabitants of the village of Namiquipa, one of the earliest and most prestigious military colonies, wrote to President Díaz in 1908. "If you do not grant us your protection we will have to abandon our homes in order to subsist."[2]

Their call as well as that of many other military colonies went unheeded. They not only lost their lands but many other rights and privileges they had long enjoyed: district chiefs and mayors appointed by the governor

---

[2] Departamento Agrario, Dirección de Terrenos Nacionales, Diversos, Chihuahua, exp. 178, Letter of the inhabitants of Namiquipa to President Porfirio Díaz, July 20, 1908.

destroyed the municipal autonomy that had been a hallmark of Chihuahuan villages. Between 1891 and 1893 these villages staged a series of uprisings against the state government. In military terms they achieved some surprising results. The small village of Tomochi, with less than a hundred men of fighting age, managed twice to defeat government units of more than five hundred men and finally succumbed after a long and bloody struggle with more than a thousand government troops. The years of combat against Apache raiders had given these men a unique fighting capacity and experience. Nevertheless, the former military colonists regained absolutely nothing from their struggles against the Porfirian regime. The expropriation of their lands and the erosion of their municipal autonomy continued. One of the main reasons for their lack of success was the fact that within the state of Chihuahua these peasants stood alone. This was not surprising. As foreign capital flowed into Chihuahua, there was a tremendous economic boom. New mines were discovered and worked, new industries were set up, and migrants from both the United States and other regions of Mexico streamed into Chihuahua. The living standards of miners, industrial workers, and the newly emerging middle class of shopkeepers, teachers, doctors, and the like were rising, and they saw no reason to participate in revolts of dispossessed peasants.

Less then twenty years later a completely different situation emerged. An economic crisis that began in 1907 put a temporary end to the economic boom and thousands of workers became unemployed. The crisis equally affected the state's emerging middle classes. Shopkeepers saw their customers dwindle away, patients could not pay their doctors, white collar workers were dismissed from their jobs. Their anger at these conditions was compounded by a state government that since the turn of the century was managed as a kind of family enterprise by Chihuahua's wealthiest family, the Terrazas-Creel clan (Almada 1964; Wasserman 1984). Only members or clients of the family received government jobs, and family-appointed judges consistently decided in their favor. When the crisis came, the family attempted to shift its losses onto the poor and middle classes. Taxes were not decreased but rather increased, and banks controlled by the same family called in outstanding loans.

When in 1910 Francisco Madero, a reform-minded member of one of Mexico's richest families, called on the people to rise against the dictatorship of Porfirio Díaz, the most diverse segments of Chihuahua's population rose in his support. Their anger was directed at Díaz and at the ruling Terrazas-Creel family in Chihuahua.

Although the Mexican Revolution was different in many respects from other major revolutions of the modern world (France, Russia, China) there were similarities. In their first stages, revolutionary movements constituted very broad coalitions of extremely heterogenous social forces. Once a revolution achieved an initial victory and the prerevolutionary government was toppled, this coalition began to disintegrate at a more or less rapid pace. Generally, in the first phase of a revolution, its leaders were men from the upper classes who wanted political but not social transformation and who tried to keep the old army and the old state intact or nearly so. They soon encountered the opposition of more radical forces who demanded profound social and economic changes and advocated the destruction of both the old army and the old state. At the same time, though, these moderate leaders were opposed by the forces of the old regime who wished to regain the power they had lost. In the ensuing conflicts, men such as Mirabeau in France or Prince Lwow and Kerensky in Russia could not resist the opposition of both conservatives and radicals. Conservative forces attempted to regain control of these countries by military coups or other plots, banking on the loss of popular support the moderates had suffered. This was the case in France when Louis XVI attempted to flee the country in 1791 and in Russia during the Kornilov putsch attempt in July 1917. These attempts either prompted or facilitated radical control of the revolutionary movement and the radical seizure of power. Radicalism was strengthened when the conservatives aligned themselves with foreign powers intent on stemming the revolutionary tide. The warfare foreign powers waged against revolutionary France strengthened the Jacobins as foreign interventions in Russia after 1917 strengthened the Bolsheviks. To fight their enemies and consolidate their hold over the country, the radicals proceeded to carry out far-reaching social transformations: the expropriation of the holdings of the old upper class and radical agrarian reform. At the same time, a reign of terror against the enemies of the revolution was unleashed.

In much of Mexico, and especially in Chihuahua, the revolution seemed to follow a somewhat similar pattern. The two moderate leaders of the revolution, Madero in Mexico City and Governor Abraham González in Chihuahua, were toppled, not by radicals as in France and Russia but by conservative officers. Their fall was like those in France and Russia: an offensive by conservative forces at a time when the moderate leadership of the revolution was losing popular support. The military coup by the conservatives and the deaths of the moderate leaders radicalized the revolutionary movement in Chihuahua. The main exponent of this new radicalism and the main leader of the new revolutionary wave that swept over Chihuahua was Villa.

When he assumed control of what was to become one of the most powerful revolutionary movements in Mexico, Villa was already a legendary figure. He was born in 1878 on a hacienda in the northern state of Durango. His parents were sharecroppers, and by the age of sixteen Villa was in conflict with the hacienda administration. Legend has it that the son of the hacendado, Lopez Negrete, raped Villa's sister and that Villa shot him and then had to flee from the estate. The legend has never been corroborated, but it is not surprising that a man with the high intelligence and rebellious and violent character of Villa would not submit to the extremely authoritarian patterns that were the rule on the northern Mexican haciendas.[3]

Villa at first roamed through the mountains of Durango but later transferred his activities to the neighboring state of Chihuahua. Here opportunities for cattle rustling were much greater than in Durango. Chihuahua was the center of Mexico's largest cattle estates, and opportunities for selling stolen beef across the U.S. borders were great. While Villa's activities led to furious persecution by both the state authorities and the hacendados, he found much sympathy among the lower classes of the state. Until 1884 much of the grazing land of Chihuahua had been open range (that is, public land). The wild cattle grazing on it were considered public property which anyone who needed meat could seize. Many inhabitants of Chihuahua considered the subsequent seizure of these lands by wealthy hacendados and the restrictions imposed on the slaughter of wild cattle violations of traditional rights. In their eyes, Villa did nothing more than restate traditional laws. A few years before the outbreak of the 1910 revolution, Villa moved his headquarters to a place near the town of San Andres, an old military colony whose inhabitants had fought a desperate battle against the state authorities. At first they fought to retain lands which had been given to them a century before and which were now being confiscated by large estate owners. Then they revolted in 1908 against tax increases the state government had imposed on them in the midst of the greatest economic crisis Chihuahua had ever suffered.[4] Villa did not participate in these uprisings, but there is little doubt that he was in close contact with the people of San Andres. Some of his men came from there, and he married

---

[3]This story is based on Villa's autobiography, which constitutes the first chapters of Martin Luis Guzman's *Memoirs of Pancho Villa* (1966). There is no corroboration other than Villa's own account, and his enemies do not accept it, considering him a common criminal (Herrera 1964).

[4]For a description and analysis of the expropriations of the lands of the former military colonists in Chihuahua, see Katz 1976; Wasserman 1984:104–16. The agrarian conflict of San Andres is dealt with in *Departamento Agrario, Seccion de Terrenos Nacionales Peticione Macario Nieto*, December 18, 1906, L.29 (06) L2E.143. For the 1908 uprising in San Andres, see Almada 1964:1.116–18.

a woman from the town. Villa's close contact with San Andres may have helped to give his instinctive hatred of state and federal authorities a more ideological tint. In 1910, Villa joined the revolution, and thanks to his natural talent as a leader, organizer, and strategist he soon became one of the two main military commanders of the revolutionary forces in Chihuahua.

Because of these capacities and in view of the fact that the other main leaders of the 1910–11 Revolution were either dead (González) or had gone over to the Huerta dictatorship (Pascual Orozco, the main military figure of the 1910–11 revolt in Chihuahua), Villa was elected by the leaders of the revolutionary movement in Chihuahua to assume command of the army and to be state governor at the end of 1913. The first measure he took showed a kind of radicalism that had not been present in the administration of his predecessor, González. Villa decreed the confiscation and state administration of all estates belonging to wealthy Mexican landowners, especially those of the Terrazas-Creel family. In the short run, revenues from these properties were to be used to finance the war. After victory, they would be devoted to social purposes: support of the widows and orphans of soldiers who had been killed and establishment of a rural bank to give credit to poor peasants. At the same time, plans were made to divide many of these lands among veterans of the revolution and to return to the villages the land that had been taken from them.[5] Villa thus seemed to be following the classic path of the Jacobins in the French Revolution or the Bolsheviks during the Russian Revolution. Villa was more moderate, however, in the use of revolutionary terror. Although he did shoot some prisoners and executed some supporters of Huerta, no mass killings on the model of the French Terror or the terror the Bolsheviks instituted against their enemies occurred in northern Mexico. Very soon, in any case, the trend toward radicalism slowed down considerably. One of the main causes of radicalism in other revolutions, foreign intervention against the revolutionaries, failed to materialize; on the contrary, the revolutionaries began to enjoy a decisive measure of foreign support.

When in February 1913 the military had toppled Madero, the classic scenario of foreign support for a conservative restoration seemed to have taken place in Mexico. All foreign representatives and foreign companies in Mexico, and especially the U.S. ambassador, Henry Lane Wilson, enthusiastically supported the coup. Only a few weeks after Madero's death, Woodrow Wilson was inaugurated as president of the United States. Presi-

---

[5]For a description of Villa's social legislation and his activities as governor of Chihuahua, see Almada 1964:2.63–75; Cervantes 1960:72–83; Katz 1979.

dent Wilson carried out a radical reversal of U.S. policy. He refused to recognize the Huerta regime and by the end of 1913 had thrown his full support to the revolutionaries (Clendenen 1961; Link 1954). The reasons for this abrupt and in some respects complete reversal of U.S. policy are still a subject of debate among historians. Some view Wilson's policies as dictated by purely idealistic motives. A strong advocate of democracy, Wilson profoundly resented the murder of Madero, with whose ideas he greatly sympathized. Wilson's aim was to impose a North American kind of democracy on Mexico. Others draw a contrary picture: Mexico's new military dictator, General Huerta, established close links to both the British government and British oil companies. Thus, it is argued, Wilson's primary aim was to dislodge the British from Mexico. In recent times historians such as Robert Freeman Smith (1972:31–33) describe a more complex picture. Wilson, Smith argues, was primarily interested in maintaining the system of free enterprise in Mexico. This could only be done, Wilson believed, if a revolutionary leadership instituted wide-ranging social and political reforms. Some lands at least would have to be divided among the peasants and some kind of political democracy instituted. At the same time, though, Wilson constantly insisted that foreign and especially American property not be touched in the process. In Wilson's eyes, Villa seemed to be the right man to carry out these changes. His charismatic personality, the authority and popularity he enjoyed in Mexico, would give him the necessary strength to implement reforms. At the same time, he had consistently shown respect for American properties and the lives of foreigners in the cities his troops occupied. In some respects, Wilson seems to have considered Villa a kind of mixture of Jesse James and Wyatt Earp. In January 1914, the French ambassador in Washington reported that a leading U.S. official (in all probability Woodrow Wilson) stated to him that

> Villa is hardly a man of no property. . . . he is an excellent horseman and a crackshot. Without fear of physical danger or the law, he already led the life of a rancher at a very early age. It is the same life many of us led until recently in distant areas of the West, in areas that lie outside of the power of the authorities, where every man was his own master . . . and created his own law. . . . He would be unable to rule but could create order quite nicely if he wanted to. If I were the president of Mexico, I would entrust him with this task; I am completely convinced that he would do it masterfully; he would also compel all the rebels to remain peaceful. In Mexico's current situation I see no one beside him who could successfully handle this task.[6]

[6]Archives du Ministère des affaires étrangerès, Paris, Correspondance politique, Nouvelle Série, Mexique, vol. 9, Jusserand to Doumergues, January 27, 1914.

Not only the Wilson administration but some of the largest American business interests that had invested heavily in the state of Chihuahua, above all the American Smelting and Refining Company, were backing Villa. In their eyes Villa was the strongest revolutionary leader and the only one who could impose order on his army and thus prevent the looting of their property. They also appreciated the fact that taxes imposed on foreigners were far lower in the territories controlled by Villa than in those where the other major revolutionary leader to emerge in northern Mexico, Venustiano Carranza, held sway (O'Connor 1937).

Ironically, this contrast between the policies of the two revolutionary leaders was a consequence of Villa's social radicalism. Carranza nominally assumed the supreme leadership of the revolutionary movement in Mexico in 1913. He had been governor of his native state of Coahuila until then and was a far more conservative man than Villa. He was an hacendado (though not a very wealthy one) and had maintained close relations with the elite of his native state for many years. Unlike Villa, he did not want to break up the great estates, believing that the hacienda system was the only viable system for Mexico. When the second phase of the Mexican Revolution broke out in 1913, both leaders were faced with an immediate task—to finance the revolution. There were basically only two sources of financing, the property of wealthy Mexicans and the wealth accumulated by foreigners. Carranza, not wanting to expropriate the holdings of wealthy Mexicans (at times he was reluctantly forced to do so), attempted to fund the revolution primarily through higher taxes that largely affected foreigners. Villa, by contrast, was interested in destroying the traditional Mexican oligarchy, so he confiscated their properties and thus, at least at the beginning, had no need to impose higher taxes on foreign companies. As a result, foreign interests viewed Villa with far greater sympathy than Carranza, in spite of the fact that Villa was far more radical in social terms than his nominal chieftain and later rival.

American businessmen expressed their support for Villa, not only by writing glowing reports about him to U.S. government officials and lobbying in his favor in Washington, but also by backing his currency. Villa issued large amounts of paper money which nevertheless depreciated less than might have been expected considering the huge quantities of it—thanks to the many American businessmen and speculators who bought up large amounts of it (Katz 1981:285–86). They hoped that after his expected victory he would redeem his paper money (or at least accept it for tax payments) at the official rate of exchange, which was far higher than the black market rate at which they bought it. Villa thus was able to exchange the paper money he printed for dollars at relatively favorable rates and could thus buy arms and supplies across the border in the United States. Though Villa did not realize it, he was practically living on credit.

Villa also received extensive support from the other side of the U.S. political spectrum. Radical intellectuals such as John Reed, who went to Mexico to cover the Villa campaign, waxed enthusiastic about both Villa and his movement. Reed (1969:113–48) considered Villa one of the greatest personalities Mexico had produced and stated that he led a genuine revolutionary movement whose aim was to put an end to the exploitation Mexico's poor had suffered for so long.

By early 1914 the Villa movement had become largely dependent on the United States. It was from its northern neighbor that it secured arms, ammunition, uniforms, and supplies. Until early 1914, while an embargo imposed by the United States on arms supplies to Mexico was still in effect, arms and ammunition were smuggled to Villa frequently with the tacit tolerance of U.S. authorities. In the spring of 1914, Wilson revoked the embargo and allowed the revolutionaries to buy arms and supplies freely across the border. A more hidden but no less effective form of dependence (though Villa was probably less aware of its implications) was the backing of Villa's currency by American corporations. In diplomatic terms, the State Department strongly supported Villa in controversies with European powers.

How did this dependence affect the Villa movement? Did Villa become a tool of U.S. government and private interest, as his enemies later charged? Did Wilson in fact buy himself a revolution? There is little doubt that the dependence on the United States profoundly influenced the character, policies, and ideology of the Villa movement. Nevertheless, one has to separate the indirect from the direct consequences of this dependence.

The first indirect consequence of Villa's links to the north was to slow the pace of land redistribution. In this respect the Villa movement was quite different from its counterpart in southern Mexico, that headed by Zapata. Zapata confiscated the huge sugar estates in his native state of Morelos, returned expropriated lands to their former owners, and operated the remaining properties as state enterprises (Womack 1968:224–55). Sugar cultivation soon dropped and was replaced by subsistence agriculture of mostly corn and beans. There was no incentive for Zapata to maintain sugar production. Morelos had no seashore and no border with another nation. Zapata could not have sold the sugar anywhere. Villa, by contrast, could easily sell both cattle and cotton from the large estates to Americans and thus gain sufficient funds to supply his troops. Had he divided up the estates immediately, or had he been unable to export their products, these sources of revenue might have disappeared. The wish to secure revenues to finance the revolution was not, however, the only thing that prevented Villa from dividing the large estates among the peasants. There were ecological and demographic factors as well: a large part of the haciendas consisted of cattle range, unsuitable for agriculture and small-scale production. The nonagricultural population was far larger in Chihuahua than in Morelos, and if Villa wished to retain the support of the urban population some revenues from the estates would have to be diverted to them. Nevertheless, Villa could theoretically have given more land to peasants and transformed the internal organization of the haciendas. He did not do so. The large estates were maintained as such, frequently under the supervision of their former administrators, who knew them best (Katz 1980). As a result, land reform was postponed until the period after the triumph of the revolution, and some peasants became disillusioned with the Villa movement.

This disillusionment was restrained by another development, the formation of a professional army. The revolutionary peasants of Zapata's Army of the South were basically paid by the land they received, and this ensured their loyalty to the Zapata movement. Villa's soldiers were paid with money, which Villa had in plentiful supply as a result of the financial backing of American corporations. In some respects, an army paid with money could be superior to a peasant army paid with land. Villa's soldiers were ready to fight anywhere in Mexico, whereas the Zapatistas tended to fight only near their villages. The drawback was that Villa's professional army might easily switch sides if another faction was able to pay more or if Villa's money lost its value.

A third consequence of Villa's close links to the United States was that conservative politicians and military men who would never have dreamed of siding with Zapata now joined Villa, firmly convinced that his close links to the United States would prevent him from becoming too radical and would allow them to influence his social policies.

These indirect consequences were matched by direct ones, that is, conscious decisions of Villa in favor of American interests. Villa's relationship to the United States was closely linked to the forms of political organization of his movement and to his style of leadership, which to a large degree still corresponded to nineteenth-century Mexican traditions. This can best be understood by contrasting it with the style of leadership of the other main revolutionary faction, led by Venustiano Carranza and Alvaro Obregón. The latter developed a strong nationalistic anti-American ideology that was partly sincere and partly utilized to deflect the attention of their supporters from social reforms their leaders did not want to carry out. In terms of organization, Carranza and Obregón used a twentieth-century style of cooptation of popular organizations. They supported unions and attempted to control them and set up peasant movements that they closely monitored and controlled. Villa, in contrast, did not propagate any comparable ideology. As in many Mexican revolutionary movements in the nineteenth century, it was not an abstract ideology but the personality of the leader that became the rallying point for his supporters. They supported him because the "centaur of the north," as Villa was frequently called, would lead them to victory and to a better life. He did not establish any mass organizations but rather replicated traditional patriarch relationships between leaders and followers that, again, were characteristic of nineteenth-century social movements. He attempted to establish close personal links with his soldiers. He ate with them, frequently slept near their campfires, knew their first names, and, instead of having his paymaster give them money on a regular basis, personally gave them gifts and money when they needed it or asked for it. This paternalistic relationship was based on the concept of very clear mutual obligations. The soldiers were expected to fight for him, and he in turn would support their families during the course of the revolution, support their widows and children if they died, and reward them after victory.

In many respects, Villa felt that Wilson had established a similar kind of paternalistic relationship with him in which mutual obligations, while never spelled out in writing, were nevertheless clear to both sides. In return for American support, Villa was ready to make substantial concessions to the U.S. administration and American companies, but he considered these concessions freely chosen; they did not make him a vassal of the United States. For Villa, both sides were bound by a code of honor to respect their mutual obligations.

Whenever Villa's troops occupied a city or a region, he took strong measures to protect American properties and holdings. Until the beginning of 1915, taxes on American properties remained low. When in April 1914 U.S. troops occupied the port of Veracruz, Villa, unlike Carranza, did not protest against the action but assured U.S. representatives that he would not oppose them in any substantial way. At the same time, he constantly emphasized to Americans that, in case of a war between the United States and Japan or a conflict between the United States and Britain over Mexico, the Americans could count on his firm support.

When radical organizers from the Industrial Workers of the World arrived in Chihuahua to set up unions among Mexican mine workers, Villa sent them back to the United States.[7] He was afraid that otherwise the

[7] *El Paso Morning Times,* July 15, 1914.

American Smelting and Refining Company would shut down its operations in northern Mexico.

These concessions, which may seem substantial to present-day observers, were not considered so by Villa. Ideology was unimportant in his eyes, and so were unions. In ideological terms, he allowed his most conservative supporters—above all, former federal general Felipe Angeles—to define his ideology for the public. As a result, the ideological pronouncements of the Villa movement were far less radical than the social measures it actually instituted. This was in stark contrast to Villa's rival, Carranza, who used radical pronouncements to mask his conservative policies.

By mid-1914, the military dictatorship of Huerta had been toppled, and a new civil war developed between the revolutionary faction headed by Carranza, on the one hand, and Villa and Zapata, on the other. Villa seemed to be in a unique position vis-à-vis the United States in this conflict. He enjoyed the support of the Wilson administration and of conservative businessmen as well as radical intellectuals. Within a year, however, Washington, American business interests, and the intellectuals turned against him. A short time later, Villa attacked Columbus, New Mexico, and nearly provoked a Mexican-American war.

What went wrong? Why did this alliance disintegrate? Few American or for that matter Mexican historians have acknowledged the existence of a genuine alliance between Villa and the United States. Those who did so generally attributed its breakdown to a simple series of factors. Villa, they argue, was defeated by the superior military skills of Carranza's most talented general, Alvaro Obregón, and thus Wilson had no choice but to recognize Carranza. At this point, furious at Wilson's betrayal, Villa attacked the United States in a fit of rage. Reality though, is far more complex than this interpretation. Relations between Villa and the United States worsened long before Wilson decided to recognize Carranza. The main reason (though not the only one) for this deterioration of relations was that different groups in the United States attempted to change what had been fundamentally an alliance into a relation of subordination. Villa expected the protection he extended to American citizens and properties (which included protection not only from the military and the bureaucracy but from union organizers as well) and the low taxes he imposed to guarantee the support of American businessmen. He expected these same measures together with his promise to hold elections and not be a candidate for the Mexican presidency, his at least partial respect for the laws of war (in response to long talks with U.S. Chief of Staff Hugh Lennox Scott, Villa had somewhat limited the execution of prisoners), the confiscation of large estates carried out with the promise of dividing them after the victory of the revolution, and the large-scale redistributive measures taken by his administration (meat taken from the large estates was sold at low prices in popular markets and unemployed workers were supplied food by Villa's army) to gain him continued support from both the Wilson administration and radical intellectuals. He was wrong on all accounts. American businessmen and at least some branches of the U.S. government wanted far more than that, and the radical intellectuals would look more to words than to actions when assessing Villa.

Influential businessmen—including John Hays Hammond, one of the most important executives of the American Smelting and Refining Company—dreamed of dividing Mexico into northern and southern regions and of exercising a large measure of control over the north. In 1913, Hammond told a representative of the Mexican federal government,

> We want and need no intervention. We want nothing more than Baja California and the entire area north of a line running from the southern tip of Baja California to Matamoros, this area will either come under our control of itself or we will occupy it; then you can come and try to take it away from us. That is what we want and we will get it without firing a shot, since you are incapable of resisting, because of your advanced internal collapse.[8]

These remarks were not made to Villa or to one of his subordinates, but such aims were frequently voiced by American businessmen and U.S. officials (around the same time Hammond made these remarks, U.S. Chief of Staff Leonard Wood made a proposal for a separate northern Mexican state to Carraza, which was refused)[9] and probably filtered down to Villa.

Villa resented the fact that American companies were utilizing the Mexican Revolution to acquire huge holdings in his country. As the revolutionary armies advanced from northern Mexico into the south, large Mexican landowners, afraid their properties would be confiscated, sold them at cut rate prices to the only buyers who knew their property would not be touched—American entrepreneurs.[10] For Villa, such sales represented a twofold blow: he was deprived of the revenues of these estates, and the influence of American companies grew enormously. He very clearly stated

---

[8] *Foreign Office Archives*, Bonn Mexico 1, vol. 37, Hintze to Bethmann-Hollweg, September 24, 1913.

[9] Haus, Hof, and Staatsarchiv, Wien, Pa, Mexico Reports 1914. Austrian ambassador in Washington, D.C., to Bechtold, January 19, 1914.

[10] Haus, Hof, and Staatsarchiv, Wien, Pa, Berichte U.S.A. 1914. Ambassador in Washington, D.C., to Bechtold, May 5, 1914.

his opposition to this situation in a confidential conversation with Duval West, Wilson's personal representative in Mexico. West reported to his chief that Villa had "stated that Mexican industry should be primarily developed by Mexican capital. I received the impression that he held to the popular demand of Mexico for the Mexicans, and that he saw an open door for foreign investors as a danger to his country." West labeled Villa a socialist: "The socialist idea even if it is not clearly articulated appears to predominate throughout this movement."[11]

Far more damaging to the Villa-United States alliance were proposals the head of the Mexican desk in the State Department, Leon Canova, presented to Villa through several intermediaries in 1915. At that time both Villa and Carranza were vying for U.S. recognition, and Canova offered to recognize the Villa faction if he would acquiesce to U.S. conditions, which in practice would have converted Mexico into a U.S. protectorate. Some of the measures Canova proposed consisted of "an agreement" that the Mexican ministries of the interior, foreign affairs, and finance would be filled by individuals enjoying the support of the Wilson administration and a ninety-nine year concession granting the United States rights to the Magdalena Bay, Tehuantepec, and to an unnamed region in the oil zone in return for a loan of $500 million to the Mexican government. This loan would be guaranteed by "a lien on the entire income of the Mexican treasury with a representative of the United States government to have supervision over Mexico's compliance with this provision" (Katz 1981:303–8). While these measures would have ensured U.S. control of Mexico, a further condition proposed by Canova—the return of all confiscated properties to their former owners—would have put an end to all contemplated agrarian reforms. In spite of his desperate financial and military situation in mid-1915, Villa rejected this offer.[12] He now became firmly convinced that Canova's proposals constituted the basic policy of the United States toward his movement and that his alliance with the Wilson administration had never been anything but a farce.

Villa's relations with the United States worsened and his social policies became more radical. An agrarian law was proclaimed by the Villa faction in the spring of 1915 (Díaz 1960:29–36) and began to be implemented in Chihuahua in the summer of that same year. At the same time, new and higher taxes were imposed on American properties.

---

[11] National Archives, Washington, D.C., State Department Files, Record Group 59, File 812.00/14622, undated report by Duval West to Secretary of State.
[12] National Archives, Washington, D.C., State Department Files, Office of the Counselor, E. B. Stone to Justice Department, March 14, 1916.

It is by no means clear that Wilson or Secretary of State Bryan (and later Lansing) knew of Canova's proposals, which had been conveyed to Villa as official U.S. policy. Nevertheless, their behavior with respect to the recognition of Carranza must have strengthened Villa's impression that he had never been considered an equal or ally but a subordinate and instrument to be manipulated at will.

By mid-1915, Villa had been decisively vanquished on the battlefield and only retained control of parts of northern Mexico. The Wilson administration did not particularly like Carranza, a committed nationalist, and would have preferred to have a coalition government in Mexico in which it could have played off one faction against the other. For this purpose it made limited concessions to Villa (it allowed him to export meat to the United States in order to be able to buy arms and prevent a complete Carranza victory), and Wilson proposed a conference of all Mexican factions to designate a leader acceptable to all, whom the United States could recognize (Cervantes 1960:504; Quirk 1960:467). Implementation of these proposals would have excluded both Carranza and Villa from the presidency. Villa agreed to these proposals and sent a representative to the United States. Before the conference could deliberate at the end of September and the beginning of October 1915, the Wilson administration again changed its policies. As the intensity of World War I in Europe increased, the possibility that the United States might be drawn into it loomed larger on the horizon. At this point, Wilson wanted a quiet Mexico and no involvement in Mexican affairs. This was the basis for the recognition of the Carranza government by the Wilson administration on October 14, 1915. Only a few weeks before this recognition, when a change of policy was already in the making, Wilson sent General Hugh Scott, one of his highest military officers, and a man on good personal terms with Villa, to meet him to arrange for the return of some American properties Villa had confiscated. Scott conveyed to Villa assurances from Wilson that Carranza would not be recognized.[13] The sense of betrayal Villa felt once his rival was recognized by the United States must have been accentuated by the way his representatives to Washington were notified of this decision. On October 29, ten days after Carranza's recognition, Villa representative Roque Gonzalez Garza wrote to Villa:

> It was a great blow to me to see that you have always been miserably deceived; possibly this took place in good faith but you were always deceived. I was

[13] Library of Congress, Washington, D.C., Scott Papers, Box 20. Scott to Garfield, October 14, 1915.

also deceived . . . after arriving in Torreon. . . . I was clearly told that from the point of view of international political relations, our situation was very good; we were one step from recognition by the United States. . . . a few days went by and you received the clearest assurances that from the point of view of international politics everything was proceeding in your favor; that only a small effort on our part was required for the United States government to take us into consideration and that the original plan of the participants of the conference would be implemented with satisfactory result for us.

Bitterly, Gonzalez Garza went on to describe how Villa's delegates at the Washington peace conference were treated by their American hosts:

Our situation was depressing, everything turned out to have been lies; we were badly off, we were not even listened to. . . . the 19th of October arrived and the participants of the conference decided to recognize Carranza. . . . this decision communicated ex abrupto to the four winds was an enormous humiliation for us since we were delegates to the Peace Conference. We were not told anything and the solemn declaration made by Wilson at an earlier date was simply discarded. All historical precedents were ignored. Even common sense was not respected since we had come to the conference ready to make peace but in an honorable way. This resolution was approved and we suffered a great blow. . . . I have seen many injustices but I have never thought that Carranza would triumph in the international political field after he played the comedy of being the most nationalist of all Mexicans and after he provoked the United States two or three times. I do not entirely know what has been decided concretely, but I am convinced that something very dark has been agreed on; for I have no other explanation for this sudden change in U.S. policy against our group and in favor of Carranza.[14]

The "something very dark" Gonzalez Garza was referring to had become very clear in Villa's mind. Carranza could have secured U.S. recognition only by agreeing to the terms Canova had offered Villa and Villa had rejected. Villa now became convinced that Carranza had transformed Mexico into a colony of United States. This impression became even stronger when Wilson allowed Carranza to do something no other Mexican faction was permitted to do—transport Mexican troops through U.S. territory. Villa suffered his last great defeat when Carranza's troops traveled through the United States to reinforce the garrison of the border city of Agua Prieta, which Villa was beseiging.

Villa believed not only that Wilson was in fact assuming control of

[14] Roque Gonzalez Garza Papers, Mexico. D. F. Roque Gonzalez Garza to Villa, October 26, 1915.

Mexico but also that he had violated that tacit agreement existing between them and thus broken the code of honor that constituted the basis of Villa's thinking and actions. In a proclamation issued in November 1915, Villa made this quite explicit.[15] He insisted that he had done everything in his power to protect both the lives and properties of Americans. Wilson though, had never kept his side of the bargain and had broken the trust between him and Villa. It was this conviction that Wilson had used him to transform Mexico into a protectorate of the United States and betrayed every element of the code of honor by which Villa lived that induced the Mexican leader to attack Columbus, New Mexico, and thus to increase enormously the risks of a war with the United States. Villa obviously felt that such a war would put an end to the American protectorate of Mexico to which, in his opinion, Carranza had tacitly agreed. In case U.S. troops entered Mexico, Carranza would be forced either to oppose them and thus forfeit U.S. support and end U.S. influence in Mexico or to openly acknowledge his close links with the Americans and thus lose popular support.

One of the most ironic facts about American attitudes toward Villa at the time was that, precisely when the Wilson administration as well as American businessmen were turning against Villa, the same could be said of some of the most radical northern intellectuals. John Kenneth Turner (1920), a longtime foe of the Díaz dictatorship in Mexico who maintained close ties to the Mexican union movement, denounced Villa as a tool of reactionaries. Lincoln Steffens (1931:715) denounced Villa as a tool of Wall Street just when Wall Street had had enough of Villa. These intellectuals were captivated by the radical rhetoric of Carranza and never looked into the practical policies that both Carranza and Villa had been carrying out. John Reed, an enthusiastic supporter of Villa in 1913–14, does not seem to have participated in these controversies. His main interests had shifted to Europe.

What consequences did the temporary alliance between the U.S. government and American business interests, on the one hand and Villa, on the other, have for both sides? For American businessmen, the alliance proved to be extremely profitable, since they were able to acquire at very cheap prices extensive Mexican holdings from Mexican owners who panicked when Villa's troops approached. In the short run, the alliance with Villa allowed the Wilson administration to weaken European influence in Mexico and to demonstrate to large segments of the American electorate that it was sincere in its desire to carry out a new policy of contributing to social

[15] *Vida Nueva*, Chihuahua, November 21, 1915.

reform in Latin America. In the longer run, however, the abrupt policy reversal and the sense of betrayal provoked in Villa and his adherents nearly caused a war that would have had tremendous consequences for the United States, since it might very well have hampered U.S. efforts to play a decisive role in the European war and in the Far East.

For Villa, the alliance with the United States had even more ironic effects. Although in the short run he profited both from the arms he received and the financial support of American corporations, in the long run the United States' embrace of Villa proved to be deadly for its recipient. The fact that Villa was able to sell the products of confiscated estates in the United States and thus acquire arms from his northern neighbor prevented him from carrying out any large-scale agrarian reform in the first stages of his movement. As a result, a chain of events was set in motion which ultimately isolated Villa from the peasantry, the basis of his movement. The administrators Villa named to the confiscated estates had a vested interest in preventing reform and constituted one of the bases of the conservative faction of the Villista movement. Villa's increasing dependence on arms from the United States made it more and more imperative for him to gain U.S. recognition and thus not to antagonize the Americans by radical social changes. The financial backing of American companies allowed him to print large amounts of paper money whose value depended on the attitude of these companies. This had a double effect. On the one hand, it made Villa extremely vulnerable to any loss of confidence by American financial interests. On the other hand, it gave him the necessary means to transform his army from a popular into a professional military force. This in turn made it less imperative for him to carry out immediate social reforms. The result of all these factors was not only Villa's defeat because of the loss of support of the peasantry but the postponement of agrarian reform in most of Mexico for many years to come.

The break between Wilson and Villa was final as far as the U.S. government was concerned. This fact was reflected in the works of U.S. diplomatic historians. Most of them (in contrast to social historians of Latin America) considered Villa a bandit and Wilson's temporary support of that Mexican leader an aberration by a president unable or unwilling to see reality. In contrast to diplomatic historians, artists, writers, film producers, social historians, as well as radical intellectuals began to "rehabilitate" Villa. Apart from the social historians, whose new insights about Villa were based on original research, movie producers in Hollywood as well as artists and writers were strongly influenced by the writings of John Reed, who painted a picture of Villa quite different from that of either the U.S. or Mexican governments. One of the first expressions of this "rehabilitation" was

Wallace Beery's portrayal of Villa in the memorable 1930s film *Viva Villa* as a bloodthirsty, primitive, but honest and sincere revolutionary. Similar portrayals in art and novels followed.

The links among the historical facts, the works of historians, artists and movie makers, and the legends about Villa in both northern Mexico and the southwest of the United States are tenuous and indirect. In northern Mexico there are several types of legend about Villa, sometimes held by groups having opposing views, sometimes superimposed on each other. There is the Robin Hood-type legend: Villa as a friend of the poor and foe of the rich. As is not surprising, this legend is especially popular among the poorer segments of society. Not surprising, either, the Villa legends among the upper classes of Chihuahuan society are of a quite different character: Villa is seen as a ruthless, unpredictable killer, shooting masses of people for the pleasure of it. Between the two is the macho image of Villa, which frequently cuts across class lines and is superimposed on both the negative and positive images of the Mexican revolutionary: Villa, the superb rider, the impetuous leader of men, the gunman, the womanizer. Boundless generosity and boundless cruelty are a definite part of this image. All these legends have been influenced in some way or other by the official Mexican attitude toward Villa, which itself has undergone changes. In the 1920s and early 1930s, when the men who held power in Mexico were basically the victors over Pancho Villa, his official image was nearly entirely bad: he was a bandit without ideology, though some merit was attached to his rebellion against Díaz and Huerta; a rebel against the legitimate government of Carranza; an opportunist who never fought for a cause; a traditional caudillo grasping only for power; a reckless adventurer who nearly precipitated a war between Mexico and the United States. In more recent times, as a new generation of politicians not directly involved in the revolution assumed power in Mexico, an attempt was made to fit Villa into the pantheon of revolutionary heros. He was still considered reckless and rebellious, but his merits, his charismatic leadership of men, were emphasized much more. He was no longer a bandit who for a short time was a revolutionary, but a revolutionary who for a short time was a bandit.

These legends and interpretations have seeped across the border to the United States, and there again they have been changed, transformed. There is the Mexican-American legend of Villa in which the positive aspects of the Mexican leader are emphasized; at times, Mexican-Americans consider him the one avenger they have had, the one man who attempted to right the wrongs suffered at the hands of Anglo-Americans. Anglo-American attitudes toward Villa in the southwest are ambiguous and mixed. On the one hand, he fits a traditional racist stereotype: the Mexican bandit who smilingly kills, tortures, and murders his victims. On the other hand, there are still strong residues of the period when Villa was seen as an extremely positive figure, protector not only of Mexico's poor but of Americans in Mexico as well. These different historical images have been adapted to Anglo-American traditions, with Villa being seen as a mixture of the rebelliousness of Jesse James and the law and order of Wyatt Earp.

References

Almada, F.
   1964   *La revolución en el estado de Chihuahua*. 2 vols. Chihuahua: Instituto Nacional de Estudios Historicos de la Revolucion Mexicana.

Cervantes, F.
   1960   *Francisco Villa y la revolución*. Mexico: Ediciones Alonso.

Clendenen, C.
   1961   *The United States and Pancho Villa*. Ithaca: Cornell University Press.

Cline, H. F.
   1953   *The United States and Mexico*. Cambridge: Harvard University Press.

Díaz Soto y Gama, A.
   1960   *La cuestión agraria en Mexico*. Mexico: Ediciones El Caballito.

Guzman, M. L.
   1966   *Memoirs of Pancho Villa*. Austin: University of Texas Press.

Herrera, Celia
   1964   *Francisco Villa ante la historia*. Mexico: Editorial Libros de México.

Katz, Friedrich
   1976   Peasants in the Mexican revolution of 1910. In J. Spielberg and S. Whiteford, eds., *Forging Nations*, pp. 61–86. East Lansing: Michigan State University Press.
   1979   Pancho Villa: Reform governor of Chihuahua. In G. W. Wolfskill and D. W. Richmond, eds., *Essays on the Mexican Revolution: Revisionist Views of the Leaders*, pp. 25–46. Austin: University of Texas Press.
   1980   Pancho Villa, peasant movements and agrarian reform in northern Mexico. In D. Brading, ed., *Caudillo and Peasant in the Mexican Revolution*. Cambridge: Cambridge University Press.
   1981   *The Secret War in Mexico*. Chicago: University of Chicago Press.

Link, Arthur S.
   1954   *Woodrow Wilson and the Progressive Era, 1910–17*. New York: Harper.

O'Connor, H.
   1937   *The Guggenheims: The Making of an American Dynasty*. New York: Covici, Friede.

Quirk, R. E.
- 1960 *The Mexican Revolution, 1914–1915.* Bloomington: Indiana University Press.

Reed, John
1969 *Insurgent Mexico.* New York: Greenwood Press.

Smith, R. F.
1972 *The United States and Revolutionary Nationalism in Mexico, 1916–1932.* Chicago: University of Chicago Press.

Steffens, Lincoln
1931 *The Autobiography of Lincoln Steffens.* New York: Harcourt, Brace.

Turner, J. K.
1920 *Hands off Mexico.* New York: Rand School of Social Science.

Wasserman, M.
1984 *Capitalists, Caciques and Revolution: The Native Elite and Foreign Enterprise in Chihuahua, Mexico, 1854–1911.* Chapel Hill: University of North Carolina Press.

Wilson, H. L.
1927 *Diplomatic Episodes in Mexico, Belgium and Chile.* Garden City: Doubleday.

Womack, J.
1968 *Zapata and the Mexican Revolution.* New York: Knopf.

CHAPTER THIRTEEN

Old Postulates and New China

Morton H. Fried

Concepts that can be used as implements of analysis have their vogue in anthropology, as in other disciplines. Many such ideas run quickly to their peaks, rapidly lose popularity, and often seem to disappear. About half a century ago, Ruth Benedict not only captured the attention of her colleagues but titillated a broad nonprofessional audience with her notion of "patterns of culture." In the next decade, Morris Opler advanced a similar concept. His idea, the analysis of particular cultures in terms of component "themes" (Opler 1946, 1951), facilitated more comprehensive analysis than did Benedict's scheme. Opler's thematic analysis of the culture of the Jicarillo Apache was both appreciated (Gladwin 1947) and criticized (Cohen 1948). It is relevant to the theme of the present essay that Cohen's critique was inspired by fear that thematic analysis might lead to an overly simplistic stereotyping of the cultures submitted to such analysis, although Jicarillo could hardly be thought of as complex. In any case, thematic analysis as such did not spread. But in 1954 an anthropologist who specialized in primitive law, E. Adamson Hoebel, published a book on that subject which included his first venture into the analysis of particular cultures in terms of "postulates," "corollaries," and "subcorollaries." The form of this analysis shows striking resemblance to Opler's earlier scheme, but the Hoebel suggestions provided for deeper and more detailed coverage.

In 1969, Francis L. K. Hsu, writing on the study of literate civilizations (Hsu 1969), sought a tool that would make it easier to carry on a comparison of several complex cultures. His search led him to Hoebel's work, which had begun with the assumption that every society must of necessity choose a limited number of behavior possibilities for incorporation in its culture and it must peremptorily and arbitrarily reject the admissibility for its own members of those lines of behavior which are incompatible with its selected lines as well as others which are merely different. (Hoebel, cited in Hsu 1969:61)

Hsu uses Hoebel's definition of postulates as broadly generalized propositions about the nature of things and what is held desirable and undesirable in a particular culture. All cultures have postulates. Hoebel emphasized that they are not "mere descriptive summaries of what the people do" (Hsu 1969:62) but statements about what a particular culture regards as desirable under most culturally available circumstances. To apply more recent terminology, postulates and their corollaries are emic statements. There may be conflicting postulates in the same system (Hoebel 1954:168; Hsu 1969:63).

One of the main criticisms of postulates and corollaries has been directed at their application to complex, class-structured societies. The core of this criticism is the complaint that the postulated system is derived from and applies primarily to one class in the society, usually the ruling class. Thus, in 1946, before Hoebel's contribution appeared, Fei Hsiao-tung (Fei Xiaotong) (1946) in a seminal article divided the peasants' ways from the customary behavior of the Chinese gentry. Stimulated by the Fei essay I entered the fray and argued that class was a form of subculture, giving evidence from fieldwork in China (Fried 1952a). The intervening years have given this problem fresh relevance. The People's Republic of China (PRC) has encouraged vast changes in what is done and the way it is done. Are such changes along with Marxist doctrine primarily imports from Europe, most particularly from the Soviet Union? Or is it more probable that much of the present culture of the PRC "New China" is the institutionalization at the state level of what previously was the obscure subculture of the peasant masses? In this essay I confront that problem directly.

Although we began this inquiry by referring to work carried out by Benedict, Opler, and Hoebel, it must be realized that there is a distinct tradition of similar ideas in disciplines other than anthropology, especially sinology—a blend of social sciences and humanities which seems, most of all, to revolve around the discipline of history. For a long time sinologists have been providing lists of what they believe to be the basic elements in Chinese culture. We also look into some of these schemes here. Let me begin, however, with a brief comment on a fairly old tradition in the treatment of China as a technological, economic, sociopolitical, and ideological whole. I refer to the concept of "Oriental despotism," which is also known, in another aspect, as the "Asiatic mode of production," based on its system of "hydraulic agriculture." These concepts, but not necessarily these terms, go back at least to the eighteenth century, for example, in Montesquieu, *L'esprit des lois*. Basically, according to this theory, the political character of such "despotisms" is a result of the interaction of a human population with the specific environmental characteristics of the regions occupied. More precisely, the focus is placed on the availability of moisture for agriculture: whether rainfall is generally adequate or not, whether it falls when needed most or not, and whether irrigation or flood control is required or not. China is seen as representing one type, a type dominated by a need for extensive irrigation and massive flood control. This is seen as causal in the emergence of a system of huge corvée labor forces under centralized, basically civilian, political control requiring a large bureaucracy as the instrument. Beneath a small, tightly defined imperial court, the bureaucracy functions in close harmony with a larger class of powerful commercial figures and wealthy landowners. The most important twentieth-century purveyor of this thesis has been Karl August Wittfogel (1929, 1957), a student of Max Weber, who had himself been inclined toward the theory. A broader range of examples of hydraulic theory is available in a collection edited by Bailey and Llobera (1981), and an anthropological critique has been suggested by Stephen Dunn (1982).

A major pillar of Oriental society is the observable weakness of private capital. This was manifest in the frequency with which the emperor and higher officialdom sentenced wealthy merchants to death or exile and impounded the wealth of their families. Nonetheless, despite common ideology to the contrary, as in the conventional view of the class system as comprising *shi, nong, gong, shi* (gentry, farmers, artisans, and merchants), wealthy merchants were regarded as equivalent to members of the gentry. It was this enlarged category of *shi* that comprised the bulk of the literate social sector. Their view of the content of Chinese culture was predominant, and it was that view that was absorbed by European clergy and other travelers to China in late Ming and early Qing times.

Events in China during the nineteenth century might have given rise to interpretations departing sharply from the politically dominant gentry view, but in fact, with few exceptions, they did not. After all, the Taiping, the folk movement that almost captured state power in the middle of that century, ultimately failed, in part because of European (largely British) support of the imperial government. In any event, the gentry position, that its own class ideology was the value system for the whole Chinese population system, remained basically unchanged until the fall of the Republic of China on the mainland. With the coming to power of the PRC, the situation was open for basic change. Now it would be possible for the values of the great mass of the Chinese people to emerge from historical darkness, perhaps becoming dominant. This might be expected unless the Chinese masses indeed held basically the same value system as did the gentry.

One of the foremost voices supporting this view was that of Francis Hsu, a prominent American anthropologist who was born and grew to maturity in China. Hsu (1969:65–78), basing his approach explicitly on Hoebel's earlier analysis, provided fourteen postulates and seventy seven corollaries and subcorollaries for Chinese culture. He anticipated criticism of the kind previously discussed with reference to work by Fei and myself and met that expected challenge directly:

> Now we must deal with some general problems. One of these concerns class ... differences. ... I think these differences are important, but still do not prevent the student from identifying the unifying features of each civilization in spite of them. For example, it is a well-established fact that while the Chinese have traditionally given much social fanfare to the "big family" ideal, field investigations showed the actual number of families with several generations under the same roof to be very small. Furthermore, it was also unmistakable that the big families with several generations under the same roof were much more likely to be found among the affluent and socially prominent than among the poor and the common men. But the poor did not have a different culture. On the contrary, it can be demonstrated that the size of household rose directly with the increase of social status. That this is not merely due to the higher infant survival rate among the rich was attested to by the fact that the bigger families were bigger not because of the number of surviving children but because of the presence of a large number of collateral relatives (Hsu 1943). In other words, the cultural model of higher and lower classes was the same, but the latter could only move toward that model when economic conditions permitted. (29)

Hsu also faced another problem quite directly:

> The communist regime has not completely changed the traditional patterns of life even in mainland China. Otherwise, it would have no need for the many continuing antilandlord, antientrepreneur, antiintellectual movements of which the latest was exemplified by the Red Guards. On the other hand, the kind of pattern described [above] is clearly visible in Taiwan today and, I am sure, still to be found in mainland China for years to come if we had the opportunity of direct observation. (29)

Ten years later, Hsu still held that view (Hsu 1979; Hsu and Chu 1979).

The argument about family structure is critical to the conflicting views of the class nature of ideologies and value systems. Unfortunately, before this question has been solved, some momentous changes have obliterated the evidence. Reference is to the PRC's recent recognition of a staggering population problem. As its solution, the PRC is attempting to limit urban families to one child and rural families to two (with certain exceptions). For most families there are no options regarding family structure in real behavioral terms. Yet, this may be an overstatement: significant variations may continue to exist. When Hsu visited his relatives in China (Hsu-Balzer, et al. 1974), he discovered that they were largely distributed in distinctly nuclear families. In my own trips to the PRC in 1977 and 1981, I found that the families of all persons I asked, or whose dwellings I visited, were either of nuclear or stem form. This includes families in two large villages that were parts of two different communes in widely separated parts of China. Both were similar in that the residents of houses were usually related and composed stem families, although one of the towns I visited was in northern Manchuria and was mainly the home of persons who had come from Korea about fifty years earlier and their descendants. The other was part of a tea-growing commune near Hangzhou with an entirely Han population. Still, such evidence not only is painfully thin, it is ambiguous at precisely the point advanced by Hsu. That is because all the individuals seen possessed relatively small capital resources, so that their family types would not be expected by Hsu to be joint.

In recent years, mainly since 1981, this situation has been complicated by the new political and economic environment. The PRC has seen the abandonment of much of the commune system; the brigade and team approach to agricultural labor is largely defunct. The new system is *zheren ze*, the "responsibility system" by which individual families operate sections of land over which they have sole decision-making power; the crops, after taxes, are theirs to market freely. This system reintroduces the premium on child labor, since the larger the family workforce the greater the return. Obviously, the present demographic policy will encounter increasing resistance.

Meanwhile, research by Greenhalgh (1982) indicates that a surprisingly large sector of the Taiwanese population goes through a cycle of family forms that includes nuclear, stem, and joint stages. A portion of the sample, however, did not display a full range of cycling but was confined to nuclear and stem forms. Greenhalgh emphasizes the positive correlation between total wealth, income, and large family size, but she is reluctant to come to a firm conclusion on the basis of her limited data. Thus, she avoids seeing relative wealth as the necessary condition for joint family structure as opposed to joint family structure as the condition (through pooling) of wealth. In either case, however, the joint families encountered by Greenhalgh do not display the feature emphasized by Hsu in one of the passages quoted above. The extended families in her sample are almost entirely constructed of several nuclear families whose fathers are siblings. Few, if any, of these families include collateral relatives. Notice that the mainland now shows the absence of joint families involving collaterals (except for non-Han populations). This is, in part, the consequence of the recent pressure on parents to limit their offspring to two children or even one child. It is premature to look for the effects of this policy. The generation of persons actively reproducing during the 1980s included many members of huge cohorts produced during a baby boom that took place in the 1950s and 1960s. It would seem to be of considerable importance that the presently enormous Chinese population undoubtedly contains an extremely high number of genetically related brothers yet has undergone sharp reduction in the frequency of joint families. If confirmed, this would tend to show that the underlying value system of the Chinese masses differs at critical junctures from that held by the gentry, who preferred joint families of which the component elementary families included many children.

It must be noted that the dismal picture offered by projections of Chinese population size does not mean a continuity of the present drive against more than one child. It is difficult to name PRC policies that have not been dropped or substantially changed over the years.

The preference for several sons is not solely dependent on ambitions regarding family structure. The frightening continuation of too high a rate of increase is tied to two specific conditions that qualify as themes, probably at the level of corollaries. The first has to do with the notion, still remarkably widely distributed in rural areas, that one or two sons are a requirement for a relatively secure old age. Despite strong governmental attempts to dispel this notion, Chinese peasants show behaviorally that they continue to believe that daughters are a financial liability who normally move out of range at marriage. In the effort to produce sons, it is often necessary to have several more children than is presently sanctioned. It is interesting that the number of births is much closer to being under control in the city. The reason for this seems to lie in the higher level of economic security enjoyed by urban workers. They are covered by pensions not found in the countryside.

The second factor that would contribute to the continuation of a high birthrate is less documented. It also would operate by placing a premium on the birth of males, leading couples without sons to keep trying for one.

This is the belief that the afterlife one experiences is closely linked to the behavior of male offspring. Having no sons is to become, at death, a homeless ghost—a pathetic, awful fate. According to official propaganda, such beliefs have to a large extent lost their hold on most peasants but remain in isolated pockets of reactionary thought. The homes of the people into which I have been taken have had few or no objects or wall hangings of any ritual significance; certainly nothing like what I used to see, years ago, in Chuxien (Ch'uhsien) or, more recently, in Taiwan. Yet the continuing high birthrate, seemingly in the face of reductions in income as a penalty, implies that some extremely powerful cultural force is at work. A reasonable hypothesis is that allegedly disappearing religious ideas remain potent.

Incidentally, when relevant statistics become available, it is likely that we shall find an exceptionally heavy frequence of stem families. This case will apply to urban and rural areas alike and for the same reasons: the scarcity of housing and the use of grandparents as surrogate parents.

It is at present the official policy of the PRC that urban couples ideally should have only one child; two is the maximum. More brings a variety of punishments of which the most common are economic penalties and public humiliation. In the countryside two children are regarded as a more reasonable maximum. It is worth noting that Chinese press reports indicate a higher level of success for these measures in urban than in rural areas. Also important is the apparent frequency with which Communist party members and officials are named and attacked in the press for failures to observe these demands for strict control of reproduction. At this point, however, before continuing with comments on the validity of Hsu's postulates, let us turn briefly to a consideration of similar propositions offered by nonanthropologists.

At the end of World War II, an anthology of original essays relating to Chinese society and culture authored by a distinguished crew of sinologists appeared under the direction of Harley F. MacNair, then Professor of Far Eastern history and institutions at the University of Chicago. The volume's first essay, devoted to the "molding forces" of Chinese culture, was written by Han Yu-shan, a scholar whose American doctorate had been in philosophy but whose academic career in China and the United States had been in history and other social sciences. His concept of molding forces was indistinguishable from the notion of "dominant ideas," the topic of the next essay, written by Derk Bodde. For Han, the first of these central conceptions was the belief in nature as a domain not antagonistic to but complementing man. Thus, nature was not to be conquered but understood and lived with in harmony. To some extent, this attitude has succumbed in recent years to a more exploitative idea of the culture-nature relationship. Probably the peak of that attitude was reached in 1958 with the "Great Leap Forward." During this brief period, Chinese in all productive sectors sought enormous increases in production. The goal was nothing less than surpassing Western industrial nations in output by the turn of the century. Such a feat could not even be thought of without significant change in the attitude toward nature. That this attitude did in fact change is shown by the damage done to productive lands by excessive efforts to expand crop yields and to replace ecologically practical cultigens with those associated elsewhere, in different environments, with impressive yields. Chinese food supplies were to suffer for many years as a consequence of this sharp turning away from the notion of man and nature in harmony.

Han's next theme is the "age-long reverence" for parents that has been celebrated in China since antiquity. This point is merely the tip of a collection of themes, including Confucian concepts of filial piety and general respect for age. Han (1946:5) sums it up: "Religion, ethics, education, art, and the conduct of affairs both great and small have been inextricably bound by this one emphasis." This point is not quite as manifest as Han represents. Furthermore, its reality is closely related to our previous discussion of family types. Respect for parents seems to vary almost directly with form of the family. Respect for father peaks in the large joint family in which father (or father's father, father's brother, and so on) has formal control over the family capital. It may be invisible in smaller, poorer families. I was amazed to see ancient and feeble parents working long days at menial tasks in Anhui, Chuxien, when I lived there in 1947–48. Less oppressive, although resented by old surviving parents, is the formerly(?) widespread practice in Taiwan whereby such old parents periodically move from the house of one son to another, where they are cared for in turn. Such movements may be monthly, constituting a hardship for elderly people.

Even more contradictory of the theme of filial piety was the behavior of large numbers of young people during the Cultural Revolution (1966–76). A feature of that period was the public denunciation of parents by their sons and daughters and of teachers by their students. The former activity was exceptionally widespread, appearing not merely among the powerless remnants of former landlords and bourgeoisie but also among elements of the new ruling stratum, of whom perhaps the foremost example was Liu Shaoqi (Liu Shao-ch'i) and his wife, Ying-mei. These two were reviled in Beijing by their daughter despite Shaoqi's standing, which was second to Mao's. The major convulsion that was the Great Proletarian Cultural Revolution has now been over for more than a decade, yet today, when one visits a school in China, it is extremely difficult to imagine those very obedient students—who are allowed to raise their hands only from their elbows, which are placed firmly on their desks—clapping dunce caps on their teachers and forcing them to march until they collapsed in the schoolyard.

For Han (1946:7), the "third pillar of Chinese society was the civil service examination system." This institution is linked with education as the prime means of social mobility. Han is rare among scholars in his acceptance of military careers as parallel to literary scholarship. He includes the military because it, too, was often associated with competitive examinations including essay writing. Although some of the most painful experiences China has undergone since 1950 have concerned schools (especially universities) and examinations, this situation seems to have stabilized at a condition resembling that characteristic of the Republic of China on Taiwan: national entrance examinations are given for which the percentage that receives the necessary minimum grade for admission to college is extremely small. Persons who do not succeed may try again, but such efforts are not encouraged. By law, except in very unusual cases, the examinations may not be taken by persons over thirty years of age. This represents an interesting shift from an institution that was famous during imperial days. At that time there was no limit on examinees, and occasionally men of great age would pass and be celebrated with considerable honor, though usually receiving no official positions. It is useful in this connection to bring up the theme of respect for age although it is not explicitly mentioned by Han. Though the examination route to a high-status position has pretty well been cut off for people over thirty, even a quick glance at the power structure of the PRC shows a predominant number of figures who are over seventy and an absolute rarity of persons under sixty. Even during the Cultural Revolution, the ages of the people constituting the central control group, the Gang of Four, included persons who in the United States would be considered well into middle age if not simply old.

Han's final two unique factors in the molding of China include its passion for history and extensive use, in conversation and writing, of proverbial sayings. The passion for history certainly remains, although older forms of historical narrative have undergone extensive changes of content. One major alteration saw a move away from the portrayal of history, excepting the twentieth century, as a process dominated by specific named individuals, particular dynasts, ministers, heroes, and villains. Emphasis is now on whole socioeconomic classes, the peasants and the workers. This attitude continues to apply both to the writing of history and the curation of museums. History dominated by named individuals cannot, however, be called dead in China. Mao still occupies a special place. Earlier, Liu Shaoqi and Confucius were linked in a major purgative campaign.

As for the continuous use of the proverb or slogan, it scarcely needs illustration. Mao was a master of the pithy phrase. For example, the four-character description of the Cultural Revolution was *jengchi guashuai* (politics in command), as opposed to the slogan that preceded and succeeded it, *jingji guashuai* (economics in command).

Derk Bodde's first generalization in considering the "dominant ideas" of Chinese culture is surprising for an anthropologist who has done intensive ethnographic research in two widely separated Chinese locales. Bodde begins by declaring that "the Chinese have been less concerned with the world of the supernatural than the worlds of nature and man" (1946:18). It is precisely because of the formulation of principles such as this that the question has arisen whether the analyses of Chinese culture into a series of themes or postulates can be said to apply to all Chinese or only to the literati or gentry. To a considerable extent Bodde's stipulation of the priority of secular concerns applies easily and snugly only to the higher social and economic classes. It does not apply broadly to the peasantry. There is somewhat less evidence for deciding the degree to which the same reservation can be made for workers, but the little relevant material we have indicates considerable importance for religious concepts in proletarian circles in both cities and small towns. There they had their own divinities (often different personae of gods otherwise worshiped).

For the mass of peasants, life was oriented around a set of ideas that had a sacred core. That core was essentially triangular: one angle rested in the ancestral complex, another in temple-organized Buddhism with strong (sometimes distinct) elements of folk Daoism. The third angle led to a battery of ideas concerned with a variety of animistic spirits extremely active in one's own locality, invariably including the often faceless and shapeless god of earth (*tudi*). Often a host of other spirits would be appeased, including a mass of homeless ghosts, the spirits of women who had died in childbirth, or men cut down by accident. The world inhabited by the people of Chuxien that I knew in the 1950s was only partly visible to my eyes; much was always going on in a dimension to which my upbringing had left me insensitive. Atheism is a vital part of the ideology of the government of the PRC today. The question is, does that official view affect what is going on among the peasant masses in China now? On my trips to the PRC I have visited temples whenever I could. In every case, the signs of recent rituals were obvious. Nor was such evidence associated only with the few priests who could be seen in attendance. It is quite usual to see old women and a much smaller number of old men offering incense in postures associated with prayer. Though the old women are often accompanied by small children, for whose day care they are undoubtedly responsible, one hardly ever sees a young or middle-aged adult of either sex. The children, it should be noted, are usually being physically involved in the motions of worship.

Derk Bodde attributes the attraction of religious ideas for members of the Chinese masses to ancient diffusions from India. This strikes me as a misreading of the evidence, which suggests a deep indigenous tradition of ancestor worship and animism. To this day, when places such as Taipei and Kaohsiung are full of tall buildings and mechanized transportation, it is not difficult to find practicing shamans whose specific repertoires may well go back to Yang Shao neolithic or even earlier horizons. Incidentally, though the primary locus of such belief systems has been securely located among the peasants for most of China's long history, we know of repeated extensions of these beliefs to members of the gentry. By and large, however, it is accurate to consider them primarily of lower-class provenance.

What has happened to this whole catalogue of beliefs in the PRC? It is still too early to say, though a respectable preliminary report may be expected from the Potters when they publish about their community in Guangdong. The book by Steven Mosher (1983) contains little material on religion (see his Chapter 11). For the moment, however, it appears that, while Islamic and Christian belief systems managed at least to some extent to survive, the same statement may not as surely be made with reference to Daoist or less institutionalized animistic beliefs. The extent to which Buddhism continues in China is also questionable. That there remain some relatively fully staffed, operating Buddhist temples is a fact verified by groups of Japanese who have been invited to visit them, but the extent to which common people still use them is difficult to determine.

In part this difficulty derives from the nature of Buddhist worship, which is rarely if ever communal, much less congregational. In Taiwan today, as in pre-Communist China, one activity that shows extensive formal participation by Buddhist clergy is the conduct of funerals. Indeed, funerals have undergone great changes in Taiwan as well as in China (Fried and Fried 1980:161–74). We have been told of an increasing deemphasis of funeral procedures in China, not only in reduction of surrounding ritual but through government encouragement of a shift to cremation. Despite such statements, reality appears to be quite complex. During a bus ride from the Li River to Gueizhou (Kweichou) city in 1977, I was surprised while traversing a forested area that extended for several miles to discover that the place was full of grave mounds, conical heaps of soil that stand four to eight feet high, beneath which people, especially mature or elderly parents, are buried. Unexpectedly, many of those grave mounds appeared to be fresh or at most only a few months old. I saw no funeral processions, but others who have seen them, especially in rural areas, have reported the return of elaborate paper constructions that are burned at the grave. I would like to register in this context a prediction. If the attitude associated with Deng Xiaoping (Teng Hsiao-p'ing) continues, I expect that ancestor tablets and other religious objects, such as idols of *genius loci* or previously popular Buddhist or Daoist figures, will reemerge from the places many of them have been carefully hidden. Less certain am I about the strong return of that extensive set of religious observances known as *jiao* (*chiao*) (commonly referred to as *pai-pai* in Taiwan, where they remain very extensive). Although known widely throughout China, this complex has been most closely associated for the past century or longer with southeastern China, especially Guangdong, Fujien, and Taiwan. The return of this complex of large-scale rituals is improbable, not merely for its association with belief systems that for centuries have been considered heterodox and subversive but because they involve excessive displays of wealth and unusual consumption of food that can deplete supplies and lead to periods of hunger.

Bodde also raises the point made earlier by Han: the Chinese ideal of fitting harmoniously into nature rather than challenging it. Bodde goes a bit farther, raising the vital conception of Chinese folk cosmogeny that the Way (*Tao*) comprises two equally important segments, *yang* and *yin*. The tremendous complex of ideas that revolve around this approach to reality clearly touched every Chinese, no matter where they lived or what their socioeconomic class; what is more, it did so for more than two thousand years. We can ask whether anything of this corpus of ideas is likely to survive the extensive ideological remolding that was Maoism.

Mao Zedong's utterances are stamped, even in translation, with that distinctive Chinese style even when the content is in realms of concern common to a wide variety of cultures. This can be seen from the hastiest inspection of that remarkable little red book, *Quotations from Chairman Mao Tse-Tung*, although it is no longer in circulation in China. Consider, for example, this passage:

> We are now carrying out a revolution not only in the social system . . . but also in technology . . . and the two revolutions are interconnected. . . . Therefore we must on no account regard industry and the socialist transformation of agriculture as two separate and isolated things, and on no account must we emphasize the one and play down the other. (Mao 1977:26–27)

Though I cannot cite a single instance in which Mao refers explicitly to the concepts of *yang* and *yin,* he is quite clear in a great many contexts about the unity of opposites. He is also quite aware of similar concepts in Marxism and Western philosophical history. Indeed, he directly addresses the "three-category" view—thesis, antithesis, synthesis—saying that, "we must take life as our starting point in discussing the unity of opposites. . . . While analysis is going on, there is also synthesis, and while synthesis is going on, there is also analysis" (Schram 1974:225). He goes on in the same talk to make the point absolutely clear:

> Engels talked about the three categories, but as for me I don't believe in two of those categories. (The unity of opposites is the most basic law, the transformation of quality and quantity into one another is the unity of the opposites quality and quantity, and the negation of the negation does not exist at all.) The juxtaposition, on the same level, of the transformation of quality and quantity into one another, the negation of the negation, and the law of the unity of opposites is "triplism," not monism. The most basic thing is the unity of opposites. . . . There is no such thing as the negation of the negation. . . . in the development of things, every link in the chain of events is both affirmation and negation. (Schram 1974:226)

As Bodde goes on to mention, the basic Daoist belief in the interaction of *yin* and *yang* sees that process as the origin of the five primary elements (fire, water, earth, wood, and metal). This in turn leads to the generation of everything else, specified in sets of five: five colors, tastes, smells, directions, and so on. The PRC continues to coin "fives." For example, the national flag shows five stars on an otherwise solid mass of red. Those stars stand for the five "races" of the Chinese nation: Han, Manchu, Moslem, Mongolian, and Tibetan.

Bodde mentions another feature of Chinese culture pervading its long history and surviving dynastic changes: "The Chinese state . . . aimed at moral suasion rather than legalist compulsion. . . . Legal codes existed, but they were subject to individual judgment and interpretation, based upon the body of traditional experience and morality known as *li*" (1946:25). This statement cannot be applied without change to the PRC, but with a few specific alterations it fits quite well. The image of the Chinese as relatively nonlitigious is questionable; in any event, observations in this century indicate that it was not the Communists who brought extensive litigation into fashion (cf. Buxbaum 1967; Moser 1980). Nonetheless, despite a tradition of law codes extending for more than two thousand years, local variation in legal norms is usually recognized at higher governmental levels. It is clearly recognized by the Communists, not merely in the application of differently phrased laws to different ethnic groups but in the frequently found stipulation that the law stands as stated unless there is a strong local precedent to the contrary. Such reservations, however, seem to have been ignored more often than not. They seem to be missing from more recent constitutional pronouncements. Still, the considerable activity that was under way in China in 1982 as a new constitution was being introduced did not obscure the stated determination of the government to revise and reissue new constitutions and new laws as needed.

Another point made by Bodde concerns the basic mobility enjoyed by individuals. China has generally lacked castelike formations. Even when groups completely detached from possibilities of social mobility existed—as when entertainers and their offspring for several generations, as well as certain hereditary servants or slaves, were rigidly excluded from the examination systems—the groups so outcast were small and insignificant. But the number of poor boys who made good was never large, although Ho P'ing-ti years ago presented before an audience of anthropologists his notion that Qing (Ch'ing) China knew a higher frequency of upward mobility than did Victorian England (Ho 1960; also see Ho 1962). We do not yet have enough material from the PRC to figure out exactly what rate of mobility has characterized it. Of course, we understand that the formal ideology calls for almost total mobility, at least to the extent that social strata continue to be recognized. The matter is complicated. We know, for example, that persons of secure worker backgrounds are reluctant to marry those whose backgrounds are bourgeois or landlord. At the same time, young people born into peasant families have virtually no chance at all of moving to cities where they may enjoy more valued careers. Youths who have been transferred from cities to the countryside frequently avoid taking any responsible positions there lest they jeopardize their chances for return. Similarly, the frequency of intermarriage between sent-down urban youth and local rurals is said to be very low.

We have already encountered the theme of the love for, and importance of, education manifest in the critical passing of examinations, and we have already heard of the continued importance of achieving the highest level of education possible. In a sense, the ongoing high status given advanced education represents a triumph of older Chinese values over those iterated by Mao. Although Mao displayed considerable erudition, he was in conflict about it. He stated proudly,

> Many of the great scholars and scientists did not go through college. Not many of the comrades in our Party's Central Committee are university graduates. (Mao, Speech at Hangchow, 21 December 1965, in Schram 1974:237)

> We shouldn't read too many books. We should read Marxist books, but not too many of them either. It will be enough to read a dozen or so. If we read too many, we can move toward our opposites, become bookworms, dogmatists, revisionists. (Schram 1974:210)

The official policy of the PRC has undergone a 180-degree shift: it has seen the return of extensive study at home and abroad. A major portion of overseas students enjoy complete governmental subsidization, but quite a few are totally supported by their families. Such expenditures represent one of the few ways private capital can be invested. Not only do such significant private savings still exist, but bank accounts receiving interest are increasing.

Moving on, we note a list of "approved attitudes and behavior patterns" offered by the late Arthur F. Wright, another outstanding sinologist (Wright and Twitchett 1962:6):

1. Submissiveness to authority—parents, elders, and superiors
2. Submissiveness to the mores and the norms (*li*)
3. Reverence for the past and present respect for history
4. Love of traditional learning
5. Esteem for the force of example
6. Primacy of broad moral cultivation over specialized competence
7. Preference for nonviolent moral reform in state and society
8. Prudence, caution, preference for a middle course
9. Noncompetitiveness
10. Courage and sense of responsibility for a great tradition
11. Self-respect (with some permissible self-pity) in adversity
12. Exclusiveness and fastidiousness on moral and cultural grounds
13. Punctiliousness in treatment of others

Wright makes clear that the distillation of these principles was basically deductive: "Some of these attitudes and behavior patterns occur again and again in our biographies. A few of them—reinforced by social conventions and institutions—appear decisive in shaping the lives of many of our subjects" (6–7). It is much to the point that the persons whose biographies composed the work Wright considered were all excellent examples of the "Confucian tradition"; indeed, the title of his book is *Confucian Personalities*. One of the most important and constantly reiterated motifs of the Cultural Revolution was "eliminate Confucianism." Yet, even at the height of that campaign, when the Gang of Four was in control, not all of the thirteen themes enumerated by Wright could be said to be under attack.

Indeed, impressionistically, it seems that many of Wright's motifs continued to enjoy wide respect after the success of the revolution. About his points 1, 5, 9, 12, and 13 there can be little doubt, as the information already scrutinized in this essay has shown. Point 6 needs a bit of revision to bring it up to date. Phrased as the "primacy of redness over expertise," it scores very high as a key slogan of the period since 1950, although its highest peak was achieved during the Cultural Revolution. Since Deng Xiaoping consolidated his power, there has been a real change; the slogan now is better written "Red *and* expert."

The one theme suggested by Wright that seems to have been almost completely washed out of the system is 4. If there are pockets of Chinese in the PRC who still cherish traditional learning, they maintain this attitude in private. Wright's motifs 7 and 8 have had a different fate. The preference for nonviolent reform, again with the return to power of Deng, reappeared. It should not be forgotten, however, that reform with violence has been characteristic of this Chinese revolution on at least two previous occasions. The first occurred during the coming to power of the Chinese Communist Party and the two years that followed it. This is not a reference to the violence that accompanied the civil war; rather, it refers to the treatment received by landlords or other bourgeois elements exposed by the Communist victories. Perhaps the best description of a real example of that process is to be found in William Hinton's (1966:114 ff.) account of the transformation of the village of Changzhou (Ch'angchou). At first, the Communist cadres were disappointed that there was no spontaneous attack by the local peasants on their former exploiters, but after the cadres pitched in and aroused them there was a violent eruption. Huge social explosions also characterized the Cultural Revolution, particularly from 1966 through 1969. It is too early to pronounce these outbreaks atypical. Many Chinese seem, as late as 1981, to be completely uncertain, holding themselves as if in fear of another sudden outbreak of such internal hostilities.

A similar analysis may be made about Wright's eighth point, the preference for a middle course. Once again the Gang of Four represent one major deviation from the desire to compromise. Their ouster by Deng Xiaoping brought about the return to favor of compromise and middle positions. It is also difficult to decide how relevant is Wright's third motif: the reverence for the past. The PRC clearly does not venerate the same version of history as did its imperial predecessors. Yet history is still of very high regard. One of the buildings surrounding Tienanmen Square—the symbolic center and heart of Beijing, perhaps of the whole country—is the National Museum of History. At the northern edge of the same square is the Forbidden City, the great residence of the Qing emperors. It is not visited only by foreigners;

at any particular moment, the gaping tourist mobs are mainly composed of Chinese. And so it is at the Great Wall and at the many other sites of historical interest scattered throughout China. The one place I found no crowd of Chinese was Zhoukoudien (Chouk'outien), the first locality at which *Homo erectus sinanthropus* was found. Despite a seeming lack of popularity, the site has been carefully landscaped and provided with a small museum and attached refreshment area. The present regime's views of history are quite different from those held by its predecessors, but that it continues to be considered of the greatest importance is widely evident. Indeed, the central place of history in the college curriculum has never been under challenge, although its content has undergone the most extensive scrutiny. Most of China's older archaeologists and cultural anthropologists are still to be found attached to departments of history. After 1950, there were no departments of anthropology anywhere in China. The first department with all four traditional subfields permitted to reopen did so at Zhungshan (Chungshan) University, just outside of Guangzhou (Kuangchou; Canton) in the fall of 1981.

In addition to sizable expenditures on historical shrines and momentos in general, the present regime continues a practice of its predecessors by restoring and refurbishing historical buildings and parks. Places where notable events in the history of the Communist party took place have been reconstructed in painstaking detail. Travelers returning to China after that long period during which they could not gain entry frequently experience déjà vu.

Returning to the postulates and corollaries proposed by Francis L.K. Hsu, I conclude with this analysis. Hsu's first postulate concerns filial piety and the absolute priority of relationships with parents. As we have already noted, the Cultural Revolution began with a period of about three or four years when filial piety was considered the cutting edge of reactionary Confucianism and therefore ridiculed and marked for extirpation. Curiously, that line was at zenith in the very years the adulation of Mao was at its height. A sharp reverse came in late 1976, and the "Great Helmsman" continues posthumously to decline in popularity. Conversely, the standing of parents, teachers, medical doctors, and most other specialists continues to rise.

We have already commented on the continued importance of male offspring apparently representing the continuation of belief in the necessity of a line of descendants. This attitude, in turn, has helped swell the population to record size. We have no information, however, on the fate of the common Chinese practice of adoption. It seems that adoption was most frequent in the southeast; it is still very common in Taiwan. But we are in the dark about its frequency in the PRC. If the regime has, indeed, affected Chinese folk belief about the necessity of male heirs for continuity and for one's own comfort after death, adoptions would lose most of their motivation. Thus, to discover continuing significant frequencies of adoption would tell us about the retention of other beliefs. Such a view will be found by most readers to be at odds with common sense. A society that controls births and insists on one child per family will provide few or no opportunities for adoption, except perhaps in the unlikely chance of the death of young parents. Such a limitation on adoption seems completely reasonable only if the presently propagandized limit on childbirth actually is the limit for the Han population at large rather than only in exemplary places. But the question is more complex. Perhaps the most usual adoptions in Chinese society saw the adoption of male children by relatives who themselves had no sons. Probably at least as frequent was the adoption of girls to assist a mother in tasks in and around the house and, ultimately, to be the wife of the son. That institution, called "buying a pig," continued throughout the Republic of China but, so far as is known, came to an end in the PRC in the early 1950s. The adoption of boys, as indicated, is usually tied to other motives that involve Chinese conceptions of the meaning of life and death. It might be, for example, that a couple that already had a (male) child might have another with the intention of giving it up for adoption by close relatives. Answers to problems such as this require more and deeper field research.

Hsu's second postulate applies to the recognition of agnatic kinship beyond the familial and sets up a secure foundation for a vital lineage (Hsu says "clan") organization and for the continuing significance of the *wufu*, the ritual designation of five categories of mourning kin. It is too early to come to a conclusion about these matters; they have not yet run their course. I received a personal note from Gueizhou (Kweichou) in 1982 remarking that funerals seen there seem to have gotten larger than I saw in 1977. An extensive complement of grave goods is mentioned, and large numbers of mourners. Can the *wufu* be taking shape again?

Hsu's third postulate is simply that women are inferior to men. Few motifs have undergone more heavy and direct government attack than this one. Has that campaign achieved reasonable success? Before attempting to reply, I must note that exceptions existed in the past but were relative rather than absolute; even rough equality was not achieved at any period in China's history. The Hakka subculture, however, has always been celebrated for its women, who were known to carry out tasks that elsewhere in China were considered men's work. Also, the ideology of the Taiping rebels in the mid-nineteenth century provided for even more equality of the sexes. It is surely relevant that the person who launched and headed the Taiping movement was Hung Hsiu-ch'uan, a Hakka.

Traveling about the PRC, one continually meets a few women in positions of power at all levels except the top. At one time one of the topmost figures, perhaps the chief of all, was a woman—Jiang Qing—but she was subsequently imprisoned. Traveling through China shortly after Jiang and her fellow oligarchs were condemned was to hear endless curses directed at her, alone of the Gang of Four. It seemed that in this passionate outpouring of rage one could see a convenient vent through which the angers and frustrations that seem to have attended the liberation of women could be released with social approval. In summary, then, "women's liberation" has appeared more heavily in government statements for internal and external consumption than behavioral reality in both city and countryside, though women receive more equal treatment in urban locations (Mosher 1983: chap. 8).

The fifth postulate deals with the attribution of wisdom to age, which is respected. At risk for only a short period, the continuation of formal patterns of superiority for the aged continue. As stated above, concern for the elderly has long been ambiguous in the Chinese countryside. This ambiguity seems to be continuing. Parents continue to be respected primarily in the context of productive functions such as child care.

Hsu's sixth postulate is that "political rulers are superior to their subjects. This can be seen more clearly when juxtaposed with his third postulate for the culture of the United States, which is that government is for the people. He then states a subcorollary to the effect that officials are regarded as the same as ordinary people (Hsu 1969:69). I cannot illuminate this point. In imperial China, there was a significant hiatus between the local people and their county magistrate. That magistrate, by the "law of avoidance," could never be a native of the region but always came from a different province, often speaking a different Chinese language. To a considerable extent this policy died with the Qing. Under the Kuomintang, county officials were elected and native to their districts. In the PRC equivalent, procedures are obscure; election and appointment seem to overlap depending on circumstances. At any rate, there are levels at which the top power holders in Beijing seem intent on keeping natives of a particular area from holding high-level posts in that area. The processes by which relatively low-level officials are chosen remains unclear. Most appear not directly elected but appointed by a committee of appropriate level. A subsequent election turns out to be a public acceptance of that decision. Under such structural conditions, it is difficult to assess popular feelings about governmental officials. On occasion—such as in early 1958 when the "hundred flowers" were urged to bloom (only to be scythed when they did) and during the early years of the Cultural Revolution, in the late 1960s, when mobs of young Red Guards directly confronted and sometimes condemned and punished officials—we have seen immediate interaction between people and officials. What went on at those times seems to have duplicated what went on in China during the past two millennia or more in the frequently bloody insurrections that were peasant wars.

In his eighth postulate, Hsu talks of the superiority of those doing mental work over manual laborers. As previously indicated, there is just a bit of a shift needed to make this fit what we see today. The fundamental distinction is now between urban and rural workers. Urban workers enjoy much better standards of living based on higher wages to begin with and further supported by access to a broader range of foods, better housing, a wider range of clothing and other consumer goods, better medical services, and so on. All these urban pleasures are at least theoretically available to the humblest urban manual workers, although their small wage will not get them many of the luxury goods. Yet, even the poorest city laborer has certain advantages. Rent costs very little, basic food and clothing is cheap, and medical care is not expensive. Such a worker, even though earning little, is likely to be able to bank a few biao every month. Rural counterparts usually find life somewhat harder.

Moving closer to the question of nonmanual jobs, we cannot help noting that, beyond the urban-rural split, this other division retains significance. The Cultural Revolution was a fierce attack on precisely this system. It involved very strong pressures to *xia-fang* (*hsia fang*), to transfer to work in the countryside. This system is largely, perhaps entirely, extinct. Even at its height, people who "went down" to the rural areas proved to be more of a burden than a help to the local farmers. It was not long before almost castelike relations between the rurals and the urbans took shape.

The ninth postulate offered by Hsu has been shown by every relevant community study to be at least as applicable to the peasantry as to higher social strata. This postulate asserts the hierarchical nature of the spirit world and the importance of gods and spirits to the living. It also includes corollaries limiting the power of gods and recognizing their fallibility. Although not anticipated by Hsu, this postulate helps explain the relative passivity of the masses after the relatively quick succession of the deaths of Zhou Enlai and Mao Zedong. Subsequent revisions and downgradings of Mao's thought are easily rationalized within the parameters of this postulate and its corollaries.

Closely related is Hsu's thirteenth postulate, which focuses on the concept of *bao* (*pao*), a kind of reciprocity: *bao* represents the reaction of the spiritual powers to particular streams of behavior; good is rewarded, bad is punished. It is difficult to evaluate this theme in recent Chinese life. Persons of exemplary behavior have run afoul of local or higher officials; specific behavior seems poorly correlated with the results that would be expected under *bao*. It is possible, however, that the seemingly universal renunciation of the pantheon of the folk religion, considered active within the lifetimes of a significant portion of the population, may well be considered a major reason for bad *bao*.

There is in contemporary China a strong relation between the tenth and fourteenth of Hsu's postulates. The tenth sums up the relations between ego and parents and ancestors. The best way to honor them is through achievement. The fourteenth declares the superiority of the Chinese way but recognizes that, since people are not equally endowed, some fall short. The connection lies in the substitution of the state for the parents. Achievement primarily glorifies the country and may not have deep significance for relatives, even parents, or ancestors. Quite revealing of this is the treatment given by Mao to his relatives and ancestors. The latter he never mentioned; he seemed to have had no interest in them at all. As for his parents, he displayed on numerous occasions his hatred and contempt for his father. He felt much closer to his mother, but even she was sometimes mentioned critically.

The twelfth postulate states a marked preference for peaceful rather than violent settlement of disputes. Stated as a preference, it is difficult to challenge. It should not, however, be thought that China has always eschewed violence. Indeed, buried within Confucianism is a precept that calls for violent vengeance against those who assault one's parents. Once again, the present regime seems to have been successful in translating this obligation to parents into an obligation to the state.

Incidentally, even before this century Chinese culture included several loci at which violence was positively encouraged. During recent centuries, extensive, organized violence between lineages, often of different ethnicity (for example, Punti versus Hakka), has characterized the southeastern provinces. Feuds often produced deaths and other casualties. Both gentry and peasantry were deeply involved in these activities. It is also apparent that, despite the feeling to the contrary expressed by many (particularly non-Chinese) scholars, military careers and activities were not invariably held in low repute, even by the gentry. The strategic place of the People's Liberation Army reflects a continuation and strengthening of this theme (Fried 1952b).

What the foregoing has shown is the remarkable extent of continuity between Chinese culture in the PRC and preceding regimes. The continuity is greater than may appear at first glance, because some currently institutionalized behavior has deep historical roots in ways that were peculiar to the masses of Chinese rather than to the small segment that was the gentry, which previously controlled the national image. As a consequence, changes are not necessarily reflective of external influences. At the same time, the continuation of some themes seems to indicate that their roots were not exclusively in the gentry subculture but in the subculture carried by the peasantry.

Perhaps most startling of all is the implication that the largest national culture in the world, the culture associated with almost a quarter of the human race, may be analyzed into relatively few and tightly related themes or postulates, capable of surviving perhaps the greatest political revolution ever to take place. Even though dimly seen, the future seems to hold many more such political and economic events. Will that future see again and again the phenomenon of rapid, seemingly radical change followed by growing evidence that those changes are of far smaller scale and more particular focus than was previously anticipated? From the viewpoint of the present, perhaps a non-Han anthropologist can make a slogan: *wenhua geming xiao, wenhua da* (Cultural Revolution is small, culture is great).

References

Bailey, Anne M., and Joseph R. Llobera, eds.
 1981 *The Asiatic Mode of Production: Science and Politics*. London: Routledge and Kegan Paul.
Bodde, Derk
 1946 Dominant ideas. In Harley F. MacNair, ed., *China*, pp. 18–28. Berkeley: University of California Press.
Buxbaum, David, ed.
 1967 *Traditional and Modern Legal Institutions in Asia and Africa*. Leiden: Brill.
Cohen, Albert K.
 1948 On the place of themes and kindred concepts in social theory. *American Anthropologist* 50:436–43.
Dunn, Stephen P.
 1982 *The Fall and Rise of the Asiatic Mode of Production*. London: Routledge and Kegan Paul.
Fei Hsiao-tung (Fei Xiaotong)
 1946 Peasantry and gentry: An interpretation of Chinese social structure and its changes. *American Journal of Sociology* 52:1–17.

Fried, Martha Nemes, and Morton H. Fried
- 1980   *Transitions: Four Rituals in Eight Cultures*. New York: W.W. Norton.

Fried, Morton H.
- 1952a   Chinese society: Class as subculture. *Transactions of the New York Academy of Sciences* 14:331–36.
- 1952b   Military status in Chinese society, with comments by Lee Shu-ch'ing. *American Journal of Sociology* 57:347–57.

Gladwin, Thomas
- 1947   Morris Opler's concept of themes. *American Anthropologist* 49:142–46.

Greenhalgh, Susan
- 1982   Demographic differentiation and income distribution: The Taiwan case. Ph.D. diss., Department of Anthropology, Columbia University.

Han Yu-shan
- 1946   Molding forces. In Harley F. MacNair, ed., *China*, pp. 3–17. Berkeley: University of California Press.

Hinton, William
- 1966   *Fanshen: A Documentary of Revolution in a Chinese Village*. New York: Monthly Review Press.

Ho, P'ing-ti (He Pingdi)
- 1960   The examination system and social mobility in China: 1368–1911. Proceedings of the 1959 Annual Spring Meeting of the American Ethnological Society, Seattle.
- 1962   *The Ladder of Success in Imperial China: Aspects of Social Mobility, 1368–1911*. New York: Columbia University Press.

Hoebel, E. Adamson
- 1954   *The Law of Primitive Man: A Study in Comparative Legal Dynamics*. Cambridge: Harvard University Press.

Hsu, Francis L. K.
- 1943   The myth of Chinese family size. *American Journal of Sociology* 48:555–62.
- 1969   *The Study of Literate Civilizations*. New York: Holt, Rinehart, and Winston.
- 1979   Traditional culture in contemporary China: Continuity and change in values. In Godwin C. Chu and Francis L. K. Hsu, eds., *Moving a Mountain: Cultural Change in China*, pp. 259–79. Honolulu: University of Hawaii Press.

Hsu, Francis L. K., and Godwin C. Chu
- 1979   Changes in Chinese culture: what do we really know? In *Moving a Mountain: Cultural Changes in China*, pp. 396–417. Honolulu: University of Hawaii Press.

Hsu-Balzer, Eileen, Richard Balzer, and Francis L. K. Hsu
- 1974   *China Day by Day*. New Haven: Yale University Press.

Mao Tze-tung (Mao Zedong)
- 1972   *Quotations from Chairman Mao Tse-tung*. Beijing: Foreign Languages Press.

Moser, Michael
　1980　　Mediation and litigation in rural Taiwan: An ethnographic study of law and dispute settlement in a modern Chinese community. Ph.D. diss., Department of Anthropology, Columbia University.

Mosher, Steven
　1983　　*Broken Earth.* New York: Free Press.

Opler, Morris E.
　1946　　Application of the theory of themes in culture. *Journal of the Washington Academy of Sciences* 36:137–66.
　1951　　Context of themes. *American Anthropologist* 51:323–25.

Schram, Stuart, ed.
　1974　　*Chairman Mao Talks to the People: Talks and Letters.* Trans. John Chinnery and Tieyun. New York: Pantheon Books.

Wittfogel, Karl A.
　1929　　Geopolitik, geographischer Materialismus und Marxismus. *Unter dem Banner des Marxismus.* 3:17–51, 485–522, 698–735.
　1957　　*Oriental Despotism: A Comparative Study of Total Power.* New Haven: Yale University Press.

Wright, Arthur F., and Dennis Twitchett, eds.
　1962　　*Confucian Personalities.* Stanford: Stanford University Press.

Epilogue

Clio Rediviva

Sidney W. Mintz

Students of John V. Murra, looking back at what he taught them, can sometimes recognize in what ways his anthropology is an idiosyncratic product of his times. During the years spanning World War II, American cultural anthropology was to a substantial extent enthralled by its opposite number, British social anthropology. In Britain in the years immediately following the war, scholars such as E. E. Evans-Pritchard, Raymond Firth, and Meyer Fortes were at the height of their powers. Graduate students in the United States had been discovering Africa (at Chicago, most of them under Murra's tutelage) and studying the remarkable monographs produced by British scholars beginning with Malinowski and Radcliffe-Brown. There was as yet no Leach, no Lévi-Strauss, no Wolf, no Geertz. British social anthropology was concentrating on its version of the primitive world.

It would be easy to argue at length about different varieties of functionalism within the British school. But I do not think that there can be much disagreement over the claim that, among its leaders, there was not only little interest in history or historical explanation but even dislike and some disdain for historical perspectives. To be sure, Gluckman set forth, in a now-famous pamphlet (1949), to criticize Malinowski's ahistoricity. Forde, trained by Kroeber in the United States, had refrained from taking an antihistorical stance. Evans-Pritchard would eventually argue, at least once

---

This essay began as a valedictory lecture delivered at Cornell University on the occasion of Professor Murra's retirement, May 4, 1982. I am indebted to Professors Ashraf Ghani, Heather Lechtman, and Patricia Netherly and to Jacqueline Mintz for invaluable criticism and advice.

in print (1961), that he considered history important, and even Fortes (1963) made a concession to it. But, although many competent British anthropologists were content to demonstrate the irrelevance of history by ignoring it without attacking it, one would have had real difficulty in finding, on the part of any of them, a convinced historical orientation. At best, most of them found history a second-order level of explanation; at worst, they held that historical "explanations" were spurious, merely concealing shoddy fieldwork.[1]

For that matter, historical anthropology was then receiving relatively little encouragement among American anthropologists, charmed as many were by the exactitude and scientism of British social anthropology. Some American directions were quite antihistorical or ahistorical. For example, Redfield and his students were seeking to replace (or to obviate) history with what were thought to be scientific concepts of social process, such as "secularization" or "disorganization." Other scholars, claiming to be evolutionary—such as White and his students—were equally nonhistorical, and for oddly analogous reasons. There were, to be sure, many persistently historical orientations, particularly among the archaeologists and their congeners. Of course, some cultural anthropologists, such as Alexander Lesser, never abandoned historical perspective. Lesser had trained students (including June Richardson Hanks, Jack Harris, Joseph Jablow, Oscar Lewis, Bernard Mishkin, and Morris Siegel) to apply a historical perspective in their work. This historicism was almost wholly devoted to the reconstruction of native America. It often provided invaluable materials for theories of culture contact and change, but only the very best of the resulting monographs aspired to more than a faithful depiction of some aspect of the precontact situation. The prototype—and surely the best—was Lesser's *Pawnee Ghost Dance Hand Game* (1978 [1933]), which documented (as prelude to its brilliant theoretical analysis of the games) the lengthy and depressing chronicle of the conquest, the painful resistance, and the cultural destruction of the Pawnee.[2]

Little history was to be found in the few anthropological studies devoted to nonprimitive, or "peasant," peoples. The monographs published in the

---

[1] I am oversimplifying; see, for example, Kuper 1973:163ff. A few scholars—particularly Monica Hunter, Isaac Schapera, and Godfrey Wilson—were exceptions. Murra (1984:9) himself has claimed that he finds the criticisms of British anthropological antihistoricity irrelevant. I do not. My basic contention is that history was simply not seen as a way to explain sociocultural phenomena among nonliterate peoples. In the case of a monograph such as Evans-Pritchard's splendid *Nuer* (1940), this perspective, which I see as a deliberate choice, did not vitiate the entire analysis, but readers can probably see how it gravely weakened it.

[2] See also Lesser's essay on the ghost dance in Mintz 1985.

Smithsonian Institution's Institute of Social Anthropology Series, though pioneering in conception and intent, are marked by a rather drab sameness of organization. Most include only a passing reference to the past and its relevance for the present. Gillin's *Moche* (1947), to mention but one, passes quickly over the fact that the community studied is embedded in a vast sugarcane plantation zone, transformed only in recent decades by swift and irreversible proletarianization, the significance of which is similarly ignored. Generally speaking, it may be fair to say that American anthropological historicism of the time was caught up principally in rediscovering and reconstituting primitive societies as they had been rather than in studying historical change or using history to document it. When anthropological scholars chose subjects that were not in the "primitive" category, their work tended to show timidity and hesitation.

Looking back, it seems remarkable that British anthropologists from Malinowski and Radcliffe-Brown onward so often studied the present of native African (and other "primitive") peoples with so little attention to either their pasts or the events that linked them to their European conquerors—whereas North American historical anthropologists so often studied the supposedly precontact pasts of native North American peoples with such scant attention to their depressing present. The differences between these approaches may be related to the fact that native North Americans represented internal colonies that had become more a nuisance than a political problem of any scale; native Africans constituted external colonies and were politically still significant, not to say potentially very troublesome.

Both in the United States and abroad, the recognition was slow in coming that much anthropological fieldwork may have been skewed by imparting to its presentation and analysis a somewhat exaggerated quality of intactness, separateness, and isolation. There are no Bovril signs in the anthropological photographs of Africa, no blue jeans in the pictures of the American pueblos. Somehow, in the two major versions of anthropology developed during the first half of this century, the most important fact about the postcontact past of nearly all non-European peoples—that they had been subjugated, against their wills—was almost entirely omitted from their study. Whatever else this omission may have been, it was markedly unhistorical.

Such was the state of American anthropology (as this reminiscer looks back at it) in January 1948, when I first met John Murra. He was preparing to take up a visiting assistant professorship at the University of Puerto Rico. He had also agreed to serve as the informal (that is, unpaid) field director of what has since come to be called the "Puerto Rico Project." The director of that project was Julian Steward, then of Columbia University. The graduate students who would participate in it came from the University of Puerto Rico and from the departments of anthropology at the University of Chicago and Columbia University. The institutional cosponsors were Columbia and the University of Puerto Rico, and financial support came from the Rockefeller Foundation.

Those of us who were fortunate enough to be chosen for that project got to know John in New York, just before he left for Puerto Rico, or soon after our arrival in Rio Piedras. He helped us find accommodations, work out our exploratory trips to the countryside, and begin conceptualizing our individual fieldwork. I thought that he was astoundingly patient with us; and though some found his ideas and advice more interesting than others, I learned an enormous amount from him at that time. My personal reactions to his way of teaching then have been echoed by multitudes of students before and since: he succeeds marvelously in conveying his irrepressible enthusiasm and in stimulating people to think systematically about their own ideas.

Murra appeared to have learned well the major lessons of Boasian historical anthropology without becoming a historian, and to have seen the beauty and usefulness of the British functionalist approach without becoming antihistorical. Of course, that is an assertion after the fact, and we who were learning from him in the field situation got most of what we learned by posing for him questions that arose in the course of the fieldwork. He read our field notes with startling care and frequently commented later on events and persons in the notes in ways that showed how much he had taken in from his reading. I can remember him invoking Eggan's work on the Cheyenne to show how Eggan had used British work on kinship without abandoning a historical stance, Lesser for his stress on the synthesis of functionalist and historical approaches, and Firth for his holistic view of institutions. One example of how he helped me understand things better may not be out of place here.

The Puerto Rico Project had been thought up by Steward to test his conception of anthropological theory as applied to modern societies. The communities chosen for study were supposed to stand for major economic adaptations, to be representative of much larger segments of the national population than the communities themselves. Quite early in the work, however, two features of the theoretical challenge became painfully clear to the fieldworkers: our steadily increasing awareness of the colonial context of the Puerto Rican case, and our strengthened realization of the need for a historical perspective if we wanted to understand the communities we were studying. We were—some of us more than others—going through a sort of discovery period. What we were finding out contradicted what we thought we knew or raised daunting questions about our methods and premises.

In the course of my work on a U.S. sugar plantation, I was struck by the superficial resemblance between the rural proletarian communities of the region and the kinds of description Robert Redfield had given us of his ideal folk society: uniformity of status, likeness of livelihood, homogeneity of belief, social isolation, and so on. It would, of course, have been laughable to read this as some sort of primitivity in the Puerto Rican case. My local hosts were illiterate, not preliterate; their clothing was Western, as was their food and their games; their language was Spanish, their music Afro-Caribbean or of Spanish origin. One of the forces that made these rural Puerto Rican workers similar to each other was the immense American corporation that had purchased the land around them, built factories, and employed them. Their isolation was not geographic, it was social; they were "a class apart." Yet they were also very much part of the modern world. They had become part of it by a well-traveled route of migration, imperialism, and colonialism that had been segregating the process of "westernization" in regions outside the West for several centuries.

When I discussed these materials with Murra, he posed for me a hypothetical situation that was immediately illuminating. Suppose, he said, one were to apply the folk-urban continuum to Puerto Rico, much as it had been applied to Yucatan; what would it reveal, and fail to reveal? Responding to his question, I said that the continuum would probably begin in the remote countryside of the Puerto Rican highlands and end in the capital, San Juan, missing the sugar plantation communities, which were the most important economic feature of the Puerto Rican landscape. But, of course, as soon as I said this, I realized what it revealed about Redfield's study of Yucatan as well: the total omission of the henequen haciendas from the Redfield scheme. The substitution of "space" (the folk-urban continuum) for time omitted the "reprimitivization" of the Yucatecan countryside in the War of the Castes, the creation of the henequen industry, and hence much of the relation between the state and the people. To that extent, it falsified or concealed, rather than explained and revealed, the nature of change, the place of historical explanation, and the objective status of the Yucatecan people.

Applied to Puerto Rico, the folk-urban construction could have been misleading as well. The economic complexion of the Puerto Rican countryside had been radically altered through time, particularly following the U.S. invasion in 1898–99. That impact was experienced differentially; American investments in Puerto Rico were not made at a steady rate, nor were they uniformly distributed across the colony. Sugar provided a more favorable investment opportunity than coffee or tobacco, and after 1900 sugar production expanded at the cost of the local economies in these other products while labor gravitated increasingly to the sugar regions. Any observations about rural proletarians in sugar, then, had to take into account the complementary processes occurring elsewhere in the Puerto Rican countryside, the role of the larger imperial system in affecting local developments, and, most of all, the importance of history. Particularly striking to me in retrospect was Murra's interest in having me understand the force of Redfield's ideas, not their limitations, and his concern that I figure out for myself the best way to characterize accurately the social framework that had grown up over time for the local community.

When the fieldwork phase of the Puerto Rico Project ended in the summer of 1949, Murra moved to New York, as did some of those who had worked with him in Puerto Rico. That fall, a group of the Columbia students began to meet in informal sessions to discuss anthropology and their own work. Though different in training and of a slightly different generation, Murra participated in the Columbia circle, where his former roommate and barracks mate, Elman Service, was completing a degree. I am not able to explain how the particular composition of that circle took shape, nor how Murra's participation in it came about. Nor do I think he was much influenced then by the ideas of others, though he contributed a good deal to the discussions. I do recall some of the issues he and others reviewed at the time. Interests and questions excited by the realization that anthropology had so far only barely engaged the significance of contact history and of colonialism in the preceding decades were affecting many students in those years. While writing their theses, getting their first teaching experience, moving to new posts and starting new research, some of them were also attempting to make their anthropology a tool for understanding the modern world rather than focusing exclusively on the conceptually segregated "primitives" in it. Their hope was that anthropology could become a speculum with which to theorize not only about change but also about nonchange—about conquest, resistance, economic and social interpenetration and absorption. They wanted to learn how societies at different points in their own evolution could assimilate, or be assimilated by, others. The notion of an intact, pristine primitivity, though important in their thinking, was viewed as a historical condition as well as an abstract, theoretical polarity. To be tested was whether anthropology had something to say about relationships among societies, and not only about relationships within them; about colony *and* metropolis as well as about societies within colonies; about the economics of European overlordship as well as about yam feasts; about what terms such as "class," "estate," "slavery," and "state" might mean if they could be freed from their association with the European historical idiom.

In the years since, Murra has won a special reputation for his contributions to the answering of just such problems; we can look forward to more work by him and his students in the coming years. But for thousands of the students who did not become specialists—and for those who did not become anthropologists at all—he is known best for opening their eyes. Discovering that one can think creatively about the world is a great discovery. Being able to teach it is a rare talent. As Andeanists admire John for his scholarship, so his students will always honor him for his teaching.

References

Evans-Pritchard, E. E.
 1940 *The Nuer*. London: Oxford University Press.
 1961 *Anthropology and History*. Manchester: Manchester University Press.
Fortes, Meyer
 1963 Time and social structure: An Ashanti case study. In M. Fortes, ed., *Social Structure*, p. 54–85. New York: Russell and Russell.
Gillin, John
 1947 *Moche: A Peruvian Coastal Community*. Smithsonian Institution Institute of Social Anthropology, Publication 3.
Gluckman, Max
 1949 *Malinowski's Sociological Theories*. Rhodes Livingstone Paper 16. New York: Oxford University Press.
Kuper, Adam
 1973 *Anthropologists and Anthropology: The British School, 1922–72*. Harmondsworth: Penguin.
Lesser, Alexander
 1978 *The Pawnee Ghost Dance Hand Game*. Madison: University of Wisconsin Press.
 [1933]
Mintz, Sidney W., ed.
 1985 *History, Evolution and the Concept of Culture: Selected Papers by Alexander Lesser*. Cambridge: Cambridge University Press.
Murra, John V.
 1984 An interview with John V. Murra. *Hispanic American Historical Review* 64:1–21.

Contributors

RONALD COHEN is Professor of Anthropology at the University of Florida.
MORTON H. FRIED (deceased) was Professor of Anthropology at Columbia University.
IRVING GOLDMAN is Professor Emeritus of Anthropology at Sarah Lawrence College.
JOHN S. HENDERSON is Professor of Anthropology at Cornell University.
FRIEDRICH KATZ is Professor of History at the University of Chicago.
HEATHER LECHTMAN is Professor of Archaeology and Ancient Technology at the Massachusetts Institute of Technology.
OLGA F. LINARES is an anthropologist at the Smithsonian Tropical Research Institute.
SIDNEY W. MINTZ is Professor of Anthropology at the Johns Hopkins University.
CRAIG MORRIS is Curator of Anthropology at the American Museum of Natural History.
PATRICIA J. NETHERLY is an archaeologist working with McMeekin International, S.A.
DENISE O'BRIEN is Associate Professor of Anthropology at Temple University.
NAN A. ROTHSCHILD is Associate Professor of Anthropology at Barnard College.
ELMAN R. SERVICE is Professor Emeritus of Anthropology at the University of California, Santa Barbara.
ROBERT J. SMITH is Professor of Anthropology at Cornell University.
BRUCE G. TRIGGER is Professor of Anthropology at McGill University.

Index

Algonquian peoples, 113–14
Andaman Islanders, 116–17
archipelago model of territorial organization, 5, 246–47
Athabascan peoples, 113–14
Australia, native peoples, 115–16
ayllu, 21, 23, 29–30
Aztec, 78, 244–45

British social anthropology, 2, 327–30

calendar, 40
ceque, 47
Charka confederacy, 20–25
Chavín, 263
chiefdom, 82–84, 121–26, 131–33
Chimor, 16–19, 28, 267
China, 130, 304–24
cloth, role in state, 5, 36, 42, 250–51, 254–59, 271–74
Confucianism, 55, 68–69
Cubeo. *See* Vaupés (Colombia), native peoples of

Diola. *See* Jola
divine kingship, 13, 51–71
dual sociopolitical organization. *See* moiety organization

Egypt, early civilization in, 75, 78, 89–92, 94–99, 101–2
Eskimo, 113
ethnic identity, 13

gender roles, 157–58, 168, 181–206, 209, 212–24; and sociopolitical hierarchy, 157–58, 181–85, 188–206
Great Plains Indians, 118–19
Guaraní, 119–20

Harappan civilization, 129–30
hierarchy, 137–59, 228–41
houses, size of, and wealth, 228–41
Huanuco, 5, 46–48

identity. *See* ethnic identity
Indus Valley, early civilization in. *See* Harappan civilization
Inka, 4, 14, 17–20, 22–24, 26, 28, 36–48, 160, 244–45, 247–52, 254–59, 262–63
Iroquois, 118

Jola, 160–77

!Kung, 115

lineage organization, 30–31

market economy, 36
Marxism, 4, 85–89, 304–5, 315
Meiji Restoration, 52–58, 62–69
Mesopotamia, early civilization in, 75, 78, 89–92, 94–99, 101, 128–29
metallurgy, 43, 245, 250–56, 259–71, 273–74
Mexican Revolution, 281–301
mitmaq, 23–24, 39, 44–45, 248
mit'a service, 20, 38–39, 48, 160, 176
Mochica (Moche), 127, 264–66
moiety organization, 5, 15–25, 27, 29–30, 145–48

Nootka, 121–22
Nuer, 120

Ona, 114

Pabir kingdom, 196–99, 201–3
preindustrial state. *See* state, archaic
pygmies, 115

quadripartite sociopolitical organization, 5, 16–19, 25, 27, 30
quipu, 248–49, 255–56

reciprocity-based economy, 36
Redfield, Robert, 331–32
Rwala Bedouin, 124

Semang, 116
shamanism, 154–56
Shang civilization, 130

Shinto, 60, 68
Shoshone, 114
Sicán, 267
state, archaic, 11–14, 126–33, 209–24; and agriculture, 160–77; and religion, 74–105
Steward, Julian, 81–82
storage, 43–44, 170–72

Tahitians, 123–24
Tawantinsuyu. *See* Inka
Teotihuacán, 126–27
Trobriand Islanders, 122–23
tumbaga, 266–71
Tungus, 120–21

Vaupés (Colombia), native peoples of, 137–59
vertical complementarity. *See* archipelago model of territorial organization
Villa, Francisco (Pancho), 281–301

White, Leslie, 76–77, 79–81
Wilson, Woodrow, 281, 287–90, 292–94, 296–99
women, sociopolitical status of, 157–58, 181–206, 209, 212–24
writing and political power, 209, 219–24

Yahgan, 114

Zapata, Emiliano, 282, 290–91, 293
Zulu, 124–25

Library of Congress Cataloging-in-Publication Data

Configurations of power : holistic anthropology in theory and practice / edited by John S. Henderson and Patricia J. Netherly.
   p. cm.
"Published in cooperation with the Society for Latin American Anthropology and the American Anthropological Association."
Includes bibliographical references and index.
ISBN 0-8014-2487-9 (alk. paper)
1. Anthropology—Methodology.   2. Anthropology—Philosophy.   3. Murra, John V.   I. Henderson, John S.   II. Netherly, Patricia.
GN33.C69   1993
301'.01—dc20   92-52759